The *Sams Teach Yourself in 24 Hours* Series

Sams Teach Yourself in 24 Hours books provide quick and easy answers in a proven step-by-step approach that works for you. In just 24 sessions of one hour or less, you will tackle every task you need to get the results you want. Let our experienced authors present the most accurate information to get you reliable answers—fast!

THE VISUAL BASIC DATATYPES.

DATATYPE	SIZE	DESCRIPTION AND RANGE
Boolean	2	Datatype that can be True or False only
Byte	1	Positive numeric value from 0 to 255
Currency	8	Dollar amounts from –$922,337,203,685,477.5808 to $922,337,203,685,477.5807
Date	8	Date and time value from January 1, 100, to December 31, 9999
Decimal	12	Numbers with 28 decimal places of accuracy (limited support)
Double	8	Numeric value from –1.79769313486232E+308 to 1.79769313486232E+308
Integer	2	Whole number from –32,768 to 32,767
Long	4	Integer from –2,147,483,648 to 2,147,483,647
Object		Special datatype that references objects
Single	4	Numeric value from –3.402823E+38 to 3.402823E+38
String		0 to 65,400 characters of alphanumeric data
Variant		Data of any datatype and other values for which the datatype is unknown

NUMERIC DATATYPE SUFFIX CHARACTERS.

CHARACTER	DATATYPE
&	Long
!	Single
#	Double
@	Currency

THE PRIMARY MATH OPERATORS.

OPERATOR	DESCRIPTION
+	Adds two values
-	Subtracts one value from another value
*	Multiplies two values
/	Divides one value by another value
^	Raises a value to a power
& (or +)	Concatenates two strings

COMPARISON OPERATORS.

OPERATOR	DESCRIPTION
<	Less than
<=	Less than or equal to
>	Greater than
>=	Greater than or equal to
=	Equal to
<>	Not equal to
IS	True if *obj1* and *obj2* are the same object
Like	Tests whether *expr1* is matched by a pattern in *expr2*

BASIC PATTERN-MATCHING CHARACTERS.

CHARACTER	DESCRIPTION
?	Matches any single character
*	Matches zero or more characters
#	Matches any single digit
[charlist]	Matches any single character in *charlist*
[!charlist]	Matches any single character not in *charlist*

SAMS

Teach Yourself Visual Basic 6

in 24 Hours

STARTER KIT

VISUAL BASIC COMMAND SYNTAX.

COMMAND	DESCRIPTION
`If condition Then statement`	If *condition* evaluates to True, *statement* is executed.

`If condition Then`
`    [statement block]`
`End If`
	If *condition* evaluates to True, the statements in the statement block are executed.

`If condition1 Then`
`    [statement block 1]`
`[ElseIf condition2 Then`
`    [statement block 2]]`
`[Else`
`    [statement block 3]]`
`End If`
	If *condition1* is True, the statements in *statement block 1* are executed. If *condition1* is False, the program tests *condition2*. When a true condition is found, the block of statements under the true condition are executed, and the program control reverts to the statement following the End If.

`Select Case testexpr`
`    [Case exprlist1`
`        [statement block 1]]`
`    [Case exprlist2`
`        [statement block 2]]`
`    .`
`    .`
`    .`
`    [Case Else`
`        [statement block n]]`
`End Select`
	The result of the evaluation of *testexpr* is tested against each Case clause in the structure. If a match is found, each of the statements in the statement block of the Case is executed. If none of the other Case clauses is successfully matched, the Case Else clause block of statements is executed. After a statement block is executed, program control reverts to the line of code after End Select.

`Switch(expr-1, value-1[,expr-2,`
`        value-2, ...[,expr-n,`
`        value-n]])`
	Each expression is evaluated in turn, and the value associated with the first expression that evaluates to True is returned. If no expression evaluates to True, Switch returns a Null value.

`Choose(index, choice-1[,` `        choice-2, ...[,choice-n]])`	Choose returns a choice from the list of *choice-1, choice-2,... choice-n* based on the value of *index*.

`Format 1: Do While condition`
`            [statement block]`
`        Loop`
 	
`Format 2: Do`
`            [statement block]`
`        Loop While condition`
	As long as *condition* is True, the statements in the statement block are executed. When *condition* evaluates to False, the program jumps to the line of code immediately following the Loop statement. In Format 2, the statement block is always executed.

`Format 1: Do Until condition`
`            [statement block]`
`        Loop`
 	
`Format 2: Do`
`            [statement block]`
`        Loop Until condition`
	As long as *condition* is False, the statements in the statement block are executed. When *condition* evaluates to True, the program jumps to the line of code immediately following the Loop statement. In Format 2, the statement block is always executed.

`While condition`
`    [statement block]`
`Wend`
	Same as Format 1 of Do While.

`For counter = start To end [Step increment]`
`    [statement block]`
`Next`
	The statements in the statement block are executed while varying values for *counter* from the *start* value to the *end* value. If the optional argument *increment* is present, it is the change value applied to *counter*.

`For Each element In group`
`    [statement block]`
`Next element`
	Similar to the For...Next except the statements in the statement block are executed for each *element* in *group*.

`With object`
`    statements`
`End With`
	A set of operations is performed on a given object without requalifying the object for each operation.

Greg Perry
Sanjaya Hettihewa

SAMS
Teach Yourself
Visual Basic® 6
in 24 Hours

SAMS

A Division of Macmillan Computer Publishing
201 West 103rd St., Indianapolis, Indiana, 46290 USA

Copyright © 1998 by Sams Publishing

International Standard Book Number: 0-672-31306-5

Library of Congress Catalog Card Number: 98-84138

Printed in the United States of America

First Printing: August 1998

00   99   98   4   3   2

Trademarks

Warning and Disclaimer

EXECUTIVE EDITOR
Christopher Denny

ACQUISITIONS EDITOR
Sharon Cox

DEVELOPMENT EDITOR
Tony Amico

MANAGING EDITOR
Jodi Jensen

COPY EDITOR
Kate Givens

INDEXERS
Christine Nelsen
Greg Pearson

TECHNICAL EDITOR
Jeff Perkins

SOFTWARE DEVELOPMENT SPECIALIST
John Warriner

TEAM COORDINATOR
Carol Ackerman

PRODUCTION
Michael Henry
Linda Knose
Tim Osborn
Staci Somers
Mark Walchle

Overview

Contents

About the Authors

GREG PERRY is a speaker and writer on both the programming and the application sides of computing. He is known for his skill in bringing advanced computer topics down to the novice's level. Greg has been a programmer and trainer since the early 1980s. He received his first degree in computer science and a master's degree in corporate finance. He is the author or co-author of more than 50 books, including *Sams Teach Yourself Windows 95 in 24 Hours*, *Absolute Beginner's Guide to Programming*, *Sams Teach Yourself Office 97 in 24 Hours*, *Absolute Beginner's Guide to C*, and *Moving from C to C++*, all by Macmillan Computer Publishing. He also writes about rental-property management and loves to travel.

SANJAYA HETTIHEWA is an accomplished Webmaster and consultant specializing in integrating Windows NT–based information systems on the Internet. He has lived in the Washington, D.C., area for the past eight years and is the Web Architect for TeraTech Inc., a Web and Visual Basic consulting company in Rockville, Maryland. Sanjaya specializes in projects that integrate capabilities of ASP, IIS, VB, and related technologies. Sanjaya is the author of *Windows NT 4 Web Development* and has co-authored seven books, including *Designing and Implementing Internet Information Server*, *Sams Teach Yourself Active Server Pages in 14 Days*, *Internet Explorer Unleashed*, and *Internet Information Server Unleashed*, all by Macmillan Computer Publishing. You can reach Sanjaya at http://www.NetInnovation.com/Sanjaya/. If you prefer to communicate the old-fashioned way, you can send e-mail to sanjaya@NetInnovation.com.

Dedication

This book is dedicated to Mary Jelacic for brightening my life with her friendship and showing me that life has no greater reward to offer than a true friend.

—*Sanjaya*

Acknowledgments

I would first like to thank Kim Spilker for getting me started writing books for Macmillan Computer Publishing and for being such a wonderful friend.

I'd like to thank Sharon Cox, Acquisitions Editor for this book, for being so wonderful and understanding throughout this project and for helping me complete this project on time. Many thanks go to Tony Amico for being such an excellent Development Editor, guiding me through this project, refining my work, and making this a better book. I am also very grateful to Jeff Perkins, the Technical Editor, for doing a superb job editing this book for technical accuracy. People like Sharon, Tony, Jeff, and the other wonderful people at Macmillan Computer Publishing are what make books like this possible.

I'd especially like to thank Greg Perry for doing such a superb job writing the first edition of this book. It was a pleasure working with Greg and coordinating everything for updating this book for Visual Basic 6. Greg is one of the nicest people I've ever had the pleasure of communicating with via e-mail!

I would like to thank Mary Jelacic for being a wonderful friend. I'm glad that I had the pleasure of meeting you. Special thanks go out to Jerry and Monique Feffer, for all their support and friendship, and to my parents for providing me with the tools to discover and explore the ever stimulating and fascinating world of computer science! I appreciate all that you've done for me.

Tell Us What You Think!

As the reader of this book, *you* are our most important critic and commentator. We value your opinion and want to know what we're doing right, what we could do better, what areas you'd like to see us publish in, and any other words of wisdom you're willing to pass our way.

As the Executive Editor for the Visual Basic programming team at Macmillan Computer Publishing, I welcome your comments. You can fax, e-mail, or write me directly to let me know what you did or didn't like about this book—as well as what we can do to make our books stronger.

Please note that I cannot help you with technical problems related to the topic of this book, and that due to the high volume of mail I receive, I might not be able to reply to every message.

When you write, please be sure to include this book's title and author as well as your name and phone or fax number. I will carefully review your comments and share them with the author and editors who worked on the book.

Fax: 317-817-7070
E-mail: vb@mcp.com
Mail: Executive Editor
          Visual Basic Programming
          Macmillan Computer Publishing
          201 West 103rd Street
          Indianapolis, IN 46290 USA

Introduction

You probably are anxious to get started with your 24-hour Visual Basic course. Take just a few preliminary moments to acquaint yourself with the design of this book, which is described in the next few sections.

Who Should Read This Book

This book is for programmers and would-be programmers who want to learn Visual Basic as quickly as possible without sacrificing the foundation necessary to master the language. Visual Basic is a product that can be used at many levels. Newcomers who have never programmed can create a complete working Windows program in less than two hours, as this book demonstrates. Those who have programmed in other languages will appreciate Visual Basic's design, which makes creating a Windows program more like designing a screen with a mouse-driven art program.

This book teaches Visual Basic on several levels. You will quickly begin creating applications by following simple examples. These applications will be fully working Windows applications with all the usual user-interface controls, such as command buttons, labels, and text boxes.

Once you become familiar with building the program's user interface, you can start honing your programming skills by learning the actual Visual Basic programming language. Fortunately, learning Visual Basic's programming language is much easier than learning others, such as C++.

As long as you are familiar with Windows, you can create applications with Visual Basic. You don't have to be a Windows expert, but you should feel comfortable working with menus, the mouse, and the Windows interface. If you've opened, closed, and resized windows, you surely have the skills necessary to create your own Visual Basic applications.

This 24-hour course teaches Visual Basic 6, the latest and greatest Visual Basic incarnation. Visual Basic 6 requires Windows 95/98 or Windows NT 4.0. The user interface introduced in Windows 95—and that now appears in Windows NT—makes working within a windowed environment enjoyable.

What This Book Will Do for You

Although this is not a reference book, you'll learn virtually everything a beginning or intermediate Visual Basic programmer needs to know to create usable, powerful, and fun applications with Visual Basic. There are many advanced technical details that most programmers will never need, but this book does not waste your time with them. I know that you want to get up to speed with Visual Basic in 24 hours, and this book fulfills that goal without sacrificing the quality of your skill set.

This book presents both the background and the theory that a new Visual Basic programmer needs. In addition to the background discussions, this book is practical and provides tons of step-by-step tasks that you can work through to create Visual Basic applications. The tasks start simple and add details as you move from hour to hour.

Can This Book Really Teach Visual Basic in 24 Hours?

Yes. You can master each chapter in one hour or less (by the way, chapters are referred to as "lessons" or "hours" in the rest of the book). Although some lessons are longer than others, the material is balanced. The longer lessons contain several tasks, and the shorter lessons contain background material. The balance of the material is provided by tasks, background, and insightful explanations and tips that make learning Visual Basic using this book fresh with every page.

What You Need

This book assumes that you have a Windows 95–compatible computer with Windows 95/98 or NT installed. In addition, you need Visual Basic 6.0 installed. As long as you have the hardware to install both Windows 95/98 (or Windows NT) and Visual Basic 6, you have everything you need to use this book and to learn Visual Basic programming.

Files on the Visual Basic Distribution CD-ROM

Some lessons refer to graphics files that are installed as part of your Visual Basic installation. In order for you to find these files on your hard drive, you have to choose to install the graphics files when you install Visual Basic. You may find the graphics files in the folder `D:\Program Files\Microsoft Visual Studio\Common\Grpahics\`. If you are unable to find the graphics files in this folder, you can use the Windows Find utility to search for the folder. Select Start | Find | Files or Folders. Search your local hard drive and the Visual Basic distribution CD-ROM for the directory `Graphics` to locate the VB graphics directory.

Conventions Used in This Book

Each lesson highlights new terms as they appear, and a question-and-answer section is provided at the end of each lesson to reinforce what you have learned. In addition, the lessons reinforce your learning further with quiz questions and exercises.

This 24-hour course also uses several common conventions to help teach the programming topics. Here is a summary of the typographical conventions:

- Commands and computer output appear in a special `monospaced` computer font.

- Words you type appear in a **`bold monospaced`** font.

- If a task requires you to choose from a menu, the book separates menu commands with a vertical bar. Therefore, this book uses File | Save As to indicate that you should open the File menu and choose the Save As command.

- When learning a programming language, you often must learn the syntax or format of a command. Lines similar to the following will be displayed to help you learn a new Visual Basic language command:

```
For CounterVar = StartVal To EndVal [Step IncrementVal]
    Block of one or more Visual Basic statements
Next CounterVar
```

  The monospaced text designates code (programming language information) that you'll enter into a program. The regular monospaced text, such as `For` and `Next`, represent keywords you must type exactly. *`Italicized monospace`* characters indicate placeholders that you must replace with your own program's values. Bracketed information, such as `[Step IncrementVal]`, indicates optional code that you can type if your program requires it.

In addition to typographical conventions, the following special elements are used to set off various pieces of information and to make them easily recognizable:

NEW TERM   The first time a *new term* appears, you'll find a New Term icon and definition to help reinforce that term.

Special notes augment the material you are reading in each hour. They clarify concepts and procedures.

You'll find numerous tips that offer shortcuts and solutions to common problems.

Caution sections warn you about pitfalls. Reading them will save you time and trouble.

Enough! Time Is Ticking!

Want to master Visual Basic? Turn the page.

A NOTE ABOUT THE MICROSOFT VISUAL BASIC 5 CONTROL CREATION EDITION

The CD-ROM accompanying this book includes the Microsoft Visual Basic 5 Control Creation Edition. We have included it at no charge to you so that you can better evaluate the Visual Basic programming environment. Keep in mind that this version of Visual Basic may not be able to compile all the samples provided in this book.

PART I
Introducing Visual Basic

Hour

HOUR 1

Visual Basic at Work

Welcome to Visual Basic! You possess one of the most powerful and enjoyable Windows development tools available today. Visual Basic really is fun, as you'll see throughout this 24-hour tutorial. Even if you have very little or no prior experience developing Windows applications, you'll feel right at home using Visual Basic—provided you are familiar with the Windows environment. In this hour you'll become familiar with the big picture of Visual Basic 6.0.

The highlights of this hour include

- What Visual Basic does
- How to start Visual Basic
- How to stop Visual Basic
- When to use the different Visual Basic windows
- How the system windows work together for you

What's Visual Basic About?

Microsoft Visual Basic 6.0, the latest and greatest incarnation of the old BASIC language, gives you a complete Windows application development system in one package. Visual Basic (or VB, as we often call it) lets you write, edit, and test Windows applications. In addition, VB includes tools you can use to write and compile help files, ActiveX controls (covered in Hour 21, "Visual Basic and ActiveX"), and even Internet applications (covered in Hour 24, "Online Visual Basic")!

NEW TERM *Controls* are tools on the Toolbox window that you place on a form to interact with the user and control the program flow.

NEW TERM A *program* is a set of instructions that make the computer do something such as perform accounting. (The term *program* is often used synonymously with *application*.)

Visual Basic is itself a Windows application. You load and execute the VB system just as you do other Windows programs. You will use this running VB program to create other programs. VB is just a tool, albeit an extremely powerful tool, that programmers use to write, test, and run Windows applications.

NEW TERM A *project* is a collection of files you create that compose your Windows application.

Although programmers often use the terms *program* and *application* interchangeably (as will be done throughout this 24-hour course), the term *application* seems to fit the best when you're describing a Windows program because a Windows program typically consists of several files. These files work together in the form of a project. The project generates the final program, which the user loads and runs from Windows by double-clicking an icon or by choosing the application from the Windows Start menu.

NEW TERM An *application* is a collection of one or more files that compile into an executable program.

As with computer hardware, the role of programming tools has evolved over the past 45 years. A programming language today, such as Visual Basic, differs greatly from programming languages of just a few years ago. Before windowed environments, a programming language was a simple text-based tool used to write programs. Today you need much more than just a language; you need a graphical development tool that can work inside the Windows system and create applications that take advantage of all the graphical, multimedia, online, and multiprocessed activities that Windows offers. Visual Basic is such a tool. More than a language, Visual Basic lets you generate applications that interact with every aspect of today's Windows operating systems.

Althougn Visual Basic is a comprehensive programming tool, VB retains its BASIC language heritage. Designers in the late 1950s developed the BASIC programming language for beginning programmers. BASIC was easier to use than other programming languages of the time, such as COBOL and FORTRAN. Microsoft never forgot VB's roots when developing Visual Basic. Newcomers to programming can learn to create simple but working Windows programs in just a short time. You will be using Visual Basic to write Windows programs before the next hour is complete!

NEW TERM *Wizards* are question-and-answer dialog boxes that automate tasks. Throughout the book, you will use wizards to facilitate the development of Visual Basic applications.

NEW TERM A *compiler* is a system that converts the program you write into a computer-executable application.

If you've taken a look at Visual Basic in the past, you'll be amazed at today's Visual Basic system. VB now sports a true compiler that creates standalone runtime .exe files that execute more quickly than previous VB programs. VB also includes several wizards that offer step-by-step dialog box questions that guide you through the creation of applications. VB's development platform, a development environment called the Developer Studio, now supports the same features as the advanced Visual C++ and Visual J++ compilers. After you learn one of Microsoft's visual programming products, you will have the skills to use the other language products without a long learning curve ahead of you.

NEW TERM The *Developer Studio* is Visual Basic's development environment.

Languages

Programming languages today are not what they used to be. The language itself isn't less important; rather, the graphical interfaces to applications have become more important.

A computer cannot understand any person's spoken language. A spoken language, such as Italian or English, is simply too general and ambiguous for computers to understand. Therefore, we must adapt to the machine and learn a language that the computer can understand. VB's programming language is fairly simple and uses common English words and phrases for the most part. The language isn't ambiguous, however. When you write a statement in the Visual Basic language, the statement never has multiple meanings within the same context.

NEW TERM   *Code* is another name for the programming statements you write.

As you progress through the next 24 hours, you will learn more and more of the Visual
Basic language's vocabulary and syntax (grammar, punctuation, and spelling rules). You
will use the VB programming language to embed instructions within applications you
create. All the code you write must work together to instruct the computer. Code is the
glue that ties all the graphics, text, and processes together within an application. Code
tells a checkbook application, for example, how to be a checkbook application and not
something else. The program code lets the application know what to do given a wide
variety of possible outcomes and user actions.

Visual Basic's Various Editions

Visual Basic 6 comes in several flavors. At the time of this writing, little is known about
Microsoft's Visual Basic marketing strategy. There are most likely going to be at least
two flavors of Visual Basic: the Standard/Professional Edition and the Enterprise Edition.

This book primarily teaches the Professional Edition's features. The Professional Edition
offers extra tools, including extra ActiveX add-in controls, better Internet programming
support, a Help file compiler, and improved database-access tools. Most professional
programmers use the Professional Edition. If Visual Basic 6.0 comes in a "Standard
Edition," also called the Learning Edition, you will be happy to know that it provides the
least expensive approach to using Visual Basic and gives you a complete development
environment, programming language, and many of the same tools the other editions
offer. Some people develop only with the Standard Edition and never need anything else.
You'll be able to use virtually the entire 24-hour course if you use the Standard Edition. I
recommend that you use the Professional Edition if possible.

The Enterprise Edition provides the client/server programmer with extended tools for
remote computing and application distribution. Microsoft enhanced VB's performance
for Enterprise Edition users working in a networked, distributed environment.

If you do not yet own a VB compiler, I highly recommend that you purchase the new
resource kit published by Sams Publishing. It is called *Sams Teach Yourself Visual Basic
5 in 21 Days: Complete Compiler Edition* (ISBN: 0-672-31315-4) and comes with the
Visual Basic Learning Edition compiler that you can use to follow along and build the
VB applications presented in this tutorial.

Most programmers need only the Standard or Professional Edition. The Enterprise Edition is aimed at developers who write network-intensive client/server applications. The Enterprise Edition is enhanced to aid such programmers who work within the special client/server environments.

The VB Programming Process

When you want to use Visual Basic, you'll follow these basic steps:

1. Start Visual Basic.

2. Create a new application or load an existing application. When you create a new application, you might want to use Visual Basic's VB Application Wizard to write your program's initial shell, as you'll do in the next hour.

3. Test your application with the debugging tools Visual Basic supplies. The debugging tools help you locate and eliminate program errors (or *bugs*) that can appear despite your best efforts to keep them out.

   NEW TERM   A *bug* is a program error that you must correct (debug) before your program will execute properly.

4. Compile your program into a final application.

5. Quit Visual Basic.

6. Distribute the application to your users.

Rarely will you perform all these steps sequentially in one sitting. The six steps are not sequential steps, but stages that you go through and return to before completing your application.

Starting Visual Basic

You start Visual Basic from the Windows Start menu. The Visual Basic development environment itself usually appears on a Microsoft Visual Basic 6.0 submenu, although yours might be called something different due to installation differences. You'll see additional programs listed on the submenu, but when you select Visual Basic 6.0 from the submenu, Visual Basic loads and appears on your screen.

A dialog box similar to Figure 1.1 appears as soon as you start Visual Basic. The exact dialog box you see may differ slightly depending on your version of VB 6.0.

FIGURE 1.1.

*The New Project
dialog box appears
when you start VB.*

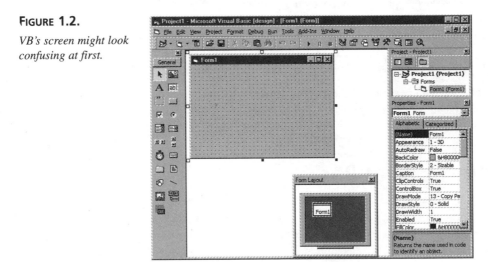

 You can always invoke the New Project dialog box by selecting File | New Project from the VB menu bar.

After you close the dialog box, the regular Visual Basic screen appears. As Figure 1.2 shows, VB's opening screen can get busy! Figure 1.2 shows the Visual Basic development environment, the environment with which you will soon be intimately familiar. From this development environment you will create Windows programs.

FIGURE 1.2.

*VB's screen might look
confusing at first.*

Although the screen can look confusing, you can fully customize the Visual Basic screen to suit your needs and preferences. Over time, you'll adjust the screen's window sizes and hide and display certain windows so that your Visual Basic screen's start-up state might differ tremendously from that of Figure 1.2.

A *dockable* window is one that you can resize and move to the sides of the screen and connect to other windows.

 Most of VB's windows are sizable and dockable, meaning you can connect them together, move them, and hide them.

The section "Mastering the Development Environment," later in this hour, explains the parts of the development environment and how to maneuver within it.

Stopping Visual Basic

You'll exit from Visual Basic and return to Windows the same way you exit most Windows applications: Select File | Exit, click Visual Basic's main window close button, press Alt+F4, or double-click VB's Control Menu icon in the upper-left corner of the screen.

If you have made changes to one or more files within the currently open project (remember that a project is the collection of files that comprise your application), Visual Basic gives you one last chance to save your work before quitting to Windows.

 Never power-off your computer without completely exiting Visual Basic, or you might lose some or all of your work for the current session!

Mastering the Development Environment

Learning the ins and outs of the development environment before you learn Visual Basic is somewhat like learning the parts of an automobile before you learn to drive; you might have a tendency to skip the terms and jump into the fray. If, however, you take the time to learn some of the development environment's fundamental principles, you'll be better able to learn Visual Basic. You then will be more comfortable within VB's environment and will have a better understanding of the related words when subsequent lessons refer to the windows and tools in the development environment.

Figure 1.3 shows the Visual Basic development environment with many of the more important screen components labeled. As you can see from the menu and toolbar, Visual Basic looks somewhat like other Windows programs on the market. Many of Visual Basic's menu bar commands work just as they do in other applications such as Microsoft

Word. For example, you can select Edit | Cut and Edit | Paste to cut and paste text from one location to another. These same menu commands appear on almost every other Windows program on the market today.

FIGURE 1.3.

Getting to know the development environment.

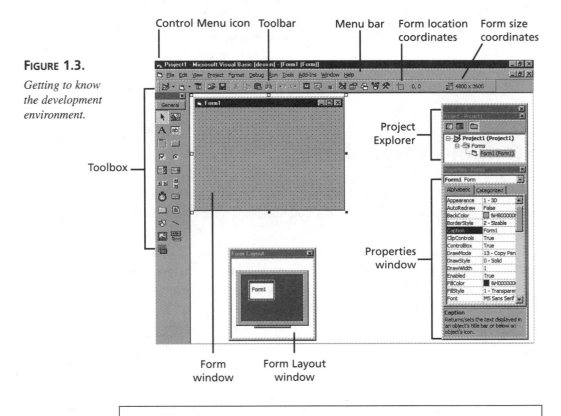

Figure 1.3 shows only a portion of the development environment's windows and components. Because you'll need additional tools such as the Menu Editor, this tutorial describes how you access those tools.

Standards: The Menu Bar and Toolbar

Visual Basic's menu bar and toolbars work just as you expect them to. You can click or press a menu bar option's hotkey (for example, Alt+F displays the File menu) to see a pull-down list of menu options that provide commands, another level of menus, or dialog boxes. Many of the menu options have shortcut keys (often called *accelerator keys*) such as Ctrl+S for the File | Save option. When you press accelerator keys, you don't first have to display the menu to access the option.

The toolbar provides one-button access to many common menu commands. Instead of selecting Edit | Paste, for example, you could click the Paste toolbar button. As with most of today's Windows applications, Visual Basic supports a wide range of toolbars. Select View | Toolbars to see a list of available toolbars. Each one that is currently showing will appear with a check mark by its name.

> VB uses twips to measure the size and location of forms and objects contained in forms. A *twip* is 1,440th of an inch (the smallest screen measurement you can adjust). Twip values usually appear in pairs. The first location value describes the x-coordinate (the number of twips from the left of the screen) and the second value describes the y-coordinate (the number of twips from the top of the screen), with 0,0 indicating the upper-left corner of the screen. The first size value describes the width of the form, and the second size value describes the height of the form. Therefore, the size coordinate pair 1000,3000 indicates that the Form window will be 1,000 twips wide and 3,000 twips tall when the program runs. As you'll learn in the next section, the Form window is the primary window for the applications you write. The location and size coordinates describe the form's location and size when you run the application.

The Form Window: Where It All Happens

The Form window is your primary work area. Although the Form window first appears small relative to the rest of your screen, the Form window makes up the background of your application. If you write a Windows-based calculator with Visual Basic, the calculator's buttons all reside on the Form window and when someone runs the calculator, the calculator that appears is really just the application's Form window with components placed there and tied together with code.

> You won't see program code on the Form window. The Form window holds the program's interactive objects, such as command buttons, labels, text boxes, scrollbars, and other controls. The code appears elsewhere in a special Code window. The Code window doesn't appear in Figure 1.3, but you can select View | Code to see it. A Code window is little more than a text editor with which you write the programming statements that tie together the application.

Consider the sample program running in Figure 1.4's window. The window shows a simple dialog box with a few options, text boxes, and command buttons.

FIGURE **1.4.**

*A simple dialog box
produced from a
running Windows
program.*

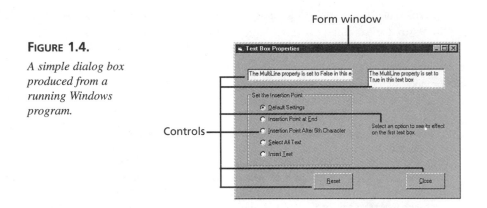

Form window

Controls

The programmer who created Figure 1.4's dialog box did so by opening a Form window, adding some controls (the items on the Form window that interact with the user—sometimes called tools), and tying the components together with some Visual Basic language code. That's exactly what you will do when writing both simple and complex Visual Basic applications. You will begin with a blank Form window and add controls to it, such as options and command buttons. Perhaps your application will even require multiple Form windows.

Some applications, such as Word, allow for several Form windows in a special mode called MDI (multiple-document interface) in which you can open multiple data documents within the same application. An application that requires only a single data window is called an SDI (single-document interface) application, such as the Windows Notepad application that lets the user open only one data document at a time. SDI applications might support multiple forms; however, these forms don't hold multiple data files but only provide extended support for extra dialog boxes and secondary work screens.

Compare Figure 1.4 with Figure 1.5. As you can see, Figure 1.5 shows the same application in the VB development environment, in its design-time state as opposed to its runtime state, which is shown in Figure 1.4. It is during design time that you design, create, edit, and correct the application. When you run the application, you can see the results of your work.

FIGURE 1.5.

The dialog box shown inside VB's development environment.

1

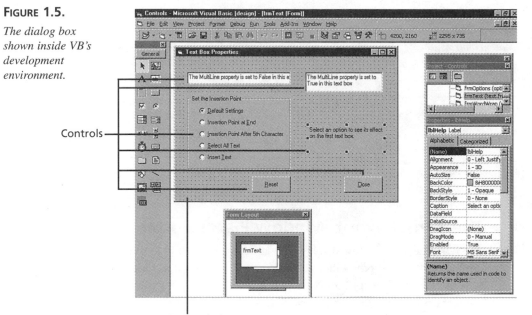

Controls

Form window

NEW TERM   The parts of the application that you create, such as the forms, the code, and the graphics that you prepare for output compose the *source program*. When you or another user compiles or runs the source program, VB translates the program into an executable program. You cannot make changes directly to an executable program. If you see bugs when you run the program, you must change the source application (which might contain multiple files in the project) and rerun or recompile the source.

The Toolbox Supplies Controls

The toolbox contains the controls that you place on the Form window. All the controls in Figure 1.5 appear on the toolbox. In the next hour, you'll learn how to place toolbox controls on the Form window. The toolbox never runs out of controls; if you place a command button on the Form window, another awaits you on the toolbox, ready to be placed.

Figure 1.6 names every tool that appears on the standard Toolbox window. These are called the intrinsic controls because all three editions of VB support these standard tools. You can add additional controls to the toolbox as your needs grow. Some extra tools come with all three editions of VB, but these extra tools don't appear on the Toolbox window until you add them through the Project | Components menu option. If you use the Professional or Enterprise Editions, you will be able to add extra controls that don't appear in the Standard Edition's collection of intrinsic and extra controls.

FIGURE 1.6.

The VB toolbox contains intrinsic controls.

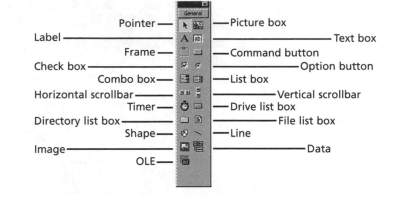

The Form Layout Window Places Forms

The Form Layout window displays the initial position and relative size of the current form shown in the Form window. For example, look back at Figure 1.5 to see the Form Layout window. The application shown is a multiple-form application. The form with the title Text Box Properties is just one of several forms. The Form Layout window always shows where the form appears in the current Form window. If you want the form to appear at a different location than the current position, you can move the form inside the Form Layout window to move the position where the form appears when the user runs the application.

This book generally doesn't show the Form Layout window in figures to give more room to the Form window and its contents. You can display the Form Layout window from the View menu, and you can hide the Form Layout window by clicking its Close button.

The Project Explorer Window

The Project Explorer window, often called the Project window, gives you a tree-structured view of all the files in the application. Microsoft changed the formal name from Project window to Project Explorer window between versions 4 and 5 to emphasize the resemblance of the window to the typical Explorer tree-structure file views prevalent in Windows NT and 95. You can expand and collapse branches of the view for more or less detail.

The Project Explorer window displays forms, modules (files that hold supporting code for the application), classes (advanced modules), and more. When you want to work with a particular part of the loaded application, double-click the component in the Project window to bring that component into focus. In other words, if the Project Explorer window displays three forms and you need to edit one of the forms, locate and double-click the form name in the Project window to activate that form in the Form window. Figure 1.7 shows a Project Explorer window that contains several kinds of files.

FIGURE 1.7.

The Project Explorer keeps track of a project's components.

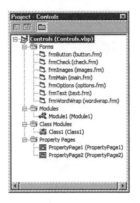

If you add a help file to your application, the Project window doesn't display the help file.

The Properties Window

NEW TERM *Properties* are detailed descriptive information about a control. A different list appears in the Properties window every time you click over a different Form window tool. The Properties window describes properties (descriptive and functional information) of the form and its controls. Many properties exist for almost every object in Visual Basic. The Properties window lists all the properties of the Form window's selected control.

Help Is at Your Fingertips

Visual Basic's online help system is one of the most advanced on the market. When you want help with a control, window, tool, or command, press F1. Visual Basic analyzes what you are doing and offers help. In addition, Visual Basic supports a tremendous help resource called Books Online. When you select Books Online from the Help menu, Visual Basic displays a tree-structured view of books about Visual Basic that you can search and read. The online help extends to the Internet as well. If you have an Internet connection, you can browse the latest help topics by selecting Help | Microsoft on the Web.

Summary

This hour quickly introduced you to Visual Basic. Perhaps you already can see that Visual Basic is more than it first appears. Programmers use Visual Basic to create extremely advanced Windows applications. Now that you understand VB's purpose and how to start and stop it, you're ready to jump right in.

The next hour describes a sample application so you can get a better picture of how Visual Basic's components work together.

Q&A

Q Must I learn a new language to use Visual Basic?

A Visual Basic is more than just a programming language. Nevertheless, learning VB's language portion is integral to writing advanced applications. Fortunately, the Visual Basic programming language is one of the easiest programming languages in existence. The language is simple but powerful because Microsoft based Visual Basic's language on BASIC, a beginner's language. VB's simplicity doesn't translate to inability, however. Visual Basic is one of the most powerful Windows programming languages on the market and supports advanced programming techniques.

Q How can I master the complicated-looking development environment?

A The Developer Studio might look complicated, but only because you are new to the development environment. The development environment is little more than a collection of windows. As you learn more about Visual Basic, you will learn which windows you need and when you need them; you can close the other windows. The Developer Studio development environment is a development platform Microsoft has integrated into most of its language products, including Visual C++, Visual InterDev, and Visual J++. Therefore, after you master the development environment, you will already understand the development environment of other languages.

Workshop

The quiz questions and exercises are provided for your further understanding. See Appendix B for the answers.

Quiz

1. What is the purpose of Visual Basic?

2. How have programming languages changed over the years?

3. What programming language is Visual Basic based on?

4. Which Visual Basic development environment window forms the background for the applications you develop?

5. What is the difference between the Form window and the Form Layout window?

6. True or false: All the tools you find on the Toolbox window when you start Visual Basic are the intrinsic controls.

Exercise

Start Visual Basic and select various options from the View window. You will see several new windows open. Look through the menu options and click any scrollbars you see. Don't save anything when prompted. Double-click over tools on the toolbox to see different tools appear on the Form window. Move the tools away from the center of the window to see more of them at one time. As you click different tools in the Form window, watch the Properties window change to reflect the current tool's properties.

HOUR 2

Analyzing Visual Basic Programs

This hour's lesson pinpoints the concepts you learned in the last hour. You will analyze a sample program in depth to learn more about how a Visual Basic application's components work together to form one executable program. Although this lesson might raise a few more questions than it answers, that's good! You need this overall walkthrough before you get your hands dirty with Visual Basic in Hour 3, "Controls and Properties."

Don't worry, this lesson isn't all theory and description. The final part of this lesson walks you through the building of a complete Visual Basic application. A little help from the VB Application Wizard will go a long way.

The highlights of this hour include

- What events are
- How to respond to events
- When to use event procedures
- How to name event procedures
- When to use the VB Application Wizard

Event-Driven Programs

Lots can happen when a Windows program executes. For example, consider the Microsoft
Excel screen in Figure 2.1. What can happen next? What exactly will the user at the keyboard do? The user might click a toolbar button, select a menu option, press F1 to get
help, scroll the window, enter additional numbers or formulas, edit existing worksheet
cells, or switch to another program.

In the old days of programming (less than a decade ago), before windowed environments
became so popular, the program dictated what the user could next do. The program
might ask a question, and the user could answer the question and nothing else until the
question was answered. The program might display a menu of options. Although the user
had a choice of options, he only had the choice of a menu selection. If he wanted to
move to another part of the program, he couldn't unless such a move was part of the currently displayed menu.

The multitasking, multiuser windowed environments changed everything. Today's
Windows program has no idea what might happen next. The program must offer a
plethora of choices that range from menu options to various controls and data-entry
locations, and the program just has to wait and see what happens.

When the programs lost control, users gained. Users can now perform any one of many tasks. The problem for the programmer is responding to users' actions when so many actions are possible. Fortunately, Microsoft designed Windows to be elegant not only for the user but for the programmer as well. When virtually anything happens in the Windows environment, Windows generates an event. An event might be a keypress, an internal clock tick, a menu selection, a mouse click, a mouse movement, a task switch, or one of many hundreds of other possible events.

NEW TERM   An *event* is something that happens, usually but not always, due to the user at the keyboard, during a program's operation.

Your program doesn't have to wait around for the user to do something specific. In text-based programming days, you would write one big program that guided the user through the execution of the code step-by-step. The program would take the user to a menu, ask the user questions, and offer only a limited set of choices. In many ways, a Visual Basic program is nothing more than a collection of small routines. These routines, called *event procedures*, handle individual events. If and only if an event occurs for which you've written an event procedure does that event procedure execute. You don't have to do anything special to execute the event procedure–just write the code. In other words, your program responds to events by supplying a matching event procedure and your program ignores events if you haven't written an event procedure.

Control Events

Every control you place on a form supports one or more events. For example, if you place a text box in the center of the Form window and run the program, you can click the text box, enter text in the text box, double-click the text box, and ignore the text box. The Text Box control happens to support events that can recognize when you've done anything to the control.

If you've written an event procedure for that text box's event, your code's instructions will execute automatically as soon as the event occurs. Therefore, if you've written code to blank out the text box as soon as the user clicks the text box and you've written another event procedure for the double-click event that fills the text box with Xs when the user double-clicks the text box, the text box fills with blanks or Xs when you run the program and click or double-click the text box.

You'll see plenty of examples in this and subsequent lessons that demonstrate the nature of event procedures.

Analyzing Sample Applications

Perhaps the best way to begin learning about VB application creation is to analyze sample applications. You will gain practice working within the development environment and master the various windows quickly.

To begin, perform these steps:

1. Start Visual Basic. If the New Project dialog box appears, close it; you will open a project without the dialog box's help.

2. Select File | Open Project (a toolbar button does this, too) to display folders from which to choose. Select the drive and directory containing the source code you retrieved from the CD that accompanies this book. You will see various project names.

3. Locate the project with the filename `Lesson 9 Int Proj.vbp` (the extension may not appear if you've turned off the display of filename extensions in Windows Explorer). The project describes a simple interest rate application that you'll learn how to create in Hour 9, "Combining Code and Controls."

Several files other than those you see in the dialog box actually reside in the `Source` folder. Visual Basic knows, however, that when you select File | Open Project, you want to open a project and not another kind of file, so Visual Basic displays only project files in the dialog box. All project files end with the `.vbp` filename extension to distinguish them from form files that end with the `.frm` extension and module files that end with `.bas` (other Visual Basic file types exist, but we won't cover them here).

The advantage that projects present to the Visual Basic programmer is that a project is a bookkeeping record of the entire collection of files that compose an application. When you write even a simple Visual Basic application, Visual Basic creates a project for that application so that as the application's functionality grows, the project can track all the files related to that project. No matter how many files go with a project, when you open the project, Visual Basic puts the project's files at your fingertips in the Project window.

Double-click the `Lesson 9 Int Proj.vbp` project file now. The Project window now displays two folders, one named Forms and one named Modules. Open the Forms folder and then double-click the form named `frmInterest` in the Project Explorer window. Your development environment changes dramatically to display the project, as shown in Figure 2.2.

FIGURE 2.2.

The Lesson 9 Int Proj *project.*

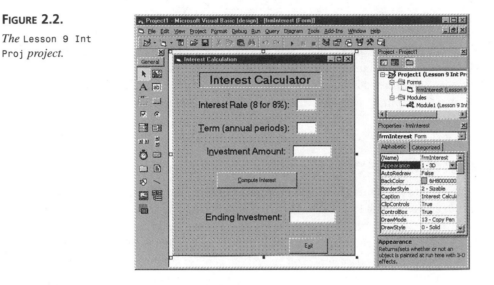

As you might guess from the name of the project and from the window in front of you, this application calculates interest rates for loans and investments. Click any plus signs you see in the Project window to expand the list. You now know that this application is a collection of two files: a form and a module file. Actually, a third file goes with the project: the Lesson 9 Int Proj.vbp project file itself, which Visual Basic keeps track of and updates as needed. (Drag the edge of the Project window to see more of the text within the window.)

The Project window describes two important aspects of a VB project: the external disk drive filenames for each project file and the internal names used inside the project. For example, the current form open in the Form window is named frmInterest. VB's title bar shows the name of the open form file and also shows that the file is a form and not another kind of file.

To every area of your project, the form is called frmInterest. This form got its name from the program writer, who named the form frmInterest. As you'll see throughout this tutorial, programmers often precede items they name with a three-letter abbreviation for the object. Thereafter, when you look through a list of object names, you'll know just from the names what the names represent.

The form isn't stored on the disk drive under the name frmInterest, however. As the Project window's parentheses show, the form named frmInterest is called Lesson 9 Int Form.frm on the disk. Rarely will the actual filename match that of the internal name used in the project. In a way, the three-letter abbreviated prefix works like a file extension in that the prefix describes the object type.

The naming rules for internal Visual Basic names differ from those of files. Therefore, you will need to give each object you create in the Project window both a filename and an internal VB name. If you don't supply a name, Visual Basic supplies one for you, but VB isn't good at assigning names to objects. VB would be happy calling every command button on your form Command1, Command2, and so on. When you name command buttons, however, you'll make up names that better match their meaning, such as cmdOK and cmdExit.

Naming Objects

As you create applications and add to them objects such as forms and modules, you'll have to come up with lots of names so that both you and Visual Basic can distinguish between the objects. Unlike filenames, a Visual Basic object name must begin with an alphabetic character and can contain letters and numbers, but it cannot contain periods or several other special characters. You can mix uppercase and lowercase as much as you want. The illegal period is the primary reason why internal object names differ from filenames.

Generally, as stated previously, programmers prefix a name with letters representing the kind of object they are naming. The prefix is often stated in lowercase letters and the rest of the name often appears as a combination of uppercase and lowercase letters. Notice that the programmer did not precede the Module1 VB name file with mdl or mod, or give the module a more appropriate internal name such as ModInterestCalc, but that doing so would better describe the file's module type.

Running Applications

You learned in Hour 1, "Visual Basic at Work," that you can execute a Visual Basic application by running the application or by first compiling the application and then running the executable compiled program. For the majority of your VB training, you'll run applications from within the Visual Basic development environment without taking the time to compile the application first. Usually, compilation is the last step a programmer takes before distributing the application to other users.

Generally, and for all of this tutorial, you'll run your applications from within the Visual Basic development environment. When you run within the development environment, you gain all kinds of advantages that your users will not need. You can stop the program in midstream and analyze values (using the debugging tools available in the development environment), you can start and stop your program at any point, you gain access to the source code faster each time you stop the program, and the program's startup is faster than having to wait for the compiler. See Hour 20, "Writing Correct Applications," for additional information about debugging your applications.

> When you are ready to distribute your application, select File | Make to start the compilation process.

Although several ways exist to run the program, the easiest is to press F5, the accelerator key for the Run | Start menu option. (A Start toolbar button also gives you quick access to the application's startup.)

Press F5 now to run the application. The application contains fields where you enter investment values. Enter an interest rate, term, and investment amount. Click the Compute Interest button to see an ending investment value such as the one in Figure 2.3. If you change a value, click the Compute Interest button once again to see how the change affects the investment. Click Exit to close the running program.

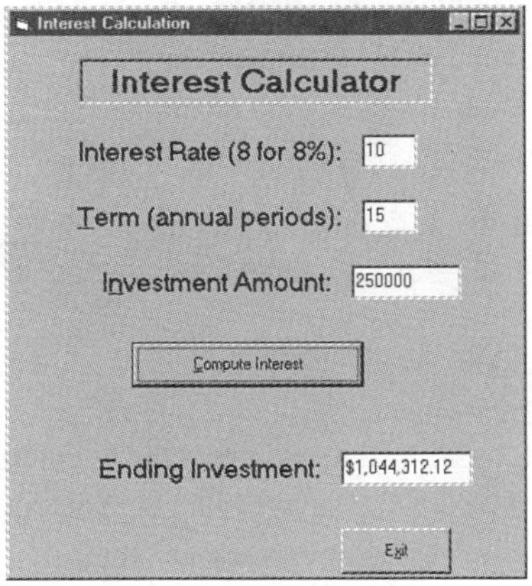

FIGURE 2.3.

Running the application.

Interest Calculation

Interest Calculator

Interest Rate (8 for 8%): `10`

Term (annual periods): `15`

Investment Amount: `250000`

Compute Interest

Ending Investment: `$1,044,312.12`

Exit

> Don't confuse the Toolbox window with the toolbar. The toolbar is the row of buttons that mimic certain menu options; it appears directly beneath the menu bar. The Toolbox window holds your tools and a collection of controls that you place on forms.

Click a button once to see that button's properties in the Properties window. Figure 2.4 shows the properties for the Compute Interest button. Each control supports a unique set of properties to differentiate the control from surrounding ones. For example, the Compute Interest button is named cmdCompute and has a Caption property value of &Compute Interest (the ampersand indicates an underlined letter) but the Exit button is named cmdExit and has a Caption property of E&xit. Although many of the two buttons' properties are identical, they contain differences that set them apart, as you see when you scroll through the Properties window.

FIGURE 2.4.

The cmdCompute
button's properties.

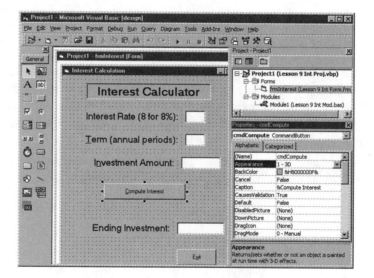

Where's the Code?

This lesson began by describing code and event procedures in detail, and yet not a word has been mentioned about those topics for several pages. The code is there as a module file, as you can see from the Project Explorer window. Actually, the interest calculation program contains two sets of code.

Controls cannot have the same name if you place them on the same form, but two forms might contain controls with the same name. A control name goes with its parent form. For example, an application might contain an About dialog box and a form that displays account information. Both forms can have a command button named cmdExit that closes the form's window. Each form contains its own code, called the *form module*, that manages and responds to the controls on that form. You won't always put code in a form's form module, but you often will.

The Project window's Modules entry also is a file with code in it. A module file that lies outside a form module is often called a standard module. You'll place event procedures for forms in the forms' form modules and you'll place common routines that work on all the forms in a standard module file that lies outside the form module but still in the project.

> As you write more code, you'll write routines that you'll want to use again, such as special calculations that are unique to your business. By storing these general-purpose routines inside modules instead of embedding them in form modules that go with specific applications, you can copy and load the standard module into multiple applications so that you don't have to type the general-purpose code more than once. Therefore, once you've written a useful procedure that calculates or processes data outside the form's boundaries, you can reuse that code and insert it into other projects as long as you keep the routines in a standard module file.

NEW TERM   You enter, edit, and view the language of VB in the *Code window*.

Visual Basic always presents you with VB code in the Code window. A Code window acts a lot like a simple text editor or word processor, in that you can insert, delete, copy, cut, and paste text. Despite the graphical nature of applications and the controls, the code you write to tie things together is still in text.

Take a brief look at the application's single module's Code window by double-clicking the Project window's Module1 entry. Visual Basic opens the module's Code window, as shown in Figure 2.5.

FIGURE 2.5.

*The module's Code
window.*

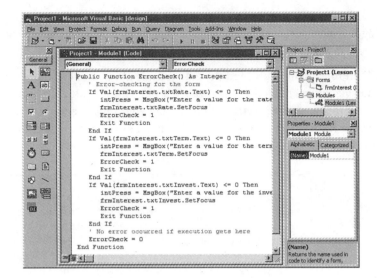

Code appears in the Code window in various colors to indicate the purpose of the code.
As you learn the Visual Basic language, you will better understand why some code is
green and some black. Scroll down through the Code window. Don't worry about understanding much or anything about the Code window at this time. As you can see, much of
the Code window contains words in English, but the structure might seem completely
odd if you've never programmed before. By the time you finish this 24-hour tutorial, you
will understand the entire program and be able to speak the Code window's language
fluently.

Click Close to close the module's Code window (not VB!) for now. When you close the
Code window, make sure that you see the Interest form before you start the next section.
If you don't see the Interest form, simply double-click the frmInterest form in the
Project window.

Event Procedures

Visual Basic makes it easy to locate event procedure code for controls on forms. Double-
click any control to see one of its event procedures. For example, if you double-click the
Exit command button, Visual Basic opens the Code window and places the text cursor in
the set of lines shown in Listing 2.1.

LISTING 2.1. THE EXIT COMMAND BUTTON'S Click EVENT PROCEDURE.

```
1: Private Sub cmdExit_Click()
2: ' Unload the form and terminate application
3: Unload frmInterest
4: End
5: End Sub
```

NEW TERM *Wrapper lines* are the first and last lines of a procedure.

NEW TERM A *block* is a section of code that goes together as a single unit.

Don't sweat the details, but become familiar with the overall event procedure. Most event procedures begin with the statement `Private Sub...` and end with `End Sub`. The `Private...End` block illustrates the first and last lines of the event procedure. The lines between these wrapper lines compose the body of the event procedure.

All controls have unique names as you saw earlier. All event procedures also have unique names. An event procedure name always takes this form:

controlName_eventName ()

> The parentheses are not actually part of the name. Some procedures require values inside the parentheses, whereas others do not. Even if an event procedure requires nothing inside the parentheses, the parentheses are still required.

The event procedure always consists of the control name, an underscore, and the procedure's event name. If you want to respond to both the click and double-click events that might be applied to the Exit command button, you would have to write an event procedure named `cmdExit_Click()` and one named `cmdExit_DblClick()`.

You don't have to memorize that the double-click event is named `DblClick` and that a keypress event is named `KeyDown`. The top of every Code window contains a drop-down list box, which contains every event possible for the control listed in the left-hand drop-down list box. The left-hand list box holds the name of every control on the form. Again, don't get too bogged down in details because when it's time to use these drop-down list boxes to select events, this lesson describes the process in detail.

The naming convention for the event procedure isn't your decision, but Visual Basic's. The `Click` event procedure for a command button named `cmdTest` will always have to be cmdTest_Click(). The two-part name makes the event procedure extremely specific; from the name, both you and Visual Basic know that the code executes only if the user clicks the cmdTest command button.

Properties and Event Procedures

This is a good time to review properties. When the programmer (that's you!) places controls on a form, she generally sets many of the control's property values at that time in the Properties window. A programmer can then write the event procedure code for the control, or she might place additional controls on the form and write event procedures later.

Many of the properties in the Properties window show up immediately during design time as you assign the properties. In other words, if you place a command button on a form and immediately click the Properties window's Caption property and type Click Here, the command button instantly reads Click Here in the Form window.

The event procedure code, however, doesn't do anything until runtime. The instructions you learn to place in the event procedures will not execute until the application's user runs the program and triggers events at runtime. The Properties window often reacts at design time, whereas the Code window often reacts at runtime. In a way, the code inside a procedure window works like a cook's recipe: the recipe describes an action that will take place once the cook begins the dish. The program describes what will happen when the program's user executes the program.

Generating an Application from Scratch

Enough already! How about a little fun? You can create your very first Visual Basic application without knowing any more than you know now about Visual Basic. The secret is Visual Basic's VB Application Wizard, a wizard that generates an application for you based on your responses to a series of dialog boxes.

NEW TERM   A *skeleton program* is a program shell that you must fill in with specific code.

Despite the ease with which you can generate an application shell with the VB Application Wizard, this book doesn't revisit the wizard after this section. You need to get well grounded in Visual Basic before you'll really understand how to add to the generated program and change the shell to suit your needs. Therefore, the VB Application Wizard arguably benefits the experienced Visual Basic programmer more than the beginning programmer because the experienced programmer will be able to decipher the generated shell and add specifics to make the program operate as needed.

Perform these steps to generate your first Visual Basic application with the VB Application Wizard:

1. Select File | New Project. Click No at the dialog box that asks if you want to save any changes to the Interest Calculation application because you don't want to over-write any changes you might have made.

2. When the New Project dialog box appears, double-click the VB Application Wizard icon to start the wizard.

3. Read through the wizard's dialog boxes and click Next when you're ready to move to the next dialog box. Keep all the default values along the way. As you'll see on the Menus dialog box (shown in Figure 2.6), the wizard gives you a choice of menu items you want to see on the generated application's menu bar. Although menus are relatively simple to place in a Visual Basic application, the wizard makes placing menus much simpler because you only need to check the boxes next to the items you want on the final application's menu bar.

FIGURE 2.6.

Selecting the menu items you want to place in the final application.

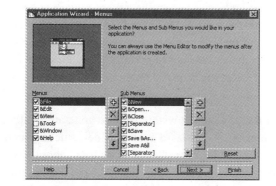

4. As you click through the wizard, look for the dialog box that describes the application's Internet connectivity. The generated application, despite being a shell, can access the Web directly. You can send your application's users to a Web page or let them view Web pages from inside your own application. The real magic is that the wizard handles all the details for you if you want the options. For now, don't select Internet Access but keep moving through the dialog boxes by clicking Next.

5. The wizard gives you a chance to interface with a database program, such as Microsoft Access, before taking you to the final dialog box, where you click Finish to watch Visual Basic's wizard perform its wizardry. Right before your eyes, the wizard will put the application together, add the forms, and build the menus.

6. Click the closing dialog box and close the final instructions. The wizard leaves your development environment fairly clean, but you know that you can double-click any object in the Project window to see forms and code modules. For now, simply run the program to see Figure 2.7's screen.

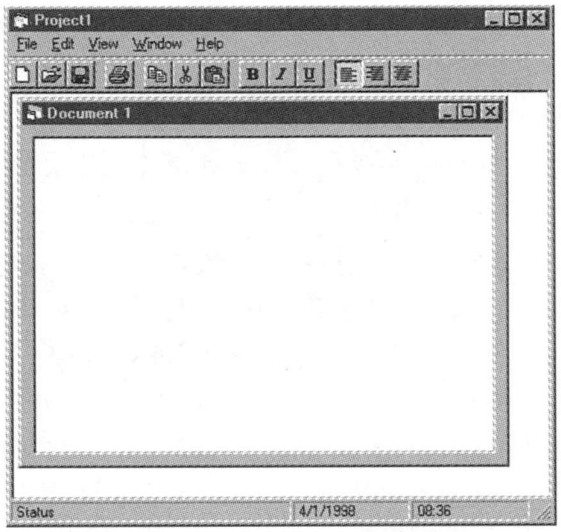

FIGURE 2.7.

The VB Application Wizard generated a working, albeit plain, application.

The generated program looks somewhat like a word processor because of the large editing area in the center of the screen. Try the menus and click the toolbar buttons. Things look good. You will find that the application doesn't respond to your keystrokes as you might expect, however. If you attempt to perform certain tasks, a small dialog box will appear telling you that what you requested has not yet been implemented by the programmer (you).

You must remember that it's not the wizard's job to generate a fully working application that performs specific tasks. The wizard's job is to construct a general application to which you can later add the specifics. As you learn more about Visual Basic, you will better appreciate how much time and effort the VB Application Wizard saves you because the simple task of adding a standard menu and toolbar buttons can take an afternoon. The generated application is a great starting point for your own applications once you and Visual Basic become better acquainted.

Summary

You've just created your first application! Actually, you got a little help from the VB Application Wizard, but that's okay. You are now beginning to understand how a Visual Basic application's components fit together. The events that the user triggers are often related directly to your application's forms or controls, and you now know where to place the code that handles the important events.

The next hour shows you how to create an application from scratch without the help of the wizard. You will better learn how the toolbox and Properties window interact and support each other's activities.

Q&A

Q How do I know which events to respond to when so many events can happen at any time?

A Your application's requirements determine the events you respond to in the application, nothing else. For example, if your application has no need to respond to a mouse click over a label you've placed on the form, don't write an event procedure for that label's Click event. If the user clicks over the label, Windows will send a message signaling the event to your program, but your program simply lets the event pass through and never responds to the event.

Q Why should I not compile my application before I run it, if compiling the application makes it more efficient?

A When you compile an application, Visual Basic translates your source code project into an executable program. The executable program often takes less disk space than all the source files, and the executable program is easier to distribute. Nevertheless, when you develop and test an application, you don't want to compile the application every time you run it to test the application and see the results. As a matter of fact, don't compile your application until you have completely finished the application and are about to distribute it to others. The compiled application is safe from modifications because a compiled program is virtually impossible to change without ruining the application's executable file. In addition, the compiled file will be faster than the project that you run from inside the development environment. Nevertheless, during development, you don't care about speed, but you do care about bugs. During debugging test runs, you want your project to execute as soon as you request it, without taking the extra time necessary to compile each time.

Q What is the difference between a form module and a standard module?

A A form module always goes with its form. The form holds controls, remember, and each of those controls can trigger and respond to events. The event procedure code that you write for the form's controls must reside in that form's form module. General-purpose routines, such as common calculations that several applications must share, should go in a standard module with the .bas filename extension. By the way, not only can other applications utilize standard module files, but you can add the same form and form module to multiple applications as well. The application's Project window will take care of the bookkeeping details.

Workshop

The quiz questions and exercises are provided for your further understanding. See Appendix B for the answers.

Quiz

1. How do windowed programs differ from programs running in text-based environments?

2. What are events?

3. Why are project component filenames not usually the same as their internal VB names?

4. What is usually the last step a VB programmer takes before distributing an application to users?

5. How does Visual Basic know which procedure to execute for a particular control's event?

6. True or false: All controls support one and only one event.

7. Which usually respond at design time: control property changes or event procedures?

Exercises

1. Scroll through the interest rate project's form module again, looking at the various event procedures coded there. Determine which events are handled and which are not. An event procedure whose name begins with Form is an event procedure for the form itself. For example, you can respond to the user's mouse click over the form differently from a mouse click over a command button. Look for the events associated with the various command buttons on the form. Most often, a command button's event procedure is a ...Click() or ...DblClick() event procedure because most users either click or double-click command buttons and the click and double-click events are the ones you often need to respond to.

2. Run the VB Application Wizard once again and, this time, test other features by including more objects (such as the Internet and database access if your disk drive contains a database file somewhere that you can locate when the wizard asks for the location) and selecting different options. Run the generated shell to see how differently the wizard's generated shell applications can act.

Hour **3**

Controls and Properties

Nobody can master Visual Basic until he masters controls and properties.
The form is the placeholder for the controls, and the controls are the really
important parts of any application. Many of the properties require different
kinds of values, and you will learn in this hour's lesson how to set those
values.

Before you finish this lesson, you also will have created your very first
application from scratch without the aid of the VB Application Wizard. You
will have created a new project, sized the form, added controls, set control
properties, and even written an event procedure using the Visual Basic programming language. As you'll soon see, Visual Basic makes all those tasks
simple.

The highlights of this hour include

- What steps are required for application creation
- How to place and size controls
- Why various properties require different setting methods
- Which naming prefixes work best
- Why your application's ToolTips give users added help

Creating New Applications

When you create an application from scratch instead of using the VB Application Wizard to generate the program shell, you control every aspect of the application's design and you place all the program's controls on the form yourself. When you place those controls, you must name the controls, position the controls, set control properties, adjust the control sizes, and hook up all the event procedure code that goes with each control.

All this may sound daunting, but Visual Basic simplifies things as much as possible. Although the task isn't quite as simple as running the wizard, you have the power to create the exact application you need. Newcomers need to learn how to create applications without the wizard so they can fully master all the ins and outs of Visual Basic.

To create a new application from scratch, start Visual Basic and double-click the Standard EXE icon. The blank Form window appears in the work area's upper-left corner next to the toolbox, ready for you to begin creating the application by placing the controls.

> The default Form window size is fairly small, especially when you realize that the Form window holds the application's background. Most applications appear either full-screen or in an initial window much larger than the Form window size that appears. Therefore, one of the first tasks you will usually perform is to increase the Form window's size.

If you double-click the Form window's title, Visual Basic expands the Form window to full screen. However, with your toolbox and other windows on the screen, you'll have to use the scrollbars to access various parts of the form. Of course, if your application is full screen, you'll need to work with the scrollbars to add controls to the full form.

> This book's Form windows typically remain a size at which you can see the entire form as well as the surrounding windows. Therefore, most of the applications in this book contain fairly small Form windows. The book's Form windows will be larger than the default size that appears when you first start Visual Basic, but the Form windows will be far smaller than full screen.

Controls Provide the Interface

The controls you select for your application's form are important because the controls (also called tools) provide the application interface for your users. Users interact with your application by clicking the controls and entering text in the controls. Placing and sizing controls are perhaps the two most important tasks you can master at this point.

Placing Controls

After you increase the Form window to a reasonable size, your job is to place controls on the form. Use either of these two methods for placing controls on the form:

- Double-click any control on the Toolbox window to place that control on the Form window. As Figure 3.1 shows, the control appears in the center of the Form window.

FIGURE 3.1.

The command button appears in the center of the Form window.

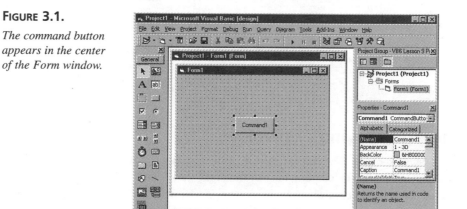

If a control appears in the center of the form already, the new control will be on top of the existing control. You can drag the new control to a different location. The eight sizing handles (the small boxes that appear around a selected control) indicate that the control is selected. If several controls appear on the Form window, the selected controls will display their sizing handles. (Typically, only one control will be selected at any one time but you can select multiple controls by holding the Ctrl key and clicking several controls.)

- If you click a toolbox control once, the toolbox highlights the control. If you then move the mouse cursor to the Form window, the mouse cursor turns into a crosshair indicating that you can place the selected control anywhere on the form. Although a control appears in the center of the Form window automatically as soon as you double-click the control, a selected control appears only when you click and drag your mouse crosshair on the Form window. The final control appears when you release the mouse.

The advantage of using this approach to placing controls over the first approach is that you don't have to move and resize the control after you've placed it. Figure 3.2 shows Figure 3.1's command button placed in the center of the form with a double-click, as well as a new command button placed on the form by dragging the control. You can place the control exactly where you want it and at the size you want it when you drag the control onto the form.

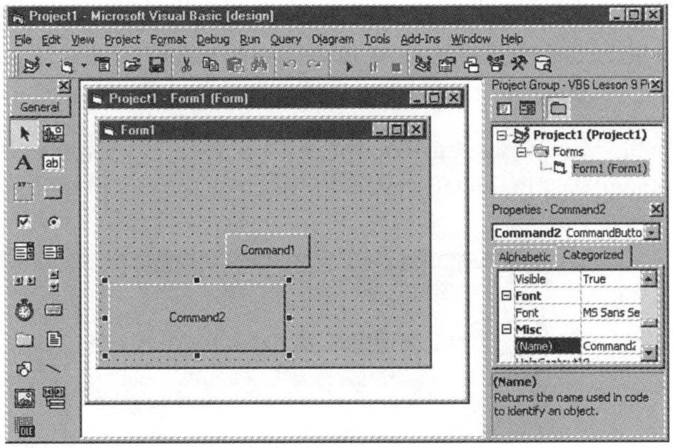

FIGURE 3.2.

The second command button is placed and sized immediately.

Sizing and Moving Controls

You can change the size of only a selected control. The eight sizing handles are the key to resizing the control. You can drag any of the eight sizing handles in any direction to increase or decrease the control's size. Of course, if you placed a control on the form by dragging the control, you won't need to resize the control as often as you would if you double-clicked the toolbox tool to place the control.

You can move a selected control to any area of the Form window by dragging the control with your mouse. After you click to select a control, click the control and hold down the mouse button to drag the control to another part of the Form window.

Sometimes you might want to drag several controls to a new location as a group. For example, perhaps you've placed a set of command buttons at the bottom of a form and after adjusting the Form window's size, you determine that you need to move the buttons down some. Although you can move the command buttons one at a time, you can more quickly select all the command buttons and move them as a group.

In addition, you can lasso the controls by dragging a selection rectangle around the controls you want to select as a group. When you release your mouse, the controls within the selected region will be selected, like those shown in Figure 3.3.

FIGURE 3.3.

Selecting multiple controls when you want to move the entire group at once.

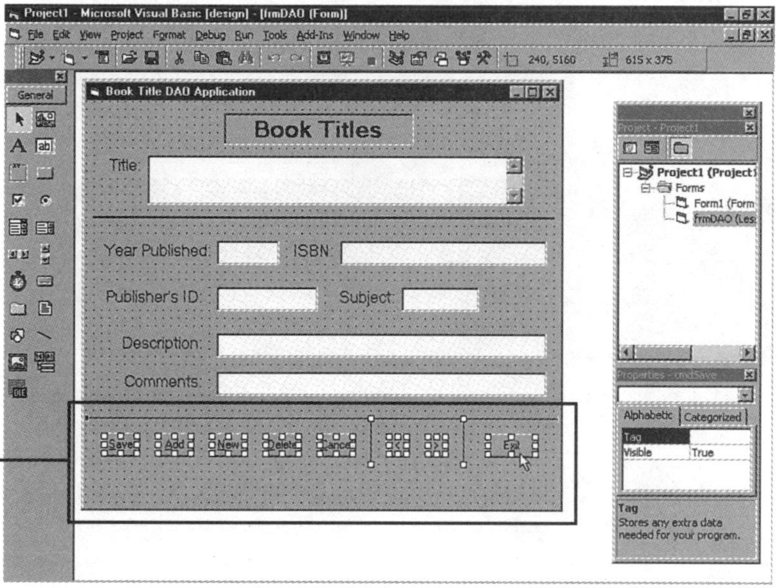

The selected controls —

Remember how to select multiple controls if you find yourself needing to change properties other than the location of controls. If you select multiple controls before changing a control property, all controls in the selected range will take on that new property value. You can only change the common properties that appear in all the selected controls.

Setting Properties

As you add controls to the Form window, the Properties window updates to show the properties for the currently selected control. The selected control is usually the control you last placed on the form. Visual Basic lets you see a control's properties in the Properties window by clicking to select the control or by selecting the control from the Properties window's drop-down list box, as shown in Figure 3.4.

FIGURE 3.4.

Selecting the control to work with.

Control object types

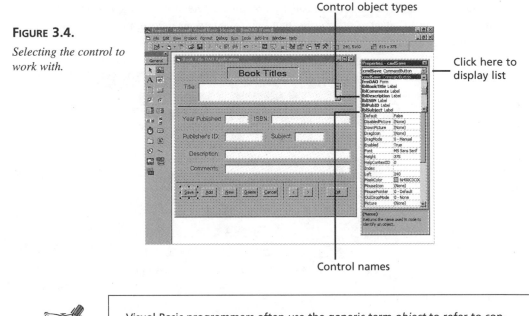

Click here to display list

Control names

Visual Basic programmers often use the generic term *object* to refer to controls, forms, menus, and various other items on the screen and in the code.

The Left, Top, Height, and Width properties are about the only properties you can set without accessing the Properties window. As you size and move a control into place, Visual Basic updates the Left, Top, Height, and Width properties according to the control's placement on the Form window and the control's size. As with the form location and size measurements, these properties appear in twips (unless you specify a different value in the ScaleMode property). Left indicates how far from the form's left edge the control appears, Top indicates how far from the top of the form the control appears, and the Height and Width properties indicate the control's size.

Even the form has properties. Click your Form window and look at the Properties window. The form will be the selected object at the top of the Properties window (Form1 is the default name for an application's initial form).

After you place and size a control, the first property you should modify is the Name property. Although Visual Basic assigns default names to controls when you place them on the Form window, the default names don't indicate the control's true purpose in your application. In addition, the default names don't contain the three-letter prefix that describes the control.

For your reference, Table 3.1 lists common prefixes used for control names. When you name your Form window's controls, you'll appreciate later that you took the time to type the three-letter abbreviations at the beginning of the names. Then you'll be less likely to assign to a text box, a property that belongs to a command button control inside an event procedure. (Such an assignment will cause a runtime error.)

The Name property is so important that Visual Basic lists the Name property first (as (Name) inside parentheses) in the Properties window instead of alphabetically in the Properties window, where the other properties reside.

3

TABLE 3.1. USE THESE PREFIX ABBREVIATIONS FOR CONTROL NAMES.

Prefix	Control
cbo	Combo box
chk	Check box
cmd	Command button
dir	Directory list box
drv	Drive list box
fil	File list box
fra	Frame
frm	Form
grd	Grid
hsb	Horizontal scrollbar
img	Image
lbl	Label
lin	Line
lst	List box
mnu	Menu
ole	OLE client

continues

TABLE 3.1. CONTINUED

Prefix	Control
opt	Option button
pic	Picture box
shp	Shape
tmr	Timer
txt	Text box
vsb	Vertical scrollbar

NEW TERM   A *ToolTip* is a pop-up description box that appears when the user rests the mouse pointer over a control.

Some property values you set by typing the values directly in the Properties window. For example, to enter a value for a control's `ToolTipText` property, click once on the Properties window's `ToolTipText` property and type the ToolTip text.

Giving Your Users Help

The ToolTip is a great feature that helps your users and is as easy to implement as typing text into the control's `ToolTipText` property. Most applications since the introduction of Windows 95 include ToolTips, and there's no reason why your applications should not include them as well.

Figure 3.5 shows a ToolTip that appears in Visual Basic when you rest the mouse pointer over the Form Layout Window toolbar button. The best time to add ToolTip text is when you adjust a new control's properties because you are more likely to remember the primary purpose for the control. Often programmers intend to add these helpful items later, after they "complete" the application, but then the items are never added.

ToolTip text

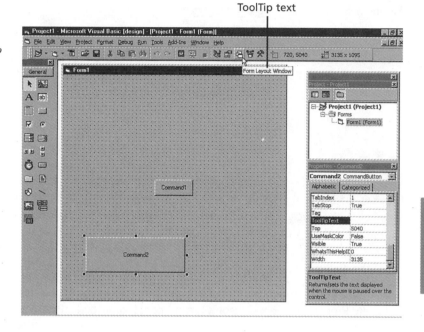

If you want to change a property value, such as the Name property, you can click the property and enter a new value. As you type, the new value replaces the original value. If instead of clicking you double-click the property, Visual Basic highlights the property value and lets you edit the existing value by pressing your cursor keys and using Insert and Delete to edit the current property value.

 As you select a property, read the text that appears at the bottom of the Properties window. The text describes the property and serves as a reminder about what some of the more obscure properties do.

Some properties require a selection from a drop-down list box. For example, Figure 3.6 shows a command button's Visible property's drop-down list box. The Visible property can either be True or False. No other values work for the property, so Visual Basic lets you select from one of those two values when you click the property value to display the down arrow and open the drop-down list box.

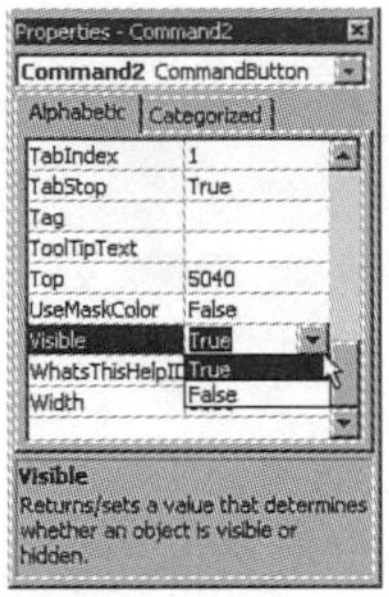

FIGURE 3.6.

Some properties require a selection from a list box.

If an ellipsis (. . .) is displayed when you click the property value, such as the Font property when you click the current Font property's value, a dialog box opens when you click the ellipsis. A Font property is more than just a style name or size. The control's Font property can take on all kinds of values. And the Font dialog box that appears from a click of the ellipsis lets you specify all available Font property parts. When you close the dialog box, the compound property is set to the dialog box's specific values.

Some programmers prefer the Categorized view of the Properties window. By default, the Properties window displays its properties alphabetically (with a possible exception at the top of the Properties window, such as the Name property). When you click the Categorized tab above the property values, the Properties window changes to show the properties in an Explorer tree view such as the one in Figure 3.7.

FIGURE 3.7.

These property values appear by category type.

If you needed to change all of a control's appearance values, such as Color and Caption, you could expand the Categorized view's Appearance entry to display all the appearance values together. That way, you can change the appearance more quickly than if you had to search through the alphabetical listing of properties.

As you can see, placing a control requires much more involvement with property values than simply moving and sizing the control. You rarely if ever have to change all the properties of a control because many default values work fine for most applications. Nevertheless, many property values work to make the control unique to your specific application.

Named Literals

A named literal, also called a named constant, is a special named value that represents a fixed value. Visual Basic comes with several named literals and you'll use many of them in your programs to assign values to controls at runtime.

Consider the drop-down list box that appears when you click a command button's MousePointer property (see Figure 3.8). The MousePointer property requires a value from 0 to 15 (or 99 for a custom value). When you set property values at design time, you simply select from the list, and the descriptions to the right of the numeric values explain what each value is for. When programming, you will be able to assign property values to properties when the user runs the program. Although you can assign 2 to the property value to change the mouse cursor to a crosshair during one part of the running application, your code will be better if you assign the named literal vbCrosshair. Although vbCrosshair is longer to type, you will know what value you assigned when you look at the project later.

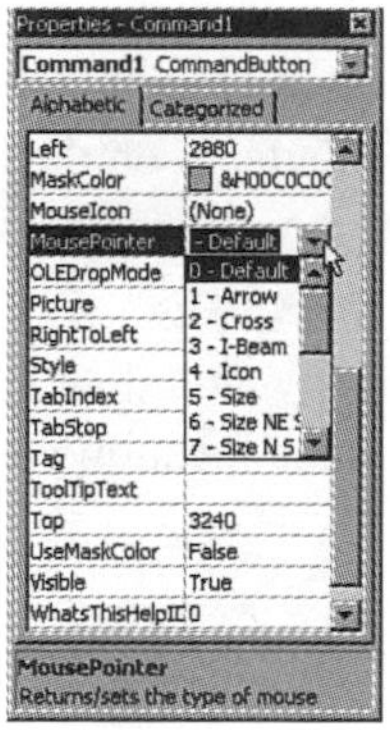

FIGURE 3.8.

You can assign a named literal to the MousePointer *property.*

We're getting slightly ahead of ourselves discussing runtime property values that change inside the code, such as event procedures. Nevertheless, keep named literals in mind as you assign values in the Properties window at design time. The named literals often closely match their Properties window counterparts.

Take a Break!

In this section, you are going to create a project from scratch without the help of the VB Application Wizard. You'll create a new project, assign controls, and write event procedure code to hook everything together. The final application will be simple, but you'll have little trouble understanding the application now that you've become more familiar with properties and event procedures.

To create your first application, follow these steps:

1. Create a new project by selecting File | New Project and choosing to create a new Standard EXE project. Don't save any changes from earlier in this lesson if you were following along during the discussion of command buttons and control placement.

2. Change the form's Name property to frmFirst and change its Caption property to My First Application. The form's Caption property text appears in the title bar when you run the application.

3. Expand the Form window to these property values: Height 7380 and Width 7095. You can either drag the Form window's sizing handles until the Form window's size coordinates to the right of the toolbar read 7095×7380 or you can set these two property values yourself by changing the values in the Properties window. If you drag the Form window to obtain this size, you can approximate the coordinates described here; you don't have to size your Form window exactly to 7,095 by 7,380 twips.

4. Click the Label control once. As you learned in Hour 1, "Visual Basic at Work," the Label control is the tool with the capital letter A on the toolbox. When you click the Label control, Visual Basic shows the control depressed as if it were a command button.

5. Move the mouse pointer onto the Form window and drag a Label control toward the top of the Form window in the approximate location you see in Figure 3.9.

FIGURE 3.9.

*A label is this form's
first control.*

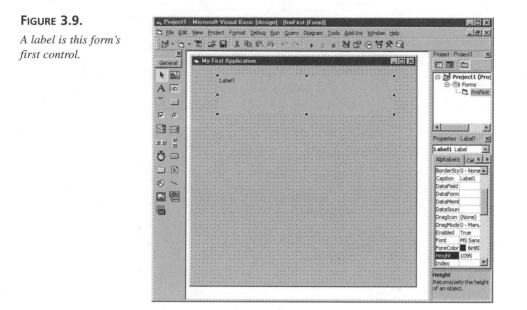

6. Change the label's Name property to lblFirst. Change the label's Caption property to VB is fun.

7. Click the label's Font property value to display the ellipsis. Click the ellipsis to display the Font dialog box for the label. Set the font size to 24 points and set the Bold property. (A point is 1/72 of an inch; 24 points is about twice the height of a word processor's character onscreen.)

   As Figure 3.10 shows, the label's text is now large enough to read, but the text isn't well centered within the label. Change the label's Alignment property to 2-Center, and the text centers just fine.

3

FIGURE 3.10.

The label needs to be centered.

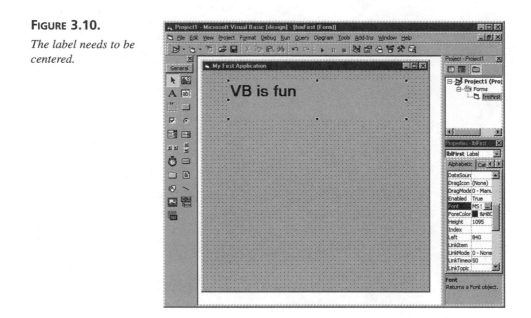

8. Change the label's `BorderStyle` property to `1-FixedSingle`. This property adds a single-line 3D border around the label. You'll see that the label's `Height` property is too large, so click the label to display its sizing handles and drag the top edge downward to center the text within the label.

9. Add a command button, but to do so, double-click the command button tool on the Toolbox window. The command button appears in the middle of the form and you can leave it where it is.

10. Change the command button's `Name` property to `cmdExit`. Change the command button's `Caption` property to `E&xit`. Watch the command button as you type the `Caption` property text. The command button's caption becomes the text you type with one exception: The x is underlined. When you precede a `Caption` property's letter with an ampersand (`&`), Visual Basic uses that letter for the control's hotkey. Users of your application will be able to select the command button not only by clicking the mouse, but also by pressing Alt+X on the keyboard.

11. The command button will be used to exit the program. When the user clicks the command button, your application should end. What happens when a user clicks a command button? A `Click` event occurs. Therefore, to respond to this event, you must write an event procedure for the command button. Visual Basic will help you

do this. Double-click the form's command button and Visual Basic instantly opens the Code window and displays the following wrapper lines for the command button's Click event procedure:

```
Private Sub cmdExit_Click()

End Sub
```

You only need to fill in the body. The name of the procedure, cmdExit_Click(), describes both the control and the event being processed by the code. Type End for the one-word body of the event procedure and close the Code window. End is now the very first Visual Basic programming language statement you've learned! End tells Visual Basic to terminate the running application, so the application will terminate when the user clicks the command button.

> Indent the body of the code from the surrounding wrapper lines as follows so you'll be able to distinguish procedures from one another when you read through a list of them:
>
> ```
> Private Sub cmdExit_Click()
>   End
> End Sub
> ```

Press F5 to run the program and watch your creation appear. As shown in Figure 3.11, the form appears with the label and command button in place.

FIGURE 3.11.

Your first running application!

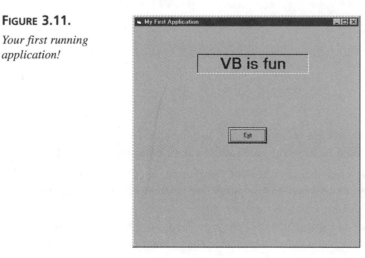

Terminate the application by clicking the Exit command button. Visual Basic regains control. (If you had compiled the application, you could run the compiled .exe file from the Windows Run command or from an icon if you assign the .exe file to an icon on the Desktop or to an option on the Start menu.)

When you save the project, Visual Basic saves all the files within the project. Select File | Save Project. Visual Basic asks for the form's name with a Save File As dialog box (remember that each element of the project is a separate file). You can select a different drive or pathname if you want. Save the form module file under the name Lesson 3 Form (Visual Basic automatically adds the .frm filename extension). Visual Basic now requests the name of the project with a Save Project As dialog box. Type Lesson 3 Proj and click Save to save the project file (Visual Basic automatically adds the .vbp filename extension). If you were to edit the project, Visual Basic would not need to request the filenames subsequently now that you've assigned them.

Take a rest before starting Hour 4, "Examining Labels, Buttons, and Text Boxes." Exit Visual Basic and give your computer's circuits a break as well. You are well on your way to becoming a Visual Basic guru, so feel good about the knowledge you've already gained in three short hours.

Summary

In this hour you learned how to place controls onto a form and how to size and move the controls. After you place controls, you must set the control property values so that the controls take on the values your application requires. (Don't you wish you could set your real estate property values just as easily?)

The next hour gets specific and describes these three common controls in detail: command buttons, labels, and text boxes.

Q&A

Q When do I double-click a toolbox control to place the control on the Form window and when do I drag the control onto the Form window?

A When you double-click a toolbox control, that control appears on the Form window immediately. The double-click requires less work from you to place the control on the form. After the control appears, however, your rest period ends because you have to move and size the control properly. By first selecting a control and dragging the control onto the form, you select, size, and move the control in one step.

Q How do I know if a property value requires a value, a selection from a drop-down list box, or a dialog box selection?

A Just click the property. If nothing happens, type the new property value. If a drop-down list box arrow appears, click the arrow to see the selections in the list. If an ellipsis appear, click it to display the property's dialog box.

Q Can I create an initial application with the VB Application Wizard and then add extra controls to the form?

A Certainly! That's the true reason for using the wizard. The wizard creates the shell, and then you add to and modify the shell to generate a final application that meets your specific needs. The only potential problem right now is that the wizard does generate a fairly comprehensive shell, especially if you add Internet and database access to the shell. Until you master more of the Visual Basic environment and language, you might find that locating the correct spots to change is more difficult than creating the application from scratch.

3

Workshop

The quiz questions and exercises are provided for your further understanding. See Appendix B for the answers.

Quiz

1. What is the fastest way to place a control on the form?
2. What are a control's sizing handles for?
3. How can you select multiple controls?
4. True or false: Some properties change automatically as you move and resize controls.
5. Which form property sets the title that appears in the form's title bar?
6. What is the difference between an object and a control?
7. When is the best time to add a ToolTip to a control?
8. Why do some controls display an ellipsis when you click certain property values?

Exercises

1. Create another application from scratch. Add two command buttons and one label between them. Make the label's Caption property blank when you place the label on the form. When the user clicks the first command button, a caption should appear

on the label that reads `Clicked!`. You'll need to place the following Visual Basic statement inside one of the application's event procedures to do this:

```
lblClick.Caption = "Clicked!"
```

Save the project and form module so you can modify the application later if you want.

2. Load the project you created in the previous exercise and add ToolTips to the two command buttons and to the label button. Run the application and test the ToolTips to see if they work.

HOUR 4

Examining Labels, Buttons, and Text Boxes

It's time to get serious about controls! This lesson dives deeply into the three most common controls and explains how you can use and manage them in your applications. By the time you complete this lesson, you will have mastered labels, command buttons, and text boxes. In addition, you will learn more about how to properly set up a form.

You'll place labels on forms to display information. Command buttons give the user push-button control within applications. Text boxes get information from the user and process that information inside the program.

The highlights of this hour include

- How to set up focus order
- When the Cancel property triggers events
- How to set a command button's Default property
- Which common properties are important
- How to adjust label sizes for long text values

Understanding Control Focus at Runtime

NEW TERM   The currently active control at runtime has the *focus*.

Before looking at this lesson's three controls, you need to master the concept of focus. Focus is a runtime concept. At runtime, only one window, form (which appears as a window), or control can have the focus. The window or form currently in focus is the form whose title bar is highlighted (typically colored blue). The control with the current focus has an outlined border or caption.

> Don't confuse focus with controls you select during design time. At design time, you select controls by clicking them to display their sizing handles. At runtime, one control always has the focus, and users can change the focus by pressing Tab or Shift+Tab.

> A control receives focus only when you run an executable VB application you compile or run a VB application from the VB compiler.

Focus is important because the focus determines what the next keystroke or Enter keypress will activate. For example, consider the screen shown in Figure 4.1. The figure shows a VB session with several windows, including two windows from the executing program. The center window is the window with the focus, and you know this because the title bar is highlighted. Therefore, the center window is the window that receives keystrokes if and when the user presses a key.

Only one control on the active window can have the focus. The AutoSize check box has the current focus. Notice the outline around the control. Despite the other windows on the screen at the time, if the user presses Enter under Figure 4.1's circumstances, the check box receives that Enter keystroke. If you understand the way check boxes work, you know that a check box is either checked or unchecked, meaning that the control determines one of two states. If the user presses Enter, the AutoSize check box will turn to unchecked.

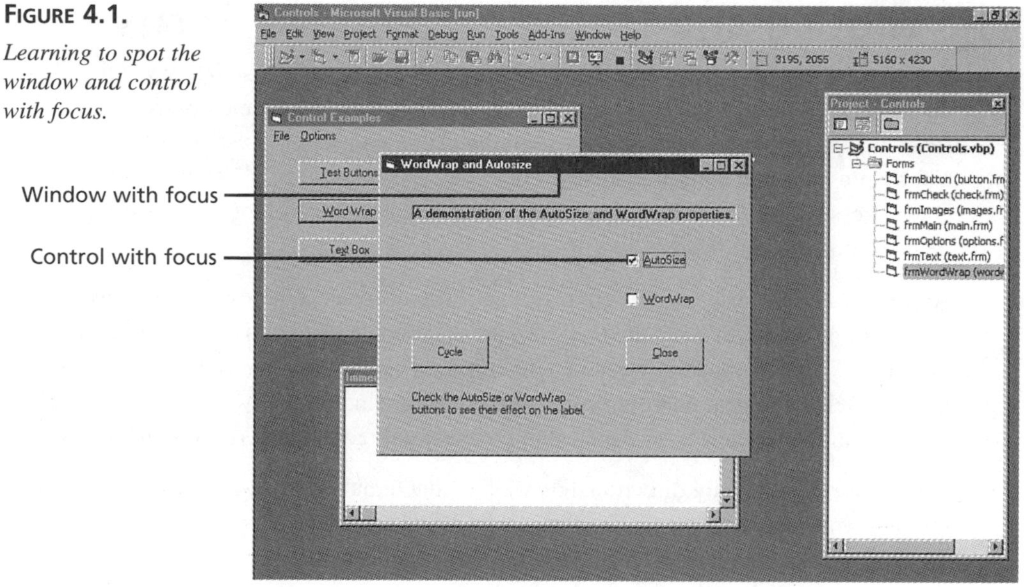

FIGURE 4.1.

Learning to spot the window and control with focus.

Window with focus ——

Control with focus ——

Of course, the user can click the AutoSize check box to uncheck the control. In addition, the user can click any control in any window on the screen and that control would receive the click. *Focus* refers to the capability of a window and control to receive keystrokes.

Different controls display the focus in different ways. Only one of the seven command buttons in Figure 4.2 can have the focus at any one time. Can you spot the command button that has the focus? The extra dotted outline around the Images command button lets you know that the Images command button has the focus and that command button will receive an Enter keypress if the user presses Enter.

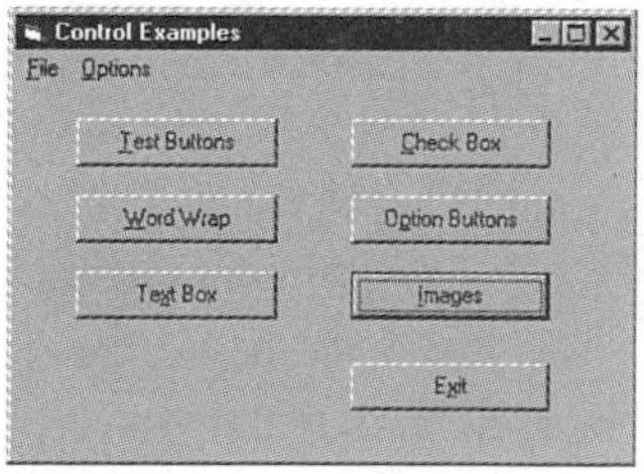

FIGURE 4.2.

One of these seven command buttons has the focus.

4

The Mouse and Hotkeys Need No Focus

As stated earlier, a mouse click doesn't have to worry about focus. Wherever the user clicks, the mouse gets the mouse click no matter which window and control had the focus before the click. In addition, within the active window, the user can select any control by pressing that control's hotkey. For example, with Figure 4.2 showing, the user could press Alt+X to select the Text Box command button even though the Images command button has the focus.

An Enter keypress has no inherent location. Without focus, Windows would have no way to determine where or what the Enter keypress is supposed to activate. With a hotkey, Windows keeps the hotkey possibility within the window with the focus. In other words, if two windows appear on your screen and both contain controls with Alt+S keystrokes, only the active window with the current focus would receive and respond to Alt+S.

The mouse is inherently directional as well as functional. When you click the mouse button over any window's control on the screen, Windows knows for certain that you wanted to click over that control. No ambiguity can exist as could happen with the Enter key. Therefore, focus doesn't apply to the mouse.

Related Properties

A command button's Cancel property relates somewhat to focus. Whereas the focus determines which control gets the Enter keypress, a command button's Cancel property determines which command button gets a simulated Click event when the user presses the Esc key.

> Often, a command button used to exit an application or close a dialog box has its Cancel property set to True. Therefore, you can close such applications or dialog boxes by clicking the command button or by pressing Esc.

A command button's Default property also relates somewhat to focus. When a form first appears, the command button with the Default property of True receives the Click event when the user presses Enter. Another control might have the focus at that time, but if a command button has a Default property value of True, that button receives a Click event when the user presses Enter—unless the user moves the focus to another command button before pressing Enter. Only one command button can have a Default value of True at any one time. As soon as you assign a command button's Default value to True, either at design time or at runtime, any other command button on the form with a `True` `Default` value immediately changes to `False`. Therefore, Visual Basic protects a form's integrity by ensuring that only one command button can have a `True Default` value at any one time.

Tab Order

The user can move the focus from control to control by pressing Tab (or Shift+Tab to move the focus backward). If you place eight controls on an application's form, what focus order will result? In other words, as the user presses Tab, will the controls get the focus from a left-to-right or from a top-to-bottom order?

VB sets the default focus order in the order you place controls on the form. Therefore, if you place the top control first and the bottom control second, and then insert a third control in the middle of the form, the focus order will not move down the form in the order the user probably expects.

You don't always place controls on a form in the same order in which you want to set the focus. Therefore, controls that can receive the focus support a property called the `TabIndex` property. The first control in the focus order has a `TabIndex` property of `0`, the second control in the focus order has a `TabIndex` of `1`, and so on. If you place controls on the form and then later want to modify the focus order, you need to change the `TabIndex` property values of controls.

4

> Not all controls can actually accept the focus. For example, a label cannot receive keystrokes, so a label never gets the focus. The Label control does include the `TabIndex` property, however. By setting the label's `TabIndex` value to one less than a text box to the right of the label, you can add a hotkey to the label's `Caption` property, and the user then has a shortcut key to the text box. Text boxes don't support hotkey keystrokes by themselves.

Command Buttons

Command buttons appear in almost every window of every Windows application. Command buttons determine when the user wants to do something such as exit the application or begin printing. In almost every case, you will perform these tasks to add a command button to an application:

1. Locate and size the command button on the form.

2. Change the command button's Name and Caption properties. (The Caption property holds the text that appears on the command button.)

3. Add code to the command button's Click event procedure.

Although the command button control supports dozens of properties, you'll set only the Name and Caption properties in most cases. In addition, although command button controls support over a dozen events, you'll write code only for the Click event in most cases. After all, a command button resides on most forms so that the user can click the button to trigger some event that she wants to start.

> By the way, you can set some properties only at design time (such as a control's Name property). You can set some properties (such as a caption) both at design time and at runtime inside event procedures and other module code, and you can set some properties (such as a list box's entries) only at runtime from within the program. All the control's properties that appear in the Properties window can be set at design time, and some you can set at runtime as well. As you learn more about Visual Basic, you will become familiar with the properties you can set only at runtime.

Although you'll set the command button's Name and Caption properties most of the time, setting the Caption property often requires that you change the font to increase or decrease the text size and style on the caption. Of course, you might want to center the caption text or, perhaps, left-justify or right-justify the text, so you also might need to change the Alignment property. In reality, you'll also set the Left, Height, Top, and Width properties when you size and locate the command button because, as you learned in Hour 3, "Controls and Properties," these properties update automatically when you place and size controls.

As you can see, although you seem to set only a few properties for most controls, the other properties really do play important roles, and you'll almost always end up setting several properties to finalize your application. Table 4.1 lists some of the most common command button properties that you'll set.

NEW TERM   An *icon* is a small graphical image that often appears on toolbar buttons. Icons are stored in a file with the .ico filename extension.

TABLE 4.1. COMMON COMMAND BUTTON PROPERTIES.

Property	Description
BackColor	Specifies the command button's background color. Click the BackColor's palette down arrow to see a list of colors, and click System to see a list of common Windows control colors. Before the command button displays the background color, you must change the Style property from 0-Standard to 1-Graphical.
Cancel	Determines whether the command button gets a Click event if the user presses Esc.
Caption	Holds the text that appears on the command button.
Default	Determines if the command button responds to an Enter keypress even if another control has the focus.
Enabled	Determines whether the command button is active. Often, you'll change the Enabled property with code at runtime when a command button is no longer needed and you want to gray out the command button.
Font	Produces a Font dialog box in which you can set the caption's font name, style, and size.
Height	Holds the height of the command button in twips.
Left	Holds the number of twips from the command button's left edge to the Form window's left edge.
MousePointer	Determines the shape of the mouse cursor when the user moves the mouse over the command button.
Picture	Holds the name of an icon graphic image that appears on the command button as long as the Style property is set to 1-Graphical.
Style	Determines whether the command button appears as a standard Windows command button (if set to 0-Standard) or a command button with a color and possible picture (if set to 1-Graphical).
TabIndex	Specifies the order of the command button in the focus order.
TabStop	Determines whether the command button can receive the focus.
ToolTipText	Holds the text that appears as a ToolTip at runtime.
Top	Holds the number of twips from the command button's top edge to the Form window's top edge.
Visible	Determines whether the command button appears or is hidden from the user. (Invisible controls cannot receive the focus until the running code changes the Visible property to True.)
Width	Holds the width of the command button in twips.

4

Labels

Labels hold the primary text that appears on a form. Often, programmers use labels to place titles in forms and to label text boxes so that users know what to type into the text box. Visual Basic supports several other ways to put text on forms, but when you use the Label control, your code can subsequently, at runtime, change the label's text so that different messages can appear when needed. Figure 4.3 shows a Form window that contains a label used for the application's title.

FIGURE 4.3.

A label forms the title on this form.

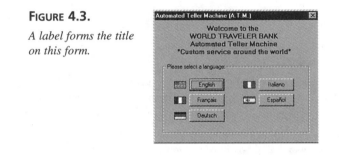

When you place labels on a form, you'll almost always set the Label control's `Name` property and type a new `Caption` value. In addition, you'll want to change the `Font` property and possibly the label's color and style. You will rarely write event procedure code for labels, so a label's overhead is fairly small and the programming effort required to manipulate labels is minimal.

Table 4.2 lists the most common Label control properties that you'll set as you work with the Label control.

TABLE 4.2. COMMON LABEL PROPERTIES.

Property	Description
Alignment	Determines whether the label's caption appears left-justified, centered, or right-justified within the label's boundaries.
AutoSize	Enlarges the label's size properties, when `True`, if you assign a caption that is too large to fit in the current label's boundaries at runtime.
BackColor	Specifies the label's background color. Click the `BackColor` palette's down arrow to see a list of colors and click System to see a list of common Windows control colors.
BackStyle	Determines whether the background shows through the label or if the label covers up its background text, graphics, and color.

Property	Description
BorderStyle	Determines whether a single-line border appears around the label.
Caption	Holds the text that appears on the label.
Enabled	Determines whether the label is active. Often, you'll change the Enabled property at runtime with code when a label is no longer needed.
Font	Produces a Font dialog box in which you can set the caption's font name, style, and size.
ForeColor	Holds the color of the label's text.
Height	Holds the height of the label's outline in twips.
Left	Holds the number of twips from the label's left edge to the Form window's left edge.
MousePointer	Determines the shape of the mouse cursor when the user moves the mouse over the label.
TabIndex	Specifies the order of the label in the focus order. Although labels cannot receive focus, they can be part of the focus order.
ToolTipText	Holds the text that shows as a ToolTip at runtime.
Top	Holds the number of twips from the label's top edge to the Form window's top edge.
Visible	Determines whether the label appears or is hidden from the user.
Width	Holds the width of the label in twips.
WordWrap	Determines whether the label expands to fit whatever text appears in the caption.

Labels can present problems if they receive text that is too large for the label boundaries. Putting captions in labels seems easy until you think about the effects that can occur if the label is too large or too small to hold the text. By using certain property combinations, you can add automatically adjusting labels for whatever text the labels need to hold.

Suppose that you design a label that contains this long caption:

```
This label's caption is extremely long-winded, just like the author.
```

A label is rarely wide enough or tall enough to hold a caption this long. If you attempt to type text into a label's Caption property that is longer than what fits within the label's size properties (Left, Height, Top, and Width), one of the following things can take place, depending on how you've set up the label:

- The text might not fit inside the label, and Visual Basic truncates the text. Figure 4.4 shows what can happen in this case.

FIGURE 4.4.

The label cannot display the entire caption.

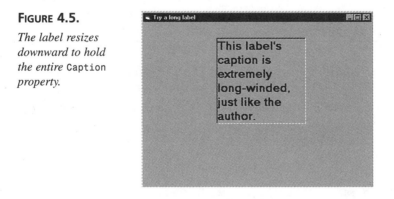

Set the `AutoSize` property to `False` if you want the label to remain the same size and not resize automatically to fit the `Caption` property value. If the code assigns long text, the label might not hold the entire caption, but the label will not expand and get in the way of other controls.

- The label automatically expands downward to hold the entire caption in a multiline label. Figure 4.5 shows the result.

FIGURE 4.5.

The label resizes downward to hold the entire `Caption` *property.*

To expand the label downward when needed to hold the caption, set both the `AutoSize` and `WordWrap` properties to `True`. Subsequently, if the code changes the caption to hold a long line of text, the label will expand to display the entire message.

Obviously, if you don't plan to change a label during a program's execution, you can size the label to fit the Caption property value at design time, and you don't have to worry about the AutoSize and WordWrap properties. You only need to concern yourself with these properties if event procedures or other code might possibly change the label's caption.

Set WordWrap to True before you set the AutoSize property to True. If you set AutoSize first, the label expands horizontally before you have a chance to set the WordWrap property.

- The label automatically expands horizontally across the screen to hold the entire caption in a long label control. Figure 4.6 shows the result.

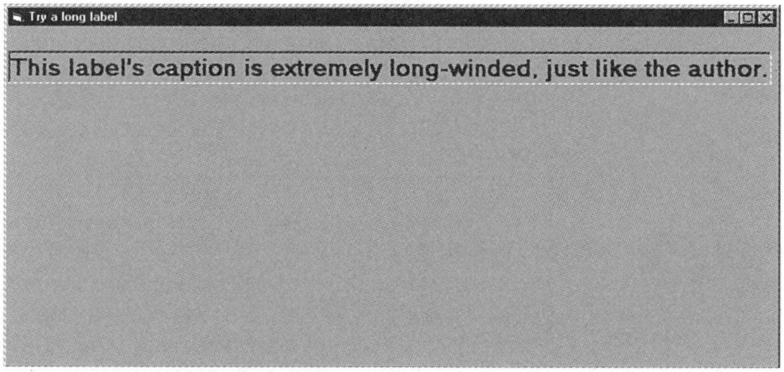

FIGURE 4.6.

A horizontally resizing label could bump off other controls.

This label's caption is extremely long-winded, just like the author.

A long label like this isn't necessarily a bad label. Depending on the length of the text you assign to the label during the program's execution, there might be plenty of screen space to display long labels. To automatically expand the label horizontally, set the AutoSize property to True but leave WordWrap set to False.

Text Boxes

Text boxes accept user input. Although several other controls accept user input, text boxes are perhaps the easiest to set up and respond to. In addition, a text box is easy for your users to use, and they see text boxes on Windows forms all the time.

You can set a default value at design time or at runtime so that the user initially sees text in the text box. The user can either change or accept the default text.

Figure 4.7 shows a running application with two text boxes that accept user input.

FIGURE 4.7.

Two text boxes request user information.

User types text here

Table 4.3 lists the common properties associated with text boxes. By familiarizing yourself with the properties now, you will be able to produce applications more quickly as you learn more about Visual Basic.

As you are beginning to see, many properties for many controls overlap. Most controls contain `Left`, `Height`, `Top`, and `Width` properties as well as the `Visible` property. Therefore, when you learn the properties for one control, you are learning properties for many other controls. When you first began learning Visual Basic just a few hours ago, you may have wondered how you could learn all the properties that go with all the possible Windows controls. You can now see that many controls support the same properties, so learning about the control properties isn't as difficult a task as it might first seem.

The `Caption` property is the most common property that displays text on a control such as a command button and a label. Text Box controls don't support the `Caption` property. The `Text` property holds text for Text Box controls.

TABLE 4.3. COMMON TEXT BOX PROPERTIES.

Property	Description
Alignment	Determines whether the text box's text appears left-justified, centered, or right-justified within the text box's boundaries.
BackColor	Specifies the text box's background color. Click the BackColor property's palette down arrow to see a list of colors and click System to see a list of common Windows control colors.
BorderStyle	Determines whether a single-line border appears around the text box.
Enabled	Determines whether the text box is active. Often, you'll change the Enabled property at runtime with code when a text box is no longer needed.
Font	Produces a Font dialog box in which you can set the Text property's font name, style, and size.
ForeColor	Holds the color of the text box's text.
Height	Holds the height of the text box's outline in twips.
Left	Holds the number of twips from the text box's left edge to the Form window's left edge.
Locked	Determines whether the user can edit the text inside the text box.
MaxLength	Specifies the number of characters the user can type into the text box.
MousePointer	Determines the shape of the mouse cursor when the user moves the mouse over the text box.
MultiLine	Lets the text box hold multiple lines of text or sets the text box to hold only a single line of text. Add scrollbars if you want to put text in a multiline text box so your users can scroll through the text.
PasswordChar	Determines the character that appears in the text box when the user enters a password, which keeps prying eyes from knowing what the user enters into a text box.
ScrollBars	Determines whether scrollbars appear on the edges of a multiline text box.
TabIndex	Specifies the order of the text box in the focus order.
TabStop	Determines whether the text box can receive the focus.
Text	Holds the value of the text inside the text box. The Text property changes at runtime as the user types text into the text box. If you set an initial Text property value, that value becomes the default value that appears in the text box when the user first sees the text box.

4

continues

TABLE 4.3. CONTINUED

Property	Description
ToolTipText	Holds the text that appears as a ToolTip at runtime.
Top	Holds the number of twips from the text box's top edge to the Form window's top edge.
Visible	Determines whether the text box appears or is hidden from the user.
Width	Holds the width of the text box in twips.

> If you are unsure how to use a particular control's property, click the property in the Properties window and press F1 to read the online help. In addition to a detailed help screen that describes the property, such as the one shown in Figure 4.8, many of the help screens also contain an example.

FIGURE 4.8.

You can press F1 to request help for any selected property.

```
Visual Basic Reference                                              _|5|X|
Help Topics  Back    Options

PasswordChar Property
See Also    Example    Applies To    Specifics

Returns or sets a value indicating whether the characters typed by a user or placeholder characters are displayed in a TextBox
control; returns or sets the character used as a placeholder.

Syntax
object.PasswordChar [= value]
The PasswordChar property syntax has these parts:

Part              Description
object            An object expression that evaluates to an object in the
                  Applies To list.
value             A string expression specifying the placeholder
                  character.

Remarks
Use this property to create a password field in a dialog box. Although you can use any character, most Windows-based
applications use the asterisk (*) (Chr(42)).
This property doesn't affect the Text property; Text contains exactly what the user types or what was set from code. Set
PasswordChar to a zero-length string (""), which is the default, to display the actual text.
You can assign any string to this property, but only the first character is significant; all others are ignored.
Note   If the MultiLine Property is set to True, setting the PasswordChar property will have no effect.
```

Form Properties

Forms have properties that you can and should set when you create an application. As the background of your application, the form's properties help set the stage for the rest of the project. The form supports more property values than the other controls described in this lesson, but Table 4.4 lists only the most common properties you'll need.

Pixel stands for picture element and represents the smallest addressable graphic dot on your monitor.

TABLE 4.4. COMMON FORM PROPERTIES.

Property	Description
BackColor	Specifies the form's background color. Click the BackColor's palette down arrow to see a list of colors and click System to see a list of common Windows control colors.
BorderStyle	Determines how the Form window appears. The BorderStyle property specifies whether the user can resize the form and also determines the kind of form you want to display.
Caption	Displays text on the form's title bar at runtime.
ControlBox	Determines whether the form appears with the Control menu icon. The Control menu appears when your application's user clicks the Control menu icon.
Enabled	Determines whether the form is active. Often, you'll change the Enabled property at runtime with code when a form is no longer needed. Generally, only multiform applications such as MDI applications need to modify a form's Enabled property.
Font	Produces a Font dialog box in which you can set the text's font name, style, and size.
ForeColor	Holds the color of the form's text.
Height	Holds the height of the form's outline in twips.
Icon	Describes the icon graphic image displayed on the taskbar when the user minimizes the form.
Left	Holds the number of twips from the form's left edge to the screen's left edge.
MaxButton	Specifies whether a maximize window button appears on the form.
MinButton	Specifies whether a minimize window button appears on the form.
MousePointer	Determines the shape of the mouse cursor when the user moves the mouse over the form.
Moveable	Specifies whether the user can move the form at runtime.
Picture	Determines a graphic image that appears on the form's background at runtime.
ScaleMode	Determines whether the form's measurements appear in twips, pixels (the smallest graphic dot image possible), inches, centimeters, or other measurements.

4

continues

TABLE 4.4. CONTINUED

Property	Description
ShowInTaskbar	Determines whether the form appears on the Windows taskbar.
StartUpPosition	Determines the state (centered or default) of the form at application startup.
Top	Holds the number of twips from the form's top edge to the Form window's top edge.
Visible	Determines whether the form appears or is hidden from the user.
Width	Holds the width of the form in twips.
WindowState	Determines the initial state (minimized, maximized, or normal) in which the window appears at runtime.

Summary

Today you learned the concept of focus. You must know about focus before continuing your work with Visual Basic controls because focus determines the order of controls and which control is active at any one time.

Most of this lesson describes the three fundamental controls that appear on almost every application's Form window: command buttons, labels, and text boxes. Many of the control properties overlap between these and other controls, so you can easily master the properties that are important.

The next hour dives head first into the Visual Basic programming language. You'll begin to build applications internally now that you've learned how to design application windows using the fundamental controls.

Q&A

Q How do I know which control has the focus?

A Generally, you'll quickly learn to recognize focus once you've worked with it a short time. The focus looks different depending on the collection of controls that appear on the form. Most of the time, the focus appears as a dotted outline around a caption or option. You'll know which window has the focus because the focus window's title bar will be colored and the others will be gray. If you really cannot determine which control has the focus, press the Tab key a few times. You will see the focus jump from control to control.

Q How can I learn all the properties?

A People who have written Visual Basic programs for years don't know every property for every control. The Properties window is always at most one menu away, and it always displays a control's properties. Therefore, don't worry about learning all the properties. Generally, if you need to adjust the location, size, look, or behavior of a control, a property probably exists to handle that operation.

Workshop

The quiz questions and exercises are provided for your further understanding. See Appendix B for the answers.

Quiz

1. True or false: A selected control (the control with its sizing handles showing) is the control with the focus.

2. True or false: When the user clicks the mouse over a control in a window that doesn't have the focus, the clicked control still gets the focus.

3. Which control works better for titles: labels or text boxes?

4. What can you do to close a Form window when the user presses Esc?

5. Which property disables a text box from triggering events when the user types or clicks the text box?

6. Why do you think labels fail to support a GetFocus event?

7. What happens if you set a label's AutoSize property to True before setting the WordWrap property to True if the label holds a long caption value?

8. Why should you avoid adding too many autosizing labels to the form at one time?

Exercises

1. Write a Visual Basic application that displays an appropriate form title and asks the user for his first and last names in two separate text boxes. Add a command button that terminates the program when the user clicks the command button, presses the command button's hotkey, or presses Esc.

2. Create an application with five command buttons. Reverse the focus order so that when you run the application and press the Tab key several times, the focus order flows upward through the command buttons.

4

3. Write an application that displays three labels with the same long label `Caption` property in each. Don't display the entire caption in the first label. Display the caption horizontally in the second label. Display the caption vertically down the window in the third label. You may have to expand the Form window to its full size (perhaps by setting the Form window's `WindowState` property to `2-Maximized`).

PART II
Coding the Details

Hour

HOUR 5

Putting Code into Visual Basic

It's time to hone your multilingual skills and learn a new language! This hour's lesson explores the Visual Basic programming language. You'll learn how code goes together to form the application, and you'll learn how VB works with data. Your applications must be capable of processing many types of data values, and you'll master those datatypes before the hour is up.

The highlights of this hour include the following:

- Which datatypes VB supports
- How to declare variables
- How to assign data to variables
- Why datatype mix-ups can occur
- When to use operators

Coding Basics

As you write more powerful programs, you'll need to insert more and more of Visual Basic's programming language into your applications. The language, although one of the easiest to master, can be tricky in places. Nevertheless, if you start with the fundamentals, you'll have no trouble mastering the hard parts.

Remember that a VB program consists of the following:

- One or more forms
- Controls on the forms
- Code written in the Visual Basic programming language

Although you can create great-looking applications just by dragging controls onto forms and setting properties, the applications don't really become useful until you add code to tie the controls together and to perform calculations and data manipulation when needed. No control exists to calculate inventory accounting values; you must add the code to do things like that. The program code that you write is just a detailed set of instructions that tells Visual Basic how to manipulate data, perform input and output (known as I/O), and respond to the user.

NEW TERM   *I/O* stands for input and output and refers to the practice of receiving data from a control, the user, or a data source such as the disk drive and sending data from your computer to the outside world, such as the screen or printer.

Before looking at specifics, you should take a moment to consider the location of the code in a VB application. You now know that much of the code in an application is comprised of small event procedures that respond to events. The form's controls often trigger the events when the user interacts with a control. Event procedures are not the only code that appears in an application, however. Code can appear in several places. This 24-hour tutorial concerns itself with code that appears in form modules and in standard modules.

NEW TERM   A *form module* is a module file that holds one or more forms and the code that goes with each form. A *standard module* is a file that holds code not related to a form.

A form module is code connected to a specific form. The form's event procedures appear in the form's form module as does other code that isn't directly connected to events, such as calculations and data-sorting routines. Every application has at least one form, so every application contains at least one form module. When you add a new form to an application, Visual Basic adds a new form module to go with the form.

Some applications, such as those that perform system utility functions and background processing tasks, never display their form. The form's Visible property is set to False.

Figure 5.1 helps illustrate the module concepts described in this section. All the application's modules reside in separate disk files, even though Visual Basic groups them together in a single project. The Project Explorer window keeps things together in an orderly manner.

FIGURE 5.1.

One or more modules can appear in an application.

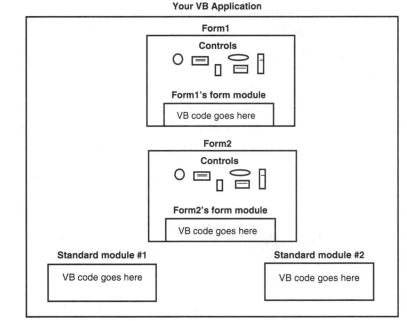

A program that supports multiple forms (and therefore, multiple form modules) is either an MDI (multiple-document interface) application or an SDI (single-document interface) application. Until version 5, VB was an SDI application. An MDI application, such as Word, can open several windows at once that contain different data documents. An SDI application, although it can contain multiple forms such as dialog boxes, supports only one data document. (The Windows Notepad application is an SDI application because when you open a new document, the current one leaves the work area.) No matter which kind of application you create, your application can contain multiple Form windows and, hence, can contain multiple form modules.

In addition to form modules, an application might contain one or more standard modules. Standard modules contain code and have no forms or controls associated with them. Although the code inside a standard module might manipulate a form or its controls, the code that you put in a standard module usually contains general-purpose code that you can use in several applications. For example, you might write some Visual Basic code that calculates wages using some special formulas that your company requires. If you need to use those calculations in several applications, store the calculations in a standard module and then add a copy of that standard module to each application instead of typing the code multiple times in multiple applications.

> You'll understand the differences in modules much more clearly as you progress through these 24 hours. For now, concentrate on getting the big picture.

Fortunately, you don't have to do much to manage projects that require multiple files; the Project Explorer window keeps track of things. As you add files to or remove files from the application (by selecting from the menu that appears when you right-click over the Project Explorer window), the Project Explorer window keeps track of the bookkeeping. When you want to modify or add to one of the items in the Project Explorer window, double-click the object's icon in the Project Explorer window, and the form or code opens in the work area (see Figure 5.2).

FIGURE 5.2.

The Project Explorer window displays the project files.

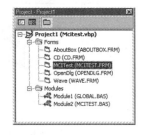

> Visual Basic also supports class modules, but this book doesn't discuss class modules in detail.

Data Basics

Now that you have a better idea of how code goes together to support a Visual Basic application, you're ready to begin the specifics. This section teaches you all about the types of data that Visual Basic can manipulate.

Before you can perform data processing, you must understand data. When you are able to represent data properly, you can learn some commands to manipulate and process that data. Data is the cornerstone for learning the rest of the Visual Basic programming language. Although writing code that manipulates data might not seem to be as much fun as working with controls, you'll soon see the tie-in between controls and the code you write. After you learn to represent and process data, you can then work with controls in ways that you could not without the language's help.

You have heard various references to data throughout this tutorial. Data simply refers to information that will be processed by your program. Data is different from the VB instructions you write. The VB instructions you write simply process the data.

Datatypes

Data falls into three broad categories: numeric, string, and special. If you want to work with a number, you'll need to use a number that fits within one of VB's datatype categories. If you want to work with text data, you'll need to use a string. Other data might fall into one of several special datatype categories, such as an item (like the value of True or False) that represents a check box.

NEW TERM A *string* is a series of zero or more characters that you treat as a single entity. VB supports both fixed-length and variable-length strings.

5

> Controls almost always supply the Variant datatype to your programs. Therefore, when your program receives a value from a control, the datatype is Variant. You can, through a conversion routine or by implicit typing (when VB converts the datatype for you as you store one datatype in a location that is designed to hold a different datatype), convert the control's datatype to another datatype. The Variant datatype lets you store data in a variable when you don't know the specific datatype of the variable.

NEW TERM *Implicit typing* is the process that VB performs when converting one datatype to another.

Table 5.1 lists the datatypes that Visual Basic supports. As you work with Visual Basic, you'll become familiar with all the datatypes (with the possible exception of Decimal, which isn't supported throughout the Visual Basic language yet).

TABLE 5.1. THE VISUAL BASIC DATATYPES.

Datatype	Description and Range
Boolean	A datatype that takes on one of two values only: True or False. True and False are reserved words in Visual Basic, meaning that you cannot use them for names of items you create.
Byte	Positive numeric values without decimals that range from 0 to 255.
Currency	Data that holds dollar amounts from −$922,337,203,685,477.5808 to $922,337,203,685,477.5807. The four decimal places ensure that proper rounding can occur. VB respects your Windows International settings and adjusts currency amounts according to your country's requirements. Never include the dollar sign when entering Currency values.
Date	Holds date and time values. The date can range from January 1, 100, to December 31, 9999. (In the years following 9999, people will have to use something other than Visual Basic!)
Decimal	A new datatype not yet supported in Visual Basic except in a few advanced situations. The Decimal datatype represents numbers with 28 decimal places of accuracy.
Double	Numeric values that range from −1.79769313486232E+308 to 1.79769313486232E+308. The Double datatype is often known as double-precision.
Integer	Numeric values with no decimal point or fraction that range from −32,768 to 32,767.
Long	Integer values with a range beyond that of Integer data values. Long data values range from −2,147,483,648 to 2,147,483,647. Long data values consume more memory storage than integer values, and they are less efficient. The Long datatype is often called a long integer.
Object	A special datatype that holds and references objects such as controls and forms.
Single	Numeric values that range from −3.402823E+38 to 3.402823E+38. The Single datatype is often called single-precision.

Datatype	Description and Range
String	Data that consists of 0 to 65,400 characters of alphanumeric data. Alphanumeric means that the data can be both alphabetic and numeric. String data values may also contain special characters such as ^, %, and @. Both fixed-length strings and variable-length strings exist.
Variant	Data of any datatype, used for control and other values for which the datatype is unknown.

Scientific Notation

NEW TERM An *exponent* is a power of 10 by which you want to multiply another value.

Table 5.1 contains Es and Ds in some numeric values. E stands for exponent, and D stands for double-precision exponent. The double-precision provides more accuracy than the regular exponent (often called a single-precision exponent). Both datatypes demonstrate a shorthand number notation called scientific notation. Scientific notation contains either uppercase or lowercase Es and Ds because the notation's letter case is insignificant.

NEW TERM *Scientific notation* is a shorthand notation for specifying extremely large or extremely small numbers.

Use scientific notation to represent extremely large and extremely small decimal numbers without typing a lot of zeros or other digits. You can convert a scientific notation value to its real value by following these steps:

1. Raise 10 to the number after the D or E. The number 5.912E+6 requires that you raise 10 to the 6th power to get 1,000,000.

2. Multiply the number at the left of the D or E by the value you got in step 1. The number 5.912E+6 requires that you multiply 5.912 by the 1,000,000 you got in the first step to get a final, meaningful result of 5,912,000.

Typing `5.912E+6` isn't much easier than typing `5912000`, but when the number grows to the trillions and beyond, scientific notation is easier. By the way, you cannot insert commas when you enter Visual Basic numbers unless your International settings use the comma for the decimal position.

> Visual Basic often displays value in the scientific notation format to save room on the screen or in a control. You need to understand scientific notation, even if you never plan to use scientific notation, so you'll recognize its meaning when you see it.

5

Specifying Values

A *literal* is a value that doesn't change. You'll sprinkle literals throughout your program. For example, if you need to annualize a monthly calculation, you'll surely multiply a value by 12 somewhere in the calculation because 12 months appear in each year. 12 is a literal and represents either a `Byte`, an `Integer`, or a `Long` datatype, depending on its context. If you multiplied the monthly value by 12.0, the 12.0 is also a literal, but 12.0 must be a `Single` or `Double` datatype due to the decimal.

When typing numeric literal values, you don't have to concern yourself with the datatype because Visual Basic takes care of things for you and attaches the best datatype for the calculation. If, however, you specify data of other datatypes, you must consider the way you type the data.

Quotation marks are required to designate a `String` literal, but the `String` literal doesn't actually contain the quotation marks. The following are literals that take the `String` datatype:

```
"Sams"       "123 E. Sycamore St."       "91829"
"#$%^&*"      "[Adam]"       "Happy birthday!"       "Angel Sue Bush"       ""
```

> The last string is called an empty string or a null string because the quotation marks are together without even a space between them.

You must embed date and time literal values (Visual Basic uses the `Date` datatype to hold these values) inside pound signs (#). Depending on your International settings, you can specify the date or time in just about any valid date or time format, as in the following:

```
#12-Jan-1999#      #14:56#      #2:56 PM#      #December 5, 1998#
```

A `Boolean` literal is always `True` or `False`, so any time you must store or retrieve a `True` or `False` value, Visual Basic uses the `Boolean` datatype to hold the value. Option and Check Box controls return their values in the `Boolean` datatype. Many programmers use the `Boolean` datatype to store two-value data such as yes/no or on/off values.

> You'll learn more about `Variant` and `Object` when you tie code to controls and forms in Hour 9, "Combining Code and Controls."

Although Visual Basic normally takes care of datatypes when you type number values, you might need to ensure that Visual Basic interprets a numeric literal as one of the specific numeric datatypes. For example, you might type the literal 86 and need Visual Basic to store or display the value as a `Long` datatype even though 86 fits within a `Byte` or `Integer` datatype.

You can use the datatype suffix characters from Table 5.2 to override the default datatype. The suffix characters let you specify the datatype for numeric literals when you need to. Occasionally, Visual Basic will also use the datatype suffix characters when displaying numeric information. Therefore, if you type 86#, Visual Basic treats the number 86 as a double-precision value.

TABLE 5.2. NUMERIC DATATYPE SUFFIX CHARACTERS.

Suffix Character	Datatype	Example
&	Long	86&
!	Single	86!
#	Double	86#
@	Currency	86@

Variables Hold Data

All your data cannot be literals. The information your program's users enter in controls such as text boxes isn't literal data because the user can change information. In addition, your program has to have a place to hold information temporarily for calculations and for in-memory storage before sending information to a disk file or to the printer. To hold data that might change due to calculations or state changes within the application, you must declare variables. A *variable* is a named location that holds data.

Variables, unlike literals, can change. In other words, you can store a number in a variable early in the program and then change that number later in the program. The variable acts like a box that holds a value. The data you store in variables doesn't have to change, but often the program does change the contents of variables.

A program can have as many variables as you need it to have. Before you can use a variable, you must request that Visual Basic create the variable by declaring the variable before using it. To declare a variable, you tell Visual Basic the name and datatype of the variable.

A variable can hold only one datatype.

5

After you declare a variable, it always retains its original declared datatype. Therefore, a single-precision variable can hold only single-precision values. When you store an integer in a single-precision variable, Visual Basic converts the integer to a single-precision number before the number gets to the variable. Such datatype conversions are common, and they typically don't cause many problems.

You use the `Dim` statement to declare variables (`Dim` stands for *dimension*). The `Dim` statement defines variables. `Dim` tells Visual Basic that somewhere else in the program the program will need to use a variable. `Dim` describes the datatype and also assigns a name to the variable.

Hour 2, "Analyzing Visual Basic Programs," describes the naming rules for controls, and you use the same naming rules for variables. Follow the naming rules when you make up names for variables. Whenever you learn a new statement, you need to learn the format for that statement. Here is the format of the `Dim` statement:

```
Dim VarName As DataType
```

`VarName` is a name that you supply. When Visual Basic executes the `Dim` statement at runtime, it creates a variable in memory and assigns it the name you give in the `VarName` location of the statement. `DataType` is one of the datatypes that you learned about in Table 5.1.

Never declare two variables with the same name in the same location. That is, you cannot declare two variables with the name `intNumber` in the same event procedure.

THE Dim STATEMENT'S LOCATION

The location of the `Dim` determines how you use the variable. If you include a special statement called the `Option Explicit` statement at the very top of a form module or at the top of a standard module (in a section called the `general` section that appears before all event procedures), you must declare all variables before you use them. Without `Option Explicit`, you can begin using a variable name without declaring the variable, but Visual Basic always assumes that the variable is a `Variant` datatype.

If `Dim` appears in an event procedure, the variable is visible (usable) only from within that event procedure and known as a local variable. If you use `Dim` in a module's `general` section, all variables in that module can access the variable (the variable is said to be global to the module). If you replace `Dim` with `Public` in a `general` section (the `Public` statement uses the same format as `Dim`), the variable is global to the entire module as well as every other module within the project. Standard module variables are almost always globally defined with `Public` so that other modules within a project that you add the standard module to can access the variables. Generally, local variables are better than global with a few exceptions (this book points out these exceptions at the appropriate times).

NEW TERM *Global variables* are variables that are available to the entire module or to the entire application. *Local variables* are variables that are available only to the procedure in which you define the variables.

The following statement defines a variable named `curProductTotal`:

```
Dim curProductTotal As Currency
```

From the `Dim` statement, you know that the variable holds the `Currency` datatype and that the variable's name is `curProductTotal`. Programmers often prefix variable names with a three-letter abbreviation that indicates the variable's datatype, but such a prefix isn't required. Table 5.3 lists these common variable prefix values. Please remember that you put these prefixes at the beginning of variable names just to remind yourself of the variable's datatype. The prefix itself has no meaning to Visual Basic and is just part of the name.

TABLE 5.3. USING VARIABLE NAME PREFIXES TO MAINTAIN ACCURATE DATATYPES.

Prefix	Datatype	Example
bln	Boolean	blnIsOverTime
byt	Byte	bytAge
cur	Currency	curHourlyPay
dte	Date	dteFirstBegan
dbl	Double	dblMicroMeasurement
int	Integer	intCount
lng	Long	lngStarDistance
obj	Object	objSoundClip
sng	Single	sngYearSales
str	String	strLastName
vnt or var	Variant	vntControlValue

5

The following statements define `Integer`, `Single`, and `Double` variables:

```
Dim intLength As Integer
Dim sngPrice As Single
Dim dblStructure As Double
```

If you want to write a program that stores the user's text box entry for the first name, you would define a string like this:

```
Dim strFirstName As String
```

You can get fancy when you define strings. This `strFirstName` string can hold any string from 0 to 65,500 characters long. You'll learn in the next section how to store data in a string. The `strFirstName` string can hold data of virtually any size. You could store a small string, such as `"Joe"`, in `strFirstName`, and then a longer string, such as `"Mercedes"`, in `strFirstName`. `strFirstName` is a variable-length string.

Sometimes you want to limit the amount of text that a string holds. For example, you might need to define a `String` variable to hold a name that you read from the disk file. Later, you'll display the contents of the string in a label on the form. The form's label has a fixed length, however—assuming that the `AutoSize` property is set to `True`. Therefore, you want to keep the `String` variable to a reasonable length. The following `Dim` statement demonstrates how you can add the `*` *StringLength* option when you want to define fixed-length strings:

```
Dim strTitle As String * 20
```

`strTitle` is the name of a `String` variable that can hold a string from 0 to 20 characters long. If the program attempts to store a string value that is longer than 20 characters in `strTitle`, Visual Basic truncates the string and stores only the first 20 characters.

Here's a shortcut: You can omit the `As Variant` descriptor when you define `Variant` variables. This `Dim` statement:

```
Dim varValue As Variant
```

does exactly the same thing as this:

```
Dim varValue
```

A good rule of thumb is to make your code as explicit as possible, so use `As Variant` to clarify your code intentions. If you begin calling a variable one name, you must stay with that name for the entire program. `curSale` isn't the same variable name as `curSales`. Use `Option Explicit` to guard against such common variable-naming errors. Visual Basic supports a shortcut when you need to define several variables. Instead of listing each variable definition on separate lines like this:

```
Dim A As Integer
Dim B As Double
Dim C As Integer
Dim D As String
Dim E As String
```

you can combine variables of the same datatype on one line. Here's an example:

```
Dim A, C As Integer
Dim B As Double
Dim D, E As String
```

Putting Data in Variables

So far you have learned how to define variables but not how to store data in them. Use the assignment statement when you want to put data values into variables. Here is the format of the assignment statement:

```
VarName = Expression
```

NEW TERM An *assignment statement* is a program statement that puts data into a control, a variable, or another object.

`VarName` is a variable name that you have defined using the `Dim` statement. `Expression` can be a literal, another variable, or a mathematical expression.

Suppose that you need to store a minimum age value of `18` in an `Integer` variable named `intMinAge`. The following assignment statement does that:

```
intMinAge = 18
```

To store a temperature in a single-precision variable named `sngTodayTemp`, you could do this:

```
sngTodayTemp = 42.1
```

The datatype of `Expression` must match the datatype of the variable to which you are assigning it. In other words, the following statement is invalid. It would produce an error in Visual Basic programs if you tried to use it:

```
sngTodayTemp = "Forty-Two point One"
```

`sngTodayTemp` is a single-precision variable, so you cannot assign a string to it. However, Visual Basic often makes a quick conversion for you when the conversion is trivial. For example, it's possible to perform the following assignment even if you have defined `dblMeasure` to be a double-precision variable:

```
dblMeasure = 921.23
```

At first glance, it appears that `921.23` is a single-precision number because of its size. `921.23` is actually a `Variant` data value. Visual Basic assumes that all data literals are `Variant` unless you explicitly add a suffix character to the literal to make the constant a different datatype. Visual Basic can easily and safely convert the `Variant` value to double-precision. That's just what Visual Basic does here, so the assignment works fine.

NEW TERM A *constant* is a value that doesn't change, whereas a literal is a certain data value.

5

In addition to constants, you can assign other variables' values to variables. Consider the following code:

```
Dim sngSales As Single, sngNewSales As Single
sngSales = 3945.42
sngNewSales = sngSales
```

When the third statement finishes, both `sngSales` and `sngNewSales` have the value `3945.42`.

Feel free to assign variables to controls and controls to variables. Suppose, for example, that the user types the value `18.34` in a text box's `Text` property. If the text box's `Name` property is `txtFactor`, the following statement stores the value of the text box in a variable named `sngFactorVal`:

```
sngFactorVal = txtFactor.Text
```

Suppose that you defined `strTitle` to be a `String` variable with a fixed length of 10, but a user types `Mondays Always Feel Blue` in a text box's `Text` property that you want to assign to `strTitle`. Visual Basic stores only the first 10 characters of the control to `strTitle` and truncates the rest of the title. Therefore, `strTitle` holds only the string `"Mondays Al"`.

You can instantly make data appear on a form by assigning the `Text` property of text boxes or the `Caption` property of labels and command buttons. No variables are required to do this. Suppose you put a command button named `cmdPress` on a form. The event procedure shown in Listing 5.1 changes the command button's `Caption` property and immediately places a new caption on the form (this occurs at runtime when this event procedure executes).

LISTING 5.1. AN EVENT PROCEDURE THAT ASSIGNS A NEW COMMAND BUTTON CAPTION.

```
1: Private Sub cmdPress_Click ()
2: cmdPress.Caption = "Brush your teeth daily!"
3: End Sub
```

No matter what the command button's `Caption` property is set to at the start of the event procedure, when the user clicks the command button, this event procedure executes and the command button's caption changes to `Brush your teeth daily!`.

Some properties accept only a limited range of values. Assign only the number when a control's property can accept a limited range of values. For example, the possible values that you can select for a label's `BorderStyle` property in the Properties window are `0-None` and `1-Fixed Single`. To assign border style directly without using a named constant, assign just 0 or 1. Don't spell out the entire property. You can assign a fixed single-line border around a label like this:

```
lblSinger.BorderStyle = 1
```

Visual Basic includes a number of named literals internally that you can use for assigning such controls when the controls require a limited number of values. You can search the property's online help to see a list of named literals that you can assign. For example, not only can you assign 0 and 1 to a label's border, but you can also assign one of the named literals, vbBSNone and vbFixedSingle. Most named literals begin with the Visual Basic prefix vb.

Expressions and Math Operators

You should learn Visual Basic's math operators so you can calculate and assign expression results to variables when you code assignment statements that contain expressions. An *operator* is a symbol or word that does math and data manipulation.

Table 5.4 describes Visual Basic's primary math operators. Other operators exist, but the ones in Table 5.4 suffice for most of the programs that you will write. Look over the operators. You are already familiar with most of them because they look and act just like their real-world counterparts.

TABLE 5.4. THE PRIMARY MATH OPERATORS.

Operator	Example	Description
+	Net + Disc	Adds two values
-	Price - 4.00	Subtracts one value from another value
*	Total * Fact	Multiplies two values
/	Tax / Adjust	Divides one value by another value
^	Adjust ^ 3	Raises a value to a power
& (or +)	Name1 & Name2	Concatenates two strings

5

Suppose that you wanted to store the difference between the annual sales (stored in a variable named curAnnualSales) and cost of sales (stored in a variable named curCostOfSales) in a variable named curNetSales. Assuming that all three variables have been defined and initialized, the following assignment statement computes the correct value for curNetSales:

```
curNetSales = curAnnualSales - curCostOfSales
```

This assignment tells Visual Basic to compute the value of the expression and to store the result in the variable named curNetSales. Of course, you can store the results of this expression in a control's Caption or Text properties, too.

If you want to raise a value by a power—which means to multiply the value by itself a certain number of times—you can do so. The following code assigns 10000 to lngValue because 10 raised to the fourth power (that is, 10 times 10 times 10 times 10) is 10,000:

```
lngYears = 4
lngValue = 10 ^ intYears
```

No matter how complex the expression is, Visual Basic computes the entire result before it stores that result in the variable at the left of the equal sign. The following assignment statement, for example, is rather lengthy, but Visual Basic computes the result and stores the value in the variable named sngAns:

```
sngAns = 8 * sngFactor - sngPi + 12 * sngMonthlyAmts
```

Combining expressions often produces unintended results because Visual Basic computes mathematical results in a predetermined order. Visual Basic always calculates exponents first if one or more ^ operators appear in the expression. Visual Basic then computes all multiplication and division—working from left to right—before any addition and subtraction.

Visual Basic assigns 13 to intResult in the following assignment:

```
intResult = 3 + 5 * 2
```

At first, you might think that Visual Basic would assign 16 to intResult because 3 + 5 is 8 and 8 * 2 is 16. However, the rules state that Visual Basic always computes multiplication—and division if division exists in the expression—before addition. Therefore, Visual Basic first computes the value of 5 * 2, or 10, and next adds 3 to 10 to get 13. Only then does it assign the 13 to Result.

If both multiplication and division appear in the same expression, Visual Basic calculates the intermediate results from left to right. For example, Visual Basic assigns 20 to the following expression:

```
intResult = 8 / 2 + 4 + 3 * 4
```

Visual Basic computes the division first because the division appears to the left of the multiplication. If the multiplication appeared to the left of the division, Visual Basic would have multiplied first. After Visual Basic calculates the intermediate answers for the division and the multiplication, it performs the addition and stores the final answer of 20 in intResult.

> The order of computation has many names. Programmers usually use one of these terms: *order of operators, operator precedence,* or *math hierarchy.*

It is possible to override the operator precedence by using parentheses. Visual Basic always computes the values inside any pair of parentheses before anything else in the expression, even if it means ignoring operator precedence. The following assignment statement stores 16 in intResult because the parentheses force Visual Basic to compute the addition before the multiplication:

```
intResult = (3 + 5) * 2
```

> Appendix A, "Operator Precedence," contains the complete Visual Basic operator precedence table. The table contains several operators that you have yet to learn about, so you might not understand the full table at this time.

The following expression stores the fifth root of 125 in the variable named sngRoot5:

```
sngRoot5 = 125 ^ (1/5)
```

As you can see from this expression, Visual Basic supports fractional exponents.

NEW TERM To *concatenate* means to merge two strings together.

One of Visual Basic's primary operators has nothing to do with math. The *concatenation operator* joins one string to the end of another. Suppose that the user entered his first name in a Label control named lblFirst and his last name in a Label control named lblLast. The following concatenation expression stores the full name in the String variable named strFullName:

```
strFullName = lblFirst & lblLast
```

There is a problem here, though, that might not be readily apparent—there is no space between the two names. The & operator doesn't automatically insert a space because you don't always want spaces inserted when you concatenate two strings. Therefore, you might have to concatenate a third string between the other two, as in

```
strFullName = lblFirst & " " & lblLast
```

Visual Basic actually supports a *synonym operator,* the plus sign (+), for concatenation. In other words, the following assignment statement is identical to the previous one

5

(although the ampersand [&] keeps ambiguity down because of the plus sign's double usage with numbers and strings):

```
strFullName = lblFirst + " " + lblLast
```

Use the ampersand for string concatenation even though the plus sign works also. The ampersand is less ambiguous and makes for better programs.

> Remember that you'll use the Code window to enter code such as that which you see in this lesson. The Code window appears when you select View | Code or when you double-click a control to open its event procedure as you saw in Hour 3, "Controls and Properties."

Summary

In this lesson you learned how to recognize and use Visual Basic data. Visual Basic supports 14 datatypes, and you must know how to specify literals and declare variables that take on those datatypes. After you know the datatypes and variables, you can perform calculations that assign the results of expressions to variables and controls.

The next hour adds to your programming power by explaining a quick and simple way to display information and receive user input.

Q&A

Q I don't like math, so will I not like VB programming?

A Visual Basic does all the math for you! That's why you learned the operators. People who don't like math use calculators, and people who don't like math can write VB programs.

Q If I want to represent a person's age value, which integer-based datatype do I use?

A The quick answer is that you should use the smallest datatype that will hold every value you'd want to assign. A person's age is rarely more than 100 and doesn't ever go past 255. Therefore, you could use a Byte datatype for a person's age. The Byte datatype is small and is much more efficient than a Long. You should now have the idea that you need to ensure that your variables can hold all the data required but that you should not use one that's too large and that will use unnecessary space. Having said that, the Byte datatype is really an exception to that rule! Byte is generally reserved for special system-level coding. Generally, the smallest integer programmers use is the `Integer` datatype, even though an `Integer` datatype is slightly less efficient than a `Byte` datatype because the computer has to transfer more information at one time when working with integers.

Workshop

The quiz questions and exercises are provided for your further understanding. See Appendix B for the answers.

Quiz

1. What is a datatype?

2. What is the difference between a `String` and a `Boolean` datatype?

3. What are two controls that behave as if they conform to the `Boolean` datatype?

4. What is the difference between a literal and a variable?

5. Which of the following are invalid variable names?

   ```
   12Months
   a
   85
   "curSalesForecast"
   Acctg98
   ```

6. Which operator performs two operations?

7. What is the difference between a fixed-length string and a variable-length string?

8. What value would Visual Basic store in the following `ans` variables?

   a. `ans = 1 + 2 + 3 + 4 / 2`

   b. `ans = 1 + 2 + 3 + (4 / 2)`

   c. `ans = 2 ^ 5`

   d. `ans = 25 - 8 / 2 ^ 2 + 1`

Exercises

1. Write code that declares these variables: your first name, your last name, your age, your tax rate, and whether you are married.

2. Write an application that accepts your age in a text box and then displays, when you click a command button, your age in dog years (your age divided by 7). Don't worry about rounding that might take place.

5

HOUR 6

Message and Input Boxes

In this and subsequent lessons, your application will need to display messages and ask questions of the user. The application needs to receive the user's response from the questions. Although the Label and Text Box controls work well for giving and receiving user information, such controls don't lend themselves to messages and questions that the program displays during execution, such as error messages and warning boxes.

For example, suppose you want to know if the user has prepared the printer for printing. To prepare a printer, the user has to turn on the printer, make sure paper is there, and ensure that the online light is on. Your program should not attempt to print a report until the user has performed these actions or an error will occur. Therefore, when the user initiates a report for printing, your application can gather the data and then ask the user if the printer is ready. If the user responds affirmatively, you can start the report's output. The form's controls simply do not provide such interaction. In this hour's lesson you'll learn how to display message boxes and input boxes that provide runtime I/O.

The highlights of this hour include

- How message boxes differ from text boxes
- Why functions benefit programmers
- When to test message box return values
- Why you should add remarks
- How to receive input box answers

A Function Preview

Visual Basic includes several built-in functions (often called intrinsic functions) that do work for you. Many functions perform common mathematical tasks such as computing a square root. Other functions manipulate string data such as converting text inside a string to uppercase or lowercase letters. Other functions, such as the functions taught in this lesson, perform input and output.

 NEW TERM A *function* is a routine that accepts zero, one, or more arguments and returns a single result. An *intrinsic* function is a function supplied with Visual Basic.

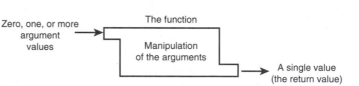 Hours 13, "Modular Programming," and 14, "Built-In Functions Save Time," describe how you can write your own functions.

A function takes zero, one, or more arguments and converts those arguments to a single return value. Figure 6.1 shows an overview of a function's job. The most important thing to remember is that a function always returns a single value.

FIGURE 6.1.

A function accepts arguments and returns a single value.

Zero, one, or more argument values → The function — Manipulation of the arguments → A single value (the return value)

 NEW TERM An *argument* is a value you pass to a function so the function has data to work with.

A function's job is to save you time. For example, if you need to compute the square root of a user-entered value, you could write the assignments and expressions to compute the square root. The square root, however, is such a common routine that Microsoft wrote the code once and stored the square root routine in an intrinsic function. Now, if you want the square root of a value, you'll pass the value as a single argument to the square root function, and after performing the necessary math, the square root function will return the root.

This lesson focuses on two intrinsic functions that don't do math. Instead, they display messages or receive user input. Don't worry too much about what a function is as long as you have the general idea. You'll become much more familiar with them before you're through with this tutorial.

This lesson spends the rest of the hour teaching you these functions:

- `MsgBox()`
- `InputBox()`

Function names, unlike variable names, usually appear with parentheses at the end. The parentheses hold the function arguments that you send to the function. Even if a function receives no arguments, the parentheses are still required when you use the functions.

A `MsgBox()` and `InputBox()` Overview

You use input boxes and message boxes when you need to ask the user questions or display error messages and advice to the user. As stated earlier, the form's controls don't often work well for such user dialog boxes. For example, suppose the user is to enter a sales code of A, B, or C to indicate a discount to be used in a total calculation. Users don't always know what's expected of them, so a message box can pop up when the user enters a bad value, and the message box can explain that the user needs to enter only A, B, or C. If the user enters an invalid code, your program could display an error message such as the one shown in Figure 6.2.

6

FIGURE 6.2.

A message box can tell the user what to do.

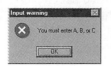

NEW TERM A *message box* is a dialog box you display to give the user information. An *input box* is a dialog box you display to ask the user questions. A message box is typically used to display a short single sentence message to the user. Program execution continues after the user acknowledges the message box. An input box, on the other hand, can be thought of as a message box with a text box. An input box displays a prompt to the user and obtains text input from the user.

> You might hear about a Visual Basic statement called the MsgBox statement (as opposed to the MsgBox() function). Although Visual Basic still supports the MsgBox statement, Microsoft recommends that you use only the MsgBox() function because of its inspection ability for a return value.

The Text Box controls that you've seen are great for getting values from the user. Other controls that you'll learn as you progress through this book also accept the user's input from the keyboard or mouse. Nevertheless, Visual Basic's controls just aren't enough to handle all the input that your program will need. Input boxes are great to use when the user must respond to certain kinds of questions. Text boxes and other controls are fine for getting fixed input from the user, such as data values with which the program will compute. Input boxes are great for asking the user questions that arise only under certain conditions. Input boxes always give the user a place to respond with an answer. In Figure 6.3, the input box is asking the user for the name of a server.

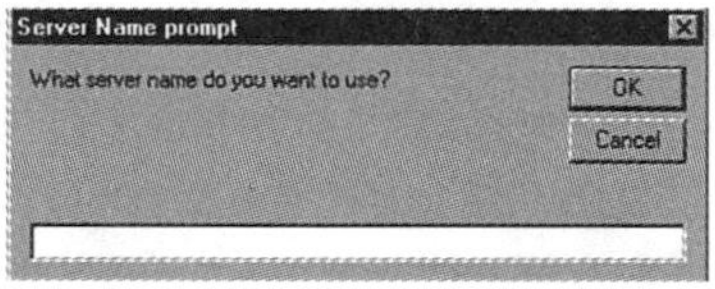

FIGURE 6.3.

Input boxes get user information.

Server Name prompt	
What server name do you want to use?	OK
	Cancel

Note that there is more than one way for the user to respond to the input box in Figure 6.3. The user can answer the question by typing the name of the server and pressing Enter or clicking OK. The user also can click Cancel whether or not the user entered the server name. Therefore, the program must be capable of reading the user's entered answer as well as responding to a Cancel command button press. Responding to message box and input box command buttons is part of the processing that you'll learn about in the remaining sections of this lesson.

Examining `MsgBox()`

Always assign a `MsgBox()` function to an integer variable. The variable will hold the return value, and that value will indicate the button the user clicked (message boxes can display multiple buttons such as OK and Cancel).

Here is the format of the `MsgBox()` function:

anIntVariable = MsgBox(*strMsg* [, [*intType*] [, *strTitle*]])

> The `MsgBox()` function's format, shown here, accepts one required (*strMsg*) and two optional (*intType* and *strTitle*) arguments. `MsgBox()` can accept more arguments, but these three are the only ones needed in most applications.

strMsg is a string (either a variable or a string constant enclosed in quotation marks) and forms the text of the message displayed in the message box. *intType* is an optional numeric value or expression that describes the options you want in the message box. Table 6.1, Table 6.2, and Table 6.3 contain all the possible values you can use for the type of message box you want displayed. (Visual Basic displays no icon if you don't specify an *intType* value.) If you want to use a value from two or more of the tables, you'll add the values together. Although you can use the integer value, if you use the built-in Visual Basic named literal, you'll more easily understand the message box's style if you ever have to change the message box in the future. *strTitle* is an optional string that represents the text in the message box's title bar. If you omit *strTitle*, Visual Basic uses the project's name for the message box's title bar text.

TABLE 6.1. SELECT THE BUTTONS DISPLAYED IN THE MESSAGE BOX.

Named Literal	Value	Description
vbOKOnly	0	Displays the OK button.
vbOKCancel	1	Displays the OK and Cancel buttons.
vbAbortRetryIgnore	2	Displays the Abort, Retry, and Ignore buttons.
vbYesNoCancel	3	Displays the Yes, No, and Cancel buttons.
vbYesNo	4	Displays the Yes and No buttons.
vbRetryCancel	5	Displays the Retry and Cancel buttons.

6

TABLE 6.2. SELECT THE ICON DISPLAYED IN THE MESSAGE BOX.

Named Literal	Value	Description
vbCritical	16	Displays Critical Message icon.
vbQuestion	32	Displays Warning Query icon.
vbExclamation	48	Displays Warning Message icon.
vbInformation	64	Displays Information Message icon.
VbSystemModal	4096	Displays a SystemModal dialog box. The user must acknowledge a SystemModal dialog box before doing anything else.

TABLE 6.3. SELECT THE DEFAULT BUTTON IN THE MESSAGE BOX.

Named Literal	Value	Description
vbDefaultButton1	0	The first button is the default.
vbDefaultButton2	256	The second button is the default.
vbDefaultButton3	512	The third button is the default.

The options that you select using the *intType* value in the MsgBox() function determine whether the message box displays an icon and controls the modality of the message box. The modality determines whether a message box is *application-specific* or *system-specific*. If it's application-specific, the user must respond to the message box before doing anything else in the application. If the message box is system-specific, the user must respond to the message box before doing anything else on the system.

NEW TERM *Modality* determines how the system handles a dialog box.

The modality often causes confusion. If you don't specify a system-modal *intType* value of 4096 (or if you don't use the named literal vbSystemModal to specify the system's modal mode), the user's application will not continue until the user closes the message box. However, the user can switch to another Windows program by pressing Alt+Tab or using the application's control menu. If, however, you do specify that the message box is system modal, the user will not be able to switch to another Windows program until the user responds to the message box because the message box will have full control of the system. Reserve the system-modal message boxes for serious error messages that you want the user to read and respond to before continuing the program. You may make a message box a System Modal message box by adding 4096 to the *intType* value of the message box.

> If you don't specify an icon, Visual Basic doesn't display an icon. If you don't specify the system modality, Visual Basic assumes that you want an application-modal message box.

The following `MsgBox()` function produces the message box shown in Figure 6.4:

```
intPress = MsgBox("Are you ready for the report?", vbQuestion + _
vbYesNoCancel, "Report Request")
```

FIGURE 6.4.

*Message boxes sup-
port several command
buttons.*

> If you need to type long VB program statements such as this `MsgBox()` function, you can break the line into more manageable lines by terminating the first line with an underscore character (_).

Remember that the `MsgBox()` values such as `vbQuestion` and `vbYesNoCancel` are not variables but named literals that Visual Basic has defined to correspond with matching integer values. The named literals `vbQuestion` and `vbYesNoCancel` produced both a question mark icon and the three buttons. A title also appeared due to the third value inside the `MsgBox()` function.

`MsgBox()`'s Return Value

The reason that you assign `MsgBox()` functions to variables is so you can tell which button the user presses. Suppose that the user clicked the Yes button in Figure 6.4. The program could then print the report. If, however, the user clicked the No button, the program could describe what the user needed to do to get ready for the report (load paper, turn on the printer, and so on). If the user pressed the Cancel button, the program would know that the user didn't want the report at all.

Table 6.4 lists the seven possible `MsgBox()` return values. You can test either for the integer or the named literal return value.

6

TABLE 6.4. MSGBOX( ) RETURN VALUES.

Named Constant	Value	Description
vbOK	1	The user clicked the OK button.
vbCancel	2	The user clicked the Cancel button.
vbAbort	3	The user clicked the Abort button.
vbRetry	4	The user clicked the Retry button.
vbIgnore	5	The user clicked the Ignore button.
vbYes	6	The user clicked the Yes button.
vbNo	7	The user clicked the No button.

You'll learn how to test for specific values in Hour 7, "Making Decisions."

Visual Basic's Code Window Help

Can you remember the named literals in this lesson's tables? How can you remember that the named literal value to display three buttons—Yes, No, and Cancel—is the vbYesNoCancel named literal?

Fortunately, Visual Basic supplies you with all the help you need. As soon as VB's Code editor recognizes that you're entering a function, the editor immediately displays pop-up help that displays the function's format, as shown in Figure 6.5.

Visual Basic gives you help not only with a function's format, but also with the function's named literals. When you get to any function argument that requires one of the named literals, Visual Basic displays a drop-down list box such as the one in Figure 6.6, from which you can select a named literal. To accept the selected named literal, press Enter, type a comma, or press the Spacebar to continue with the program.

The format and argument list box pop-up help appear all throughout Visual Basic. As you learn additional Visual Basic statements, you'll see the pop-up Code window help more often.

FIGURE 6.5.

Visual Basic displays the function's format for you.

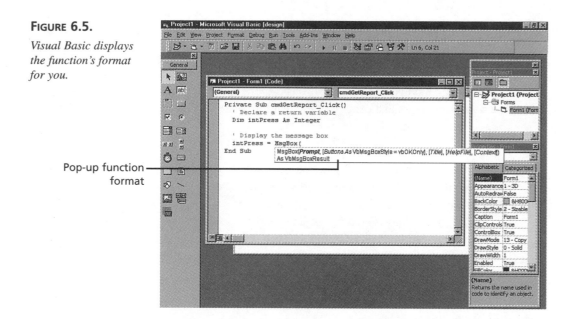

Pop-up function
format

FIGURE 6.6.

Visual Basic displays the function's named literals.

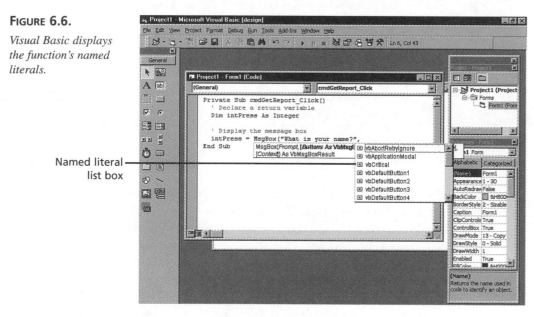

Named literal
list box

6

A Short Detour: Remarks

Figures 6.5 and 6.6 show two new program statements you've not yet seen. Two remark statements appear in each figure. Remarks help both you and other programmers who might modify and update your Visual Basic applications in the future. Remarks offer descriptive messages that explain in English (or whatever language you prefer) what's going on in the program's code.

It's said that a program is written once and read many times. That saying is true because of the nature of applications. Often, you'll write a program that helps you or your business compute required calculations and keep track of daily transactions. Over time, requirements change. Businesses buy and sell other businesses, the government changes its reporting and taxing requirements, and people's needs change. You should realize that after you write and implement a program, you will make modifications to that program later. If you use the program in a business, you'll almost certainly make many modifications to the program to reflect changing conditions.

> If you program for someone else or as part of a team, the chances are high that others will modify the programs that you write and that you'll modify programs that other programmers write. Therefore, as you write programs, think about the future modifications that you and others will make. Write your programs clearly, using ample spacing and indentation, and add remarks that explain complex sections of code.
>
> The most useful remarks are those that point out assumptions made when doing the complex sections of code. For example, in an insurance program, you might identify the actuarial table that was used to provide variables in a computation.

A remark is a message that you put inside a program's code. Programmers concerned with maintenance know that ample remarks help clarify code and aid future maintenance. Visual Basic completely ignores any and all remarks because those remarks are for people looking at your program code. Users don't see remarks because users don't see the program's code; rather, users see a program's output.

Programmers often add remarks to their programs for the following purposes:

- To state the programmer's name and the date that the program was written.
- To describe in the general section the overall goal of the program. (The general section appears before all the program's procedures and is the location Hour 5, "Putting Code into Visual Basic," described when it talked about declaring global variables.)

- To describe at the top of every procedure the overall goal of that procedure.

- To explain tricky or difficult statements so that others who modify the program later can understand the lines of code without having to decipher cryptic code.

Even if you write programs for yourself, and if you are the only one who will modify your programs, you should still add remarks to your programs. Weeks or months after you write a program, you'll have forgotten the exact details of the program, and remarks that you interspersed throughout the code will simplify your maintenance and help you find the code that you need to change.

> Add remarks as you write your programs. Often, programmers say to themselves, "I'll finish the program and add remarks later." Trust me—the remarks don't get added. It's only later, when programmers need to modify the program, that they notice the lack of remarks and regret it.

Add remarks to your program so that you and others can more quickly grasp the nature of the program and can make modifications to it more easily when needed. Visual Basic supports two kinds of remarks:

- Remarks that begin with the Rem statement

- Remarks that begin with the apostrophe (')

The Rem statement is more limiting than the apostrophe and isn't as easy to use. Nevertheless, you'll run across programs that use Rem statements, so you should learn how Rem works. Here is the format of the Rem statement:

```
Rem The remark's text
```

You can put anything you want in place of The remark's text. The following are examples of remarks:

```
Rem Programmer: Sanjaya Hettihewa, Date: Mar-27-1998
Rem
Rem This program supports the check-in and check-out
Rem  process for the dry-cleaning business.
Rem
Rem This event procedure executes when the user
Rem  clicks on the Exit command button. When pressed,
Rem  this event procedure closes the program's data
Rem  files, prints an exception report, and terminates
Rem  the application
```

6

The first of these remark sections consists of a one-line remark that tells the programmer's name and the date that the program was last modified. If someone else must modify the program later, that person can find the original programmer if needed to ask questions about the program's code. The second remark describes the program's overall goal by starting with a high-level description of the program's purpose. The third remark might appear at the top of a command button's `Click` event procedure.

As you can see, you can add one or more lines of remarks depending on the amount of description needed at that point in the program. Visual Basic ignores all lines that begin with `Rem`. When someone looks at the program code later, that person will know who the programmer is, the date that the program was written, the overall purpose of the program, and the overall description of each procedure that includes a remark section.

Say that you used apostrophes in place of the `Rem` statement in the previous remarks. The following rewritten remarks demonstrate that the remarks are even more effective because `Rem` doesn't get in the way of each remark's text:

```
' Programmer: Sanjaya Hettihewa, Date: Mar-27-1998
'
' This program supports the check-in and check-out
'   process for the dry-cleaning business.
'
' This event procedure executes when the user
'   clicks on the Exit command button. When pressed,
'   this event procedure closes the program's data
'   files, prints an exception report, and terminates
'   the application
```

The remarks don't have to go at the beginning of event procedures. You can place remarks between lines of code, as shown here:

```
Dim intRec As Integer
Rem Step through each customer record
For intRec = 1 To intNumCusts
' Test for a high balance
If custBal(intRec) > 5000 Then
Call PayReq
End If
Next intRec
```

Don't try to understand the details of this code yet. Concentrate now on the remarks. The code contains some advanced features (Visual Basic arrays and subroutine procedures) that you'll learn about in the last half of this book.

You can place apostrophe remarks at the end of Visual Basic statements. By placing a remark to the right of certain lines of code, you can clarify the purpose of the code. Consider how the following code section uses a remark to explain a specific line of code:

```
a = 3.14159 * r * r     ' Calculate a circle's area
```

Perhaps only a mathematician could interpret the formula without the remark. The remark helps even non-mathematicians understand the purpose of the statement. There is no reason that you should have to re-examine code every time you look at it. By reading remarks, you can glean the code's purpose without taking the time to interpret the Visual Basic code.

The wrong kinds of remarks won't help clarify code, though, so don't overdo them. As a matter of fact, many lines of code need no remarks to explain their purpose. The following remark is redundant and wastes both your programming time and the time of anyone who may maintain the program later:

```
Dim Sales As Single   ' Define a variable named Sales
```

Do not use the remarks when looking for a bug. Too often a programmer will read only the remarks and ignore the code because it's easier that way, but it's not very conducive to fixing a bug!

Examining InputBox()

You'll find that the InputBox() function is easy because it acts much like the MsgBox() function. The InputBox() function receives answers that are more complete than the MsgBox() function can get. Whereas MsgBox() returns one of seven values that indicate the user's command button press, the InputBox() function returns a string data value that holds the answer typed by the user.

Here is the format of the InputBox() function:

```
strVariable = InputBox( strPrompt [, [strTitle] [, strDefault]
➥ [, intXpos, intYpos]]])
```

strPrompt works a lot like the strmsg value in a MsgBox() function. The user sees *strPrompt* inside the input box displayed onscreen. *strTitle* is the title inside the input box's title bar. *strDefault* is a default string value that Visual Basic displays for a default answer, and the user can accept the default answer or change the default answer.

6

The *intXpos* and *intYpos* positions indicate the exact location where you want the input box to appear on the form. The *intXpos* value holds the number of twips from the left edge of the Form window to the left edge of the input box. The *intYpos* value holds the number of twips from the top edge of the Form window to the top edge of the input box. If you omit the *intXpos* and *intYpos* values, Visual Basic centers the message box on the form.

> Input boxes always contain OK and Cancel command buttons. If the user clicks OK (or presses Enter, which selects OK by default), the answer in the input box is sent to the variable being assigned the returned value. If the user clicks Cancel, a null string ("") returns from the InputBox() function.

The following statement displays an input box that asks the user for a company name. The user either enters a response to the prompt or clicks the Cancel command button to indicate that no answer is coming:

```
strCompName = InputBox("What is the name of the company?",
➥ "Company Request", "XYZ, Inc.")
```

> You can offer a default answer that the user can accept or change in the *strDefault* argument. The input box function returns the answer to the string variable to which you assign the function.

Figure 6.7 contains the message box displayed from this InputBox() function.

FIGURE 6.7.

The InputBox() *function is used to ask a question from the user.*

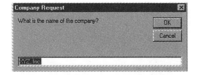

Summary

Message boxes display output, and input boxes get input. The message and input boxes offer ways for your programs to request information that regular controls can't handle. Use controls to display and get data values that are always needed. Use message and input boxes to display messages and get answers that the program needs in special cases, such as for error conditions and exception handling.

The next hour explains how to test the return values from this hour's functions as well as additional operators with which your applications can make decisions.

Q&A

Q When do I use controls and when do I use message and input boxes?

A You use Form controls when the user is to interact with a form and enter values the form module will process. The Toolbox controls are extremely useful for guiding the user through a list of choices. The message box is a program feature you can use to display one-time notes and warnings to your users. The input box is a great one-time dialog box you can display to ask the user questions when needed during the execution of the program.

Q Why should I add remarks to my code?

A You'll modify your programs over time. The more you modify a program, the faster that modification (called maintenance) will go if you add ample remarks at the time you create the program. The remarks help you remember what a particular section of code is for. In addition to remarks, use named literals when available for options such as the message box button type because the named literal mnemonics are easier to remember than their numeric equivalents.

Workshop

The quiz questions and exercises are provided for your further understanding. See Appendix B for the answers.

Quiz

1. What is the difference between a message box and a text box?
2. Which stays on the user's screen during the majority of a program's execution: a text box or an input box?
3. Why do the named literals provide for better program maintenance?
4. What are the two kinds of remark statements?
5. Whom are remarks for?
6. What does modal mean?
7. How many icons can you display with message boxes?

6

8. True or false: You can pass multiple arguments and receive multiple return values from functions.

9. What role do default values play in input boxes?

10. True or false: The `MsgBox()` function can return one of seven values.

Exercises

1. Write three remarks for the top of a program that calculates sales tax. The first remark should hold your name, the second should hold the date that you write the remark, and the third should span at least two lines and should describe the purpose of the program.

2. Write an input box function that asks users for their ages. Display a default value of 25.

HOUR 7

Making Decisions

You learned Visual Basic's mathematical operators in Hour 5, "Putting Code into Visual Basic," but Visual Basic supports several more operators, as you'll learn in this lesson. The operators described here are known as comparison operators because they compare data and determine the results of the comparison. By using comparison operators, you can write your programs so that they make certain runtime decisions based on the comparison results.

The highlights of this hour include

- Which comparison operators to use
- How to form `If` statements
- When to use an `Else` branch
- How `Select Case` statements streamline `If...Else`

Comparison Operators

All comparison operators produce true or false results. In other words, the comparison is either true or the comparison is false. The mathematical operators produce numeric values, whereas the comparison operators produce only true or false values. The rest of the program can use the true or false comparison operator result to make decisions. If a comparison operator returns `False` when comparing whether an employee worked the last pay period, the rest of the program knows not to print a paycheck for that employee.

 NEW TERM   *Comparison operators* are operators that compare data values against each other and produce true or false results.

> This section describes just the operators; subsequent sections in this lesson describe new programming statements that can make use of the comparison operators.

Table 7.1 describes VB's six comparison operators. The comparison operators always compare data, and that comparison is either true or false because data either compares as expected or does not.

> Two values can be equal to one another or one can be greater than the other. Keep these possibilities in mind as you read through Table 7.1.

TABLE 7.1. THE COMPARISON OPERATORS DETERMINE HOW DATA COMPARES.

Operator	Use	Description
>	lblSales. Caption > Goal	The *greater than* operator returns `True` if the value on the left side of > is numerically or alphabetically greater than the value on the right.
<	Pay < 2000.00	The *less than* operator returns `True` if the value on the left side of < is numerically or alphabetically less than the value on the right.
=	Age = Limit	The *equal to* operator (or equal operator) returns `True` if the values on both sides of = are equal to each other.
>=	FirstName >= "Mike"	The *greater than or equal to* operator returns `True` if the value on the left side of >= is numerically or alphabetically greater than or equal to the value on the right.

Operator	Use	Description
<=	Num <= lblAmt.Caption	The *less than or equal to* operator returns True if the value on the left side of <= is numerically or alphabetically less than or equal to the value on the right.
<>	txtAns.Text <> "Yes"	The *not equal to* operator returns True if the value on the left side of <> is numerically or alphabetically unequal to the value on the right.

 Remember that if a comparison operator doesn't produce a true result, the result must be false.

As you can see from Table 7.1, the comparison operators compare either variables, literals, control values, or combinations of all those data sources. The comparison operators work on both numeric and alphabetic values. You can compare any kind of number against another number, or any kind of string against another string.

The Comparison's Nature

When you compare strings, Visual Basic uses the ASCII table to determine how to compare the characters. For example, the ASCII table says that the uppercase letter *A*—with an ASCII numeric value of 65—is less than the uppercase letter *B*, which has an ASCII numeric value of 66. Notice that all uppercase letters are less than lowercase letters. Therefore, the abbreviation *ST* is less than *St*.

NEW TERM   An *ASCII table* contains a list of characters with corresponding unique numeric representations.

To understand how comparison operators work, you must understand how to use their true or false results. The If statement, introduced in the next section, explains how you can use true and false results to make decisions in your program. Before you read the next section, make sure that you understand how these operators compare values. Make sure that you understand the Result column of Table 7.2 before you go any further.

7

TABLE 7.2. RELATIONSHIP RESULTS.

Relation	Result
4 > 2	True
4 < 1	False
4 < 8	True
"Apple" <= "Orange"	True
"Macmillan" < "Mc millan"	True
0 >= 0	True
0 <= 0	True
1 <> 2	True
2 >= 3	False

Keep Each Side's Datatype Consistent

Take extra care that the expressions on both sides of a comparison operator conform to the same datatype or at least compatible datatypes. In other words, you cannot compare a string to a numeric datatype. If you try, you will receive a type mismatch error because the datatypes don't match. You can compare any numeric datatype against any other numeric datatype most of the time. In other words, you can test whether a single-precision value is less than or greater than an integer value.

Be careful when you compare nonintegers for equality. Precision numbers are difficult to represent internally. For example, if you assigned 8.3221 to a single-precision variable and assigned 8.3221 to another single-precision variable, Visual Basic might return a false result if you compare the values for equality. Internally, one of the variables might actually hold 8.322100001 because of rounding errors that occur in insignificant decimal places. You can safely compare two currency values for equality, however, because Visual Basic maintains and compares their accuracy to two decimal places.

The comparison operators are sometimes known as *conditional* operators because they test conditions that are either true or false.

The `If` Statement

Perhaps the most important statement in a program is the `If` statement and its cousin statements. With logic that `If` provides, your application can begin to analyze data and make decisions based on that analysis. For example, your program can display a three-button message box and determine, with the `If` statement, which command button the user clicked to close the message box.

`If` uses the comparison operators you learned earlier in this lesson to test data values. `If` performs one of two possible code actions, depending on the result of the comparison. In other words, `If` uses comparison operator results to test data. `If` might execute one or more lines of subsequent code, depending on the result of a comparison.

Before `If`, the code you wrote executed sequentially, one statement after another. `If` lets your program be more decisive and execute only parts of the program if the data warrants partial execution. For example, suppose you were writing an invoicing system. In such a system, no sales tax should be computed for tax-exempt organizations, so your program would skip over the tax computation code when processing such organizations.

`If` makes decisions. If a comparison test is true, the body of the `If` statement executes. (In fact, the previous sentence is almost identical to Visual Basic's `If` statement!) Here is one format of `If`:

```
If comparisonTest Then
   One or more Visual Basic statements
End If
```

`End If` tells Visual Basic where the body of the `If` statement ends. Suppose that the user enters a sales figure into a Text Box control named `txtSales`. The following `If` computes a bonus amount based on the sales:

```
If (txtSales.Text > 5000.00) Then
   sngBonus = txtSales.Text * .12
End If
```

Data enters a control such as a text box as a `Variant` datatype. When you perform arithmetic with a `Variant` and the `Variant` datatype holds a numeric value, Visual Basic converts the `Variant` to a number for the calculation.

Remember that Visual Basic stores `0` in all numeric variables that you don't first initialize. Therefore `sngBonus` has a `0` before the `If` executes. When `If` executes, the code

7

changes the `sngBonus` variable only if the value of the `txtSales.Text` property is more than `5000.00`. In a way, the `If` reads like this:

If the sales are more than $5,000.00, then compute a bonus based on that sales value.

Visual Basic stores a null zero in string variables that you have not yet initialized. If you use an uninitialized `Variant` datatype variable, the variable holds a null value that becomes zero if you assign the variable to a numeric variable.

The body of an `If` can have more than one statement. The body is often known as a block. The following `If` calculates a bonus, the cost of sales, and a reorder amount based on the value of the `txtSales` text box entry:

```
If (txtSales.Text > 5000.00) Then
  sngBonus = txtSales.Text * .12
  curCostOfSales = txtSales.Text * .41
  curReorderCost = txtSales.Text * .24
End If
```

The three statements that make up the body of the `If` execute only if the condition `txtSales.Text > 5000.00` is true. Suppose that this code contains another assignment statement immediately after `End If`. That assignment statement is outside the body of the `If`, so the true or false result of the condition affects only the body of the `If`. Therefore, the tax computation in the following routine executes regardless of whether the sales are more or less than $5,000.00:

```
If (txtSales.Text > 5000.00) Then
  sngBonus = txtSales.Text * .12
  curCostOfSales = txtSales.Text * .41
  curReorderCost = txtSales.Text * .24
End If
sngTax = .12 * txtSales.Text
```

> The parentheses are not required around the comparison test in an `If`, but they help separate the test from the rest of the code. In addition, the indentation helps illustrate the code that appears inside the `If` statement's body.

Can you see how the program makes decisions using `If`? The body of the `If` executes only if the comparison test is true. Otherwise, the rest of the program continues as usual.

There is a shortcut form of `If` that you might run across. The single-line `If` statement has a format that looks like this:

```
If comparisonTest Then VBStatement
```

The single-line `If` doesn't require an `End If` statement because the comparison test and the body of the `If` reside on the same line. Single-line `If` statements don't provide for easy program maintenance. If you decide that you want to add to the body of the `If`, you must convert the single-line `If` to a multiple-line `If`, and you might forget to then add `End If`. Therefore, even if the body of an `If` statement takes only one line, code the `If` as a multiple-line `If...End If` statement to make the program more maintainable.

The `If` Statement's `Else` Branch

Whereas `If` executes code based on the comparison test's true condition, the `Else` statement executes code based on the comparison test's false condition. `Else` is an optional part of the `If` statement. `Else` specifies the code that executes if the comparison test is false. The complete format of the `If` statement with `Else` is as follows:

```
If comparisonTest Then
  One or more Visual Basic statements
Else
  One or more Visual Basic statements
End If
```

Typically, programmers call this full-blown `If` statement the `If...Else` statement. The `If...Else` statement is sometimes called a mutually exclusive statement. The term *mutually exclusive* simply means that one set of code or the other executes, but not both. The `If...Else` statement contains two sets of code—that is, two bodies of one or more Visual Basic statements—and only one set executes, depending on the result of the `If`. An `If` statement is either true or false because the `If`'s comparison produces either a true or false result. Therefore, either the first or the second body of code in an `If...Else` executes.

Suppose that a salesperson receives a bonus if sales are high (more than $5,000.00) or suffers a pay cut if sales are low (less than $5,000.00). The `If...Else` shown next contains the code necessary to reward or punish the salesperson. The `If` code body computes the bonus, as you saw in the previous section. The code body of the `Else` subtracts $25 from the salesperson's pay, which is stored in the `curPayAmt` variable, if the sales quota isn't met. The following code computes such a payment amount based on the quota:

```
1: If (txtSales.Text > 5000.00) Then
2:    sngBonus = .05 * txtSales.Text
3: Else
4:    curPayAmt = curPayAmt - 25.00
5: End If
6: curTaxes = curPayAmt * .42
```

The fourth line of code might surprise you at first. The assignment appears to make the statement that the pay is equal to the pay minus 25. You know that nothing can be equal

7

to itself minus 25. In math, the equal sign acts as a balance for the two sides of the equa-
tion. In Visual Basic, when the equal sign isn't used inside an `If`'s comparison test, it is
an assignment that takes everything to the right of the equal sign and stores that value in
the variable to the left of the equal sign. Therefore, the fourth line subtracts the 25 from
the value stored in `curPayAmt` and assigns that result back to `curPayAmt`. In effect, it
lowers the value of `curPayAmt` by 25.

> When a variable appears on both sides of an assignment's equal sign, the
> variable is being updated in some way.

To further your understanding of the `If...Else` statement and to demonstrate testing for
an input box's return value, study how Listing 7.1 uses `If...Else` to respond to an input
box. The code asks the user for a company name and then accepts the name or recognizes that the user clicked Cancel to close the input box without answering it. (When a
user clicks Cancel in response to an input box, the input box returns a null string, `""`.)

LISTING 7.1. CHECKING AN INPUT BOX'S RETURN VALUE.

```
 1: Dim strCompName As String
 2: Dim intPress As Integer    ' MsgBox return value
 3:  ' Ask the user for a name
 4:  ' Use XYZ, Inc. for the default name
 5: strCompName = InputBox("What is the company name?", _
 6: "Company Request", "XYZ, Inc.")
 7:  ' Check the return value
 8: If (strCompName = "") Then
 9: ' The user clicked Cancel
10: intPress = MsgBox("Thanks anyway")
11: Else
12: ' The user entered a company name
13: intPress = MsgBox("You entered " & strCompName)
14: End If
```

Compound Comparisons with the Logical Operators

Visual Basic supports three additional operators—`And`, `Or`, and `Not`—that look more like
commands than operators. `And`, `Or`, and `Not` are logical operators. *Logical operators* let
you combine two or more comparison tests into a single compound comparison.

Table 7.3 describes the logical operators, which work just like their spoken counterparts.

TABLE 7.3. THE LOGICAL OPERATORS.

Operator	Use	Description
And	If (A > B) And (C < D)	Produces True if both sides of the And are true. Therefore, A must be greater than B *and* C must be less than D. Otherwise, the expression produces a false result.
Or	If (A > B) Or (C < D)	Produces True if either side of the Or is true. Therefore, A must be greater than B *or* C must be less than D. If both sides of the Or are false, the entire expression produces a false result.
Not	If Not(strAns = "Yes")	Produces the opposite true or false result. Therefore, if strAns holds "Yes", the Not turns the true result to false.

As you can see from Table 7.3, the And and Or logical operators let you combine more than one comparison test in a single If statement. The Not negates a comparison test. You can often turn a Not condition around. Not can produce difficult comparison tests, and you should use it cautiously. The last If in Table 7.3, for instance, could easily be changed to If (strAns <> "Yes") to eliminate the Not.

Your code often must perform an assignment, print a message, or display a label if two or more conditions are true. The logical operators make the combined condition easy to code. Suppose that you want to reward the salesperson if sales total more than $5,000 and if the salesperson sells more than 10,000 units of a particular product. Without And, you have to embed an If statement in the body of another If statement like this:

```
If (sngSales > 5000.00) Then
  If (intUnitsSold > 10000) Then
    sngBonus = 50.00
  End If
End If
```

Here is the same code rewritten as a single If. It is easier to read and to change later if you need to update the program:

```
If (sngSales > 5000.00) And (intUnitsSold > 10000) Then
   sngBonus = 50.00
End If
```

7

How can you rewrite this `If` to pay the bonus if the salesperson sells either more than $5,000 in sales or if the salesperson sells more than 10,000 units? Here is the code:

```
If (sngSales > 5000.00) Or (intUnitsSold > 10000) Then
   sngBonus = 50.00
End If
```

Listing 7.2 contains an `If...Else` that tests data from two divisions of a company and calculates values from the data.

LISTING 7.2. CALCULATING SALES FIGURES FOR A COMPANY'S DIVISIONS.

```
1: If (intDivNum = 3) Or (intDivNum = 4) Then
2:   curDivTotal = curDivSales3 + curDivSales4
3:   curGrandDivCosts = (curDivCost3 * 1.2) + (curDivCost4 * 1.4)
4: Else
5:   curDivTotal = curDivSales1 + curDivSales2
6:   curGrandDivCosts = (curDivCost1 * 1.1) + (curDivCost5 * 1.9)
7: End If
```

If `intDivNum` contains either a 3 or a 4, the user is requesting figures for the East Coast, and the code in the first `If` branch executes to produce an East Coast pair of values. If `intDivNum` doesn't contain a 3 or a 4, the program assumes that `intDivNum` contains a 1 or a 2, and the West Coast pair of values is calculated in the `Else` portion.

Notice how easy it is to spot the variable's datatype in code that names variables with a datatype prefix such as `cur` (for currency) and `sng` (for single-precision). Use datatype prefixes in all your variable names. Although you must type a little extra, your program code will be much clearer.

Multiple Choice with `Select Case`

`If` is great for data comparisons in cases where one or two comparison tests must be made. When you must test against more than two conditions, however, `If` becomes difficult to maintain. The logical operators help in only certain kinds of conditions. At other times, you must nest several `If...Else` statements inside one another.

Consider the `If` statement shown in Listing 7.3. Although the logic of the `If` statement is simple, the coding is extremely difficult to follow.

LISTING 7.3. NESTED If...Else STATEMENTS QUICKLY BECOME COMPLEX.

```
 1: If (intAge = 5) Then
 2:    lblTitle.Caption = "Kindergarten"
 3:    Else
 4:      If (intAge = 6) Then
 5:        lblTitle.Caption = "1st Grade"
 6:      Else
 7:        If (intAge = 7) Then
 8:          lblTitle.Caption = "2nd Grade"
 9:        Else
10:          If (intAge = 8) Then
11:            lblTitle.Caption = "3rd Grade"
12:          Else
13:            If (intAge = 9) Then
14:              lblTitle.Caption = "4th Grade"
15:            Else
16:              If (intAge = 10) Then
17:                lblTitle.Caption = "5th Grade"
18:              Else
19:                If (intAge = 11) Then
20:                  lblTitle.Caption = "6th Grade"
21:                Else
22:                  lblTitle.Caption = "Advanced"
23:                End If
24:              End If
25:            End If
26:          End If
27:        End If
28:      End If
29: End If
```

Visual Basic supports a Select Case statement that handles such multiple-choice conditions better than If...Else. Here is the format of the Select Case statement:

```
Select Case Expression
  Case value
    One or more Visual Basic statements
  Case value
    One or more Visual Basic statements
  [Case value
    One or more Visual Basic statements]
  [Case Else
    One or more Visual Basic statements]
End Select
```

Select Case is a good substitute for long, nested If...Else conditions when several choices are possible. You set up your Visual Basic program to execute one set of Visual Basic statements from a list of statements inside Select Case.

7

The Select Case format makes the statement look as difficult as a complex nested If...Else, but you will soon see that Select Case statements are actually easier to code and maintain than their If...Else counterparts.

Expression can be any Visual Basic expression—such as a calculation, a string value, or a numeric value—provided that it results in an integer or a string value. Each *value* must be an integer or a string value that matches *Expression*'s datatype.

The Select Case statement is useful when you must make several choices based on data values. Select Case can have two or more Case *value* sections. The code that executes depends on which *value* matches *Expression*. If none of the *values* match *Expression*, the Case Else body of code executes if you code the Case Else. Otherwise, nothing happens and control continues with the statement that follows End Select.

> Don't use Select Case when a simple If or If...Else will suffice. Test logic is often so straightforward that a Select Case would be overkill and even less clear than an If. Unless you need to compare against more than a couple values, stick with the If and If...Else statements because of their simplicity.

The fastest way to learn Select Case is to see an example of it. Listing 7.4 contains a Select Case version of the child grade assignments shown in Listing 7.3. Select Case organizes the multiple-choice selections into a more manageable format.

LISTING 7.4. USING Select Case TO SIMPLIFY COMPLEX NESTED If...Else STATEMENTS.

```
 1: Select Case intAge
 2:    Case 5:  lblTitle.Caption = "Kindergarten"
 3:    Case 6:  lblTitle.Caption = "1st Grade"
 4:    Case 7:  lblTitle.Caption = "2nd Grade"
 5:    Case 8:  lblTitle.Caption = "3rd Grade"
 6:    Case 9:  lblTitle.Caption = "4th Grade"
 7:    Case 10: lblTitle.Caption = "5th Grade"
 8:    Case 11: lblTitle.Caption = "6th Grade"
 9:    Case Else: lblTitle.Caption = "Advanced"
10: End Select
```

> Use Select Case instead of embedded If...Else because Select Case keeps the code much simpler and easier to maintain.

Here's how the `Select Case` works: If the `intAge` variable holds the value 5, the label is assigned `"Kindergarten"` in the second line. If the `intAge` variable holds the value 6, the label is assigned `"1st Grade"` in the third line. The logic continues through the `Case 11:` statement. If `intAge` holds a value that doesn't fall within the range of 5 through 11, the final `Case Else` assigns `"Advanced"` to the label.

The body of each `Case` can consist of more than one statement, just as the body of an `If` or `If...Else` can consist of more than one statement. Visual Basic executes all the statements for any given `Case` match until the next `Case` is reached. When Visual Basic executes a matching `Case` value, it skips the remaining `Case` statements and continues with the code that follows the `End Select` statement.

Notice the colons after each `Case value` statement in Listing 7.4. The colons are optional, but they do help separate the case being tested from its code that executes.

Programmers often trigger the execution of complete procedures, such as event procedures, from within a `Case` statement. As you will learn in Hour 13, "Modular Programming," instead of putting several statements in the body of an `If...Else` or a `Case`, you can execute a procedure that contains all the statements that execute when a given condition is true.

Two Additional `Select Case` Formats

The two additional formats differ only slightly from the standard `Select Case` that you learned about in the previous section. They enable you to extend the power of `Select Case` so that Visual Basic can make `Case` matches on both comparison tests and ranges of values. Here is the first additional format:

```
Select Case Expression
  Case Is Relation:
    One or more Visual Basic statements
  Case Is Relation:
    One or more Visual Basic statements
  [Case Is Relation:
    One or more Visual Basic statements]
  [Case Else:
    One or more Visual Basic statements]
End Select
```

Relation can be whatever comparison test you want to perform against *Expression* at the top of the `Select Case`. The standard `Select Case` statement, discussed in the previous section, compared the *Expression* value against an exact `Case` match. When you use the comparison `Is Select Case` option, each `Case` can be matched on a comparison test.

7

The format of the second extra `Select Case` format is as follows:

```
Select Case Expression
  Case expr1 To expr2:
    One or more Visual Basic statements
  Case expr1 To expr2:
    One or more Visual Basic statements
  [Case expr1 To expr2:
    One or more Visual Basic statements]
  [Case Else:
    One or more Visual Basic statements]
End Select
```

The `Case` lines require a range, such as `4 To 6`. The `To Select Case` option enables you to match against a range instead of a relation or an exact match.

 You can combine the extended formats of `Select Case` with the standard `Select Case` so that two or more kinds of `Case` formats appear within the same `Select Case` statement.

Study Listing 7.5 to learn how to combine different `Select Case` statements to test for various values.

LISTING 7.5. USING `Select Case` TO SIMPLIFY COMPLEX NESTED `If...Else` STATEMENTS.

```
 1: Rem The following Select Case to End Select code
 2: Rem    assigns a student's grade and school name
 3: Rem    to the label on the form. The code checks
 4: Rem    to make sure that the student is not too
 5: Rem    young to be going to school.
 6: Select Case intAge
 7: ' Check for too young...
 8: Case Is <5:  lblTitle.Text = "Too young"
 9:
10: ' Five-year olds are next assigned
11: Case 5: lblTitle.Text = "Kindergarten"
12:
13: ' Six to eleven...
14: Case 6 To 11:  lblTitle.Text = "Elementary"
15: lblSchool.Text = "Lincoln"
16:
17: ' Twelve to fifteen...
18: Case 12 To 15: lblTitle.Text = "Intermediate"
19: lblSchool.Text = "Washington"
20:
21: ' Sixteen to eighteen
```

```
22: Case 16 To 18: lblTitle.Text = "High School"
23: lblSchool.Text = "Betsy Ross"
24:
25: ' Everyone else must go to college
26: Case Else: lblTitle.Text = "College"
27: lblSchool.Text = "University"
28: End Select
```

If the age is less than 5, the title label becomes Too young, and the school name remains blank. If the age is exactly 5 (intAge is obviously an integer value), the title gets Kindergarten, and the school name still remains blank. Only if the child is 5 or older are both the title and school name initialized.

If you were to rewrite this code using embedded If...Else logic, the code would become a nightmare. The Select Case's range testing, such as Case 16 to 18, saves a tremendous amount of If...Else logic.

Summary

In this hour you learned how to write Visual Basic programs that make decisions. When your programs are able to test data values against certain conditions, they begin to make execution decisions and perform smarter calculations. Visual Basic offers several forms of the If and the Select Case statements to make comparisons. The comparison operators, especially when combined with the logical operators, produce advanced compound conditions.

The next hour explains how to write looping statements so that your programs can repeat logic as often as needed.

Q&A

Q **Which testing statement is better: If, If...Else, or Select Case?**

A No testing statement is better than another in all situations. The If statement is the fundamental building block for testing data, and If is extremely common in most applications. When you need the application to execute one block of code or another, depending on the result of an If test, use If...Else. If you need to embed several If...Else statements together because you've got to test for multiple comparisons, the Select Case almost always makes a better comparison statement than If...Else. You would not, however, save effort or program clarity if you used Select Case when a simple If...Else would do. The bottom line is that your application determines the best statement to use at any one time.

7

Q Why is the `Not` operator considered so bad?

A `Not` isn't considered bad, really, but the negative logic that `Not` produces often makes for confusing logic. Some logic is best performed with `Not`, but you can almost always turn the `Not` logic into positive and simpler logic by reversing the comparison.

Workshop

The quiz questions and exercises are provided for your further understanding. See Appendix B for the answers.

Quiz

1. How do comparison operators differ from mathematical operators?

2. What role does the ASCII table play in comparison logic?

3. Do the following statements produce true or false results?

   a. 25 <= 25

   b. "a" >= "B"

   c. 0 < –1

   d. 234.32 > 234.321

4. When do you code the `Else` portion of an `If` statement?

5. True or false: The `End If` statement isn't needed for one-line `If` statements.

6. Which statement replaces nested `If...Else` logic?

7. Which `Case` option checks for a range of values?

8. What happens if every `Case` fails and there is no `Case Else` option?

9. What role do code blocks play in `Select Case` statements?

10. What is wrong with this `If` statement?

    ```
    If (intA < 1) And (intC >= 8) Then
      lblDraft.Caption = "Overdrawn"
    Else
      lblDraft.Caption = "Underdrawn"
    End Else
    ```

Exercises

1. Rewrite the following nested `If` statement using a single `If` with a logical operator:

```
If (A > 3) Then
  If (B > 10) Then
    lblAns.Caption = "Yes"
  End If
End If
```

2. Rewrite the following `If` to eliminate the `Not` and to clarify the code:

```
If Not(X < 10) Or Not(Y >= 20) Then
```

7

HOUR **8**

Visual Basic Looping

You've now mastered sequential logic and decision-making logic. This hour's lesson explains how to write programs that contain looping logic. A loop is a set of program instructions that execute repeatedly. Your programming preferences and application dictate how many times the loop must repeat.

Loops play important roles in programs because you'll need to repeat sections of a program to process multiple data values. For example, you might need to calculate a total of past due charges for all past due customers. A loop can read each customer's past due charge and add that amount to the running total. As you learn more about Visual Basic in subsequent lessons, you will see additional uses for loops.

The highlights of this hour include

- What a loop is
- How you code a Do loop
- Why several Do loop formats exist
- When to use For
- How the Exit statements interrupt execution

The `Do While` Loops

Visual Basic supports several versions of the `Do` statement. The `Do While` loop is perhaps the most common looping statement that you'll put in Visual Basic programs. `Do While` works with comparison expressions just as the `If` statement does. Therefore, the six comparison operators that you learned about in the previous lesson work as expected here. Rather than controlling the one-time execution of a single block of code, however, the comparison expression controls the looping statements.

Like the `If` statement (covered in Hour 7, "Making Decisions") that ends with an `End If` statement, a loop will always be a multiline statement that includes an obvious beginning and ending of the loop. Here is the format of the `Do While` loop:

```
Do While (comparison test)
   Block of one or more Visual Basic statements
Loop
```

The block of code continues looping as long as *comparison test* is true. Whether you insert one or several lines of code for the block doesn't matter. It's vital, however, for the block of code to somehow change a variable used in *comparison test*. The block of code keeps repeating as long as the `Do While` loop's *comparison test* continues to stay true. Eventually, *comparison test* must become false or your program will enter an infinite loop and the user will have to break the program's execution through an inelegant means, such as pressing the Ctrl+Break key combination.

NEW TERM   An *infinite* loop is a loop that never terminates.

> Guard against infinite loops and always make sure that your loops can terminate properly. Even if you provide an Exit command button or a File | Exit menu option in your application, the program will often ignore the user's exit command if the program enters an infinite loop.

The `Do While` loop continues executing a block of Visual Basic statements as long as *comparison test* is true. As soon as *comparison test* becomes false, the loop terminates.

> **THE LOOP'S TERMINATION**
>
> As long as *comparison test* is true, the block of code in the body of the loop continues executing. When *comparison test* becomes false, the loop terminates. After the loop terminates, Visual Basic begins program execution at the statement following the Loop statement because Loop signals the end of the loop.
>
> As soon as Do While's *comparison test* becomes false, the loop terminates and doesn't execute even one more time. The Do While's *comparison test* appears at the top of the loop. Therefore, if *comparison test* is false the first time the loop begins, the body of the loop will never execute.

Listing 8.1 contains a section of an event procedure that contains a Do While loop that asks the user for an age. If the user enters an age less than 10 or greater than 99, the program beeps at the error and displays another input box asking for the age. The program continues looping, asking for the age, as long as the user enters an age that's out of range.

LISTING 8.1. THE Do While LOOP EXECUTES AS LONG AS *comparison test* IS TRUE.

```
 1: Dim strAge As String
 2: Dim intAge As Integer
 3: Dim intPress As Integer
 4:
 5:  ' Get the age in a string variable
 6: strAge = InputBox("How old are you?", "Age Ask")
 7:  ' Check for the Cancel command button
 8: If (strAge = "") Then
 9: End    ' Terminates the application
10: End If
11:
12:  ' Cancel was not pressed, so convert Age to integer
13:  ' The Val() function converts strings to integers
14: intAge = Val(strAge)
15:
16:  ' Loop if the age is not in the correct range
17: Do While ((intAge < 10) Or (intAge > 99))
18: ' The user's age is out of range
19: intPress = MsgBox("Your age must be between " & _
20: "10 and 99", vbExclamation, "Error!")
21: strAge = InputBox("How old are you?", "Age Ask")
22:
23:  ' Check for the Cancel command button
```

continues

LISTING **8.1.** CONTINUED

```
24: If (strAge = "") Then
25: End   ' Terminate the program
26: End If
27: intAge = Val(strAge)
28: Loop
```

Figure 8.1 shows the message box error that Listing 8.1 displays if the user enters an age value that's less than 10 or greater than 99. Listing 8.1 does nothing with `MsgBox()`'s return value stored in `intPress`. The user simply presses Enter to close the message box, so checking for `intPress`'s value would not help this particular section of code.

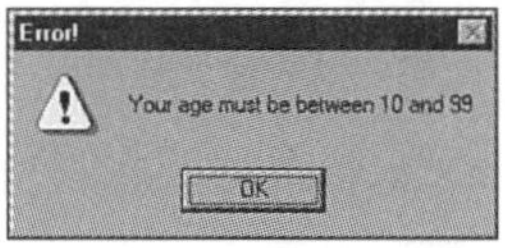

FIGURE 8.1.

The user sees this message as long as the age is out of range.

Error!
⚠ Your age must be between 10 and 99

OK

Listing 8.1 uses the built-in `Val()` function. `Val()` accepts a string argument and converts that string to a number (assuming that the string holds the correct digits for a number). The `InputBox()` function returns a string so that the value the user enters into the input box must convert to an integer before you store the value in the integer variable named `intAge`.

The code contains some redundancy. For example, two lines contain almost the same `InputBox()` function, and the same check for a Cancel button press appears twice in the program. There are other looping statements that you'll learn about later in this lesson; those statements can help simplify this code by removing some of the redundancy.

Perhaps the most important thing to note about the `Do While` loop in Listing 8.1 is that the body of the loop provides a way for *comparison test* to terminate. The code contains an `intAge` variable that the body of the loop reassigns each time the loop's block of code executes. Therefore, assuming that the user enters a different value for the age, the loop will test against a different set of comparison values, the comparison test will fail (which would mean that the age is inside the range), and the program will stop looping. If the loop body did nothing with the *comparison test* variable, the loop would continue forever.

The `Do Until` Loop

Whereas the `Do While` loop continues executing the body of the loop as long as the comparison test is true, the `Do Until` loop executes the body of the loop as long as the comparison test is false. The program's logic at the time of the loop determines which kind of loop works best in a given situation.

`Do Until` works almost exactly like the `Do While` loop except that the `Do Until` loop continues executing the body of the loop until the comparison test is true. Like the `Do While`, the `Do Until` is a multiline looping statement that can execute a block of code that's one or more lines long.

Here is the format of `Do Until`:

```
Do Until (comparison test)
    Block of one or more Visual Basic statements
Loop
```

Remember that the *comparison test* must be false for the loop to continue.

You can use the `Do While` or the `Do Until` for almost any loop. Listing 8.2 contains the age-checking event procedure that contains a `Do Until` loop. The loop ensures that the age falls between two values. As you can see, *comparison test* for the `Do Until` is the opposite of that used in Listing 8.1's `Do While` loop.

WHICH LOOP IS BEST?

Use the loop that makes for the cleanest and clearest *comparison test*. Sometimes, the logic makes the `Do While` clearer, whereas other loops seem to work better when you set them up with `Do Until`.

`Do Until` continues executing a block of Visual Basic statements as long as *comparison test* is false. As soon as *comparison test* becomes true (the loop is said to `Do` a loop until the condition becomes false), the loop terminates and the program continues on the line that follows the closing loop statement.

There is really no technical advantage to using `Do While` instead of `Do Until`. Use whichever one seems to flow the best for any given application.

LISTING 8.2. THE Do Until LOOPS UNTIL *comparison test* BECOMES TRUE.

```
 1: Dim strAge As String
 2: Dim intAge As Integer
 3: Dim intPress As Integer
 4:
 5:   ' Get the age in a string variable
 6: strAge = InputBox("How old are you?", "Age Ask")
 7:
 8:   ' Check for the Cancel command button
 9: If (strAge = "") Then
10: End     ' Terminate the program
11: End If
12:
13:   ' Cancel was not pressed, so convert Age to integer
14: intAge = Val(strAge)
15:   ' Loop if the age is not in the correct range
16: Do Until ((intAge >= 10) And (intAge <= 99))
17: ' The user's age is out of range
18: intPress = MsgBox("Your age must be " & _
19: "between 10 and 99", vbExclamation, "Error!")
20: strAge = InputBox("How old are you?", "Age Ask")
21: ' Check for the Cancel command button
22: If (strAge = "") Then
23: End     ' Terminate the program
24: End If
25: intAge = Val(strAge)
26: Loop
```

The 16th line provides the only real difference between Listing 8.1 and Listing 8.2. The age must now fall within the valid range for the loop to terminate.

The Other Do Loops

Another pair of Do loops work almost exactly like the two previous loops. Do...Loop While and Do...Loop Until look very much like their counterparts that you learned about earlier. But these new loop formats check their comparison tests at the bottom of the loop rather than at the top.

If a loop begins with a single Do statement, the loop ends with either Loop While or Loop Until. Here is the format of Do...Loop While:

```
Do
    Block of one or more Visual Basic statements
Loop Until (comparison test)
```

That Do looks lonely by itself, doesn't it? The purpose of the Do is to signal the beginning of the loop. The loop continues until the Loop Until statement. The *comparison test* appears at the bottom of the loop if you use the Do...Loop While loop statement. The body of the loop always executes at least once. The body of the loop executes more than once as long as the *comparison test* stays true. There is a corresponding Do...Loop Until statement that checks for a false condition at the bottom of the loop's body.

Notice that the Do...Loop While loop's *comparison test* appears at the bottom of the loop instead of at the top of the loop. You'll use the Do...Loop While loop when you want the body of the loop to execute at least one time. Often, by placing *comparison test* at the bottom of the loop, you can eliminate redundant code that otherwise might be required if you used Do While.

To complete the loop statements, Visual Basic also supports a Do...Loop Until statement. Like the Do...Loop While, the Do...Loop Until statement tests *comparison test* at the bottom of the loop. Therefore, the body of the loop executes at least once, no matter what *comparison test* turns out to be. The loop continues as long as the *comparison test* result stays false.

Listing 8.3 contains the age-checking procedure that's much shorter than the previous versions. *comparison test* appears at the bottom of the loop, so the extra InputBox() function call isn't needed.

LISTING 8.3. USING THE Do...Loop While TO CHECK THE COMPARISON AT THE BOTTOM OF THE LOOP.

```
 1: Dim strAge As String
 2: Dim intAge As Integer
 3: Dim intPress As Integer
 4:
 5: Do
 6: strAge = InputBox("How old are you?", "Age Ask")
 7: ' Check for the Cancel command button
 8: If (strAge = "") Then
 9: End    ' Terminate program
10: End If
11: intAge = Val(strAge)
12:
13: If ((intAge < 10) Or (intAge > 99)) Then
14: ' The user's age is out of range
15: intPress = MsgBox("Your age must be between " & _
16: "10 and 99", vbExclamation, "Error!")
17: End If
18: Loop While ((intAge < 10) Or (intAge > 99))
```

The loop begins almost immediately. The loop's body will always execute at least once, so InputBox() appears right inside the loop. By placing the InputBox() function inside the loop, you eliminate the need to put this function in the code twice (once before the loop and once inside the loop, as was necessary using the previous looping statements in Listings 8.1 and 8.2).

> In this simple application of the looping statements that you've seen here, Do...Loop While required less code than the Do While and Do Until loops. By changing the Do...Loop While's *comparison test*, a Do Until would also work. These last two loops will not, in every case, produce less code as they do here. The logic of the application determines which loop works best.

The For Loop

The For loop (sometimes referred to as the For...Next loop) also creates a loop. Unlike the Do loops, however, the For loop repeats for a specified number of times. The format of the For loop looks a little more daunting than that of the Do loops, but after you master the format, you'll have little trouble implementing For loops when your code needs to repeat a section of code for a specified number of times.

There isn't one correct loop to use in all situations. The For statement provides the mechanism for the fifth Visual Basic loop block that you'll learn. A For loop always begins with the For statement and ends with the Next statement. Here is the format of the For loop:

```
For CounterVar = StartVal To EndVal [Step IncrementVal]
    Block of one or more Visual Basic statements
Next CounterVar
```

A simple example will help demonstrate how the For loop works. The loop in Listing 8.4 computes the total of the numbers from 1 to 10.

LISTING 8.4. ADD THE NUMBERS FROM 1 TO 10.

```
1: intSum = 0
2: For intNumber = 1 To 10
3: intSum = intSum + intNumber
4: Next intNumber
```

intNumber is the CounterVar in the format of the For loop. The CounterVar must be a variable and not a control or a literal. 1 is the For loop's StartVal. The StartVal can be either a number, an expression, or a variable. 10 is the EndVal. EndVal can be either a number, an expression, or a variable. There is no Step specified here. In the For statement's format, the Step IncrementVal is optional (as you can tell from the format's square brackets). If you don't specify a Step value, Visual Basic assumes a Step value of 1. Therefore, both of the following For statements do the same thing:

```
For intNumber = 1 To 10
```

```
For intNumber = 1 To 10 Step 1
```

Listing 8.4's summing For loop initially assigns the StartVal to the CounterVar in the second line. Therefore, intNumber is assigned 1 at the top of the loop. Visual Basic then executes the body of the loop using the value 1 for intNumber. With intNumber being equal to 1, the third line works as follows, the first time through the loop:

```
intSum = intSum + 1
```

When Visual Basic executes the Next intNumber statement, Visual Basic returns to the top of the loop (the For statement), adds the Step value 1 to intNumber, and continues the loop again using 2 as intNumber in the loop's body. Therefore, the second time through the loop, the third line becomes this:

```
intSum = intSum + 2
```

The loop continues, adding the default Step value 1 to intNumber each time the loop executes. When intNumber becomes 10 (the format's EndVal), the loop finishes and the statement following the Next statement continues.

> Remember, the For loop terminates when the CounterVar becomes larger than the EndVal. There's an exception to this: If you code a negative Step value, the loop terminates when the CounterVar becomes smaller than the EndVal, as you'll see a little later in this section.

You don't need a For statement to sum the values 1 through 10. You could code one long assignment statement like this:

```
intSum = 1 + 2 + 3 + 4 + 5 + 6 + 7 + 8 + 9 + 10
```

You could also code back-to-back assignment statements like this:

```
IntSum = IntSum + 1
IntSum = IntSum + 2
IntSum = IntSum + 3
IntSum = IntSum + 4
IntSum = IntSum + 5
IntSum = IntSum + 6
IntSum = IntSum + 7
```

```
IntSum = IntSum + 8
IntSum = IntSum + 9
IntSum = IntSum + 10
```

Neither of these approaches is extremely difficult, but what if you needed to add the first 100 integer numbers? The previous assignments could become tedious indeed, but with the For loop it's as easy to add the first 100 integers as it is to add the first 10 integers, as Listing 8.5 demonstrates.

LISTING 8.5. ADD THE NUMBERS FROM 1 TO 100.

```
1: IntSum = 0
2: For intNumber = 1 To 100    ' Only this line changes
3: IntSum = IntSum + IntNumber
4: Next intNumber
```

The following loop displays five message boxes:

```
For intCtr = 1 To 20 Step 4
   intPress = MsgBox("This is a message box")
Next intCtr
```

The loop counts up from 1 to 20 by fours, putting each count into the counter variable named intCtr and printing a message box each time. The Step value changes how Visual Basic updates the CounterVar each time the loop iterates.

NEW TERM   An *iteration* is one complete cycle through a loop.

If you specify a negative Step value, Visual Basic counts down. The following loop rings the PC's speaker five times:

```
For intCtr = 5 To 1 Step -1
   Beep
Next intCtr
```

The Beep statement simply buzzes the speaker on your computer.

If you specify a negative Step value, EndVal must be less than StartVal or Visual Basic will execute the loop only once.

Listing 8.6 contains a fairly comprehensive `For` loop that computes compound interest for an initial investment of $1,000.00. The code appears inside the `Click` event procedure for a command button named `cmdIntr`. With compound interest, each year the amount of money invested, including interest earned so far, compounds to build more money. Each time period, normally a year, means that another year's interest must be added to the value of the investment. A `For` loop is perfect for calculating interest. Listing 8.6 uses five compound cycles.

LISTING 8.6. USING A `For` LOOP TO CALCULATE COMPOUND INTEREST.

```
 1: Sub cmdIntr_Click ()
 2:  ' Use a For loop to calculate a final total
 3:  ' investment using compound interest.
 4:  '
 5:  ' intNum is a loop control variable
 6:  ' sngIRate is the annual interest rate
 7:  ' intTerm is the number of years in the investment
 8:  ' curInitInv is the investor's initial investment
 9:  ' sngInterest is the total interest paid
10: Dim sngIRate As Single, sngInterest As Single
11: Dim intTerm As Integer, intNum As Integer
12: Dim curInitInv As Currency
13:
14: sngIRate = .08
15: intTerm = 5
16: ' Watch out... The Code window might convert the
17: ' following literals, 1000.00 and 1.0, to double-
18: ' precision literals with the suffix # to ensure
19: ' accuracy.
20: curInitInv = 1000.00
21: sngInterest = 1.0   ' Begin at one for first compound
22:
23: ' Use loop to calculate total compound amount
24: For intNum = 1 To intTerm
25: sngInterest = sngInterest * (1 + sngIRate)
26: Next intNum
27:
28: ' Now we have total interest,
29: ' calculate the total investment
30: ' at the end of[]years
31: lblFinalInv.Caption = curInitInv * sngInterest
32: End Sub
```

This analysis focuses on the loop and not on the interest calculation. The most important thing that you can do at this point is to master the `For` looping statement. The code's remarks contain variable descriptions so that anyone looking at the code or changing the code later will know what the variables are for.

After the program defines all the variables, the variables are initialized with startup values. If you use this event procedure, be sure to add a label named `lblFinalInv` to a form and add a command button named `cmdInt` to the form. The middle lines will seem to give you trouble as you type them unless you remember the description of data suffix characters you learned in Hour 5, "Putting Code into Visual Basic." Visual Basic uses the pound sign (#) to indicate double-precision values, and Visual Basic will assume that `1000.00` is a double-precision value (I don't know why) and will convert the `1000.00` to `1000#` as soon as you press Enter at the end of the line. In addition, Visual Basic converts the `1.0` to `1#` on the next line. Don't worry about Visual Basic's pickiness here.

The most important part of this program is the `For` loop that iterates through each interest rate period (five of them) and compounds the interest on top of the investment to date. Again, don't let the financial part worry you. The calculation is less important than understanding the looping process. After the loop finishes, the event procedure places the compounded investment in the label's `Caption` property.

YOU CAN TERMINATE LOOPS EARLY

Sometimes, you'll be processing user input or several data values using looping statements, and an exception occurs in the data that requires an immediate termination of the loop. For example, you might be collecting sales values for a company's 10 divisions inside a `For` loop that iterates 10 times. However, the user can enter `0` for a division's sales value, indicating that there is no sales data for that division. Rather than completing the loop, your program might need to quit the loop at that point because the full divisional report information can't be gathered at the time.

The `Exit Do` and the `Exit For` statements automatically terminate loops. No matter what the `Do` loop's comparison test results in, or how many more iterations are left in a `For` loop, when Visual Basic encounters an `Exit Do` or `Exit For` statement, it immediately quits the loop and sends execution down to the statement following the loop.

Typically, an `If` statement triggers one of the `Exit` statements like this:

```
For intDivisions = 1 To 10
   ' Code to get a sales value
   If (cngSales <= 0.0) Then
      Exit For        ' Quit the loop early
   End If
   ' Process the rest of the code
Next intDivisions
```

The `If` ensures that the `Exit For` executes only under one specific condition (a missing sales value). Without that specific condition triggering the `Exit For`, the loop cycles normally. Visual Basic also supports the `Exit Sub` statement that terminates a procedure early.

I don't recommend that you rely on the Exit statement to bail out of control blocks and procedures. Most experienced programmers will not use the exit function. The Exit statement has a nasty habit of creating multiple exit points for a block of code, which normally makes the code harder to understand and maintain.

8

Summary

In this hour you learned how you can add loops to your programs. Computers do not get bored. Your program will execute the same series of instructions over and over until you terminate the loop. Visual Basic supports several forms of looping statements. The Do and For loops provide you with the power to write any kind of looping section your program needs. Which loop you choose to use is up to your style and coding preference more than anything else.

The next hour moves away from the theory you've been learning in the last few lessons to take you back to the keyboard and freshen up your application design and construction skills.

Q&A

Q How can I guard against infinite loops?

A All loops continue as long as a condition is true or as long as a condition is false. Therefore, somewhere inside the loop's body your code must modify the condition used for the loop. The For loop's control variable must reach its ending value or something inside the Do loop's condition must change inside the loop's body. If the body of a loop doesn't change the controlling condition, the loop will execute forever.

Q How do I terminate an infinite loop?

A As the lesson states, you must press Ctrl+Break to terminate an infinite loop. Until this lesson, you had not heard of Ctrl+Break, but the keystroke has been the program-stopping keystroke for many versions of the BASIC language through the years. In addition, you can click on VB's End toolbar button or select Run | End from the menu.

Workshop

The quiz questions and exercises are provided for your further understanding. See Appendix B for the answers.

Quiz

1. Why might your program need a loop?

2. How many forms of `Do` are there?

3. True or false: The `Do...Loop While` and the `Do While` are identical in every respect.

4. What is the difference between `Do...Loop While` and `Do...Loop Until`?

5. Which loop checks its condition at the top of the loop: `Do Until` or `Do...Loop Until`?

6. Why do programmers often use the `Val()` function on control values and `InputBox()` returns?

7. True or false: A `For` loop can count down.

8. How many times does the following loop iterate?
   ```
   intI = 10
   do While intI >= 1
   intI = intI - 1
   Loop
   ```

9. What default `Step` value does Visual Basic use if you don't supply a `Step` value?

10. True or false: The `Exit` statement exits the current application.

Exercises

1. Write a program that contains a text box and a command button. Put a label above the text box that tells the user to type a number from 1 to 10 inside the text box. When the user clicks the command button, check the text box for a valid number and issue an error message box if the number isn't inside the expected range. If the user entered a valid number, use a `For` loop to issue a beeping sound equal to the number entered in the text box.

2. Rewrite Listing 8.3 so that the error message box that you display tells the user that the age entered is too low if the age is less than 10 or that the age entered is too high if the age is more than 99.

PART III
Putting Code to Work

Hour

HOUR 9

Combining Code and Controls

This hour's lesson takes a short break from the theory you've seen in the past few lessons. In this lesson you'll put some of the code you've seen into a fairly large application and run the application to work with the results. You've already learned a lot about Visual Basic. Nevertheless, as this lesson illustrates, you have many exciting things yet to learn over the next few lessons.

This lesson's primary goal is to refresh your Visual Basic knowledge once again by putting together the big picture. You'll build a simple but complete application just to practice working with both code and the controls you've learned so far. After you refresh your application-building skills, the next lesson teaches more controls from the toolbox. The more controls you learn to use, the more powerful your applications become.

The highlights of this hour include

- Where to place the initial form
- What a control array is

- How default properties speed development
- Where and how to add external code modules
- How to write your own functions

The Interest Calculation Application

The previous lesson describes how to compute compound interest using a For loop. You studied the code in the previous lesson, and this lesson will build a simple application around that interest calculation.

 In creating an application from scratch, this hour lets you review the application, controls, form, and standard modules. Therefore, when the next lesson begins to teach some more advanced controls, you'll be better prepared for them.

Figure 9.1 shows the application that you'll create today.

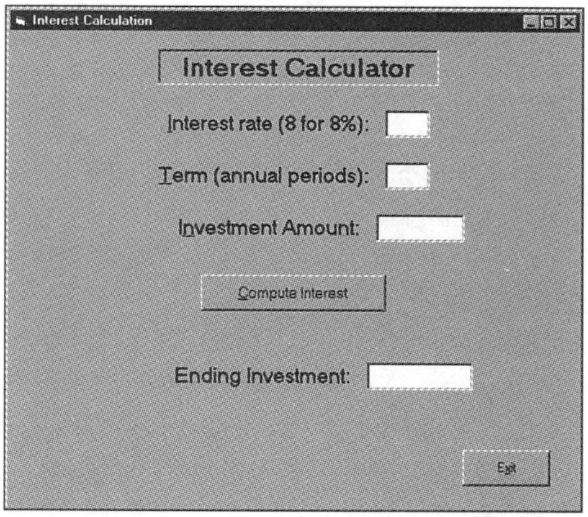

FIGURE 9.1.

The interest calculating application's window.

Interest Calculation
Interest Calculator
Interest rate (8 for 8%):
Term (annual periods):
Investment Amount:
Compute Interest
Ending Investment:
Exit

Perform these steps to create the interest calculating application:

1. Start a new Standard EXE project by selecting File | New Project or double-clicking the Standard EXE icon (the icon you'll most often choose for regular applications).

2. Change the form's Name property to frmInterest. Change the Caption property to Interest Calculation.

3. Change the form's `StartUpPosition` property to `2-CenterScreen`. You haven't seen the `StartUpPosition` property yet; it determines the location of the Form window when the user runs the program. Let Visual Basic center the form on your user's screen because you don't know the exact measurements of the screen that your users will use. If you set `StartUpPosition` to `2-CenterScreen`, Visual Basic always places the form in the middle of the screen no matter what the user's screen size and resolution are. (Use the `WindowState` property to open the Form window in its maximized state if you want a full-screen Form window when the application starts.)

9

 The `StartUpPosition` property makes the Form Layout window unnecessary in most cases. `StartUpPosition` gives you much more accurate placement of the form than the Form Layout window.

4. Now you need to add the labels and text boxes. The form's title label is easy to generate. Place a label on the form and set the following properties:

```
Name:              lblTitle

Alignment:         2-Center

BorderStyle:       1-Fixed Single

Caption:           Interest Calculator

Font:              Bold 18

Height:            495

Left:              2090

Top:               240

Width:             3855
```

You now must set up a series of three label/text box pairs. Notice that the labels in Figure 9.1 all have hotkeys. Although a label cannot accept the focus, pressing Alt+hotkey sends the focus to the next control in line, which will be the text box next to the label (assuming that you place the text box right after you place the corresponding label).

5. Set the interest rate label as follows:

Name:	lblRate
Alignment:	1-RightJustify
Caption:	&Interest rate (8 for 8%):
Font:	Regular 14
Height:	375
Left:	2040
Top:	1080
Width:	2895

6. Set the interest rate text box as follows:

Name:	txtRate
Alignment:	0-LeftJustify
Font:	10
Height:	375
Left:	5160
ToolTipText:	Annual rate investment grows
Top:	1080
Width:	615

7. Blank out the Text property so nothing appears in the text box at startup (this can be done by deleting the default value of the Text property). Notice that you're adding ToolTipText at the same time you add the control that the user interacts with.

Design time is the best time to add ToolTipText because the control's meaning is clearest in your mind then.

Using Control Arrays

This is a great time to introduce a new concept called control arrays. A *control array* is a group of more than one control of the same control type. You will better understand control arrays after you learn about data arrays in Hour 10, "List Boxes and Data Lists," but the interest rate application makes this a great project to introduce them.

Notice that the interest calculator's Term and Investment Amount labels and text boxes look similar to the Interest rate label and text box you just placed on the form; the font information and Height properties are all the same. Therefore, although you could enter the remaining labels and text boxes, you can utilize the Windows Clipboard to make the job go faster.

Highlight both the existing Interest rate label and text box. You can select multiple controls by pressing the Ctrl key while you click each control, or you can lasso the controls by dragging a rectangle around the two controls. When you select both controls, sizing handles appear around them (see Figure 9.2).

FIGURE 9.2.

The sizing handles show that two controls are selected.

The selected controls —

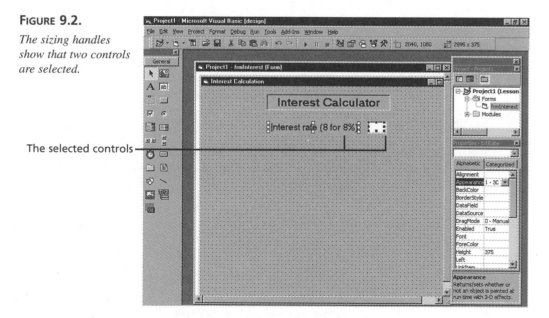

Select Edit | Copy to copy the selected controls to the Windows Clipboard. Now select Edit | Paste, and Visual Basic pops up a warning dialog box that says You already have a control named 'lblRate'. Do you want to create a control array?

A control array is a set of multiple controls that have the same name. You distinguish between the controls inside the array with an index value. For this particular example, you should not create a control array (you will learn how to create one in the next lesson). Answer No to the dialog box and answer No again when Visual Basic asks you about creating a control array for the text box.

Visual Basic saw that you wanted to paste two controls on the form that already had controls with those same names. Visual Basic cannot replace existing controls when you paste new ones with the same name, so Visual Basic guessed (in this case incorrectly) that you wanted to add a control array named txtRate. When you refused the control array, Visual Basic made up its own name for the new label (Label1) and the new text box (Text1).

Move the pasted label and text box to their correct positions under the first pair and set these properties for the label:

```
Name:                     lblTerm

Caption:                  &Term (annual periods):

Left:                     2040

Top:                      1800

Width:                    2895
```

The Height and Font properties are already correct because you borrowed these properties from the control you originally copied from. Set these properties for the text box:

```
Name:                     txtTerm

Left:                     5160

ToolTipText:              Number of periods

Top:                      1800

Width:                    615
```

As you can see, you don't have to set as many properties when you paste from an existing similar control.

NEW TERM *Default properties* are the properties Visual Basic assumes if you don't set the properties at design time or within the application's code at runtime.

Click the form and select Edit | Paste once more (the Clipboard still holds those first two controls you sent there). Refuse the control array and set the following properties for the new label:

Name:	lblInvest
Caption:	I&nvestment Amount:
Left:	1920
Top:	2520
Width:	2895

Set the text box's properties to the following:

Name:	txtInvest
Left:	5160
ToolTipText:	Money you invested
Top:	2520
Width:	1215

Your screen should look similar to Figure 9.3.

FIGURE 9.3.

Proper form design takes awhile.

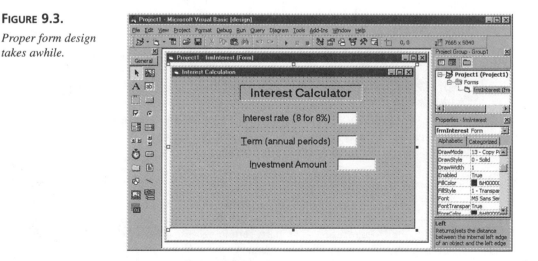

Finishing the Form

You can quickly finish the form now. While the label and text box still reside on the Windows Clipboard, this would be a good time to add the Ending Investment label and text box. Select Edit | Paste once again and set the pasted label's properties as follows:

Name:	lblEnding
Caption:	Ending Investment:
Left:	1800
Top:	4560
Width:	2895

Set the text box's properties as follows:

Name:	txtEnding
Left:	4920
Locked:	True
TabStop:	False (so the user cannot send the focus to this text box)
Top:	4560
ToolTipText:	Compounded Investment
Width:	1455

The new property you set just now is the Locked property. When you lock a control, Visual Basic allows no user editing of the control. Therefore, the code beneath the form can modify the text box's Text property but the user cannot. The final text box will be a holding place for the calculated compound investment amount, so the user should not be allowed to edit the control even though it's a Text Box control.

You might wonder why the application uses a text box and not a read-only control such as a label. The Label control would work just as well and would not require a Locked property setting because labels can never be changed by the user. Nevertheless, the text box keeps a uniform appearance throughout the form, so we're using a text box here.

Add a command button named `cmdCompute`, add the caption `&Compute Interest`, and add a `ToolTipText` value of `Click to compute final investment`. Place and size the command button as follows: `Height: 495`, `Left: 2640`, `Top: 3360`, and `Width: 2535`. Add a final command button named `cmdExit` to the lower-right corner with the `E&xit Caption` property.

 Building an application can be tedious, but your productivity is greater with Visual Basic than with virtually every other application-development system available. Although you've seen most of this lesson's concepts before, this is the first lesson that truly ties things together by walking you through the entire application-creation process.

9

Adding Code

Often, programmers run their applications as they build them despite the fact that no code exists yet to make the application do real work. You should be able to run your application now to make sure that the labels and text boxes all look correct. Check out the ToolTip text to ensure you've entered the text properly. Click the toolbar's End button to stop the program so that you can add the final code.

The code is going to borrow a bit from the interest calculation routine you learned about in Hour 8, "Visual Basic Looping." You'll have to modify the routine somewhat so the data comes from the Text Box controls you've set up. You want the calculation to take place when the user clicks the center command button, so add the following code to the command button's `Click()` event procedure. Double-click the Form window's Compute Interest command button to open the `cmdCompute_Click ()` event procedure to complete the code that follows:

```
Private Sub cmdCompute_Click()
  ' Use a For loop to calculate a final total
  ' investment using compound interest.
  '
  ' intNum is a loop control variable
  ' sngIRate is the annual interest rate
  ' intTerm is the number of years in the investment
  ' curInitInv is the investor's initial investment
  ' sngInterest is the total interest paid
    Dim sngIRate As Single, sngInterest As Single
    Dim intTerm As Integer, intNum As Integer
    Dim curInitInv As Currency
```

```
sngIRate = txtRate.Text / 100#
intTerm = txtTerm.Text

curInitInv = txtInvest.Text
sngInterest = 1#    ' Begin at one for first compound

' Use loop to calculate total compound amount
For intNum = 1 To intTerm
sngInterest = sngInterest * (1 + sngIRate)
Next intNum

' Now we have total interest,
' calculate the total investment
' at the end of [] years
txtEnding.Text = curInitInv * sngInterest

End Sub
```

This is basically the same code that you saw in the previous lesson when studying For loops. This code does include a few minor differences so that the application's control names properly initialize and receive values.

Visual Basic supports default properties for most controls. The default property is the property Visual Basic uses if you don't explicitly specify a property. For example, if you use a Text Box control in code and don't type the Text property, Visual Basic assumes you mean Text (as long as you don't specify a different property). Therefore, the first assignment in the application is now sngIRate = txtRate.Text / 100#, but the following statement is identical in every respect because Visual Basic assumes that you are using the text box's Text property: sngIRate = txtRate / 100#.

You must also add the terminating code for the Exit command button. Here's a simple way the Code window lets you add new procedures:

1. Click the drop-down object list box (the left list box, directly beneath the toolbar) and select cmdExit.

2. Select the event for which you want to add code in the right drop-down list box whose ToolTip reads Object. (The default procedure listed for command buttons is Click, so in this case you don't need to select a different procedure.)

Add the following code for the command button's event procedure:

```
Private Sub cmdExit_Click()
' Unload the form and terminate application
Unload frmInterest
End
End Sub
```

The Unload Statement

The Exit command button's Click event procedure contains a statement you haven't seen until now. The Unload statement unloads a form from memory. If the form to unload is currently displayed, Visual Basic removes the form and returns all the form's control values back to their design-time state.

In most cases the Unload statement is unnecessary, especially when your application contains only a single form. If you add multiple forms to the application, however, the user could have closed one of the Form windows (by clicking the form's window close buttons), and the End statement could fail to release that form's resources properly.

The Unload statement lets you use a shortcut that looks like this:

```
Unload Me
```

Me is a special object that refers to the currently active form. Use Unload Me when the application contains only a single form if you don't want to type the full form name. For a multiple-form application, however, be sure to unload all the forms before terminating the program.

Finishing Touches

Run your application and enter some sample values. Figure 9.4 shows the application with some sample data entered for a five-year investment. As shown in Figure 9.4, if you invested $1,000 today at 11% interest, in five years you will have approximately $1,685.

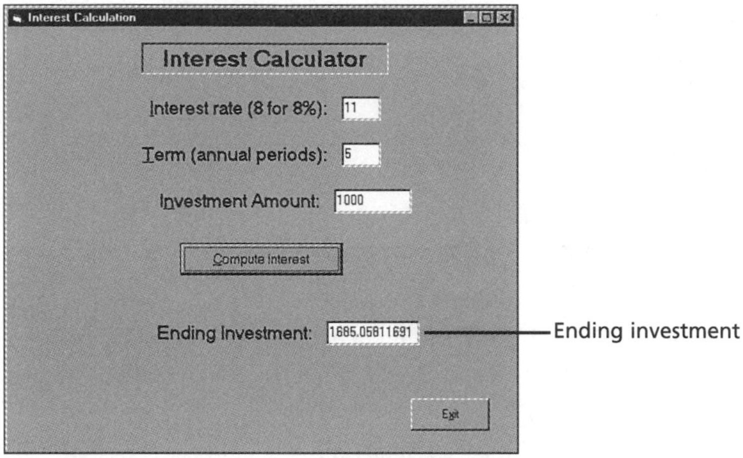

FIGURE 9.4.

The running application computes the final investment amount.

Interest Calculation

Interest Calculator

Interest rate (8 for 8%): `11`

Term (annual periods): `5`

Investment Amount: `1000`

Compute Interest

Ending Investment: `1685.05811691` ─────── Ending investment

Exit

The application is not really complete and ready for distribution. Although you've mastered the mechanics of this simple application, more is needed to make the application professional. Obviously, the ending investment's decimal place precision is far too high.

You need to format the value shown in the Ending Investment text box. When you format a value, you don't change the value, but you change the value's look. Visual Basic includes a built-in function called Format() that formats numeric and string values so you can display such values as dollars and cents, area code formats, or whatever formats you want to use. Although Hour 14, "Built-In Functions Save Time," explains Format() in detail, you can use the Format() function now to spruce up your application.

NEW TERM   To *format* is to change the way a value appears to the user.

At the end of the cmdCompute_Click() event procedure, change the ending investment's assignment to this:

```
txtEnding.Text = Format(curInitInv * sngInterest, "$###,##0.00")
```

Some formats get lengthy, so programmers often declare a string variable and assign the format to the variable. They then use the variable inside the Format() function instead of using the string literal for the format. If you use the same format in several locations within the code, the variable means less typing on your part, and if you ever change the format, you only have to change the format in one place.

The `Format()` function's basic format is this:

```
Format(expression, strFormat)
```

Visual Basic changes the look of `expression` to match that of the format string you supply. Therefore, the format string "`$###,##0.00`" instructs Visual Basic to display the value with a dollar sign, floating numbers with the # (if the number is less than $100,000.00 the numbers will move left to touch the dollar sign instead of leaving a gap for the missing digits), commas in the amount if the amount is over $1,000, and a decimal point with two decimal places showing. If the value happens to be `$0.00`, the zeros ensure that the value prints, whereas if you used a # in place of each `0`, the # would show nothing if the result were zero.

After you format the value and rerun the application with the numbers used earlier, you'll see a result that looks better, as Figure 9.5 shows.

FIGURE 9.5.

The `Format()` *function improved the output.*

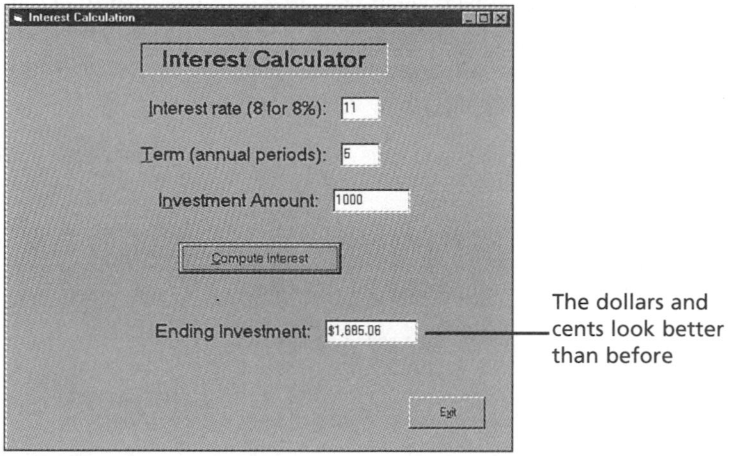

The dollars and cents look better than before

Error Checking

A big problem still exists with the application if you plan to distribute it to others. The problem is not in the logic, calculation, or form. The problem is the application's lack of error checking. If the user doesn't enter a value in one or more of the text boxes, the calculation will not work properly. Even worse, an error such as a divide-by-zero error could occur and stop the running program. Mathematically, one cannot divide by zero, and Visual Basic stops the program and issues a runtime error message if a divide-by-zero occurs. Any time you write an application that performs division, you should check to make sure that you never divide by zero.

You'll need to add error checking to the application to ensure that the user enters positive values greater than 0 in each of the text boxes before clicking the computational command button.

The error checking can be fairly simple. Convert the text box values to numbers, and if any text box contains zero or less, perform the following:

1. Tell the user about the problem with a message box.
2. When the user closes the message box, set the focus on the control with the bad value so the user can more easily enter a corrected value.
3. Test the controls again before any calculation is performed to ensure that the problem is fixed.

Several approaches exist for handling this error. The approach this lesson uses is slightly advanced, but it gives you a chance to see an external standard module added to an application (an external code module that is different from the form module), and you'll get a glimpse of the function-writing code you'll learn in Hour 13, "Modular Programming." You will actually create your own function instead of using one of the built-in functions supplied with Visual Basic.

First, assign the hook to the other function in your `cmdCompute_Click()` event procedure like this:

```
Private Sub cmdCompute_Click()
  ' Use a For loop to calculate a final total
  ' investment using compound interest.
  '
  ' intNum is a loop control variable
  ' sngIRate is the annual interest rate
  ' intTerm is the number of years in the investment
  ' curInitInv is the investor's initial investment
  ' sngInterest is the total interest paid
    Dim sngIRate As Single, sngInterest As Single
    Dim intTerm As Integer, intNum As Integer
    Dim curInitInv As Currency

    ' Error-checking
    If ErrorCheck() = 1 Then
    Exit Sub
    End If

    sngIRate = txtRate.Text / 100#
    intTerm = txtTerm.Text
```

The rest of the procedure is identical to the earlier listing. You only need to add the four lines that follow the variable declarations.

ErrorCheck() is a procedure you'll add that checks the form for bad values. You'll add this procedure in a separate module, not at the bottom of the form module. Notice that you use the ErrorCheck() procedure just as you use built-in functions: You call the function with an empty argument list (no arguments are necessary), and the function returns a value. If that value is 1, the form contains an error, so you use the Exit Sub statement to terminate the event procedure and return the user to the form. (The previous lesson described other forms of the Exit statement such as Exit For.) If no error exists, the ErrorCheck() procedure will not return a 1, and the processing continues as normal.

New Term A *function procedure* is a procedure that you write that accepts zero or more arguments and returns a single value. A *subroutine procedure* is a procedure that you write that accepts zero or more arguments but does not return a value.

You must now add the ErrorCheck() procedure. Unlike the event procedures you've been writing until now, the ErrorCheck() procedure is a function procedure and not a subroutine procedure. A function procedure always returns a value, whereas a subroutine procedure never returns a value. (Again, you'll learn more about function and subroutine procedures in Hour 13.)

To add an extra module to your project, perform these steps:

1. Select Project | Add Module to add a new module (that you can view in a Code window) to the project. You could also right-click over your Project window and add the module from the pop-up menu.

2. Click the Module icon that appears in the Add Module dialog box. Visual Basic adds a new module with the default name Module1 (and the filename Module1.bas). Figure 9.6's Project window shows the new module in your project. Your Code window will now display a blank module where you can type the module's code.

FIGURE 9.6.

You've now added another code module to the project.

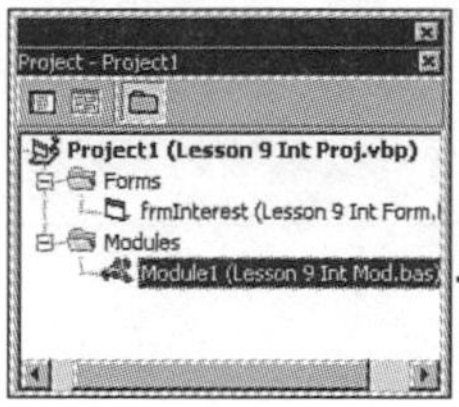

The new module

3. Maneuver between modules and the form by double-clicking the Project window object you want to work with. For now, however, stay inside the new module.

Type the following function procedure inside the new module's Code window:

```
Public Function ErrorCheck() As Integer

IntPress As Single

    ' Error-checking for the form
    If Val(frmInterest.txtRate.Text) <= 0 Then
        intPress = MsgBox("Enter a value for the rate", vbCritical)
        frmInterest.txtRate.SetFocus
        ErrorCheck = 1
        Exit Function
    End If
    If Val(frmInterest.txtTerm.Text) <= 0 Then
        intPress = MsgBox("Enter a value for the term", vbCritical)
        frmInterest.txtTerm.SetFocus
        ErrorCheck = 1
        Exit Function
    End If
    If Val(frmInterest.txtInvest.Text) <= 0 Then
        intPress = MsgBox("Enter a value for the investment", vbCritical)
        frmInterest.txtInvest.SetFocus
        ErrorCheck = 1
        Exit Function
    End If
    ' No error occurred if execution gets here
    ErrorCheck = 0
End Function
```

The first difference you'll notice between the function procedure and the event subroutine procedures you've seen so far is the difference between the opening and closing statements. The keyword Function distinguishes the function procedure from a subroutine procedure. The procedures you've seen until now were subroutine procedures that used the Sub keyword to define them. In addition, the function procedure's opening line ends with As Integer. This qualifier tells Visual Basic that the function procedure will return an integer value. Functions can return any datatype as long as you define the function to return the proper datatype with the As keyword.

The function then checks each text box on the form. All form references include the form name. Therefore, instead of referring to the interest rate text box as txtRate, the code qualifies the text box with a form name as follows: frmInterest.txtRate. Remember that an external standard module, such as this one, is not part of a form's code found in the form module. A standard module might need access to several forms in the same project, so the standard module needs the qualifying form name before each control name.

After a text box is found to hold a bad value, a message box describes the problem. The module then sets the focus to that control. Therefore, the focus goes straight to the problem so the user can edit the control without having to find it first when the error message box goes away.

> SetFocus is not a property or an event. SetFocus is known as a method. Controls usually support all three: properties, events, and methods. A *method* is a built-in routine attached directly to a control. In a way, the control executes its own method. You'll append method names to the end of a control as done here. Read the methods from right to left to understand them fully. For example, frmInterest.txtTerm.SetFocus tells Visual Basic to set the focus on the control named txtTerm located on the frmInterest form.

Finally, the code sets the function's return value to 1 if an error occurs and exits the function (and therefore the module) and returns the return value to the calling code, which is the form module. To return a value from a function procedure, simply assign the value that you want to return to the function name.

Figure 9.7 shows the message box that appears if the user enters a term value that's zero or less.

FIGURE 9.7.

The user must enter valid data.

Save your project (Lesson 9 Int Proj would be a good name). When you save the project, Visual Basic asks for a form name and a module name as well (use Lesson 9 Int Form and Lesson 9 Int Mod to follow the naming convention that this 24-hour tutorial uses).

Summary

This hour develops a complete application. Through the development process, you saw how even a simple project can require detailed components such as error checking and proper form management. Too many books rush to the theory without hands-on work or rush to the hands-on without explaining the process. This lesson gives your 24-hour tutorial a needed boost with both hands-on development that strengthens what you already know, and some new topics to consider such as function procedures and form placement.

The next hour describes important list-based controls. You'll learn how to produce drop-down list boxes and how to initialize and work with such lists.

Q&A

Q **Why doesn't `End` terminate an application properly? `End` seems to work fine without the extra `Unload` statement.**

A `End` does work fine for single-form applications. Problems can arise, however, if you create applications with multiple forms. In certain cases, the `End` statement might fail to release every form's resources. In today's multitasking, multiuser networked world, you need to release resources as soon as you can so that other processes have access to those resources (such as memory and CPU time). The `Unload` statement takes care of closing forms properly.

Q **How can I find the default properties for all controls?**

A Surprisingly, Visual Basic's online help doesn't list the default properties. The default properties are the most common properties referenced for a control. Therefore, the default property for a text box is the `Text` property, and the default property for a label is the `Caption` property. Generally, using a control's default property makes for less typing, but default properties can add confusion later when you try to figure out the code and change it. If you use default properties, use them only for the Label and Text Box, but specify all other controls' default properties explicitly so that your code is as clear as possible.

Workshop

The quiz questions and exercises are provided for your further understanding. See Appendix B for the answers.

Quiz

1. What does the form's `StartUpPosition` value do?

2. Why do label captions often show hotkey letter combinations?

3. When is the best time to enter `ToolTipText` properties and why?

4. What is a control array?

5. Why does Visual Basic like to offer a control array when you paste a control on a form that has the source of the paste already on the form?

6. Why might you want to lock a Text Box control?

7. What is the proper way to terminate an application?

8. What happens when you attempt to divide by zero?

9. True or false: The following two statements are identical:
   ```
   lblTitle = "The Sound of Multimedia"

   lblTitle.Caption = "The Sound of Multimedia"
   ```

10. What is the difference between a function procedure and a subroutine procedure?

Exercises

1. Change this lesson's application's form properties so the user cannot resize the form. Search through the form properties until you find the property that will do this.

2. Add input box routines to the application so that the user sees the error message in the input box and can enter the replacement values in the input box. The code then places the input box's value into the form. Once the form gets a replacement value, check the controls again to make sure that the replacement value is correct. You might want to add a `Do...While` loop around the input box routines so that the user keeps seeing the input box warnings until the user enters a value greater than zero.

HOUR **10**

List Boxes and Data Lists

Often the user will need to select from or add to a list of items such as pay code abbreviations or division names. Visual Basic supports two controls, List Box and Combo Box, that you use to display lists from which the user can select items.

After you master the List controls, two additional VB programming topics are simple: data arrays and control arrays. You can combine the List controls and the arrays to work in harmony when processing lists of information, as you'll see in this lesson.

The highlights of this hour include

- How to add list boxes
- What differences exist between list boxes and combo boxes
- How to initialize lists
- When to use drop-down list boxes
- How to declare and use arrays
- Why control arrays streamline coding

The List Box Control

Figure 10.1 shows the Editor Format tab of the Options dialog box, which appears when you select Tools | Options and click the Editor Format tab. The dialog box illustrates a List Box control. You've seen list boxes throughout your work with Windows; list boxes appear on many forms and dialog boxes. The List Box control gives the user a choice of several values. The user selects an option instead of typing a value into a text box. The list box ensures that the user always chooses one of the available options.

FIGURE 10.1.

The List Box control gives the user a choice of options.

The selected list box item

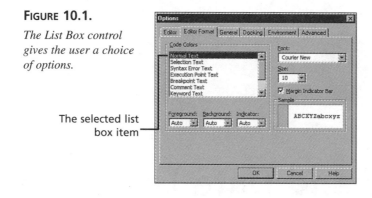

The list box displays scrollbars if the list box isn't tall enough or wide enough to display all its data.

As you place the list box on the form, think about the data the list box will hold and try to size the list box so that it's large enough to hold the data. Of course, you don't always know a list box's data in advance because the data might come from a disk file or from the user at the keyboard. Your form's size and surrounding controls might limit the size of your list box, so the scrollbars often appear.

Any list box can have a single or multiple columns. In many situations the single column makes data selection easier for your users, but they will have to scroll through more values to locate the item they want to find. Figure 10.2 shows a form with two list boxes; the first list box is a single-column list box, and the second displays three columns. (The Columns property determines the list box's number of columns.)

FIGURE 10.2.

A list box with one column and one with three columns.

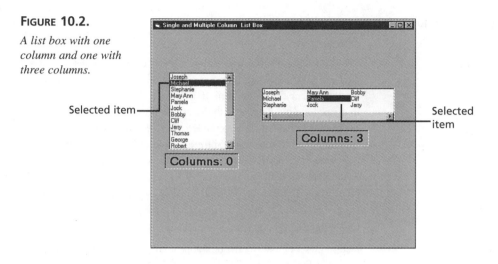

To familiarize yourself with list boxes as quickly as possible, look over the property values in Table 10.1. You'll work with other properties at runtime because you often initialize the list box at runtime and not at design time.

TABLE 10.1. THE BASIC LIST BOX PROPERTIES.

Property	Description
BackColor	Specifies the list box's background color.
Columns	Determines the number of columns. If 0, the list box scrolls vertically in a single column. If 1 or more, the list box items appear in the number of columns specified (one or more columns), and a horizontal scrollbar appears so that you can see all the items in the list.
ForeColor	Specifies the list box's text color.
Height	Indicates the height of the list box in twips.
IntegralHeight	Determines whether the list box can display partial items, such as the upper half of an item that falls toward the bottom of the list box.
List	Holds, in a drop-down property list box, values that you can enter into the list box at design time. You can enter only one at a time, and most programmers usually prefer to initialize the list box at runtime.

continues

10

TABLE **10.1.** CONTINUED

Property	Description
MultiSelect	The state of the list box's selection rules. If 0-None (the default), the user can select only one item by clicking with the mouse or by pressing the Spacebar over an item. If 1-Simple, the user can select more than one item by clicking with the mouse or by pressing the Spacebar over items in the list. If 2-Extended, the user can select multiple items using Shift+click and Shift+arrow to extend the selection from a previously selected item to the current one. Ctrl+click either selects or deselects an item from the list.
Sorted	Determines whether the list box values are automatically sorted. If False (the default value), the values appear in the same order in which the program added the items to the list.
Style	Determines whether the list box appears in its usual list format or, as shown in Figure 10.3, with check boxes next to the selected items.

FIGURE 10.3.

You can add check boxes to list box items.

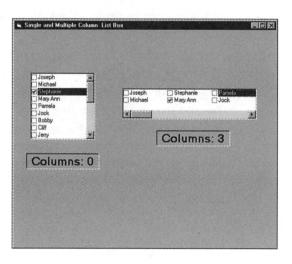

You can add a command button that operates in conjunction with the list box in many situations. The user can, therefore, select a value from the list box and then click the command button to inform your application of the selected value. You can also add a double-click event procedure to the list box so that when the user double-clicks a list box item, that item is selected. If you set up the command button first, the double-click event procedure is simple because you can trigger the command button's Click() event procedure from within the double-click procedure with this one line:

```
CmdAccept_Click     ' Triggers the button's click event
```

Table 10.2 describes the methods available to the list box. Remember that methods are routines a control knows how to execute. List boxes use methods more than any other control you've learned about so far. The methods help the user initialize, add items to, and remove items from list boxes.

TABLE 10.2. COMMON LIST BOX METHODS.

Method	Description
AddItem	Adds a single item to the list box.
Clear	Removes all items from the list box.
List	A string array that holds items from within the list box.
ListCount	The total number of list box items.
RemoveItem	Removes a single item from the list box.

Perhaps the most important method is the AddItem method, which adds items to the list box. AddItem is to list boxes what the assignment statement is to variables. A method always appears between the control name and a period. For example, the following AddItem method sends the value of Joseph to a list box named lstOneCol:

```
lstOneCol.AddItem "Joseph"
```

> The one-column list box shown in Figure 10.2 is named lstOneCol and that's the name used throughout the next couple of examples.

You'll often initialize a list box in the Form_Load() event procedure that initializes the form and the form controls right before the form appears on the screen. The following code sends several people's names to the list boxes shown earlier:

```
lstOneCol.AddItem "Joseph"
lstOneCol.AddItem "Angel Sue Bush"
lstOneCol.AddItem "Michael"
lstOneCol.AddItem "Stephanie"
lstOneCol.AddItem "Mary Ann"
lstOneCol.AddItem "Pamela"
lstOneCol.AddItem "Jock"
lstOneCol.AddItem "Bobby"
lstOneCol.AddItem "Cliff"
lstOneCol.AddItem "Jerry"
lstOneCol.AddItem "Thomas"
lstOneCol.AddItem "George"
lstOneCol.AddItem "Robert"
```

10

You'll initialize both single-column and multiple-column list boxes the same way with AddItem. The number of columns the list box contains has no bearing on how you initialize the list box.

Each item in a list box contains an associated subscript. The subscript is a number that begins at 0 for the first item, the second subscript is 1, and so on. Therefore, if you apply the RemoveItem method as follows, the third item is removed (because of the first item's 0 subscript):

```
lstOneCol.RemoveItem(2)    ' 3rd item has a subscript of 2
```

NEW TERM A *subscript* is a value that distinguishes one array item from the other array items.

As you remove list box items, the remaining item subscripts adjust upward accordingly. Therefore, if a list box contains seven items, each item has a subscript that ranges from 0 to 6. If you remove the fourth item, the list box items will then range from 0 to 5; the subscript 5 will now indicate the same item that the subscript 6 indicated before RemoveItem removed the fourth item.

You can remove all items from the list box with Clear, like this:

```
lstOneCol.Clear      ' Remove all items
```

You can assign individual items from a list box that contains data using the List method. You must save list box values in String or Variant variables unless first you convert the items to a numeric datatype using Val(). The following statements store the first and fourth list box items in two String variables:

```
strVar1 = lstOneCol.List(0)
strVar2 = lstOneCol.List(3)
```

The List method requires a subscript so Visual Basic knows which value from the list to assign to the variable. The value remains in the list after the assignment, but now the value appears in the variable as well.

You use ListCount to determine the number of items in the list box currently defined. The following statement stores the number of list box items in a numeric variable named intNum:

```
intNum = lstOneCol.ListCount
```

You use `ListCount` to loop through an entire list box with a `For...Next` loop.

You use `Selected` to determine whether a user has selected a list box item. `Selected` returns `True` for one or more list box items if the item's `MultiSelect` property is set to either `1-Simple` or `2-Extended`. Those properties indicate that the user can select more than one item at once. Figure 10.4 shows a list box with several items selected at the same time.

FIGURE 10.4.

A list box with a `MultiSelect` *property set to 1 or 2.*

Five selected items—

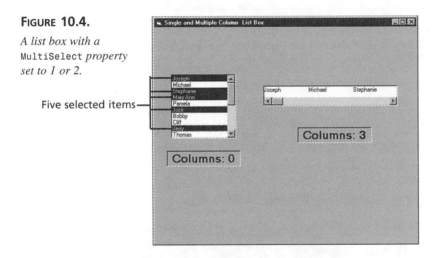

Combo Boxes

Combo boxes work much like list boxes except that the user can add items to a combo box at runtime, whereas the user can only scroll and select items from a list box at runtime. Visual Basic supports three kinds of combo boxes, and the kind you select depends on the combo box you want to display on the form and on the ability you want the user to have. All the list box methods that you learned about in the previous section apply to combo boxes.

Here are the three kinds of combo boxes:

- Drop-down combo box—Takes up only a single line on the form unless the user opens the combo box (by pressing the combo box's down arrow) to see additional values. The user can enter additional items at the top of the drop-down combo box and select items from the combo box.

- Simple combo box—Displays items as if they were in a list box. The user can add items to the combo box list (whereas the user cannot with a normal list box).

- Drop-down list box—Doesn't let the user enter new items, so it's similar to a list box. Unlike a list box, however, the drop-down list box normally appears closed to a single line until the user clicks the down arrow button to open the list box to its full size. Technically, drop-down list boxes are not combo box controls but work more like list boxes. The reason drop-down list boxes fall in the combo box control family is that you place drop-down list boxes on forms by clicking the combo box control and setting the `Style` combo box property.

> Think of a combo box as a combination of the List Box and Text Box controls. The user sees items in the list but then enters additional items in the text box portion of the combo box.

Figure 10.5 shows the three kinds of combo boxes. Each combo box contains the names of people that you saw in Figure 10.4. The first combo box, the drop-down combo box, is normally closed; when the user clicks its down arrow, the combo box opens. The third combo box, the drop-down list box, is left unopened. If the user opens the drop-down list box, the user will see a list of people's names but will not be able to add to the names because no data entry is possible in drop-down list boxes.

FIGURE 10.5.

Use `Style` *to change the combo box appearance.*

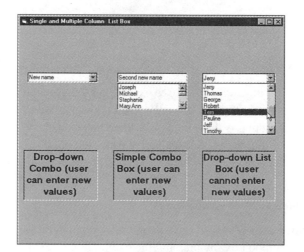

Study your form's design and determine the best list control to use. If the user must enter values, you should use either a drop-down combo box or simple combo box. If the user only selects a value from a list, use a list box if you have enough form space or use a drop-down list box if you don't have much room to display a full-sized list box.

Table 10.3 describes some of the combo box properties.

TABLE 10.3. THE FUNDAMENTAL COMBO BOX PROPERTIES.

Property	Description
BackColor	The combo box's background color.
ForeColor	The combo box's foreground text color.
Height	The height, in twips, of the closed combo box.
IntegralHeight	Determines whether the combo box can display partial items, such as the upper half of an item that falls toward the bottom of the combo box.
List	A drop-down property list box where you can enter values into the combo box at design time. You can enter only one at a time, and most programmers prefer to initialize the combo box at runtime.
Sorted	Determines whether the combo box values are automatically sorted. If False (the default value), the values appear in the same order in which the program added the items to the combo box.
Style	Determines the type of combo box your application needs. If 0-DropDown Combo, the combo box is a drop-down combo box. If 1-Simple Combo, the combo box turns into a simple combo box that remains open to the height you used at design time. If 2-DropDown List, the combo box turns into a drop-down list box that remains closed until the user is ready to see more of the list.

10

The user's entered value doesn't add to the Drop-down Combo Box control or to the Simple Combo Box control unless you add the capability to capture the user's entry. The combo box by itself, without code, cannot handle the addition of items automatically. You need to write, in the combo's `Change` or `LostFocus` event procedure, enough code to add the new item (that always appears in the combo's `Text` property) to the combo box list, like this:

```
cboBox.AddItem cboBox.Text  ' Adds user's value to the box
```

You can also add a command button that adds the combo box value entered by the user if the user clicks the command button.

Data Arrays

Now that you've mastered list boxes and combo boxes, you will have little trouble understanding data arrays. An array is nothing more than a list of variables. Regular nonarray variables, as opposed to arrays, have separate names such as the following:

```
curSales98      sngTaxRate      intCount      blnIsRecorded
```

Variables in an array all have the same name. Therefore, an array that holds a list of 10 division sales figures might be named `curDivSales`. Your program must be capable of distinguishing between an array's variables, and with the single name, this distinction might seem impossible. Nevertheless, as with list boxes, your program can distinguish between array variables by using a subscript. The subscript works just like an index value. The first value in the array would be subscripted as `curDivSales(0)` (subscripts start at `0` unless you use the `Option Base 1` statement in a `general` module to start the array's subscripts at `1`). The second value in the array would be `curDivSales(1)`, and so on.

NEW TERM   An *array* is a list of items with the same name and type.

Figure 10.6 illustrates how an array such as the 10-element `curDivSales` resides in memory.

FIGURE 10.6.

Distinguishing array elements with subscripts.

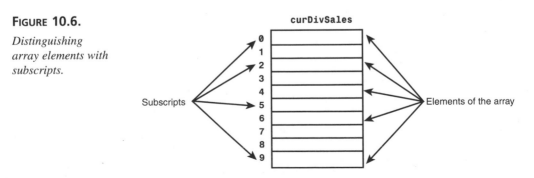

To declare an array, you use `Dim` or `Public` just as you declare regular nonarray variables. In the declaration, specify the number of elements (in parentheses) that the array is to hold. The following `Dim` statement declares the 10-element `Currency` array named `curDivSales`:

```
Dim curDivSales(10) As Currency
```

All elements in an array must be the same datatype.

Here's the great benefit that arrays give you over separate variable names: When you need to work with a group of variables, if you don't use an array, you must list each variable. Therefore, if you want to add all the divisions' sales figures and they are stored in separate nonarray variables, you would have to code something like this:

```
curTotal = curDivSales0 + curDivSales1 + curDivSales2 + _
curDivSales3 + curDivSales4 + curDivSales5 + _
curDivSales6 + curDivSales6 + curDivSales7 + _
curDivSales8 + curDivSales9
```

If you want to break a long statement into two or more lines, terminate each continued line with the underscore character, as shown in the `CurTotal` assignment.

An array makes stepping through and totaling the data much simpler. Here is the code that uses a `For...Next` loop to add the items in an array:

```
curTotal = 0    ' Zero out the total
 ' Step through the elements
For intCtr = 0 To 9
curTotal = curTotal + curDivSales(intCtr)  ' Add elements
Next intCtr
 ' curTotal now holds the sum of all 10 values
```

With only 10 variables, the array doesn't seem to offer a lot of space advantages or coding shortcuts. But what if there were 1,000 variables that you needed to track and total?

10

By making a simple change to the `For...Next` loop, you can easily add together all 1,000 elements, like this:

```
curTotal = 0    ' Zero out the total
 ' Step through the elements
For intCtr = 0 To 999
curTotal = curTotal + curDivSales(intCtr)  ' Add elements
Next intCtr
 ' curTotal now holds the sum of all 1,000 values
```

Suppose you need to ask the user for several values, such as the names of children in a class. By declaring a string array, a `For...Next` loop makes getting the names simple, as you can see here:

```
For intCtr = 1 To 10
   strChildName(intCtr) = InputBox("What is the next child's name?")
Next intCtr
```

Control Arrays

A control array is a list of controls with the same name. Instead of using four command buttons with four separate names, you can place a command button control array on the form, and that control array holds four command buttons. The control array can have a single name, and you'll distinguish the controls from each other with a subscript.

> Use a control array if several controls on your form are to look and act similar to each other, such as multiple command buttons or two or more list boxes.

One of the best reasons to use a control array is that you can add the first control to your form and set all its properties. When you create a control array from that first control, all the elements in the control array take on the same property values. You then can change those properties that need to be changed without having to set every property for every control individually.

NEW TERM   A *control array* is an array of several controls that you reference with an `Index` property value that acts as the subscript. The controls in a control array must be of the same control type.

Control arrays have a lot in common with data arrays. A control array has one name, and you distinguish all the array's controls from each other with the zero-based subscript. (The `Index` property holds the control's subscript number.) All the control array elements must be of the same datatype.

As soon as you place a control on a form that has the same name as an existing control, Visual Basic makes sure that you want to begin a control array by issuing the warning message shown in Figure 10.7. The message box keeps you from accidentally creating a control array when you actually want to add a different control. You'll see Figure 10.7's message box when you copy an existing control to the Clipboard and paste the copy elsewhere onto the form. If you click No, Visual Basic uses a default control name for the placed control.

FIGURE 10.7.

Visual Basic asks whether you want a control array.

10

All event procedures that use controls from a control array require a special argument value passed to them to determine which control is being worked on. For example, if your application contains a single command button named `cmdTotal`, the `Click()` event procedure begins and ends as follows:

```
Private Sub cmdTotal_click ()

End Sub
```

If, however, you created a control array named `cmdTotal`, the `Click()` event procedure begins and ends like this:

```
Private Sub cmdTotal_click (Index As Integer)

End Sub
```

The procedure uses the `Index` argument as the control index number (the subscript) that the user clicked. If you want to change the clicked command button's `Caption` property inside the `cmdTotal_Click()` procedure, you would do so like this:

```
cmdTotal(Index).Caption = "A new Caption value"
```

The `Index` value holds the command button's index that the user clicked to generate the event procedure. You will always respond to the proper clicked control if you use `Index` after the control array name.

Summary

In this hour you learned how you can add lists of items to your application. The first kind of list, the List Box control, lets your users select from a list of items that your application displays. The Combo Box control works like a List Box control but lets the user enter new values into the list.

Data and control arrays help you streamline your programs. Instead of working with separate variable or control names, you can work with a single name and use a subscript value to distinguish between the items. The code to process 10 or 100 array items is virtually the same, as this lesson demonstrated.

Hour 11, "Additional Controls," teaches several new controls that you can add to your applications.

Q&A

Q When do I use a list box and when do I use a combo box?

A A list box presents a user with a list of items. The user can select from the list. The user cannot add new items to the list box. If you want to present a list of items to the user and let him enter new items, use a combo box. A combo box works a lot like a combination of a list box and a text box.

Q What's the difference between a combo drop-down list box and a regular list box?

A The only difference is that the drop-down list box remains closed until the user opens it. Therefore, the list box doesn't consume a lot of form space until the user is ready to see the values in the list. If your form contains lots of extra room, you might want to use a regular list box so your users can see more values at one time. If form space is tight, use a drop-down list box.

Q Should I use 0 or 1 for the starting array subscript?

A You can use either unless you've added the `Option Base 1` statement to a module's `general` section, in which case your subscripts will have to begin at 1. If you don't use `Option Base 1` and you ignore the 0 subscript, however, make sure you declare enough array elements to hold all your data. If you need 15 elements and you use 1 for the starting subscript, you must declare 16 values to access subscripts 1 through 15.

Workshop

The quiz questions and exercises are provided for your further understanding. See Appendix B for the answers.

Quiz

1. When do you normally initialize a list box?

2. What method adds new items to a list box?

3. Which method determines the number of items in a list box?

4. True or false: Visual Basic will automatically keep list box items sorted if you set a certain property to `True`.

5. How many combo boxes are there?

6. How do you specify the type of combo box you want to add to an application?

7. True or false: The drop-down list box is one of the Combo Box controls, so users can enter new values in the drop-down list box just as they can other Combo Box controls.

8. What is an array?

9. What is the highest subscript in a 10-element array if you don't use `Option Base 1` and you use element `0`?

10. True or false: A control array exists when two or more controls have the same `Name` property.

10

Exercises

1. Write an application that builds a list as the user enters new values. (Hint: Use a Combo Box control for the list.) The list should hold the user's favorite book titles. As the user enters more and more titles, the list should grow. Add a command button to the form with the caption Add To; when the user clicks the command button, the title just entered goes to the list. Keep the list sorted at all times.

2. Write an application that contains four command buttons. The command buttons should be blue and have boldfaced, italicized captions that read Change Color, Change Bold, Change Height, and Change Width. When the user clicks one of the command buttons, the appropriate property should change inside the `Click()` event procedure. Use a `Select Case` statement to determine which property should change based on the event procedure's `Index` argument.

Hour **11**

Additional Controls

Now that you've added several programming statements to your Visual Basic language repertoire, you can learn about additional controls to add new features to your applications and to take advantage of some of the more powerful commands you now know. As you learn about new controls, your programming ability grows by leaps and bounds because your programs become richer in functionality and user interaction.

You'll learn about the selection controls, how to program scrollbars, and how to set the Timer control to let your application know when a predetermined amount of time has passed.

The highlights of this hour include

- How option buttons differ from check boxes
- When to change the check box's style
- Why scrollbars contain unusual properties
- How to set the Timer control to record time passing as an application executes

Option Buttons

Figure 11.1 shows an application with four option buttons. An option button gives your user a choice. By clicking the option button or by sending the focus to the option button and pressing the Spacebar to choose the option, the user selects or deselects an option button. When selected, the option button has a black center inside its circle.

FIGURE 11.1.

A form with four option buttons.

Conference Selection

Conference Site

- ○ Florida
- ⊙ California
- ○ Texas
- ○ New York

Return

Select a state for the conference

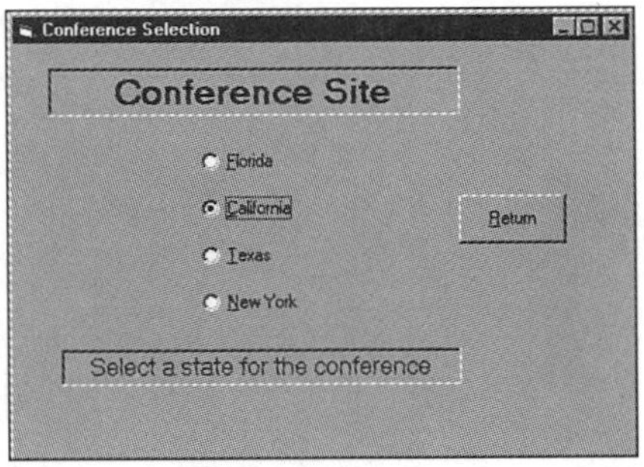

Option buttons act in a mutually exclusive fashion. Only one option button can be selected at any one time. Therefore, in Figure 11.1, the user could not select two or more of the options. If the user were to click Texas, the California option would no longer be selected. You don't have to do anything special to ensure that only one option button is selected at any one time; Visual Basic takes care of removing the former option's selection when the user selects a subsequent option button.

Option buttons are sometimes known as *radio buttons*. Older car radios used to have five or six buttons that selected preset stations. The listener could only select one station; as soon as the listener pushed a button, the previous station's button popped out.

The option button supports several of the properties you're already familiar with, such as the Appearance and Alignment properties. The Alignment property determines whether the option button text resides to the left or right of the option button. Figure 11.2 shows the option buttons with their Alignment property set to 2-Right Justify. The alignment you set depends on where the option buttons are to fall in relation to other controls.

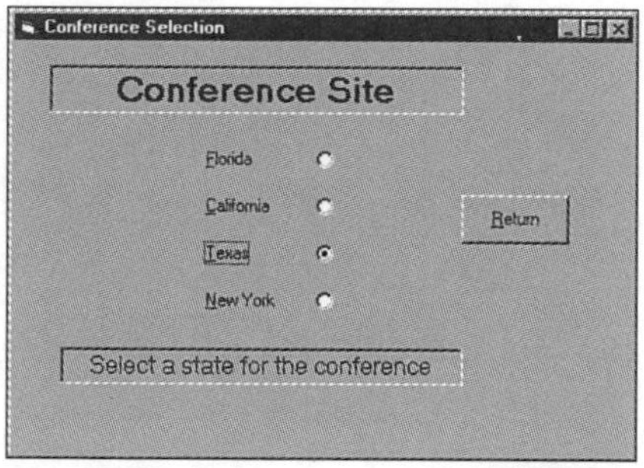

Figure 11.2.

These option buttons have a right-justified Alignment *property.*

An option button control array simplifies setting option button properties such as the Alignment property. Several option buttons almost always appear together, and the control array lets you set only one's property and the others will receive the same property settings. If you don't create an option button control array, you can change all the option button properties at once, even without a control array, by first selecting all the option button controls and then setting the properties for all of them at once.

The Value property is perhaps the most important option button property because the Value property changes at runtime and determines whether the option button is currently selected. By the way, the user can select only one option button at a time, but the application may start up without any option buttons being set if you don't set any in the Properties window or in code.

Frames and Option Buttons

Figure 11.3 shows an application with two sets of option buttons. The option buttons let you select a computer type and operating system. Figure 11.3 seems to violate the option button's primary rule: More than one option button is selected at the same time (the Pentium option button and the Windows 95 option).

11

FIGURE 11.3.

Two option buttons are set.

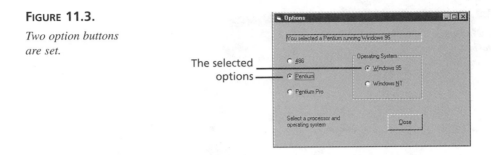

The selected options ———

Sometimes a form will need several sets of option buttons, just like the form in Figure 11.3. In each set the user should be allowed to select only one option button, but one option button should be set from each set at the same time. Therefore, you must revise the previous rule, which states that only one option button can be set at one time. The truth is that only one option button inside a frame can be set at one time.

NEW TERM A *frame* is a rectangular region on a form that holds other controls and groups the controls into a single set. It is a rectangular outline with an optional title. When you want to place multiple sets of option buttons on a form, first place the frame or frames onto the form. (You can place any control on a frame, but the frame especially helps group option buttons so you can offer multiple option button sets.)

> The form acts as a default frame. Therefore, two sets of option buttons reside on Figure 11.3's form: One set resides in a frame and the other set resides on the form itself. You can consider the latter set framed as well, even though no specific frame control surrounds it.

The frame control does support properties that determine the frame's look and caption and a frame does support a few events, but most programmers use the frame as a holding place to group other controls. After you place controls in a frame, you can move the frame and all the frame's controls move with it. Therefore, adjusting framed controls is relatively easy to do.

> Always place a frame on the form before putting controls in the frame. If you simply move controls from elsewhere on the form to the frame, the controls will not be in the frame but will exist simply on top of the frame. Visual Basic will not consider them framed together. To add additional controls to a frame with controls, click one of the framed controls before adding the new control.

Figure 11.4 shows an application that contains three frames that determine how text appears inside a label. The user can select only one option button inside each frame. As soon as the user changes one of the options, the option button's Click() event responds to the change and sets the Label property accordingly. Listing 11.1 contains the complete form module code that takes care of the user's action. The label is initialized in the Form_Load() event procedure (the procedure that executes right before the user sees the form), and the remaining event procedures are the responses to various user clicks on the form's controls. The controls are named well enough so that you will know where the controls appear in Figure 11.4.

FIGURE 11.4.

A form with three frames.

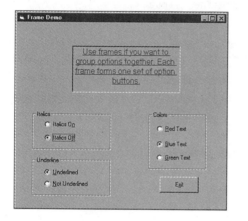

LISTING 11.1. THE FRAMED OPTION BUTTON CODE.

```
 1: Private Sub Form_Load()
 2: ' Initialize the label's text
 3: Dim strLabel1 As String
 4: Dim strLabel2 As String
 5: Dim strLabel3 As String
 6: Dim strLabel4 As String
 7:
 8: strLabel1 = "Use frames if you want "
 9: strLabel2 = "to group options together. "
10: strLabel3 = "Each frame forms one set "
11: strLabel4 = "of option buttons."
12:
13: lblFrames.Caption = strLabel1 & strLabel2 & _
14: strLabel3 & strLabel4
15:
16: ' Set the label's properties
17: lblFrames.FontItalic = True
```

continues

LISTING 11.1. CONTINUED

```
18: optItalicTrue.Value = True
19:
20: lblFrames.FontUnderline = True
21: optUnderTrue.Value = True
22:
23: lblFrames.ForeColor = vbBlue
24: optBlue.Value = True
25: End Sub
26:
27: Private Sub optItalicTrue_Click()
28: lblFrames.FontUnderline = True
29: End Sub
30:
31: Private Sub optItalicFalse_Click()
32: lblFrames.FontUnderline = False
33: End Sub
34:
35: Private Sub optRed_Click()
36: lblFrames.ForeColor = vbRed
37: End Sub
38:
39: Private Sub optBlue_Click()
40: lblFrames.ForeColor = vbBlue
41: End Sub
42:
43: Private Sub optGreen_Click()
44: lblFrames.ForeColor = vbGreen
45: End Sub
46:
47: Private Sub optUnderTrue_Click()
48: lblFrames.FontItalic = True
49: End Sub
50:
51: Private Sub optUnderFalse_Click()
52: lblFrames.FontItalic = False
53: End Sub
54:
55: Private Sub cmdExit_Click()
56: Unload Me
57: End
58: End Sub
```

COLOR NAMED LITERALS

Listing 11.1 demonstrates the use of named literals. The background colors assigned to the label are named literals that come with Visual Basic. Table 11.1 lists the named literal colors that you can assign to any property that uses color values, such as the background and foreground colors of several controls.

Given that Windows supports millions of possible colors, the eight colors that Table 11.1 lists represent a small number of colors you can possibly set. (Named literals don't exist for other color values.) Visual Basic supplies several ways to specify colors so that you can set a color from among the millions possible. For the sake of simplicity, Table 11.1's named literals work for most applications.

TABLE 11.1. THE COLOR NAMED LITERALS.

Literal	Color
vbBlack	Black
vbRed	Red
vbGreen	Green
vbYellow	Yellow
vbBlue	Blue
vbMagenta	Magenta
vbCyan	Cyan
vbWhite	White

Check Boxes

Figure 11.5 shows a form with check boxes. The Check Box control works just like the option button, with two differences: A selected check box shows the selection with a check mark, and check boxes are never mutually exclusive. Therefore, the user can select one or more check boxes even if those check boxes reside in the same frame or on the same form.

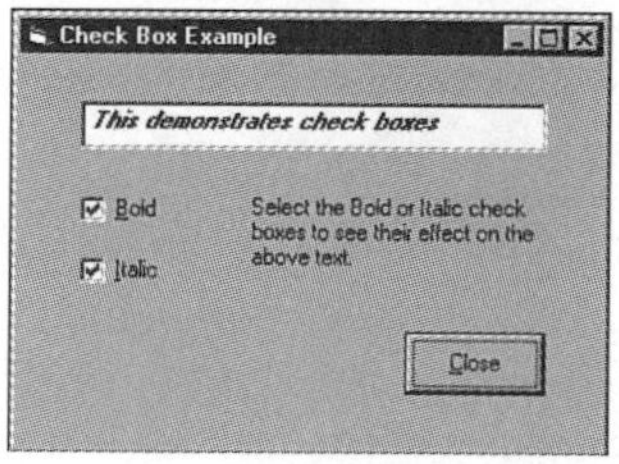

FIGURE 11.5.

A Form with two check boxes.

The Check Box control supports the same fundamental properties as the option button, except that the Value property determines not only if the box is checked (if 1) or unchecked (if 0), but also if it is grayed (if the Value property contains 2). Users sometimes use a grayed check box to determine whether part of a selected option is true. In addition, the programmer may gray out a box to show that the selection is unavailable under the current conditions.

Visual Basic version 5 added a new Style value to the Check Box control's property list. The available Style property values are 0-Standard and 1-Graphical. The graphical style value makes the check box look a lot like a command button that stays pressed (when selected) or unpressed (when not selected).

Figure 11.6 shows a form that illustrates the various Check Box property options available to you.

FIGURE 11.6.

Some Check Box control property options.

Scrollbars

Scrollbars let users control value changes. Rather than type specific values, the user can move the scrollbars with the mouse to specify relative positions within a range of values. The toolbox includes both a Horizontal Scrollbar and a Vertical Scrollbar control.

Table 11.2 contains a list of important scrollbar properties that determine the behavior of the scrollbar.

TABLE 11.2. FUNDAMENTAL SCROLLBAR PROPERTIES.

Property	Description
LargeChange	Specifies the amount that the scrollbar changes when the user clicks within the scrollbar's shaft area.
Max	Indicates the maximum number of units that the scrollbar value represents at its highest setting. The range is from 1 to 32,767 (the default Max value).
Min	Indicates the minimum number of units the scrollbar value represents at its lowest setting. The range is from 1 (the default Min value) to 32,767.
SmallChange	Specifies the amount that the scrollbar changes when the user clicks an arrow at either end of the scrollbar.
Value	Contains the unit of measurement currently represented by the position of the scrollbar.

When you place a scrollbar on a form, you must decide at that time what range of values the scrollbar is to represent. The scrollbar's full range can extend from 1 to 32,767. Set the Min property to the lowest value you want represented by the scrollbar. Set the Max property to the highest value you want represented by the scrollbar.

When the user eventually uses the scrollbar, the scrollbar arrows control small movements in the scrollbar's value, determined by the SmallChange property. Clicking the empty part of the shaft on either side of the scrollbox produces a positive or negative change in the value represented by the LargeChange property. The user can drag the scrollbox itself to any position within the scrollbar shaft to jump to a specific location instead of changing the value gradually.

Suppose, for example, that a horizontal scrollbar represented a range of whole dollar amounts from $5 to $100. When the user clicks the scroll arrows, the scrollbar's value changes by $1. When the user clicks the empty shaft on either side of the scrollbox, the scrollbar's value changes by $5. Here are the property values that you would set that determine how VB interprets each click of the scrollbar: Min: 5, Max: 100, SmallChange: 1, and LargeChange: 5.

The physical size of the scrollbar has no bearing on the scrollbar's returned values when the user selects from the scrollbar. Adjust the scrollbars on your form so that the scrollbars are wide enough or tall enough to be appropriately sized for the items that they represent.

NEW TERM   The *thumb* is the scrollbar's moving scrollbox (the elevator-like box).

11

Figure 11.7 shows an application that uses a vertical scrollbar to change the size of a label's font size. As the user clicks the top scrollbar arrow, the font size shrinks by the SmallChange value. As the user clicks the bottom scrollbar arrow, the font size increases by the SmallChange value. (The application's SmallChange property value is 1.) If the user clicks in the scrollbar's shaft on either side of the scrollbar's thumb, the LargeChange property value of 5 is either added to or subtracted from the font size.

FIGURE 11.7.

The vertical scrollbar determines the label's font size.

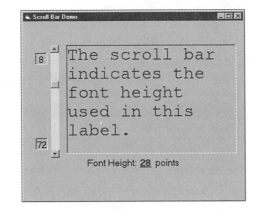

Listing 11.2 shows the code behind Figure 11.7. The code isn't lengthy because the scrollbar's Click() event procedure must change only the label's text font size and the label that displays the current font size. Any time the user changes the scrollbar, the scrollbar's Change() event procedure executes.

LISTING 11.2. THE CODE BEHIND THE SCROLLBAR APPLICATION.

```
1: Private Sub vsbHeight_Change()
2: lblScroll.FontSize = vsbHeight.Value
3: lblFontHeight.Caption = vsbHeight.Value
4: End Sub
```

VB's Clock: The Timer Control

The Timer control acts unlike any other control you've seen so far. The Timer control always works in the background, and the user never sees the timer on the form. You will see the Timer control during design time because you need to be able to select the control and change its properties. Nevertheless, the timer's purpose is to work in the background, triggering an event every once in a while according to the clock ticks.

Your computer has an internal clock to keep things running smoothly. The hardware requires an accurate clock for memory refreshes and CPU cycle coordination efforts. Software such as Visual Basic can tap into the internal clock and use its timing to control certain time-based events that your application may need to perform.

Figure 11.8 shows the Timer control as it appears when you place the control on a form. The Timer control supports only seven properties because the Timer control never appears on the form at runtime. Therefore, the control has no need for many of the style and size properties used for other controls that the user sees.

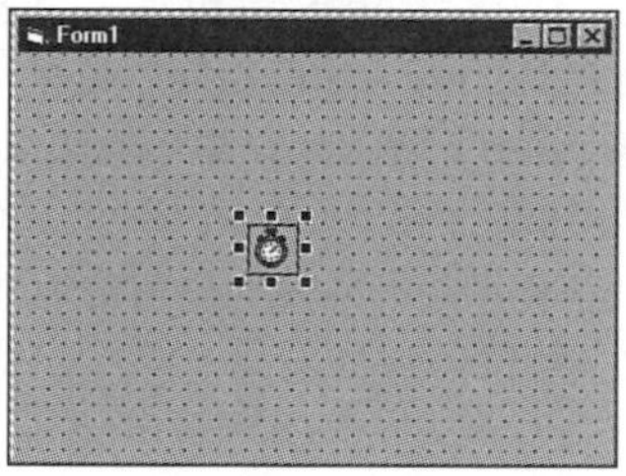

FIGURE 11.8.

The Timer control appears on the form only at design time.

You can place the timer out of the way of your form's other controls because its physical location is trivial. After you place the timer on the form, you should set its `Interval` property; `Interval` is the most important timer property. The `Interval` property contains a value that must range from 1 to 65,535. The value is in milliseconds (or thousandths of a second), so an `Interval` value of `500` would equate to half a second. The Timer control generates only one event: the `Timer` event. The Timer control triggers a `Timer` event after each interval of time goes by. Therefore, if you named a Timer control `tmrClock`, and if you set the control's `Interval` property to 1000, Visual Basic would execute the `tmrClock_Timer()` event procedure approximately every second.

NEW TERM A *millisecond* is one-thousandth of a second.

The Timer control isn't a perfect timer, just a good timer. Other processes occurring inside your computer can cause the Timer control to be off by a few milliseconds. The smaller the `Interval` value, the more likely the `Timer` event will be off. Fortunately, the Timer control works without much of a timing hitch, especially given today's faster computers.

11

If you need an interval that's larger than the 65,535 Interval value allows (this maximum Interval value provides only about a 10-second interval), insert some If logic at the top of the Timer() event procedure that checks to see if the required amount of time has passed since the last interval. (To do this, you will need some of the time functions described in Hour 14, "Built-In Functions Save Time.")

Summary

In this hour you learned about several new controls that allow you to begin adding more user interactivity to your applications. The option buttons and check boxes work almost exactly alike except that the option buttons are mutually exclusive and provide your users with a single option from a selection. The scrollbars let your users select values based on a range, using either a horizontal or vertical scrollbar. The Timer control keeps track of time passing during your application's execution and triggers a Timer() event every time the Interval value of time has passed.

Hour 12, "Dialog Box Basics," builds further on your I/O skills by demonstrating how to create common dialog boxes. Your users will be able to use the dialog boxes to enter and select values.

Q&A

Q Can I program check boxes to be mutually exclusive or do I have to use option buttons?

A Check boxes are not mutually exclusive by design. Option buttons are. Therefore, a Visual Basic application's user can only select one option button at a time within any one frame or on the form. If you want to change the behavior of check boxes and make them act like option buttons, be warned that you are giving your users mixed signals. Users are familiar with being able to select as many check boxes as they want. If your application prevents them from doing the usual, they might begin to dislike your application. Users feel comfortable when an application follows de facto standards.

Nevertheless, you can make the check boxes act like option buttons, but you will have to put code in the check boxes' Click() event procedures to remove the check from the current check box when the user clicks another check box. The code is fairly trivial, but again, your users will adapt more easily to your application if you use option buttons in mutually exclusive cases.

Q How can I trust the Timer control if it isn't accurate?

A The Timer control is accurate, but your computer cannot always let Windows respond to events exactly when needed. A multitasking operating system such as Windows does a lot of things at once. If a `Timer()` event occurs, the operating system cannot always, at that exact millisecond, go back to the running application and signal that the event occurred. Therefore, your applications sometimes take a back seat to system operations. Today's fast computers have much less of a time-accuracy problem than in the past, so you shouldn't worry too much about the potential millisecond miss now and then.

Workshop

The quiz questions and exercises are provided for your further understanding. See Appendix B for the answers.

Quiz

1. True or false: Option button captions always appear to the right of the buttons.
2. What happens if the user clicks an option button that isn't currently selected?
3. Why would you gray out a Check Box control?
4. What happens if the user clicks a check box that isn't currently selected?
5. True or false: An application can begin with none of its option buttons or check boxes selected.
6. What kind of control can you place on a frame?
7. What is the difference between a scrollbar's `SmallChange` and `LargeChange` properties?
8. Which property changes when the user clicks one of the scrollbar's arrows?
9. True or false: The Timer control works like an alarm clock ready to go off at a preset time of day.
10. True or false: If you need a timer interval greater than approximately 10 seconds, you must use multiple Timer controls.

Exercises

1. Create an application that mimics the frame application used with Listing 11.1. Instead of using separate option buttons, use an option button array for each frame's option button, making a total of three option button arrays. Change

Listing 11.1 to reduce the number of event procedures in the application. Use a `Select Case` statement based on the event procedure `Index` argument to set the appropriate label property.

2. Change the application you wrote in exercise 1 so that no frames appear on the form. Remove the Underline and Italic option buttons (keep the Framed Color option buttons) and add these check box controls in their place: Underline and Italic. Change the code so that the text will appear underlined if the user clicks the Underline check box, and the text will be italicized if the user clicks the Italic check box. Both or only one might be checked at any one time.

Duplicate this lesson's scrollbar application that lets the user set the label's text size with the scrollbar. Completely remove the scrollbar, however, and add a `Timer` property. Every second, add 5 to the label's font size. When the font size grows to 70 or more points, send the size back down to 8 and start increasing the size once again.

HOUR 12

Dialog Box Basics

You'll be an expert at displaying and responding to dialog boxes before this hour is over! Visual Basic makes the displaying of dialog boxes painless when you use the Common Dialog Box control. The Common Dialog Box control displays professional-looking dialog boxes inside your application so that the user can select from familiar dialog boxes and so your application will look as if you spent hours mimicking the cool dialog boxes found in best-selling Windows applications such as Excel.

The highlights of this hour include

- What the Common Dialog Box control does
- How to distinguish between dialog boxes
- Where to prepare the dialog box's design-time properties
- How to use named literals to display a font selection
- How consistent dialog boxes make users comfortable

What the Common Dialog Box Does

The Common Dialog Box control is perhaps the most powerful control available because of its capability to become one of several common dialog boxes you've surely seen in Windows applications. In Hour 10, "List Boxes and Data Lists," you learned that the Combo Box control is multifaceted because the control acts like one of three kinds of combo boxes, depending on the Style property you set. The common dialog box goes far beyond the combo box's capability to take on different looks and purposes.

When you place a common dialog box on a form, you won't be able to resize it because the control, like the Timer control, will not appear on the form at runtime, at least not right away. Your runtime code will have to display the common dialog box, and the look of the common dialog box displayed depends on what your code needs at the time.

If you are going to work with a data file, you could display the File Open dialog box, shown in Figure 12.1.

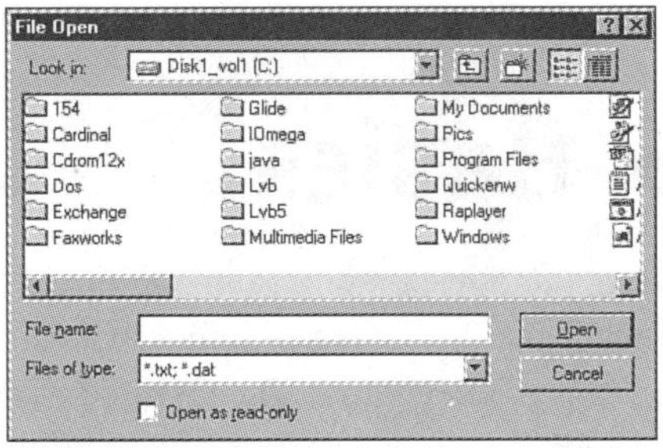

FIGURE 12.1.

Using the common File Open dialog box to request a filename and location.

The *quick viewer* is a Windows application that pops up when you right-click a filename. The quick viewer application displays the file in its native format without requiring you to own the original format's parent application (such as Lotus 1-2-3).

You've seen the File Open dialog box in many Windows applications. The dialog box works just as it does in Microsoft Word and other applications; the user can select a pathname or a filename, change the view by clicking one of the View buttons, open the file as read-only so no changes are made to the file, and even select another drive or computer to choose from by clicking the drop-down list box.

The Common Dialog Box control creates the same File Open dialog box that you see in other applications, in every respect. For example, you can right-click any folder or file displayed inside the dialog box, and a pop-up menu appears with which you can rename the object, quick view the object (if your system contains a quick viewer application for the selected file's type), open the object, copy, cut, or perform a number of other tasks.

The Common Dialog Box control also presents a similar file-related dialog box, shown in Figure 12.2, that produces a File Save dialog box. The user will also be familiar with the File Save dialog box. Your application can control the type of files displayed (by setting an appropriate filename extension type value) and can respond to the user's selection.

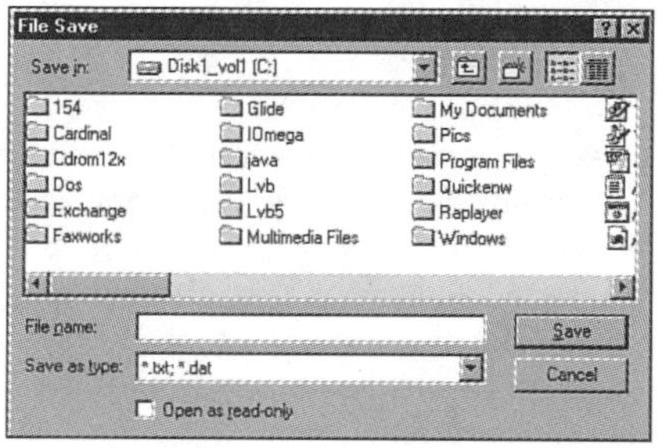

FIGURE 12.2.

The File Save dialog box is also familiar to Windows users.

WHY COMMON DIALOG BOXES?

You do not have to use the Common Dialog Box control. A dialog box is nothing more than a form with controls on it. You can add a new form to any project (with Project | Add Form) and put any controls you want on the form. The toolbox includes several file-related controls such as the File List Box control and the Directory List Box control that you can place on the form.

The Common Dialog Box control, however, makes sure that your dialog boxes that mimic those found in numerous other applications perform in the same way as those in other applications. You want to present the same set of common dialog boxes that your users are used to seeing in other applications, or they will not adapt to your application as quickly as they might otherwise. In addition, using the Common Dialog Box control and setting a few properties is much simpler and gives you much more time than you would have if you created these dialog boxes from scratch.

Figure 12.3 shows another common dialog box that the Common Dialog Box control can generate. Your applications can display the Color dialog box any time you want the user to select a color for an application such as a drawing application. Windows supports

12

several million colors, and the Color dialog box shows only a few at a time. However, the user can locate the exact color desired from the Color dialog box or define his or her own custom colors by clicking the dialog box's Define Custom Colors button.

FIGURE 12.3.

The Color dialog box is used by the user to pick a color.

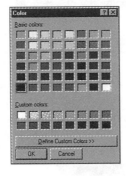

The Common Dialog Box controls are front-end shells that present your users with a standard dialog box they can respond to. Your code must take over as soon as the user responds to the common dialog box and inspect the values the user selected. In other words, just because the user selects a file-name in a File Open dialog box does not mean that your application opens that file as soon as the user clicks OK. The job of the common dialog box is only to give the user a typical dialog box interface. When the dialog box goes away, you must inspect the dialog box's return values and perform all the coding to open the file the user selected. The same is true of other common dialog boxes because they only return to your application the user's selection, but they do nothing with that selection on their own.

The Font dialog box, shown in Figure 12.4, is another common dialog box that the Common Dialog Box control can display for you. When your application works with text, you should give your user the chance to select a font name or style. Your application cannot always know in advance which fonts the user will have on his system. The Font dialog box will, however, give the user a chance to select font information from his own computer. Once selected, your application can use the user's selection values to generate the text in the selected font.

FIGURE 12.4.

*The Font dialog box
shows font information
from the user's system.*

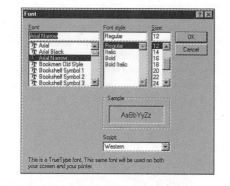

The Print dialog box, shown in Figure 12.5, displays a common printer dialog box that you can display before printing any information to the printer. The dialog box returns information the user selects about the pending print job. As with the other controls, the Print dialog box only returns information to your application; it's up to your application to look at all relevant return information and respond accordingly. Therefore, if the user elects to print six copies, your code that follows the display of the Print dialog box must print six copies of the printed output.

FIGURE 12.5.

*The Print dialog box
lets the user select a
printer for output.*

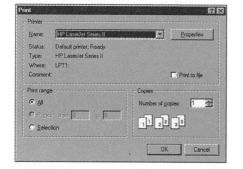

12

Want to add fax capabilities to your application? No problem; just display a Print dialog box. As long as the user has installed a Windows-aware fax driver, such as WinFax Pro or Microsoft Fax, the user can select that fax driver from the Print dialog box's Name list box. Your output, as long as you set your application's printer to the user's selected value, goes to the fax machine instead of to the printer.

The Print dialog box that appears on your system might be very different from the one shown in Figure 12.5. All the Common Dialog Box control's dialog boxes display available information based on their own computer settings. Therefore, your application will use these dialog boxes to let the user select from the properties of his own computer, depending on how those properties differ from yours.

The final dialog box that the Common Dialog Box control can display is a Help window, such as the one in Figure 12.6. The Help window is linked to a help file that you generate. Generating help files is not a trivial task, as you'll see in Hour 23, "Distributing Your Applications." Therefore, this lesson doesn't show you how to connect a help file to your application. However, the Common Dialog Box control's Help dialog box can produce the front-end dialog box your user interacts with when you learn more about providing help in Hour 23.

FIGURE 12.6.

The Help dialog box lets the user request the help needed.

Adding the Common Dialog Box Control

Although the Common Dialog Box control is known as a standard control, the control doesn't appear on your toolbox until you add it. Perform these steps to add the Common Dialog Box control to your toolbox:

1. Select Project | Components (Ctrl+T is the equivalent shortcut key for this option) to display the Components dialog box shown in Figure 12.7.

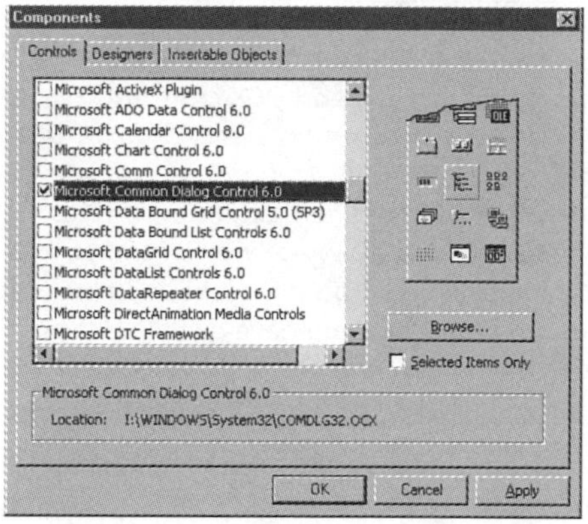

FIGURE 12.7.

*You can select
additional tools
to add to your
Toolbox window.*

2. Scroll to the control named Microsoft Common Dialog Control 6.0 and select it.

3. Click OK. The Common Dialog Box control will now appear at the end of your Toolbox window.

4. Double-click the Common Dialog Box control to add the control to your Form window.

> Search the Internet and Microsoft's home pages for additional ActiveX controls you can drop into your toolbox by selecting the tool from the Components dialog box. (You may have to click the Browse button to locate controls found in places other than your Windows\System folder.) An ActiveX control is identical to the toolbox's intrinsic controls and performs work when you set its properties and when you use methods and events related to the control.

12

You can add ActiveX controls to your Toolbox window. If a tool you need doesn't appear on the toolbox, that tool might appear as an ActiveX control in the Components dialog box or even as an add-on tool you can download from an online service.

You cannot use 16-bit VBX custom controls (controls used in earlier versions of Visual Basic), but you can add OCX controls that Visual Basic began using in version 4. An ActiveX control is identical to an OCX control except that a true ActiveX control does a little more, such as work across the Internet. All ActiveX controls end in the .ocx extension, so it is sometimes difficult to tell whether you are looking at an ActiveX control or at a pre-ActiveX OCX control. All OCX controls work, both the old and new kinds of OCX controls, but VBX controls do not. When you have a choice, select the more current ActiveX OCX version over the pre-ActiveX OCX version.

When you add the Common Dialog Box control, you'll see several other controls listed in the Components dialog box. At any time you can add these other controls to your toolbox if you think you can use their help. For example, you can add the Microsoft Calendar control if you need to display calendar information in a Visual Basic application. You can add any ActiveX control to your toolbox, and Visual Basic comes with several that you see when you display the Components dialog box.

If you use the Professional or Enterprise Editions of VB, you'll see more available controls than will users of the Standard Edition.

Only after adding the control to your project's Toolbox window can you add the control to the project's forms. When you place the control on the form, the control doesn't look like any of the controls it becomes (see Figure 12.8) because you, through properties, determine what appearance the control will take and when the control will appear.

FIGURE 12.8.

*You can select
additional tools to
add to your Toolbox
window.*

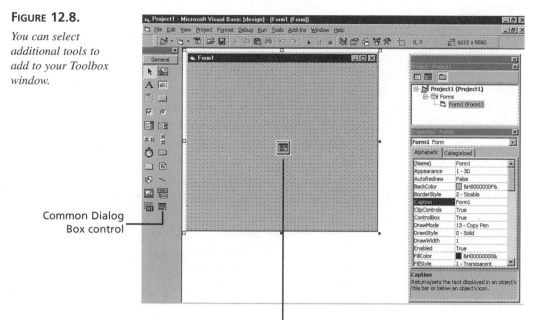

Common Dialog
Box control

Common Dialog Box control
placed on a form

Generating Common Dialog Boxes

When you add a Common Dialog Box control to your toolbox and then double-click the
control to add a dialog box to your Form window, Visual Basic offers an extra Properties
window property, Custom, that can be used to set multiple properties. This special Property
Pages dialog box is reached by right-clicking the Common Dialog Box icon and selecting Properties.

Figure 12.9 shows the tabbed Property Pages dialog box that appears when you click the
Custom property. You'll see tabs across the top that display properties sheets for
Open/Save As, Color, Font, Print, and Help dialog boxes. The properties sheets don't
offer all properties, but they do simplify entering the most common properties for each
kind of dialog box.

12

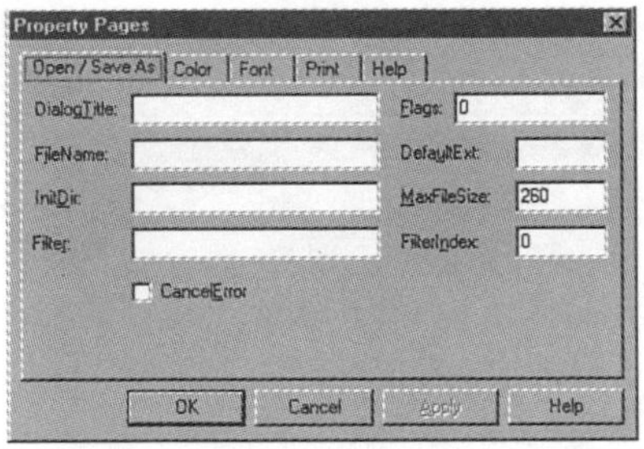

FIGURE 12.9.

The Custom *property makes entering design-time common dialog box properties simple.*

You use the Custom properties sheets to set as many properties at design time as you can. Your code can set the rest. For example, if you prefer to display text using the Arial font that appears on most Windows systems, you can type Arial in the Custom Font properties sheet for the FontName property. When the user runs the application and displays the Font dialog box, Arial will be selected. Of course, the user might change the selection, and if Arial doesn't exist on the user's system, the Font dialog box may make a different font the default font. Therefore, your code must check the dialog box's FontName property when the dialog box returns control to your application to see if the user selected a different font.

Fill in as many of the Custom values as you can at design time. (You can also change them or initialize these properties at runtime.) The more you fill in, the more you narrow the user's required selections. For example, if your application can open only files that end in the .mdb or .asc filename extensions, type this value for the Filter property in the Custom dialog box: *.mdb; *.asc. The subsequent File Open dialog box will then show only those files; you've limited the number of files the user must wade through to select a possible file because no other filename will show up. (The user can display a different set of files by changing the dialog box's Files of type drop-down list box, but she might inadvertently display and select a different kind of file that your application cannot read.)

The Common Dialog Box Methods

To display a particular dialog box, your application must specify one of these methods:

- ShowColor
- ShowFont
- ShowHelp

- ShowOpen
- ShowPrinter
- ShowSave

Therefore, if your Common Dialog Box control is named `cdbFile`, your application can display the File Save dialog box with this statement:

```
cdbFile.ShowSave
```

The next few sections quickly show you how to set up each type of common dialog box.

Adding the File Dialog Boxes

To display a File Open dialog box, your application might contain the following statements:

```
cdbDialog.DialogTitle = "File Open"
cdbDialog.Filter = "*.txt"    ' Show only text files
cdbDialog.FileName = "*.txt"  ' Default filename
cdbDialog.ShowOpen            ' Trigger the dialog box
```

All the File Open dialog box buttons and list boxes have property names. Therefore, you can initialize the File Open dialog box to have any default value that best matches your application's needs. When the user selects from and closes the dialog box, your application will have to test the dialog box's `FileName` and `IntDir` properties to locate the file the user selected.

To display a File Save dialog box, your application might contain the following statements:

```
cdbDialog.DialogTitle = "File Save"
cdbDialog.Filter = "*.*"            ' Show all files
cdbDialog.FileName = "test.txt"     ' Default filename
cdbDialog.ShowSave                  ' Trigger the dialog box
```

Notice that the methods at the end of these last two code fragments have triggered the dialog box's display for the user.

The Color Dialog Box

To display a Color dialog box, you only need to change the `DialogTitle` property and issue the correct method, like this:

```
cdbDialog.DialogTitle = "Select a Color"
cdbDialog.ShowColor     ' Display the dialog box
```

12

The dialog box's `Color` property will hold the selected color when the user closes the dialog box and your code regains control. You can assign this `Color` property to other Visual Basic properties that require color values.

The Font Dialog Box

To display a Font dialog box, you only need to change the `DialogTitle` property, select a default font name and style if you want, set the kind of font to display, and then use the `ShowFont` method, like this:

```
cdbDialog.DialogTitle = "Font"
cdbDialog.FontName = "Arial"
cdbDialog.Flags = cdlCFEffects Or cdlCFBoth
cmdDialog.ShowFont
```

The `Type` property is required, or you will cause the error shown in Figure 12.10. `cdlCFEffects` and `cdlCFBoth` are named literals that you can use with the Font dialog box. These literals tell Visual Basic to display the user's TrueType fonts as well as any printer and screen fonts that appear on the system.

FIGURE 12.10.

The Font dialog box cannot find the correct fonts.

> Search the online help for `Flags` Property (Font Dialog) for an exhaustive list of font type named literals you can use to control the fonts shown. (The Color, File Open, File Save, and Print dialog boxes also support numerous named literals you can use.)

The Printer Dialog Box

To display a Printer dialog box, you only need to change the `DialogTitle` property and use the `ShowPrinter` method, like this:

```
cdbDialog.DialogTitle = "Select a Printer"
cdbDialog.ShowPrinter
```

Summary

This hour you have learned about the many facets of the Common Dialog Box control. Depending on the properties you set and the method you use to display the Common Dialog Box control, your user will see one of several dialog boxes. The dialog boxes look and act just like other professional Windows dialog boxes. The Common Dialog Box control lets you add powerful dialog boxes with only a few lines of code.

Hour 13, "Modular Programming," moves back into a little theory by describing how to write better programs using modular, structured coding techniques.

Q&A

Q How do I know what controls I can add to my Toolbox window?

A This book examines a few more of the controls, so you'll become familiar with more of the extra controls as you progress through the book. In addition, you can click the Components dialog box's Browse button and search your hard disk (or your network) for additional controls in other locations. For example, if you subscribe to The Microsoft Network online service, you will find several ActiveX controls in the Microsoft Network folder. Any ActiveX control, whether or not it comes with Visual Basic, will work as a Toolbox control.

Q How do I know all the properties of the six dialog boxes?

A This lesson does not list all the properties available for all the dialog boxes, but then again, this entire book has yet to list all properties for any control described. Some properties are simply not useful enough to warrant a lot of attention. This book, although extremely complete, is not an encyclopedic reference to Visual Basic, but you do have access to such a reference: the online help and, especially, Books Online. In addition, the online help describes the various named literals available for several of the Common Dialog Box controls. This book gives you the tools you need to begin developing Visual Basic applications as soon as you can, but exhaustive property and named literal lists would become too cumbersome for this text.

12

Workshop

The quiz questions and exercises are provided for your further understanding. See Appendix B for the answers.

Quiz

1. How many different dialog boxes can the Common Dialog Box control produce?

2. What are two advantages to using the Common Dialog Box control over your own dialog boxes that you create?

3. True or false: You can add an ActiveX control to your toolbox.

4. True or false: Visual Basic includes these five controls that you can add to your toolbox: File Open, File Save, Colors, Font, and Help.

5. What property limits the files displayed to a particular set of extensions?

6. Name the methods that display all six common dialog boxes.

7. Why does the following code not display a Font dialog box?

```
cbdDialog.DialogTitle = "Font"
cbdDialog.ShowFont
```

8. How do you know which file was selected by the user after a File Save dialog box closes?

9. True or false: The Color dialog box limits the user to a few limited color values.

10. Why does a file not begin printing as soon as the user selects a printer and closes the Printer dialog box?

Exercises

1. Press Ctrl+T to display the Components dialog box once again. Search through the controls you can add to your toolbox. Add a few interesting controls and study their properties. You can add as many as you want. You also can delete one of these extra controls from the Toolbox window by pressing Ctrl+T and deselecting it.

2. Write a simple Color dialog box application that lets the user display a Color dialog box simply by clicking a command button. When the user selects a color and closes the Color dialog box, set the command button's BackColor property to the user's selected color.

3. Run the application you created in exercise 2 and click the Define Custom Colors button to see how the Color dialog box changes. Aren't common dialog boxes simple to use?

4. Display a File Open dialog box (attach the display to a command button so you can display the dialog box when you are ready) that displays, by default, all files in the selected folder that end with .txt and .bat extensions. Set the default folder to your computer's root directory (C:\) and make Autoexec.bat the default filename selected when the user first sees the dialog box.

PART **IV**

Programming with Data

Hour

HOUR 13

Modular Programming

This lesson covers the theory of good, structured programming techniques. By breaking your application into several procedures, you'll streamline your coding efforts, write more accurate code, and speed subsequent maintenance. Before you can successfully write well-structured code, you'll have to master argument passing. This lesson examines Visual Basic's two argument-passing methods and describes when and why you would choose one over the other.

The highlights of this hour include

- What benefits structured programming offers
- Why short, numerous procedures beat long procedures
- How to write your own functions and subroutines
- When to use functions
- How to code argument lists
- Why VB uses two argument-passing methods
- How to protect passed arguments

Structured Programming

You already know the best way to structure programs because you can use Microsoft's Visual Basic design as a guide. The small event procedures you've seen and coded are perfect examples of the correct way to code. Don't write long routines that do everything; instead, write small code procedures that each perform only one task, such as respond to a user's keystroke. If the keystroke is to trigger a bunch of things, keep the event procedure small and call other small procedures that do the detailed work.

Structured programming is a programming method you use to break long programs into numerous small procedures, putting off the details as long as possible.

For example, suppose that you need to perform the following tasks when the user clicks a Reconcile command button in a checkbook application:

1. Display checks next to cleared items.
2. Total the cleared items.
3. Total the uncleared items.
4. Recommend an action if the manual checkbook balance and the checkbook computer file's balance don't match.
5. Print a reconciliation report.

Such a detailed response to a single command button click would take many screens of code. Nevertheless, the Click() event procedure doesn't have to be many screens. Instead, you could insert a series of procedure calls that do the detailed work and keep the Click() procedure small like this:

```
Private Sub cmdReconcile_Click ()
    Call ClearItems ()
    Call UnClearItems ()
    If ChkBkIsBalanced () Then
        Call OutBalanceAction ()
    End If
    Call ReconcilePrint ()
End Sub
```

You are now learning about a topic known as *structured programming*. In structured programming you delay coding details for as long as you can. Keep subdividing your code procedures so that they simply control procedures that call more detailed procedures until you finally reach the point where a task cannot be further subdivided.

All the procedures called by a subroutine should be as small as possible and only perform a single task, or a series of calls to other procedures. When you follow this simple advice, your code becomes a structured, manageable set of routines where each subroutine performs a single task or controls other tasks.

Not only does structured programming make writing code easier, it makes managing code simple. If your application contains a bug, you can more easily locate the bug because you follow the thread of procedures until you get to the routine that controls the logic with the bug. If your uncleared balance is incorrect, you can go directly to the procedure that computes that balance and then locate the problem without affecting lots of other code around that routine.

NEW TERM   The *called* procedure is the procedure called by another procedure. The *calling* procedure is the procedure that triggers another's execution.

Calling Procedures and Returning from Them

The previous section discusses calling procedures. You have learned about the `Call` keyword, but you haven't been exposed to `Call` before now. That is, you haven't been directly exposed to `Call` even though you have performed a similar action by using the built-in `Val()` and `Format()` functions.

When one procedure contains a `Call` statement, the `Call` statement puts the current procedure on hold and executes the called procedure. Here is one of the formats of the `Call` statement:

```
Call Procedure
```

> The `Call` keyword is sometimes optional, as you'll see later in this lesson. The `Call` keyword is rarely used in VB programs.

13

When one procedure's execution reaches its `Call` statement, that procedure is put on hold and execution begins at the called *Procedure*. After the called procedure ends (whether it ends with the `End Sub` statement or an `Exit Sub` statement or by other means), the called procedure returns control to the calling procedure. The same thing happens when you call the built-in functions because a built-in function is a special kind of procedure: Your code temporarily stops, and the built-in function's code takes over and uses the argument(s), and finally returns a value as well as control back to your code.

You've seen event procedures and you've executed the built-in function procedures, and Visual Basic supports two other kinds of procedures:

- Standard subroutine procedures
- Standard function procedures that you write

A standard subroutine or function procedure doesn't respond to an event. A standard procedure only executes when called from elsewhere in the program.

> If a procedure is defined with the `Private` keyword, only procedures elsewhere within that module can call that procedure. If a procedure is defined with the `Public` keyword, all procedures in the project can call the procedure.

Standard procedures, whether they are subroutines or functions, can reside either inside a form module (following the event procedures) or inside an external module file you add to your project. Figure 13.1 illustrates the difference between subroutines and functions. The calling code calls both and they both do work. The subroutine doesn't return a value to the calling procedure. The function does return a value to the calling procedure, and the calling procedure must do something with that value such as assign the value to a variable or control. By the way, you'll understand all that's happening in Figure 13.1 before this lesson is over, so if some of it confuses you right now, don't be alarmed.

WHY CODE EXTERNAL MODULES?

Generally, programmers put general-purpose `Public` procedures in their external modules (modules that are not form modules). These general-purpose subroutines and functions perform work such as calculations and printed output that you may want to repeat in several different applications. For example, if you want to incorporate Visual Basic code that prints your letterhead in two or more applications, you can write the code once, store the code in a standard module, and then add that module to whatever application needs the letterhead printed. The application's regular form module code might call the external module's letterhead routine when ready for the printed letterhead, such as before the body of a specific report prints.

To add an external module to a project, simply right-click the Project Explorer window and select Add Module. The extra module appears in the Explorer window and in the Code window. You then can switch between modules by double-clicking the module name in the Explorer window.

The Sub keyword indicates that you're coding a subroutine and Function indicates that you're writing a function. Of course, you can put standard subroutines and functions inside form modules and you should do that if your event procedures get too long. Standard procedures help to break down longer problems into more manageable structured routines, as described earlier in this lesson.

FIGURE 13.1.

Both subroutines and functions do work, but only functions return values.

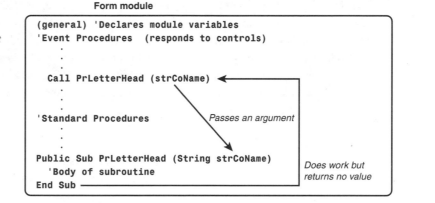

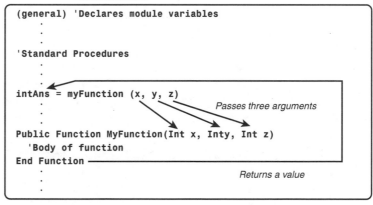

As Figure 13.1 illustrates, when you want to write a procedure that performs a task but doesn't need to return a value, write a subroutine procedure. If you need to write a procedure that performs a task and returns a value, such as a calculated result, write a function procedure. You can pass arguments to either kind of procedure.

13

NEW TERM — A *standard function* procedure is a standalone nonevent procedure that does work when called by another procedure and returns a single value to that called procedure. A *standard subroutine* procedure is a standalone nonevent procedure that does work when called by another procedure.

Coding Subroutines

You'll find uses for subroutines as you begin writing larger applications. For example, suppose you were writing a company sales status program. You might need a specialized routine that calculates a cost of sales value and displays that value in a label. By putting that code in a subroutine procedure, you help separate the task from other tasks and make the application more manageable. In addition, if several procedures in the application need the calculation, you can call the procedure from every place that needs it instead of repeating the same code in every place.

To create a subroutine procedure, perform these steps:

1. Make up an appropriate name for the procedure using the same naming rules as you use for variables. Give the procedure a meaningful name such as `CostOfSales`.

2. Determine whether you want to put the procedure in the form module or in a separate external module. If you think you'll use the code in other applications, add a new module to your Project Explorer window, but if the code goes with this application only, you can add the code to the current form module.

3. Open the Code window and scroll to the bottom. On a blank line below the last line type `Private Sub CostOfSales()`. (If you fail to type the parentheses, Visual Basic adds them for you because all procedure names terminate with the parentheses to hold possible arguments.) As soon as you press Enter, Visual Basic adds the end of the procedure, as shown in Figure 13.2's Code window.

FIGURE 13.2.

You must fill in the procedure's body.

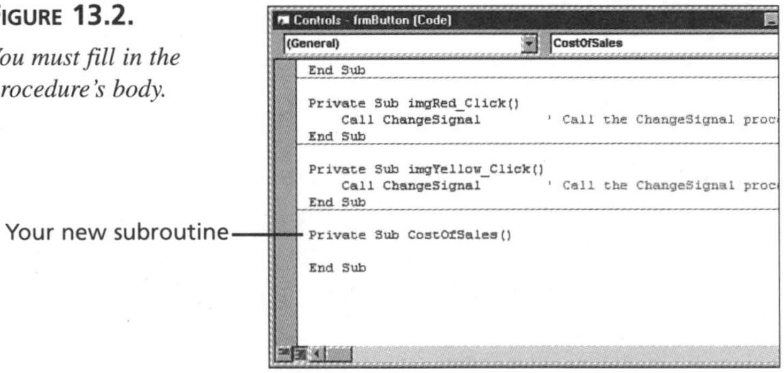

Your new subroutine ──────

```
Controls - frmButton [Code]
(General)                              CostOfSales
    End Sub

    Private Sub imgRed_Click()
        Call ChangeSignal        ' Call the ChangeSignal proc
    End Sub

    Private Sub imgYellow_Click()
        Call ChangeSignal        ' Call the ChangeSignal proc
    End Sub

    Private Sub CostOfSales()

    End Sub
```

Instead of locating the end of the module and typing the first line, you could also select Tools | Add Procedure to open the Add Procedure dialog box (see Figure 13.3) and set up a new subroutine (or function) procedure.

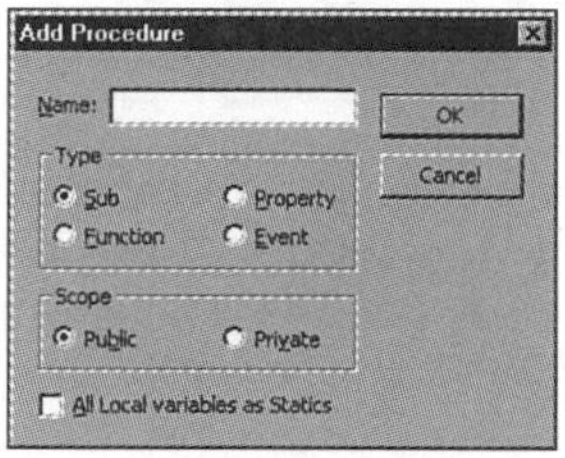

FIGURE 13.3.

You can insert new procedures from the Add Procedure dialog box.

After Visual Basic creates the place for the procedure, you can add the body of the code. For example, Listing 13.1 shows how you might code a cost of sales subroutine procedure. The procedure's job is to calculate the cost of sales from text box values and assign the cost to a label named lblCost.

If you put code such as Listing 13.1 in an external module, you must precede all control names with the form name that contains those controls. Therefore, precede the text boxes and labels with the form name that contains those text boxes and labels (for example, frmSales.txtTotalInv.Text and frmSales.lblCost.Caption).

LISTING 13.1. A COST OF SALES SUBROUTINE.

```
 1: Private Sub CostOfSales()
 2: ' Computes a cost of sales and
 3: ' displays that code in a label
 4: Dim curGrossSales As Currency
 5: Dim curCostSales As Currency
 6: Dim sngOverHead As Single
 7: Dim sngInventoryFctr As Single
 8: Dim sngPilferFctr As Single
 9:
10: ' Store initial variable values from controls
11: curGrossSales = txtGross.Text
12: sngInventoryFctr = txtTotalInv.Text * 0.38
13: sngPilferFctr = txtPilfer.Text
14: sngOverHead = 0.21 ' Fixed overhead percentage
15:
```

13

continues

LISTING 13.1. CONTINUED

```
16: curCostSales = curGrossSales - (sngInventoryFctr * curGrossSales)
17: curCostSales = curCostSales - (sngPilferFctr * curGrossSales)
18: curCostSales = curCostSales - (sngOverHead * curGrossSales)
19: lblCost.Caption = Format(curCostSales, "Currency")
20: End Sub
```

Use default property values for the text boxes and labels if you want to shorten your code. Coding just txtTotalInv accomplishes the same purpose as coding txtTotalInv.Text because Text is the default property for all text boxes. Caption is the default property for labels.

To call this procedure, another procedure (such as a Click() event procedure or another standard procedure) can issue either of these statements:

```
Call CostOfSales()    ' Calls the CostOfSales() subroutine

CostOfSales           ' Calls the CostOfSales() subroutine
```

If the subroutine uses no arguments, you don't need to use Call and the parentheses to trigger the subroutine's execution. If CostOfSales() did use one or more arguments, you would not need Call or the parentheses around the list of arguments.

Coding Functions

You can write your own general-purpose function procedures that are not tied to specific events. You can call these functions from any Visual Basic application just as you can subroutine procedures. Function procedures work just like subroutine procedures in every way; you call them from elsewhere in the code. Unlike subroutine procedures, however, a function procedure always returns a value.

If you run across a needed calculation and Visual Basic has no built-in function equivalent, you can write your own function that returns that calculated value. When you call the function, you must do something with the returned value. You cannot put a function call on a line by itself as you can with a subroutine. If CalcTax() is a function, you cannot call the function like this:

```
CalcTax ()   ' Problem!
```

The CalcTax() function will return a value and you must do something with that value. Therefore, you'll usually assign the return value like this:

```
lblAmt.Caption = CalcTax()    ' Okay
```

You can also use the function call inside an expression, like this:

```
curAmount = Estimate * .2 + CalcTax() * .14
```

> You should code as though the function call becomes its return value. In other words, when `CalcTax()` returns from doing its job, the return value temporarily replaces the function call inside the expression.

The functions that you write aren't quite as built-in as Visual Basic's built-in functions, but they behave the same way. Your functions never become part of VB's repertoire, but you can put them in any module that needs to access them. Over time, you will write many general-purpose function and subroutine procedures and you might want to keep a module library of common routines that you'll use throughout different applications. To use one of the procedures that you write, you can add that procedure's module to whatever application needs the procedure.

You will write new function procedures the same way you write new subroutine procedures (with Tools | Add Procedure or by typing the first function procedure's line at the end of the module). Use the `Function` keyword in place of `Sub`. The following statements would code the beginning and ending statements from a `CalcTax()` function:

```
Public Function CalcTax () As Single
End Function
```

You'll notice something extra on that function's opening statement: `As Single`. In addition to using the `Function` keyword, you must also specify the function's return value datatype in the function's opening declaration line. Therefore, this `CalcTax()` function returns a single-precision datatype.

Listing 13.2 contains a function that computes the postage for a letter or package using the following rules:

1. The post office charges 32 cents for 8 ounces or less.

2. Add 15 cents for each 4 ounces above the first 8.

3. The weight cannot exceed 24 ounces.

The function's code assumes that the letter or package weight appears in a text box control named `txtWeight.Text`. In addition, the weight must appear as ounces. Therefore, any application that uses this function must make sure these conditions are met before calling the function.

13

The function procedure in Listing 13.2 uses no arguments. You'll learn how to code arguments in the next section.

LISTING 13.2. CALCULATING POSTAGE WITH A FUNCTION PROCEDURE.

```
 1: Public Function Postage() As Currency
 2: ' Calculate postage based on the
 3: ' weight of a letter or package
 4: Dim curPostHold As Currency
 5: Dim intWeight As Integer
 6: Dim intPress As Integer   ' MsgBox() return
 7:
 8: ' Grab the weight from the text box
 9: ' and convert to number for comparison
10: intWeight = Val(txtWeight.Text)
11:
12: Select Case intWeight
13: Case Is <= 8:  curPostHold = 0.32
14:
15: Case Is <= 12: curPostHold = 0.47
16:
17: Case Is <= 16: curPostHold = 0.62
18:
19: Case Is <= 20: curPostHold = 0.77
20:
21: Case Is <= 24: curPostHold = 0.92
22:
23: Case Is > 24:
24: intPress = MsgBox("Weight is too heavy", _
25: vbExclamation, "Error")
26: curPostHold = 0#
27: End Select
28:
29: Postage = curPostHold    ' Return the value
30: End Function
```

Listing 13.2 demonstrates the way you return the value from a function. There is no Postage variable declared, yet the second-to-last line assigns a value to Postage. Postage is the name of the function, not a variable. Inside a function procedure, when you assign a value to the function's name, the function uses that value as the return value. This function doesn't actually end until the End Function statement is reached, but the return value is set right before the terminating statement.

> If you ever need to terminate a subroutine or function from somewhere in
> the body of the routine instead of at its normal termination point, use the
> `Exit Sub` or `Exit Function` statement. Be sure to set a return value of some
> kind to the function name before terminating a function because the func-
> tion requires a return value.

Coding Arguments

Variables that are local to a procedure can only be used inside that procedure. Variables
declared inside a module's `general` section are global to the module and available
throughout the entire module. Variables declared with `Public` instead of `Dim` inside the
`general` section are global to the entire project.

You've seen throughout the first part of this book that you should avoid global variables
as much as possible and use only local variables. If, however, you only use local variables but you write lots of small procedures (as you should), how can the procedures
share data? If all the data is local, a called procedure has no access to the calling procedure's data. As you probably suspect, you'll share data through argument lists. When one
procedure must call another procedure, and the called procedure needs information from
the calling procedure, the calling procedure can send that information inside the argument list.

Suppose one procedure calculates a value and a second procedure must use that value in
a different calculation before displaying a result on the form. You need to know how to
pass local data from the procedure that defines the local variable to other procedures that
need to work with that value.

When you call a built-in function, you pass one or more arguments to the function so
that the function's internal code has data to work with. When you call your own subroutine and function procedures, you also can pass arguments to them. The arguments
are nothing more than the passing procedure's local variables that the receiving procedure needs to work with.

After you pass data, that data is still local to the original passing procedure, but the
receiving procedure has the opportunity to work with those values for the time of the
procedure execution. Depending on how you pass the arguments, the receiving procedure
might even be able to change those values so that when the passing procedure regains
control, its local variables have been modified by the called procedure.

13

The passed argument name (or names) doesn't have to be the same as you used in the receiving procedure. Therefore, you might call a subroutine with Call CalcIt(X) and the subroutine begins with this declaration line: Public Sub CalcIt(Y As Int). Although in this case both X and Y refer to the same value, the receiving subroutine procedure uses a different name from the passing procedure. The only argument list requirements are that the calling and receiving argument lists must match in number of arguments and they must match in datatype order.

You must declare the receiving argument list's datatypes for each argument. If you pass or receive more than one argument, separate the arguments with commas. The following statement passes the three values to a subroutine:

```
Call RecProc(I, J, K)
```

The following statement declares the RecProc() procedure:

```
Public Sub RecProc (I As Integer, J As Integer, K As Single)
```

The calling procedure already knows the datatypes of I, J, and K, but those values are unknown to RecProc(). Therefore, you'll have to code the datatype of each received argument so that the receiving function knows the datatype of each sent argument.

If a subroutine or function procedure is to receive arrays, don't indicate the array subscripts inside the argument list. The following Sub statement defines a general-purpose subroutine procedure that accepts four arrays as arguments:

```
Public Sub WriteData (GNames() As String, CBalc() As Currency,
➡CDate() As Variant, CRegion() As Integer)
```

The built-in UBound() function returns the highest subscript that's defined for any given array. The following statement, which might appear inside the WriteData() subroutine, stores the highest possible subscript for the CNames() array, so the subroutine won't attempt to access an array subscript outside the defined limit:

```
intHighSub = UBound(CNames)
```

Receiving by Reference and by Value

Visual Basic lets you pass arguments two ways: by reference and by value. The way you use them determines whether the receiving procedure can change the arguments so that those changes remain in effect after the calling procedure regains control. If you pass and receive by reference (the default method), the calling procedure's passed local variables may be changed in the receiving procedure. If you pass and receive by value, the calling procedure can access and change its received arguments, but those changes don't retain their effects in the calling procedure.

> Passing by reference is sometimes called passing by address. In some languages, by address and by reference mean two different things, but not in Visual Basic.

When passing by reference, subroutines and functions can always use their received values and also change those arguments. If a receiving procedure changes one of its arguments, the corresponding variable in the calling procedure is also changed. Therefore, when the calling procedure regains control, the value (or values) that the calling procedure sent as an argument to the called subroutine may be different from the time before the call.

NEW TERM *By reference* is a way in which you pass values and allow the called procedure to change those values, also called by address. *By value* is a way in which you pass values and protect the calling procedure's passed data so that the called procedure cannot change the original data.

Arguments are passed by reference, meaning that the passed arguments can be changed by their receiving procedure. If you want to keep the receiving procedure from being able to change the calling procedure's arguments, you must pass the arguments by value. To pass by value, precede any and all receiving argument lists with the ByVal keyword, or enclose the passed arguments in parentheses.

> If you want to be explicit, use the ByRef keyword. Passing by reference is the default method if you don't specify ByRef.

13

It's generally safer to receive arguments by value because the calling procedure can safely assume that its passed values won't be changed by the receiving procedure. Nevertheless, there may be times when you want the receiving procedure to permanently change values passed to it. In such cases, you'll need to receive those arguments by reference.

Listing 13.3 shows two subroutine procedures. One, named Changes(), receives arguments by address. The second procedure, NoChanges(), receives its arguments by value.

Even though both procedures multiply their arguments by two, those changes affect the calling procedure's variables only when Changes() is called but not when NoChanges() is called.

LISTING 13.3. SOME PROCEDURES CAN CHANGE THE SENDING PROCEDURE'S ARGUMENTS.

```
 1: Sub Changes(N As Integer, S As Single)
 2: ' Receives arguments by reference
 3: N = N * 2 ' Double both
 4: S = S * 2 '    arguments
 5: ' When the calling routine regains control,
 6: ' its two local variables will now be twice
 7: ' as much as they were before calling this.
 8: End Sub
 9:
10: Sub NoChanges(ByVal N As Integer, ByVal S As Single)
11: ' Receives arguments by value
12: N = N * 2    ' Double both
13: S = S * 2        '    arguments
14: ' When the calling routine regains control,
15: ' its two local variables will not be
16: ' changed from their original values.
17: End Sub
```

As you can see, Changes() receives its arguments by reference. (Remember that the default passing method is by reference, even if you omit ByRef.) Therefore, when the procedure doubles the arguments, the calling procedure's argument variables change as well.

In NoChanges(), the procedure receives its arguments by value. Therefore, nothing NoChanges() does can change those values in the calling procedure.

Summary

In this lesson you learned how to write programs that are properly structured so that you can more easily and quickly write and debug the code. By coding small and numerous modules, and by putting off details until you're ready to code a procedure that performs a single task (although that task may take a few statements), you'll write code that you can easily debug and modify later.

After you break a program into several procedures, however, you must be careful when you pass arguments to the procedures that need them. The way you pass arguments determines how the passing procedure's argument values change. If you pass by value, the passing procedure's values are protected and always left unchanged, no matter what the called procedure does to them.

Now that you've learned how to write your own procedures, you're ready for Hour 14, "Built-in Functions Save Time," which describes many of Visual Basic's built-in functions that you can use in your own programs.

Q&A

Q I've always coded long procedures and my programs work, so why should I write structured code now?

A If your way works well, the structured way would be working even better. When you test your applications, you must wade through lots of code, searching for problem areas. When you test structured applications, however, you can usually narrow the bug down to one or two small procedures. Making a change to correct the bug rarely affects other procedures, but when your code is in a few long procedures that do lots of work, a change could adversely affect surrounding code.

Q If I'm careful, what does it matter how I receive arguments?

A The method you use to pass and receive arguments, either by reference or by value, doesn't just protect data. Sometimes you want a called procedure to change the calling procedure's argument values. A function procedure can only return a single value, but if you want a function procedure to modify several values, pass those values by reference and then make the function procedure (or even the subroutine procedure) modify each of those values. When the calling procedure regains control, the passed arguments will hold values changed by the called procedure.

Workshop

The quiz questions and exercises are provided for your further understanding. See Appendix B for the answers.

Quiz

1. What are two reasons for writing structured programs?
2. True or false: Structured code is useful for getting to code details as fast as possible.
3. True or false: You can write your own functions.
4. What is wrong with the following subroutine declaration?
   ```
   Public Subroutine DoItSub ()
   ```
5. When is the `Call` keyword optional in subroutine calling?

13

6. The following code appears in a form module's general section. Is X a local, module-global, or project-global variable? What about Y? Would your answers be different if this appeared in an external module as opposed to a form module?

```
Dim X As Integer
Public Y As Integer
```

7. What is wrong with the following function declaration?

```
Public Function DoCalc(intAge As Integer, strCoNames(45) As String)
```

8. Why does the called procedure need to know the datatypes for passed values?

9. How does one procedure get local data from a calling procedure?

10. Which keyword is optional: ByRef or ByVal?

Exercises

1. Write a general-purpose standard function procedure that accepts a numeric integer argument and returns that argument multiplied by 10.

2. Write a standard subroutine procedure that accepts three single-precision arguments and displays those three values in labels named lblSng1, lblSng2, and lblSng3.

Built-In Functions Save Time

This lesson gives you a reference for many of the most common built-in functions. You will learn about the numeric, string, time, date, and formatting functions that Visual Basic supplies. By using the built-in functions Visual Basic gives you, you won't have to spend a lot of time writing your own code for common routines. For example, you never need to write code that extracts a square root because Visual Basic supplies a built-in square root function for you.

As with all functions, the built-in functions return values and, optionally, accept arguments that you pass to the functions when you call the functions. Some built-in functions don't accept arguments; although the style is inconsistent, you don't specify the parentheses after the built-in function names that don't accept arguments. Without the parentheses, it is easy to confuse the function with a regular Visual Basic statement. Fortunately, only a few built-in functions don't take arguments.

The highlights of this hour include

- Which numeric functions exist
- How to use string functions to manipulate strings
- Which date and time functions let you modify date and time values
- How the data-testing functions inspect data
- When to convert data from one type to another with the data-conversion functions
- How to format your data to look the way you want it to look

Many Functions

Many built-in mathematical functions exist, including data conversion functions, common math functions, trigonometric and logarithmic functions, and formatting functions. The next few sections explain how to use many of the more common kinds of numeric functions you might need to use in your own applications.

Numeric Functions

Visual Basic includes several numeric functions you can use to help calculate expressions. To start with, you might as well learn the square root function described in the previous section. Here is the format of Visual Basic's built-in square root function:

```
Sqr(argument)
```

Remember that a function accepts one or more arguments and returns a value based on the argument list. Figure 14.1 illustrates the Sqr() function. The function accepts a single argument and returns the square root of that argument.

FIGURE 14.1.

The Sqr() function returns the square of the argument you pass to it.

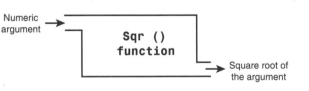

Suppose you wanted to store the square root of a builder's measurement in a control named txtSqrMeas. You could do so like this:

```
txtSqrMeas.Text = Sqr(sngMeas)
```

Table 14.1 lists several additional mathematical functions you can use.

TABLE 14.1. COMMON BUILT-IN NUMERIC FUNCTIONS.

Function	Description
Abs()	Returns the argument's absolute value. The absolute value is the positive equivalent of the argument, so the absolute value of both -87 and 87 is 87. Use absolute values for distance calculations and weight differences because such values must always be positive.
Atn()	Returns the argument's arc tangent, expressed in radians. To compute the arc tangent in degrees (or any other trigonometric function), multiply the argument by pi (approximately 3.14159) and then divide by 180.
Cos()	Returns the argument's cosine value, expressed in radians.
Exp()	Returns the argument's natural logarithm base.
Len()	Returns the number of memory characters required to hold the argument.
Log()	Returns the argument's natural logarithm.
Sin()	Returns the argument's sine value, expressed in radians.
Tan()	Returns the argument's tangent value, expressed in radians.

NEW TERM *Pi* (π) is a mathematical value that approximates 3.14159 and is used in many area calculations.

You don't need scientific, logarithmic, or trigonometric functions? That's fine, but many financial calculations use such functions, so these routines are not just for highly scientific calculations. Visual Basic will keep them ready in case you do need them.

If you use a retail version of VB, search Visual Basic's online help for Derived Math Functions, which provides an exhaustive list of built-in numeric functions.

String Functions

Unlike the numeric functions, Visual Basic's string functions return a string and often work with one or more string arguments. Table 14.2 lists several of the more common string functions you'll work with. The string functions accept controls as well as variables, literals, and expressions.

14

Table 14.2 includes the argument format because some string functions require multiple arguments.

TABLE 14.2. COMMON BUILT-IN STRING FUNCTIONS.

Function	Description
Chr(int)	Returns the ASCII character that matches the numeric argument.
LCase(str)	Returns the argument in all lowercase letters. If any character in the argument is already lowercase, no change takes place for that character.
Left(str, int)	Returns the far-left int characters from the string argument.
Len(str)	Returns the number of characters in the string. (Notice that Len() works on numeric arguments as well.) Also, Len() doesn't return a string even though Len() works with string arguments.
LTrim(str)	Returns the string argument, with any leading spaces trimmed off.
Mid(str, intStart [, intLen])	Returns a substring of the string argument, starting with the character at intStart and continuing until the entire string is extracted or until the optional intLen characters have been extracted. Mid() is called the midstring function because it can return the middle portion of a string.
Right(str, int)	Returns the far-right int characters from the string argument.
RTrim(str)	Returns the string argument, with any trailing spaces trimmed off.
Str()	Converts its numeric argument to a string with the numeric digits in the string.
UCase(str)	Returns the argument in all uppercase letters. If any character in the argument is already uppercase, no change takes place for that character.

NEW TERM   A *substring* is part of a string.

Suppose you want to determine whether a string variable's value will fit inside a text box before you attempt to assign the string to the Text Box control (assume that the text box doesn't have AutoSize set to True). If the text box is large enough to hold 20 characters, the following If statement fragment will be True if the string fits in the text box:

```
If (Len(strVar) <= 20) Then     ' String fits
```

Suppose you need to compare two password string values. Given that the user may have entered the password in all uppercase or a case mixture, the following code tests the stored password against one entered in a string variable, and the code uses UCase() to ensure that they compare with the same case matches:

```
If UCase(strUser) = UCase(strPassword) Then
' This If leg is true if the passwords match
```

The LTrim() function is often useful for trimming the leading blank from strings you make from numbers. For example, Str(123) returns the string literal " 123" (notice the leading blank). Sometimes, when writing certain kinds of files, you need to write strings of data instead of numbers and Str() comes in handy. If, however, you need to strip off the leading blank, you can embed Str() within LTrim() to return the string digits without the leading blank, like this: LTrim(Str(123)).

Left() returns the left part of a string or control value that Visual Basic converts to a string. Therefore, the following stores only the first five characters from the string argument into strAns:

```
strAns = Left(txtUser.Text, 5)
```

Whereas Left() returns the left part, Right() returns the right part of a string. Mid() can return the middle part of a string. Therefore, the following expression becomes "der" when Mid() returns the middle three letters: Mid("Federal", 3, 3). Because of the optional third argument, Mid() works like the Right() function if you omit the third argument because Mid() returns all characters from the starting position to the end of the string if you don't put the third argument inside Mid()'s argument list.

A Mid STATEMENT?

Visual Basic includes both a Mid() function and a Mid statement. The difference is subtle, so you should understand how the Mid()s compare. Mid is a statement if Mid appears on the left side of an assignment. The Mid() statement replaces part of a string with another value.

14

> If the string variable named strSentence holds "I flew home", you can replace the verb flew with rode, like this: Mid(strSentence, 3, 4) = "rode". If you omit the third argument from this Mid statement, Visual Basic will use as many characters as possible to fill the string. In this example, the third argument does nothing but clarify the programmer's intent because the replacement string is four characters long. If you were to specify a third argument value less than 4, Mid() replaces fewer characters.

Date and Time Functions

Applications need to be able to access and work with date and time values. Many applications are written for business and scientific purposes, where recording the date and time of the program run is vital to the success of the project. Visual Basic includes the date and time functions described in Table 14.3.

> The date- and time-returning functions Date, Now, and Time don't require arguments, so they don't use parentheses.

TABLE 14.3. DATE AND TIME FUNCTIONS.

Function	Description
Date	Returns the current date.
DateSerial(intYr, intMo, intDay)	Returns an internal date value for the three arguments.
DateAdd(strIntrvl, intN, dteDate)	Adds the intN value to the date specified by dteDate for the given strIntrvl.
DateDiff(strIntrvl, dte1, dte2)	Returns the number of time intervals (specified by strIntrvl) between the two dates.
DatePart(strIntrvl, dteDate)	Returns the strIntrvl portion of the dteDate.
Now	Returns the current date and time in the date format.
Time	Returns the current time.
Timer	Returns the number of seconds since midnight.
TimeSerial(hour, min, sec)	Returns the current date and time in the internal date format for the time specified.

You may think that Table 14.3 is ambiguous in places, but Visual Basic gives you many ways to manipulate and test date and time values. You'll probably use a limited set, depending on your data needs. Most of the time your application simply needs to know the current date or time to display the date or time on a form or report. Use Date, Time, or Now (for both) to return the current date, time, or both.

> The returned value is the internal Date datatype format Visual Basic uses for variables declared as Date datatype variables. You can assign and work with dates returned from Date, Time, and Now by assigning them to and from variables declared as Date datatype variables. When you print the value, Visual Basic respects your computer's International Windows settings and prints the date or time in your country's format. You can use the Format() function described in this lesson's final section to format the date into a form you need.

The serial date and time functions let you convert a three-part date into a date that matches the internal Date datatype so that you can work with variables that hold dates you specify. For example, if you want to store the value July 18, 1998, in a Date datatype variable named dteDue, you can do so like this:

```
dteDue = DateSerial(1998, 7, 18)
```

If the year falls within the 20th century, you can omit the 19 before the year. If you try to store a value that doesn't correspond to a proper date or time value, the IsDate() function (described in the next section) will return False to let you know that a bad date or time appears in the Date datatype variable.

In a similar manner, TimeSerial() returns an internal Date datatype when you specify the three time parts, like this:

```
dteTimePaid = TimeSerial(14, 32, 25)   ' Stores 2:32:25 P.M.
```

The time works on a 24-hour clock, so 14 represents 2:00 in the afternoon. The Date datatype holds dates, times, and date and time values, so your Date variable will hold whatever date or time combination you send.

> The DateSerial() and TimeSerial() functions let you specify expressions inside their argument lists to manipulate specific date and time portion values. For example, the expression DateSerial(1998, 7, 18-31) returns the date 31 days before July 18, 1998. Therefore, you don't have to worry about the number of days in a month or anything else. Such calculations are useful for aging accounts receivable balances. Use an expression inside TimeSerial() to eliminate worry with going past midnight, as in this example: TimeSerial(14-20, 30, 16). Such an expression represents 20 hours before 2:30:16 p.m.

14

`DateAdd()`, `DateDiff()`, and `DatePart()` require a special string interval value that comes from Table 14.4. The interval tells these date functions how to process the date argument.

TABLE 14.4. DATE AND TIME INTERVAL STRING VALUES.

Interval	Description
h	Hour
d	Day
m	Month
n	Minute
q	Quarter
s	Second
y	Day of year
w	Weekday
ww	Week
yyyy	Year

Suppose the user entered a date value into a control or variable and you needed to work with a date 30 days after that date to remind the user after 30 days that a project is due. You can add 30 days to a date value without worrying about days in each month or year changes (as would happen if the date fell in late December) by specifying the following expression that adds 20 days to the date and returns another date 20 days in the future: `DateAdd("d", 20, dteUserDate)`. You can subtract 20 days using a negative interval. Suppose you want the date one year from the user's date? Code this expression anywhere you need the future date in a year and you don't have to worry about leap year: `DateAdd("yyyy", 1, dteUserDate)`.

The `DateDiff()` function uses Table 14.4's interval string value to return the number of intervals between two dates. For example, the following expression returns the number of weeks between two date values: `dateDiff("ww", dteUser1, dteUser2)`.

Use Table 14.4's interval value and the `DatePart()` function to obtain the integer number that represents the specified value. You can determine the day of the week (assuming that the week starts with Sunday being 1) that you were born by coding this expression: `DatePart("d", dteUserBDay)`.

Visual Basic includes three additional functions that strip off the day, month, and year values from a `Date` datatype variable: `Day()`, `Month()`, and `Year()`. If you want to work with the current year, you can strip off the year from the current date like this:

```
intYear = Year(Date)    ' Get this year
```

The `Timer` function (see line 6 of Listing 14.1) is useful for determining the amount of time that has passed between two time values. `Timer` requires no arguments or parentheses. To use `Timer`, save the value of `Timer` in a variable and when you are ready to know how much time has elapsed since the first time, you can compare or save the current value of `Timer` again. Listing 14.1 demonstrates the `Timer` function that tests your arithmetic speed.

LISTING 14.1. USING `Timer` TO TIME THE USER'S MATH SKILLS.

```
 1: Dim lngBefore As Long
 2: Dim lngAfter As Long
 3: Dim lngTimeDiff As Long
 4: Dim strAns As String
 5:
 6: lngBefore = Timer    ' Save seconds since midnight
 7: Do
 8: strAns = InputBox("What is 150 + 235?", "Hurry")
 9: Loop Until Val(strAns) = 385
10:
11: lngAfter = Timer     ' Save seconds since midnight now
12:
13:   ' The difference between the stored time values
14:   ' is how many seconds the user took to answer
15: lngTimeDiff = lngAfter - lngBefore
16: MsgBox ("That took you only " & Str(lngTimeDiff) & _
17: " seconds!")
```

The code uses the two saved `Timer` values to determine how long the user took to answer. If the user doesn't answer correctly, the time keeps ticking. If the user happens to run this right before midnight, the results will not be accurate because of the day change.

Data-Testing Functions

The `Is...()` functions are called the data inspection functions. When you store a value in a variable declared as a `Variant` datatype variable, the data inspection functions can test that variable to see what kind of datatype the variable can be. The data inspection functions are especially useful for working with user entries in controls and variables. Table 14.5 describes the data inspection functions.

14

NEW TERM   *Data inspection functions* are functions that inspect data and return information about the datatype.

TABLE 14.5. DATA INSPECTION FUNCTIONS FOR TESTING DATATYPES.

Function	Description
IsDate()	True if the argument can convert to a Date datatype.
IsEmpty()	True if the argument has not been initialized with any value since the argument's declaration. IsEmpty() works with variable arguments only, not controls.
IsNull()	True if the argument holds Null (such as an empty string) and works for controls as well as variables.
IsNumeric()	True if the argument can convert to a Numeric datatype.

Notice that Visual Basic supports no IsString() function. If you want to test for a String value, you must use a different kind of function. If you need more specific information about a datatype, you can use the VarType() function, which returns a value that indicates the exact datatype an argument can be. If you expect the user to enter an integer, for example, you can test with VarType() to see if the argument is a valid integer. Use Table 14.6 to determine if the return type is your expected datatype.

TABLE 14.6. THE VarType() RETURN VALUES.

Return	Named Literal	Describes
0	vbEmpty	Empty and not initialized argument
1	vbNull	Invalid data or a null string argument
2	vbInteger	Integer argument
3	vbLong	Long argument
4	vbSingle	Single argument
5	vbDouble	Double argument
6	vbCurrency	Currency argument
7	vbDate	Date argument
8	vbString	String argument
9	vbObject	Object argument
10	vbError	Error argument
11	vbBoolean	Boolean argument
12	vbVariant	Variant argument

Return	Named Literal	Describes
13	vbDataObject	Data Access Object (DAO) argument; an advanced database value such as a field or record
14	vbDecimal	Decimal argument
17	vbByte	Byte argument
8192+int	vbArray	Array argument of the type specified by the int addition to 8192

If VarType(dataVal) returns a number greater than 8192, subtract 8192 from the return value to arrive at the datatype (such as 12 for a Variant datatype). A return value of 8194, therefore, represents an integer array.

Data Conversion Functions

After you determine what kind of value a Variant variable or a control holds, you can convert that argument to its associated datatype. The conversion functions shown in Table 14.7 describe the conversions you can perform.

TABLE 14.7. THE DATA CONVERSION FUNCTIONS.

Function	Description
Asc()	Converts its string argument to the ASCII number that matches the first (or only) character in the string
CCur()	Converts the argument to an equivalent Currency datatype
CDbl()	Converts the argument to an equivalent Double datatype
CInt()	Rounds its fractional argument to the next highest integer
CLng()	Converts the argument to an equivalent Long datatype
CSng()	Converts the argument to an equivalent Single datatype
CStr()	Converts the argument to an equivalent String datatype
CVar()	Converts the argument to an equivalent Variant datatype
Fix()	Truncates the fractional portion
Int()	Rounds the number down to the integer less than or equal to its arguments
Hex()	Converts its numeric argument to a hexadecimal (base-16) value
Oct()	Converts its numeric argument to an octal (base-8) value

14

NEW TERM *Hexadecimal* is the base-16 number system. *Octal* is the base-8 number system.

Normally, the following assignment stores `.1428571` in a label named `lblValue`:

```
lblValue.Caption = (1 / 7)
```

The following, however, adds precision to the label for a more accurate calculation to assign `.142857142857143` to the label:

```
lblValue.Caption = CDbl(1 / 7)
```

Use these conversion functions when you need the exact datatype for more precision in calculations or controls.

Format Function

Visual Basic cannot read your mind, so it doesn't know how you want numbers displayed in your applications. Although Visual Basic sometimes displays none, one, or two decimal places for currency values, you'll almost always want those currency values displayed to two decimal places with a dollar sign and commas when appropriate.

As with the date and time functions, if you've set your computer's international settings to a country other than the United States, your formatted currency values may differ from those shown here. (This book uses U.S. settings.) Some countries use commas to indicate decimal places, whereas the United States uses the decimal point.

`Format()` returns a `Variant` (convertible to a `String`) datatype formatted to look the way you want. `Format()` doesn't change a value, but `Format()` changes the way a value looks. Here is the format of `Format()`:

```
Format(Expression, strFormat)
```

Often, you'll assign the result of `Format()` to other variables and controls. Generally, you'll perform all needed calculations on numeric values before formatting those values. After you've performed the final calculations, you'll then format the values to `String` (or `Variant`) datatypes and display the resulting answers as needed.

Expression can be a variable, an expression, or a constant. `strFormat` must be a value from Table 14.8. Visual Basic contains many format strings in addition to the ones shown in Table 14.8. You can even develop your own programmer-defined format strings, although this book doesn't go into those.

TABLE 14.8. THE strFormat VALUES.

strFormat	Description
"Currency"	Ensures that a dollar sign ($) appears before the formatted value, followed by a thousands separator (a decimal point or comma for values over 999; your country setting determines whether the thousands separator is a comma or a decimal). Two decimal places will always show. Visual Basic displays negative values in parentheses.
"Fixed"	Displays at least one digit before and two digits following the decimal point, with no thousands separator.
"General Number"	Displays the number with no thousands separator.
"Medium Time"	Displays the time in 12-hour format and the a.m. or p.m. indicator.
"On/Off"	Displays On if the value contains a nonzero or True value and displays Off if the value contains zero or a False value.
"Percent"	Displays the number, multiplied by 100, and adds the percent sign to the right of the number.
"Scientific"	Displays numbers in scientific notation.
"Short Time"	Displays the time in 24-hour format.
"True/False"	Displays True if the value contains a nonzero or True value, and displays False if the value contains zero or a False value.
"Yes/No"	Displays Yes if the value contains a nonzero or True value and displays No if the value contains zero or a False value.

YOU'LL RARELY NEED FORMAT CODES

If the predefined formats from Table 14.8 don't match the format you need, you can define your own using special formatting codes. This lesson would be twice as long as it is if all the programmer-defined formats were taught here. The good news is that, when you do define your own formats, you'll almost always use just a combination of the pound sign and zeros to format the values you need.

Each pound sign in the format indicates where a digit goes, and the zero indicates that you want either leading or trailing zeros. The following assignment displays the value of Weight to three decimal places:

```
lblMeas.Caption = Format(Weight, "######.000")
```

You could also request that no decimal point should appear by formatting a fractional value such as Weight, and Visual Basic will round the number as needed to fit the target format. The following assignment displays Weight with no decimal places shown on the screen:

```
lblMeas.Caption = Format(Weight, "######")
```

14

Listing 14.2 contains a series of formatting function calls that convert numeric and logical values to formatted `Variant` datatypes that you can display.

LISTING 14.2. FORMATTING NUMERIC AND LOGICAL VALUES.

```
 1: Dim FormValue (8) As String
 2: ' Change 12345.678 to $12,345.68
 3: FormValue(1) = Format(12345.678, "Currency")
 4:
 5: ' Change 12345678 to 12345.68
 6: FormValue(2) = Format(12345.678, "Fixed")
 7:
 8: ' Change .52 to 52.00%
 9: FormValue(3) = Format(.52, "Percent")
10:
11: ' Change 1 to Yes
12: FormValue(4) = Format(1, "Yes/No")
13:
14: ' Change 0 to No
15: FormValue(5) = Format(0, "Yes/No")
16:
17: ' Change 1 to True
18: FormValue(6) = Format(1, "True/False")
19:
20: ' Change 0 to False
21: FormValue(7)= Format(0, "True/False")
```

> If you use VB's Professional or Enterprise Editions, you can add the Masked Edit ActiveX control, which lets you specify an edit mask that formats data in a manner similar to `Format()`.

NEW TERM An *edit mask* is a format string, such as `"#,###.##"`, that specifies how you want numeric and string data to appear. For additional information on using special numeric formats, search the online documentation for `User-Defined Numeric Formats` (`Format Function`).

Summary

You now have many new tools for your programming utility belts because you now have a good understanding of Visual Basic's built-in functions. The functions calculate, manipulate strings, work with time and date values, convert data, and format output data. You don't have to add special controls to the toolbox to use the built-in functions because Visual Basic's programming language supports all these functions automatically.

Now that you've mastered the functions, you can learn how to access large amounts of data to work with. Hour 15, "Visual Basic Database Basics," describes how to use the Data control so that your application can write and read data to and from external database files.

Q&A

Q Why would I want to perform date arithmetic?

A Date arithmetic is useful for determining the exact date (or time) after another period of time goes by. For example, suppose you need to know the exact day that three months from today's date falls on. You cannot just add 3 or 90 (3 times 30 days) to a date value; not only can you not add to a Date datatype, but even if you could, such math doesn't take into account leap years, number of days in the months, and year changes. By using DateAdd() and DatePart(), you can perform such calculations with date values and be assured that the result will fall on a valid date.

Q If Timer returns the number of seconds since midnight, how can I use Timer to determine how much time has passed for a given task?

A The key to using Timer is to save the value of Timer before the task begins and then save the value of Timer after the task ends. You then can subtract the values to determine how many seconds elapsed between the two tasks. A single Timer reading would not be very beneficial by itself, but the two before and after values can be very helpful indeed.

Workshop

The quiz questions and exercises are provided for your further understanding. See Appendix B for the answers.

Quiz

1. What preparation must you do before the built-in functions are available to you?

2. What is the value stored in each of the following assignment statements?

```
a. strA = Left("abcdefg", 3)

b. strB = Right("abcdefg", 3)

c. strC = Mid("abcdefg", 2, 3)

d. strD = Mid("abcdefg", 2)
```

14

3. Is the following `Mid()` a function or a statement?

   ```
   Mid(strTest, 2, 4) = "abcd"
   ```

4. Is the following `Mid()` a function or a statement?

   ```
   strAns = Mid(strTest, 2, 4)
   ```

5. What is the value stored in each of the following assignment statements?

   a. `intA = Int(20.34)`

   b. `intB = CInt(20.34)`

   c. `intC = Fix(-2.8)`

   d. `intD = Int(-2.8)`

6. What value appears in `varAns` after the following assignment?

   ```
   varAns = Val(LTrim(Str("10")))
   ```

7. What is the 24-hour time for 12:56 p.m.?

8. What is a thousands separator?

9. True or false: You must use `Format()` to properly format date and time values because the built-in date and time functions cannot interpret your International settings.

10. True or false: `Now` returns information for both the current date and the current time.

Exercises

1. Write a program that stores the 256 ASCII characters (from ASCII 0 to ASCII 255) in a string array that's defined to hold 256 characters.

2. Write a subroutine procedure that asks the user for the time that he clocked into work and then for the time he clocked out. Display, in three labels, the total number of seconds worked, the total number of minutes worked, and the total number of hours worked.

3. Write a subroutine procedure that asks the user for her birthday. If the user entered a valid date (check to make sure and keep asking if the user did not enter a date), display a message box telling the user how many years until she reaches the retirement age of 65. If the user is older than 65, congratulate her on a long life!

Hour 15

Visual Basic Database Basics

Rarely do Visual Basic programmers use the file-related controls you see on the toolbox, such as the File List Box control. More often, programmers use the File Open and File Save dialog boxes that you can produce from the Common Dialog Box control (refer to Hour 12, "Dialog Box Basics"). The dialog box gives users the capability to select files and link to other networked computers and files.

You must make additional file-related decisions besides which controls to use to select files. In addition to the controls you display for the user, you must decide if you want to write file-access routines yourself or use database controls that come with Visual Basic. The file routines are tedious, old-fashioned, and difficult to debug; the database controls are sometimes overkill, especially if you don't use an external database or if your application uses only a small data file.

This lesson gives you the best of both worlds. You'll learn how to write file-access routines for small file-related data, and you'll master the database control as well. Even if you don't work with files at the file-access level, the first part of this lesson prepares you for the concepts you need to use the Data control.

The highlights of this hour include

- What file terms you need to master
- When you open and close files
- How to write to a file
- How to read from a file
- When to use the Data control
- What bound controls offer
- How to use the Data Form Wizard

File Concepts

If you've collected data from the user and stored that data in variables and arrays, you can save the data to the disk for later retrieval. Also, you can access disk files from within Visual Basic for product inventory codes, amounts, customer balances, and whatever else your program needs from the long-term data file storage. Visual Basic supports several ways in which you can store information to and retrieve information from disk files. This section introduces several new file-related terms.

Several database access controls exist that read and write the data you've put in databases, using products such as Microsoft Access and Paradox. Even though these controls provide more power and ease than you can get by programming alone, you'll still need to understand fundamental disk access routines. After you learn the more primitive disk access statements taught in the next several sections, you will more quickly understand the internal workings of the Data control that the last part of this lesson teaches.

NEW TERM   A *file* is a collection of related data as well as programs that you buy and write, documents from your word processor, and data that your applications write to disk.

Although you already know what a file is, this lesson works with data files, and it often helps to understand specific terminology as soon as possible. Actually, your application can read any file whether or not the file is a data file, but the file's format determines how you'll read that file, as you'll learn here. Generally, you'll use Visual Basic to create and access data and text files stored on the disk.

Although you can use Visual Basic to write utility programs that read other kinds of files such as system and program files, this book doesn't cover such file I/O.

NEW TERM A *data file* holds data on the disk.

The files discussed in this lesson are data files that can be textual or stored in a database format. Every file is stored under a unique filename to its folder (often called a directory) and disk drive. There can't be two or more files with the same filename unless the files reside in different folders or on different disks.

Data files can take on all kinds of formats. Generally, newcomers to Visual Basic should stick with data files that are textual in nature. Reading and writing text files is rather simple when you use standard statements that have existed in BASIC-like languages for many years. After you learn these fundamental file statements, you can begin to use more advanced database files to add power to your applications.

Text files are readable by virtually any kind of program, and virtually any program can produce text files. Sometimes, text files are called *ASCII files* because text files consist of strings of ASCII characters, as opposed to *binary files*, which are only readable by special programs and system utilities.

Before Visual Basic can access a file, you or the user will have to direct Visual Basic to the exact location on the exact disk where the file is stored. If your user is selecting a file, you can display the File Open dialog box to give the user the ability to easily change drives, folders, and filenames. When your program accesses a file that the user doesn't know about, such as a data file that holds temporary program data, your program will have to supply the drive, folder, and filename.

Opening Files

The Open statement performs various tasks such as locating a file, making sure the file exists if needed, and creating some folder entries that manage the file while it's open. A Visual Basic program always has to open a file, using Open, before the program can read or write data to the file (unless you use the Data control described later in this lesson).

 Think of the Open statement as doing for Visual Basic what an open file drawer does for you when you want to retrieve a file from a filing cabinet. The Open statement locates the file and makes the file available to Visual Basic.

Here is Open's format:

```
Open strFileName [For Mode] As [#]intFileNumber
```

strFileName must be a string value or string variable that holds a filename. The file-name must reside on the default drive or folder unless you specify the full path to the file in *strFileName*. Visual Basic includes a CurDir() function that returns the current directory folder as a string; you can append this folder name or specify the full path inside the *strFileName* string argument.

The *Mode* value must be a named value from Table 15.1. Visual Basic supports additional mode values, but this book doesn't cover the more advanced or esoteric *Mode* values. The Mode tells Visual Basic exactly what your program expects to do with the file once Visual Basic opens it.

TABLE 15.1. THE Open STATEMENT'S Mode VALUES.

Mode	Description
Append	Tells Visual Basic that your program needs to write to the end of the file if it already exists. If the file doesn't exist, Visual Basic creates the file so that your program can write data to the file.
Input	Tells Visual Basic that your program needs to read from the file. If the file doesn't exist, Visual Basic issues an error message. As long as you use a file-selection frame properly, Visual Basic will never issue an error because the file-selection frame forces the user to select a file or cancel the selection operation.
Output	Tells Visual Basic that your program needs to write to the file. If the file doesn't exist, Visual Basic creates it. If the file does exist, Visual Basic first erases the existing file and creates a new one under the same name, thereby replacing the original one.

The pound sign (#) is optional, although most Visual Basic programmers specify it out of habit (some previous versions of the BASIC language required the pound sign). The *intFileNumber* value represents a number from 1 to 255 and associates the open file with that number. After you open a file successfully (assuming that there are no errors such as a floppy disk not being inserted in the drive bay), the rest of the program uses file I/O commands and functions to access the file. The file number stays with the file until you issue a Close command (see the next section) that releases *intFileNumber* and makes the number available to other files.

> The file number is sometimes called the file *channel*.

As with all DOS and Windows file descriptions, you can specify the drive, directory, and filename using uppercase or lowercase characters.

If your application uses multiple files, you can open more than one file simultaneously within a single application. Each command that accesses one of the files directs its activity toward a specific file using that file's *intFileNumber*. The following Open statement creates and opens a data file on the disk drive and associates the file to file number 1:

```
Open "d:\data\myfile.dat" For Output As #1
```

If you knew that the file already existed and you needed to add to that data file, you could use the Append mode to add to the file with this Open statement:

```
Open "d:\data\myfile.dat" For Append As #1
```

> As you can see, the Open statement's mode prepares the file for the type of processing your application will perform.

One Visual Basic program can have more than one file open at the same time. If the #1 *intFileNumber* argument were in use by another file that you had opened earlier in the application, you could assign the open file to a different number like this:

```
Open "d:\data\myfile.dat" For Append As #5
```

Any currently unused *intFileNumber* works; you can't associate more than one file at a time to the same *intFileNumber* value.

The following Open statement opens the same file for input if another application needs to use the data:

```
Open "d:\data\myfile.dat" For Input As #2
```

Visual Basic supplies a helpful built-in function named FreeFile() that accepts no arguments. FreeFile() returns the next available file number value. For example, if you've used #1 and #2 for two open files already in the application, without closing one of them, the next value returned from FreeFile() will be 3. FreeFile() is most helpful when you write general-purpose subroutine and function procedures that need to open files, and the procedures may be called from more than one place in an application. Each calling location might open a different number of files at the time. Any procedure can determine the value of the next available file number like this:

```
intFileNum = FreeFile()
```

Subsequent Open (and Close) statements could use the file number returned. No matter how many files are open, the procedure will always use the next file number in line to open its file.

The Open command associates files using file numbers with which the rest of the program will access the file. The three *Mode* values determine how Visual Basic uses the file. If you want to write to a file, you can't use the Input mode, and if you want to read from a file, you can't use Output or Append.

Closing Files

The Close statement performs the opposite job from Open. Close closes the file by writing any final data to the file, releasing the file to other applications, and giving the file's number back to your application in case you want to use that number in a subsequent Open statement. Eventually, every program that opens files should close those files. Use Close to close files.

Here are Visual Basic's two formats for Close:

```
Close [[#]intFileNumber] [, ..., [#]intFileNumber]
```

and

```
Close
```

The first Close format closes one or more open files, specifying the files by the file numbers you used to open the files. The pound sign is optional in front of any of the file numbers. The second form of Close closes all files that are currently open. Close closes any open file, no matter what mode you used to open the file.

If you create a file by opening the file with the Output mode, and then close the file, you can reopen the same file in the same program in the Input mode to read the file.

The following statement closes the two open files that were opened and attached to file numbers 1 and 3:

```
Close 1, 3    ' Closes 2 files
```

The following statement closes all files, no matter how many are open:

```
Close    ' Closes ALL files
```

Deleting Files

You can use Visual Basic's `Kill` command to delete one or more files. If you want to delete a file from within a Visual Basic program, follow `Kill` with a string that contains the filename, including an optional disk and drive path. For example, `Kill "C:\Dat\MyData.dat"` deletes the file named `MyData.dat` located on drive `C:` within the `Dat` folder. `Kill` doesn't perform the same action as `Close`; `Close` puts the file away in a safe area and releases the file from its I/O link; `Kill` permanently deletes the file from your disk.

Writing to Files with `Write #`

The `Write #` command is perhaps the easiest command to use for writing data to a file. `Write #` writes data of any datatype to a file. Using corresponding input statements that you'll learn here, you'll be able to read data that you sent to a file with the `Write #` command.

`Write #` lets you write data of any format to any disk file opened in the `Output` or `Append` modes. `Write #` writes strings, numbers, constants, and variables in any and all combinations to a disk file.

Here is the format of `Write #`:

```
Write #intFileNumber [, ExpressionList]
```

`intFileNumber` must be a file number associated with a file opened for output. If you don't specify variables or values to write, `Write #` writes a carriage return and line feed character (an ASCII 13 followed by an ASCII 10) to the file, putting a blank line in the file. If you specify more than one value in `ExpressionList`, Visual Basic writes that data to the file using the following considerations:

- `Write #` separates multiple items on the same line by adding commas between the values.
- `Write #` always adds a carriage return and line feed character to the end of each line written.
- `Write #` adds quotation marks around all strings in the file. The quotation marks make for easy reading of the strings later.
- `Write #` writes date and time values using the following format:
  ```
  #yyyy-mm-dd hh:mm:ss#
  ```

- `Write #` writes `#NULL#` to the file if the data contains a null value (a `VarType()` value of 1).

- `Write #` writes logical values using the following format:
  ```
  #True#
  #False#
  ```

- `Write #` writes nothing when the data value is empty (a `VarType()` of 0), but does separate even empty values with commas if you write more than one value on a single line.

The following statement writes five values to the disk file opened on file number 3:

```
Write #3, intAge, blnChecked, curSal, dteEnd, strName
```

This `Write #` statement writes a single line to the open disk file. The line might look like this:

```
47, #True#, 17423.61, #1-5-1998 14:21:10#, "Angel Sue"
```

If the application contained multiple `Write #` statements, or if the `Write #` statement appeared inside a loop, a new line would write to the file each time `Write #` executed.

> End the `Write #` with a semicolon (;) if you want the next `Write #` to continue on the same line in the data file.

NEW TERM *Append* means to add to the end of something.

If you open a file using the `Append` mode, `Write #` adds to the end of the file. If the file were open in `Output` mode, the first `Write #` would overwrite the file's contents and start a new file.

You can write data to files from variables as well as from controls on the form. Wherever you've got data that needs to be written, Visual Basic's `Write #` command will write that data to a disk file that you've opened.

Listing 15.1 contains a subroutine procedure that accepts four arrays of four different datatypes and writes that array data to a disk file named `Values.dat` opened in the procedure. Notice how you can use a simple `For` loop to write large amounts of data to a data file. The fifth argument sent to the subroutine is assumed to contain the total number of elements defined for the arrays so that the procedure can properly step through the entire array.

LISTING 15.1. WRITING ARRAY DATA TO A FILE.

```
1: Private Sub WriteData (CNames As String, CBalc() As _
2: Currency, CDate() As Variant, CRegion() As Integer)
3: ' Writes array data to a file
4: Dim intCtr As Integer    ' For loop control
5:
6: ' Assumes that each array has the
7: ' same number of elements defined
8: Dim intMax As Integer
9: intMax = UBound(CNames)     ' The maximum subscript
10:
11: ' Write intMax lines to the file
12: ' with four values on each line
13: Open "c:\Mktg.dat" For Output As #1
14: For intCtr = 1 To intMax
15: Write #1, CNames(intCtr), CBalc(intCtr), _
16: CDate(intCtr), CRegion(intCtr)
17: Next intCtr
18: Close #1
19: End Sub
```

Here are six lines from `Mktg.dat` that the program in Listing 15.1 might write:

```
"Adams, H", 123.41, #1998-11-18 11:34:21#, 6
"Enyart, B", 602.99, #21:40:01#, 4
"Powers, W", 12.17, #1999-02-09#, 7
"O'Rourke, P", 8.74, #1998-05-24 14:53:10#, 0
"Grady, 0", 154.75, #1999-10-30 17:23:59#, 6
"McConnell, I", 9502.32, #1999-07-12 08:00:03#, 9
```

The pound signs around the date and time `Variant` values help Visual Basic when you subsequently read the data values back into variant variables. As you can see, the date might have a missing time or the time might have a missing date. `Write #` still writes as much of the date and time as is available within that `Variant` value.

Inputting with `Input #`

`Input #` reads data from files and stores the file data in your program's variables and controls. `Input #` is the mirror image statement to `Write #`. You use `Input #` to read any data that you send to a file with `Write #`. The `Input #` statement reads data into a list of variables or controls. Here is the format of `Input #`:

```
Input #intFileNumber [, ExpressionList]
```

Again, the bottom line to using `Input #` is that `Input #` is the mirror image of the `Write #` statement that produced the file data. When you write a program that must use data from a data file, locate the program's Write # statement that originally created the data file and use that same format for the Input # statement.

The following Input # statement would read one line of values written with Listing 15.1's Write # statement:

```
Input #1, CNames(intCtr), CBalc(intCtr), _
CDate(intCtr), CRegion(intCtr)
```

NEW TERM   A *record* is a row in a file.

When reading data from a file, you can easily cause an error by attempting to read more data than the file holds. For data files that hold data such as customer balances and employee pay values, the number of records varies because you'll add and remove records as transactions take place.

Use the built-in Eof() function to test when input reaches the end of the file. Here is the format of Eof():

```
Eof(intFileNumber)
```

Eof() returns True if the most recent reading of the input file just reached the end of the file, and it returns False if the input file still has data left to be read. Most data input programs loop until the Eof() function returns True. Perhaps the best way to use Eof() is with a Do Until-Loop that follows this general format:

```
Input #1, VariableList       ' Read first record
Do Until (Eof (intFileNumber) = True)
  ' Process the record just read
  Input #1, VariableList    ' Get more data
Loop
```

If there are 0, 1, 10, or 400 records in the file, this format of Do Until will keep reading, but will stop as soon as the end of the file is reached. Many programmers often increment an integer counter variable inside the loop to count the number of records read. The counter is useful later if you're reading the file's data into arrays. If you read file data into arrays, be sure to dimension more than enough array elements to hold the maximum number of records expected.

Line Input Records

Line Input # reads data from open data files. Unlike Input #, Line Input # reads each line of data in the file into a string variable. You don't have to specify separate variable names after a Line Input # because Line Input # requires a single string value. Line Input # reads data from any file whose lines end with a carriage return and line feed sequence. (Most file records end this way.)

15

The `Line Input #` command is easy to use for reading entire records into a single variable. Whereas `Input #` reads each record's values individually, `Line Input #` reads an entire record, including all data, commas, quotation marks, and everything else. The string receives the record's contents. Here is the format of `Line Input #`:

```
Line Input #intFileNumber, strVariableName
```

No matter how many record values appear in the file associated with file number 3, the following `Line Input #` statement reads an image of the record into the `String` variable named strARecord:

```
Line Input #3, strARecord
```

Introduction to Database Processing

NEW TERM   A *database system* is a program that organizes, manipulates, retrieves, and reports data.

If you use a database for your data, you can take advantage of Visual Basic's Data control to access the database from within your Visual Basic applications. The Data control makes it easy for you to retrieve data and display values from a database file without using any of Visual Basic's specific file-related commands that you learned about in the first part of this lesson.

An organization's information is more likely stored these days in a database than in a file readable by the file commands you learned about in the previous sections. Nevertheless, the file commands are useful for simple files, especially text files that your Visual Basic application creates and manages. Also, some data files that other applications create don't appear in a database format but in a record format you can read with those file statements. In addition, the file concepts you learned will help you master the Data control faster and appreciate the Data control more because the Data control takes so much work out of your hands by automating database access.

The Data Control

If you use any of the following database applications, you'll be able to write a Visual Basic application that accesses the data within your database without resorting to the file-related commands described earlier in this lesson: Microsoft Access, dBASE, Excel, FoxPro, Lotus, Paradox, and text-based data files.

The Data control makes database access simple.

NEW TERM   A *field* is a column of data inside a file.

A database application manages your data in a record and field format. The database, however, doesn't necessarily store your data in records and fields in a table-like format, but the database makes the data appear to your program in that format. Visual Basic takes advantage of this format and retrieves data in the record and field format no matter how the database physically stores the data.

One challenge when using database access is that you must often describe parts of the database to Visual Basic. Visual Basic cannot magically understand your database structure. When you place the Data control on your form, you'll have to tell the control the structure of your data and tell the Data control which parts of the data to access so that the control can properly retrieve data. For example, by setting appropriate property values, you must tell the Data control the name of your database, the table, and the fields to access.

NEW TERM   A *table* is a logical collection of data in a database. A database might contain several tables.

Some databases, such as Microsoft Access, store all the related database files in a single global file called the *database file*. Inside the database, the individual groups of records and fields are called *tables*. Other database systems, such as dBASE, keep track of a database's data in multiple files. When you use a database such as Microsoft Access, as this lesson does, you must describe both the overall database and the individual table name within the database that the Data control is to use.

This lesson doesn't provide you with a table of Data control property descriptions because too many of the descriptions are database related and too advanced for this discussion. You might not need to know more properties than described in the small data application at the end of this lesson in most cases. You'll probably be surprised at the amount of power the Data control gives you.

Figure 15.1 illustrates a Data control in use. Notice that the Data control works much like a VCR's series of buttons. You can step through the database one record at a time. The control itself doesn't display data. Instead, the control simply lets you regulate the access of data. You'll have to supply other controls, such as labels or text boxes, to display and collect data for the database. In other words, if you want the user to be able to move to a particular record, you'll supply a Data control that the user can push to get the record in the database. Then your application can display the data on the form using label controls.

FIGURE 15.1.

The Data control sends database data to your application.

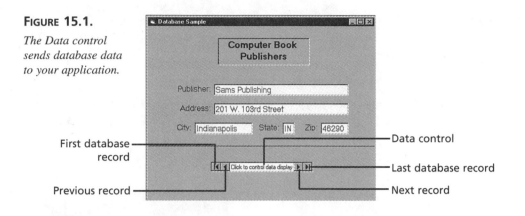

First database record

Previous record

Data control

Last database record

Next record

 NEW TERM   A *bound control* is a control you can link to a database, via the Data control, that displays and updates database records if the user modifies the data in the bound control.

The Data control is a two-way street; not only does it display database data, but your user can modify the data that the Data control displays, and the Data control makes sure that the changes are made to the underlying database through bound controls. If you don't want the user to be able to change data displayed from a Data control, you can use a label and not a text box to display the database data. You can bind several other controls to the Data controls and make the control read-only so that the user cannot change the underlying database.

A Simple but Powerful Application

Figure 15.1's text boxes are bound to the Data control on the form. Therefore, if the user changes the data in any text box that displays a value from the database, the underlying record's field value changes as well. The application is required to do nothing.

Figure 15.1 shows an application that you are about to build. Do you want to be really shocked? The application will contain no code whatsoever. The entire database access and update can be done just with the controls on the form!

> In most database applications, code is required. If the user is to add new records and delete old ones, for example, code is needed. For simple displaying and updating of existing data, however, the Data control, labels, and text boxes can do all the work.

Figure 15.1's book publisher application uses a database that comes with Visual Basic named `Biblio.mdb`. The database is a Microsoft Access database and contains computer book titles and publishers.

Perform these steps to build Figure 15.1's application:

1. Create a new project and name the form `frmData`. Add a caption that says `Database Sample`. Resize the form to a `Height` property of `5775` and a `Width` property of `7170`.

2. Add a label with these properties:

   ```
   Name:                lblAnnounce
   Alignment:           2-Center
   BorderStyle:         1-Fixed Single
   Caption:             Computer Book Publishers
   Font:                Bold 14 points
   Height:              855
   Left:                2160
   Top:                 360
   Width:               2895
   ```

3. Add five additional field labels as follows:
   - **Field 1**

     ```
     Name:                lblPub
     Alignment:           1-Right Justify
     Caption:             Publisher:
     Font:                12 points
     Left:                720
     Top:                 1800
     Width:               1215
     ```

   - **Field 2**

     ```
     Name:                lblAddress
     Alignment:           1-Right Justify
     Caption:             Address:
     ```

```
Font:                   12 points
Left:                   720
Top:                    2400
Width:                  1215
```

- **Field 3**

```
Name:                   lblCity
Alignment:              1-Right Justify
Caption:                City:
Font:                   12 points
Left:                   840
Top:                    3000
Width:                  495
```

- **Field 4**

```
Name:                   lblState
Alignment:              1-Right Justify
Caption:                State:
Font:                   12 points
Left:                   3360
Top:                    3000
Width:                  735
```

- **Field 5**

```
Name:                   lblZip
Alignment:              1-Right Justify
Caption:                Zip:
Font:                   12 points
Left:                   4800
Top:                    3000
Width:                  495
```

4. Before adding the text boxes, add the Data control. To begin, double-click the Data control to send the control to the center of the form. Change these property values:

Name:	dtaBiblio
Caption:	Click to control data display
Left:	1920
Top:	4200
Width:	3255

   The text that appears in the center of the Data control is the caption—never data. The Data control doesn't display data. Instead, it regulates the display of data, and you use other fields to hold the displayed data. The text boxes that you place in the next two steps will display the data. You'll bind the text boxes to the Data control, and the Data control will be connected to the database. You must now make that connection; click the DatabaseName property, and then click the ellipsis that appears. Select the Biblio.mdb database from VB's folder (you might have to locate the folder from the file list that appears). Now that the Data control is connected to the database, you can add the text boxes.

   The database named Biblio.mdb, now connected to the dtaBiblio Data control, contains several tables. Therefore, not only must you tell the Data control which database to use, you must also specify the table source for the data. Select Publishers from the RecordSource property's drop-down list box. The Data control will now produce records only from Biblio.mdb's Publishers table.

5. Add a text box to the form with these properties:

Name:	txtPublisher
BackColor:	(select the ToolTip color)
BorderStyle:	1-Fixed Single
Left:	2040
Top:	1800
Width:	4215

   Now you must inform the text box that its data source is the Data control named dtaBiblio. Set the DataSource property to dtaBiblio by selecting dtaBiblio from the DataSource property's pull-down list box. (dtaBiblio is the only item that appears, but if the form contained additional Data controls, you would have to select the proper one for the text box's data source.) The Publishers table, controlled by the Data control, contains several fields. Therefore, not only must you tell the text box which Data control to connect to, but you must also specify the field. Change the `DataField` property to `Company Name`. `Company Name` is the database's field name that holds the publisher name. Set `Font` to 12.

6. Add the following four text box controls:

- **Control 1**

Name:	txtAddress
BackColor:	ToolTip yellow
BorderStyle:	1-Fixed Single
DataField:	Address
DataSource:	dtaBiblio
Font Size:	12
Left:	2040
Top:	2400
Width:	4215

- **Control 2**

Name:	txtCity
BackColor:	ToolTip yellow
BorderStyle:	1-Fixed Single
DataField:	City
DataSource:	dtaBiblio
Font Size:	12
Left:	1440
Top:	3000
Width:	1815

- **Control 3**

Name:	txtState
BackColor:	ToolTip yellow
BorderStyle:	1-Fixed Single
DataField:	State
DataSource:	dtaBiblio
Font Size:	12
Left:	4200
Top:	3000
Width:	555

- **Control 4**

Name:	txtZip
BackColor:	ToolTip yellow
BorderStyle:	1-Fixed Single
DataField:	Zip
DataSource:	dtaBiblio
Font Size:	12
Left:	5400
Top:	3000
Width:	1055

7. Add a separating line with the Line control that has these properties:

X1:	0
X2:	7080
Y1:	3720
Y2:	3720

Run the application, and you'll be looking at the first record in the database. Click the Data control's buttons to move through the database records. If you change a value, you'll be changing the actual database itself because of the bound text box controls. Despite the fact that the application requires a lot of controls, no code is required because of the Data control's powerful database retrieval and update capabilities.

In order to run the examples on the CD-ROM, the Data control's database property needs to point to the database on your system.

After you master the Data control, you can learn Visual Basic's powerful Data control methods that, with code alone, let your application step through database records, update fields, and compute values from tables. In addition, the Visual Basic language supports special industry-standard database instructions called SQL (pronounced "see-quel") that you can apply to data to select and sort information from within a database.

The Data Form Wizard

The Data Form Wizard analyzes a database, locates the fields for you (you don't have to know the format of the database ahead of time), and automatically builds a form that contains an appropriate title, field names, Text Box controls for the fields, and the Data control you can use to move between the records. If you want to follow along with this exercise, start a new VB project and remove any projects currently loaded in VB.

NEW TERM An *add-in application* is a tool that extends Visual Basic's development environment.

To access the Data Form Wizard, select Add-Ins | Add-In Manager. When the Add-In Manager dialog box appears, select the VB 6 Data Form Wizard and check the Loaded/Unloaded check box. Click OK to continue. Now select Add-Ins | Data Form Wizard. Visual Basic displays the Data Form Wizard's opening window. When you click Next, you see the database-selection dialog box shown in Figure 15.2.

FIGURE 15.2.

The Data Form Wizard's database selection tool.

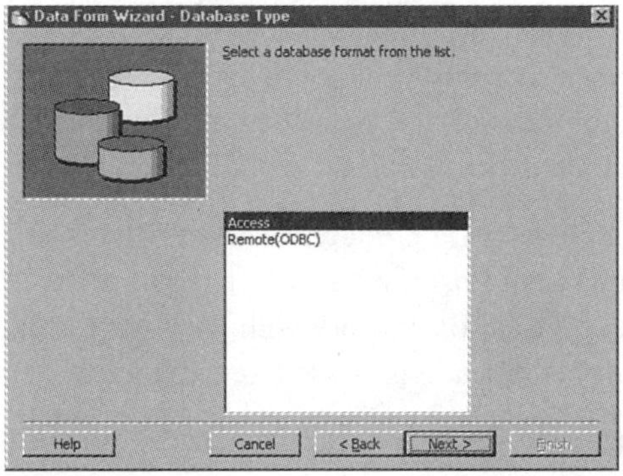

Continue following the wizard's requests to create the form. For example, you will have to tell the wizard the kind of database for which you want to create a form. After you select a database, the next dialog box asks you for the database name (which you can browse for) and a data source such as a table or query. Select the kind of form and then on the Record Source dialog box, you must select a table. Copy all the fields you want from that table to the final form. You then can click the options you want and click Finish to generate the form.

The form that the Data Form Wizard generates might not be as unique as the one you create yourself, but the form does include buttons that let the user not only change the database data, but also add and delete records as well, as Figure 15.3 shows.

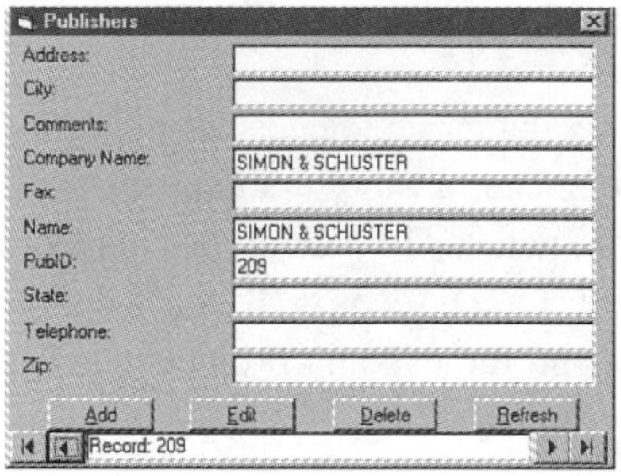

FIGURE 15.3.

*The Data Form
Wizard creates a nice
form.*

You can insert the Data Form Wizard's form into another application and
then display the form with the Show method.

Summary

In this hour you learned about two important aspects of files and Visual Basic. You
learned about regular data files that your applications can create, append to, and read.
You also learned how to use the Data control and its bound controls such as the Text Box
control to give the user a way to change the data in an underlying database.

If you have yet to select a database product, consider Microsoft Access because of its
close ties to Office and Visual Basic. With Access, you need to do only a minimal
amount of work to make Visual Basic work with your Access database. Access now
includes Visual Basic for Applications, a VB-like language.

The next hour describes how your application can access the printer to produce output.

Q&A

Q What if I don't have a database?

A If you don't have a database and if you don't see a need for one, you might not
need the Data control. You can perhaps get by with the file-related statements in
Visual Basic's language such as Write # and Input #. If you feel adventurous,
check out VB's Add-Ins | Visual Data Manager. This add-in application gives you
the ability to use Visual Basic to design, create, and analyze database files in several formats even if you don't have a database program available. Although the
Visual Data Manager doesn't take the place of a full-functioned database management system such as Microsoft Access, you can begin using the Data control to
access a database that you create with the Visual Data Manager.

Q What if I don't know the fields or tables in my database?

A If you write an application that manages and updates a database that you did not create and with which you are not familiar, you can still use Visual Basic because the Data control and bound controls are able to interpret most database formats. Therefore, when you select a database for the Data control, the Data control will display a list of tables from that database when you open the Data control's RecordSource drop-down list box. In addition, any bound controls, such as text boxes or labels, that you connect to the Data control will display an available list of fields that you want to bind to those controls.

Workshop

The quiz questions and exercises are provided for your further understanding. See Appendix B for the answers.

Quiz

1. What is the difference between a file and a database?

2. What is the difference between a record and a field?

3. What is the difference between a table and a file?

4. What happens if you open an existing file in `Output` mode?

5. What happens when you write to a file in `Append` mode?

6. Which files does the following statement close?

    `Close`

7. True or false: Your form must contain a different Data control for every table in the database.

8. What advantage does a bound text box provide for the programmer who wants to write an application that lets the user update a database field?

9. A database field is a Yes/No Access data field that can only take one of two values. Which Visual Basic control would best serve to represent that field?

10. What's the simplest way to create a form based on a database?

Exercises

1. Write an application that stores the names of your five favorite friends, their ages, and their phone numbers in five records in a disk file. Use `Write #` to write each three-value record and `Input #` to read each record. Call the data-entry and file-writing procedures from one procedure and the file-reading and display procedure from another procedure.

2. Write a database application that displays the `Biblio.mdb`'s book title table's first three fields. Don't let the user update the fields; you must be careful what kind of controls you use to display the field data.

3. Use the Data Form Wizard to generate a table based on the entire `Biblio.mdb`'s book title table. Connect the generated form to a command button's `Click()` event on the main form so that the data form appears for the user when the user clicks the command button.

Hour **16**

Printing with Visual Basic

This lesson describes how you can integrate the Windows printer driver into Visual Basic applications that you write. Visual Basic communicates with it so that you can send text and even graphics to the printer.

The highlights of this hour include

- Where your application sends printed output
- Which advantages spooled printing provides
- How to use the `Printer` object
- When to use `Printer` object methods
- How the `Print` method routes details to your printer

Introducing Printing

Surprisingly, no Printer control exists. Unlike most things in Visual Basic, sending output to the printer can be a tedious process. Printing requires that you send a fairly long list of instructions to your printer that describe exactly the way the output is to look. As easily as Visual Basic enables you to add and manage controls, one would have thought that the printing could be made easier.

Despite the tedium sometimes associated with printing, you will soon see that you can control every aspect of printing, including the font of individual characters that your application sends to the printer. The tedious control needed for printing provides pinpoint accuracy that lets you control all printing details.

NEW TERM   The Windows *print spooler*, also known as the print queue or the printer subsystem, controls all printed output in Windows.

When your application sends output to the printer, Windows intercepts those printer commands. Rather than sending output directly to the printer attached to your computer, Visual Basic actually sends printed output to the Windows print spooler.

The print spooler determines how all printed output from all Windows programs eventually appears. Therefore, when your Visual Basic application attempts to send printed output directly to the printer, the Windows print spooler intercepts those commands and might change the output before the printer ever sees it.

The Windows print spooler knows how to communicate with any printer supported by Windows. There are hundreds of different kinds of printers now recognized by Windows, and most of these printers require specialized commands. If every program that you bought had to provide support for every kind of printer that you or your users might own, programs would require even more disk space than they already do. In addition, programs would cost more because each software developer would have to spend time writing the program to produce output onto every kind of printer available.

Rather than require that every software developer support all printers, the Windows print spooler requires that every software developer support only one kind of printed output: the kind required by the Windows print spooler. If the applications that you write need to produce printed output, Visual Basic produces that output in a form required by the Windows print spooler. Figure 16.1 shows that Visual Basic applications send output directly to the Windows print spooler. The Windows print spooler then converts that output into the individual commands needed by whatever printer is attached to the system.

FIGURE 16.1.

Windows intercepts printer output.

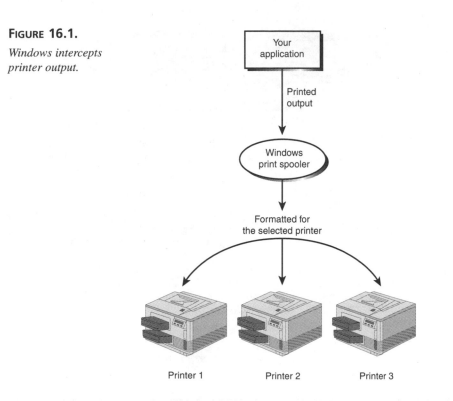

16

Suppose that you had both a laser printer and a color ink-jet printer attached to your computer. Without the Windows print spooler, you would need to provide two sets of printer commands for every Visual Basic application you write. With the Windows print spooler, you need to provide only one generic set of printer output commands. Before running the application, you can use commands available in the Windows print spooler to select one of your two printers. When you run the program, Windows will convert the Visual Basic output into commands needed by whatever printer is selected.

Preparing the User for Printing

A user could be caught unaware if your application begins printing without first warning him that the printer must be ready. Always remind the user to turn on the printer, make sure that the printer has paper, and ensure that the printer is *online*, or ready for printing. If the user's printer isn't first turned on and ready with an ample paper supply, the user will receive a Windows print spooler error message similar to the one shown in Figure 16.2.

FIGURE 16.2.

The printer isn't ready.

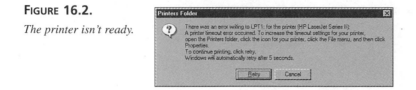

The function procedure in Listing 16.1 provides you with a useful MsgBox() call that you might want to incorporate into your own programs before printing. Of course, if you use common dialog boxes, you don't have to use this message box because the Print common dialog box serves good notice that printing is about to begin.

LISTING 16.1. TELLING THE USER ABOUT AN UPCOMING PRINT JOB.

```
1: Public Function PrReady() As Boolean
2: ' Make sure the user is ready to print
3: Dim intIsReady As Integer
4: intIsReady = MsgBox("Make sure the printer is ready", _
5: vbCritical + vbOKCancel, "Printer Check")
6: If (intIsReady = vbCancel) Then
7:    PrReady = False ' A Cancel press returns a False value
8: Else
9:    PrReady = True   ' User pressed OK so return True
10: End If
11: End Function
```

Figure 16.3 shows the message box presented by Listing 16.1.

FIGURE 16.3.

The user can now prepare the printer.

After the user reads the message and responds to the message box, the function's return value determines whether the user wants to see the output (assuming that the user has properly prepared the printer for printing) or cancel the printing. The return value of True or False can be checked as follows from another procedure that prints based on the user's response:

```
If PrReady() Then       ' If function is true...
  Call PrintRoutine      ' then print from sub
End If
```

Introducing the `Printer` Object

Visual Basic applications send all printed output to a special Visual Basic object called the `Printer` object. The `Printer` object supports several property values and methods with which you determine the look of the printed output.

The `Printer` keyword specifies the `Printer` object to which your applications will direct all output. There is no Printer control on the Toolbox window. All access to the `Printer` object must take place using Visual Basic code.

The commands that your application sends to the `Printer` object are generic Windows printer commands. The Windows print spooler converts those generic commands to a specific printer's commands. Therefore, you only worry about what you want printed and let the Windows print spooler worry about how the output is produced.

Throughout this book, when you have learned about a new object such as the Command Button control, you have learned about the properties that relate to that object. Before using the `Printer` object, you should see the properties available for it so that you'll know what you can do with printed output from within Visual Basic. All the `Printer` object's properties are listed in Table 16.1.

TABLE 16.1. THE `Printer` OBJECT'S PROPERTIES.

Property	Description
ColorMode	If 1 (or if set to the vbPRCMMonochrome named literal), output prints in monochrome (shades of white and black) even if you use a color printer. If 2 (or if set to the vbPRCMColor named literal), output prints in color.
Copies	Specifies the number of copies to print.
CurrentX	Holds the horizontal print column from the upper-left corner of the page, measured either in twips or the scale defined by the ScaleMode properties.
CurrentY	Holds the vertical print row from the upper-left corner of the page, measured either in twips or the scale defined by ScaleMode properties.
DeviceName	The name of the output device, such as a printer driver, to which you want to print.
DrawMode	Determines the appearance of graphics that you draw on the printer.
DrawStyle	Specifies the style of any graphical lines that your application draws.
DrawWidth	Specifies the width of lines drawn, from 1 (the default) to 32,767 pixels.

continues

TABLE 16.1. CONTINUED

Property	Description
DriverName	The name of the printer driver (don't specify the driver's extension).
Duplex	If 1 (or if set to the named literal vbPRDPSimplex), printing will occur on one side of the page. If 2 (or if set to the named literal vbPRDPHorizontal), printing will occur on both sides (if your printer supports double-sided printing) using a horizontal page turn. If 3 (or if set to the named literal vbPRDPVertical), printing will occur on both sides (if your printer supports double-sided printing) using a vertical page turn.
FillColor	Specifies the color of printed shapes. Determines the shading density for noncolor printed output.
FillStyle	Contains the style pattern of printed shapes.
Font	Returns a font that you can use for setting font attributes.
FontBold	Contains either True or False to determine whether subsequent printed output will be boldfaced.
FontCount	Specifies the current printer's number of installed fonts.
FontItalic	Holds either True or False to determine whether subsequent output will be italicized.
FontName	Holds the name of the current font being used for output.
Fonts	Contains a table of values that act as if they were stored in a control array. Fonts(0) to Fonts(FontCount-1) holds the names of all installed fonts on the target computer.
FontSize	Holds the size, in points, of the current font.
FontStrikeThru	Holds either True or False to determine whether subsequent output will be printed with a strikethrough line.
FontTransparent	Holds either True or False to determine whether subsequent output will be transparent.
FontUnderline	Holds either True or False to determine whether subsequent output will be underlined.
ForeColor	Specifies the foreground color of printed text and graphics. (The paper determines the background color.)
hDC	A Windows device context handle for advanced Windows procedure calls.
Height	Holds the height, in twips, of the current printed page.

Property	Description
Orientation	If 1 (or if set to the named literal vbPRORPortrait), output prints in portrait mode (printing occurs down the page). If 2 (or if set to the named literal vbPRORLandscape), output prints in landscape mode (printing occurs across the page).
Page	Contains the page number currently being printed and updated automatically by Visual Basic.
PaperBin	Specifies which paper bin the print job will use. You can search the online help for the PaperBin property for several named literals you can use to specify different kinds of bins.
PaperSize	Specifies the size of paper the print job will use. You can search the online help for the PaperSize property for several named literals you can use to specify different sizes of paper.
Port	Specifies the printer port, such as LPT1:.
PrintQuality	Determines how fine the print quality will appear. If -1 (or set to the vbPRPQDraft named literal), the printing quality is the least, but the print completes quickly. If -2 (or set to the vbPRPQLow named literal), printing occurs in a low-resolution mode. If -3 (or set to the vbPRPQMedium named literal), printing occurs in a medium resolution mode. If -4 (or set to the vbPRPQHigh named literal), printing is the slowest but the highest quality.
ScaleHeight	Specifies how many ScaleMode units high each graphic will be upon output.
ScaleLeft	Specifies how many ScaleMode units from the left of the page subsequent printed output appears.
ScaleMode	Sets the unit of measurement for all subsequent printed output that appears.
ScaleTop	Specifies how many ScaleMode units from the top of the page all subsequent printed output appears.
ScaleWidth	Specifies how many ScaleMode units wide each graphic will be upon printed output.
TrackDefault	If True, the specified printer changes if you change the default printer at the operating system level. If False, the specified printer remains the same during the program's operation even if the system's default printer changes during the program's execution.
TwipsPerPixelX	Specifies the number of screen twips that each printer's dot (or *pixel*) height consumes.

16

continues

TABLE 16.1. CONTINUED

Property	Description
TwipsPerPixelY	Specifies the number of screen twips that each printer's dot, or pixel, width consumes.
Width	Holds the size of the page width (measured in twips).
Zoom	Specifies the percentage at which printed output prints. A negative value scales the output down (smaller), 0 requests no scaling, and a positive value scales the output up (larger).

Table 16.1 contains many printer properties; fortunately, you'll use only a few of the properties for most of your printing needs. The font-related printer properties take care of just about all your printing jobs that are textual in nature.

> The graphics-related printer properties and methods aren't covered in this lesson. After you master graphics in the next part of this book, you'll be more prepared to understand the graphics-related Printer object's properties. Most of the Printer object's properties are reserved for controlling extremely advanced graphics output. For typical applications, you'll rarely bother to specify any properties because the default values work well for normal reporting requirements.

Unlike most of Visual Basic's control objects, the Printer object's methods are much more important than its property values. Table 16.2 contains a complete list of the methods supported by Visual Basic's Printer object.

TABLE 16.2. THE Printer OBJECT'S METHODS.

Method	Description
Circle	Draws a circle, an ellipse, or an arc on the printer.
EndDoc	Releases the current document, in full, to the print spooler for output.
KillDoc	Immediately terminates the output and deletes the current print job from the print spooler.
Line	Draws lines and boxes on the page.
NewPage	Sends a page break to the printed output so that subsequent output appears on the next page.
PaintPicture	Draws a graphic image file on the printer.
Print	Prints numeric and text data on the printer.

Method	Description
PSet	Draws a graphical point on the printed output.
Scale	Determines the scale used for measuring output.
ScaleX	Converts the printer's width to ScaleMode's measurement unit.
ScaleY	Converts the printer's height to ScaleMode's measurement unit.
TextHeight	Determines the full height of text given in the scale set with Scale.
TextWidth	Determines the full width of text given in the scale set with Scale.

16

By far the most widely used Printer object methods are the Print, EndDoc, and NewPage methods. After you master these three methods, you'll rarely need to use any other methods.

The Print Method

The Printer object's Print method handles almost all printed output. Print supports several different formats. With Print, you can print messages, variables, constants, and expressions on the printer. The Print method is by far the most commonly used printing method in Visual Basic.

Here is the format of the Print method:

```
[Printer.]Print [Spc(n) ¦ Tab(n)] Expression
```

The format makes Print look more confusing than it really is, but the portion of the Print method that appears to the right of Print takes some explanation. The next several sections explain the various options available for the Print method.

Printing Literals

The Print method easily prints string and numeric literals. To print a string or numeric literal, place the literal to the right of the Print method. The following methods send the numbers 1, 2, and 3 to the Printer object for output:

```
Printer.Print 1
Printer.Print 2
Printer.Print 3
```

When execution hits these three lines of code, Visual Basic sends 1, 2, and 3 to the Printer object with each number appearing on a subsequent line. Every Print method sends a carriage return and line feed sequence to the printer. A lone Print method on a line by itself, such as the following, sends a blank line to the printer:

```
Printer.Print
```

> Print adds a space before all positive numeric values printed on the page. The space is where an invisible plus sign appears.

The following code sends two lines of text to the `Printer` object:

```
Printer.Print "Visual Basic makes writing programs"
Printer.Print "for Windows easy."
```

When the Windows print spooler obtains these two lines of output, the following appears on the printer's paper:

```
Visual Basic makes writing programs
for Windows easy.
```

Printing Variables and Controls

In addition to literals, the `Print` method prints the contents of variables and controls. The following initializes a string variable and an integer variable and then prints the contents of the variables on the printer:

```
FirstName = "Charley"
Age = 24
Printer.Print FirstName
Printer.Print Age
```

Here is the output produced by these `Print` methods:

```
Charley
24
```

> Remember that Visual Basic won't send anything to the `Printer` object until the code that contains `Print` executes. You would insert `Print` methods at appropriate places in the code's procedures where printed output is required. For example, if there is a command button labeled Print Report, that command button's `Click()` event procedure will contain `Print` methods.

Printing Expressions

If you could print only individual strings, numeric constants, and variables, `Print` would be extremely limiting. Of course, `Print` isn't that limited. You can combine literals, variables, and expressions to the right of `Print` methods to produce more complex printed output. The following `Print` method prints 31:

```
Printer.Print 25 + (3 * 2)
```

The expression can contain variables, controls, and constants, like this:

```
Printer.Print sngFactor * lblWeight.Caption + 10
```

If you want to send special characters to the printer, you can do that by using the `Chr()` function. The following expression produces a message that includes embedded quotation marks inside the printed string:

```
Printer.Print "She said, " & Chr(34) & "I do." & Chr(34)
```

When execution reaches the former `Print` method, this is what the print spooler writes to the printer:

```
She said, "I do."
```

> You wouldn't be able to print the quotation marks without the `Chr()` function. Usually, Visual Basic uses quotation marks to determine where string literals begin and end.

Printing Multiple Values

When you need to print several values on one line, you can do so by separating those values with semicolons and commas. The semicolon forces subsequent values to appear right next to each other in the output. The comma forces values to appear in the next print zone.

NEW TERM   A *print zone* occurs every 14 columns on the page.

The following two messages print on different lines:

```
Printer.Print "The sales were"
Printer.Print 4345.67
```

By using the semicolon, you can force these values to print next to each other:

```
Printer.Print "The sales were "; 4345.67
```

The semicolon also acts to keep automatic carriage returns and line feeds from taking place. The following `Print` method ends with a trailing semicolon:

```
Printer.Print "The company name is ";
```

The trailing semicolon keeps the printer's print head at the end of the message for subsequent output. Therefore, the subsequent `Print` statement shown next, no matter how much later in the code the `Print` appears, would print its output right next to the previous `Print`'s output:

```
Printer.Print lblComName.Caption    ' Finish the line
```

The semicolon is nice for printing multiple values of different datatypes on the same line. The following `Print` prints all its data on the same line of output:

```
Printer.Print "Sales: "; curTotsales; "Region:"; intRegNum
```

The comma is used to force subsequent values to print in the next print zone. The following `Print` prints a name every 14 spaces on the printed line:

```
Printer.Print strDivName1, strDivName2, strDivName3
```

No matter how long or short each division name is, the next division name will print in the next print zone. The previous `Print` might produce output similar to the following:

```
North         NorthEast      South
```

When you print lists of numbers or short strings, the comma enables you to easily align each column.

Using the Fonts

Most Windows-compatible printers support a variety of fonts. The font-related properties are often useful for printing titles and other special output messages in special font sizes and styles.

You can add special effects to your printed text by using the font modifying properties in Table 16.1. For example, the following code first puts the printer in a boldfaced, italicized, 60-point font (a print size of one full inch), and then prints a message:

```
Printer.FontBold = True
Printer.FontItalic = True
Printer.FontSize = 60
Printer.Print "I'm learning Visual Basic!"
```

The font properties affect subsequent output. Therefore, if you print several lines of text and then change the font size, the text that you've already printed remains unaffected. Visual Basic prints only the subsequent output with the new font.

Better Spacing with Spc() and Tab()

The Print method supports the use of the embedded Spc() and Tab() functions to give you additional control over your program's output. Spc() produces a variable number of spaces in the output as determined by the argument you send to Spc(). The following Print method prints a total of 10 spaces between the first name and the last:

```
Printer.Print strFirstName; Spc(10), strLastName
```

The argument you send to the embedded Tab() function determines in which column the next printed character appears. In the following Print, the date appears in the 50th column on the page:

```
Printer.Print Tab(50), dteDateGenerated
```

As these examples show, if you print values before or after the Spc() and Tab() functions, you separate the functions from the surrounding printed values using the semicolon.

> Spc() and Tab() give you more control over spacing than the comma and semicolon allow.

Listing 16.2 contains some code that computes and prints two housing pricing taxation values.

LISTING 16.2. USING Spc() AND Tab().

```
 1: Tax1 = TaxRate * HouseVal1
 2: Tax2 = TaxRate * HouseVal2
 3:
 4: TotalVal = HouseVal1 + HouseVal2
 5: TotTaxes = TaxRate * TotalVal
 6:
 7: Printer.Print "House Value"; Tab(20); "Tax"
 8: Printer.Print Format(HouseVal1, "Currency");
 9: Printer.Print Tab(20); Format(Tax1, "Currency")
10: Printer.Print Format(HouseVal2, "Currency");
11: Printer.Print Tab(20); Format(Tax2, "Currency")
12:
13: Printer.Print  ' Prints a blank line
14: Printer.Print "Total tax:"; Spc(5); Format(TotTaxes, "Currency")
15: Printer.NewPage
16: Printer.EndDoc
```

Here is a sample of what you may see after Listing 16.2 executes:

```
House Value     Tax
$76,578.23      $9,189.39
$102,123.67     $12,254.81

Total tax:      $21,444.20
```

The Tab(20) function call ensures that the second column, which contains the tax information, is aligned. Also, notice that the trailing semicolons let you continue the Print methods on subsequent lines without squeezing long Print method values onto the same line. The code uses Spc() to insert five spaces between the title and the total amount of tax. The last two lines ensure that the printing stops properly.

Starting to Print

The physical printing doesn't begin until all output is released to the print spooler, or until your application issues the EndDoc method.

As you send Print methods to the print spooler via the Printer object, the print spooler builds the page or pages of output but doesn't release that output until you issue an EndDoc method. EndDoc tells the print spooler, "I'm done sending output to you; you can print now."

Without EndDoc, Windows would collect all the application's output and not print any of the output until the application terminates. If you were to write an application that the user runs throughout the day and that prints invoices as customers make purchases, you would need to issue an EndDoc method at the end of each invoice-printing procedure if you wanted each invoice to print at that time.

Listing 16.3 prints a message on the printer and then signals to the print spooler that output is ready to go to paper. Without EndDoc, the print spooler would hold the output until the application containing the code terminated.

LISTING 16.3. USING EndDoc TO RELEASE PRINTED OUTPUT.

```
1: Printer.Print "Invoice #"; invnum
2: Printer.Print "Customer:"; cust(CCnt); Tab(20); "Final Sales"
3: Printer.Print "Amount of sale:"; Tab(20); Format(SaleAmt, "Currency")
4: Printer.Print "Tax:"; Tab(20); Format(tax, "Currency")
5: Printer.Print
6: Printer.Print "Total:"; Tab(20), Format(TotalSale, "Currency")
7:
8:  ' Release the job for actual printing
9: Printer.EndDoc
```

The program containing Listing 16.3's code might continue to run and process other sets of data. The EndDoc method ensures that the output built in the preceding Print methods is sent to the physical printer immediately. If other Print methods appear later in the program, the print spooler begins building the output all over again, releasing that subsequent output only for an EndDoc procedure or when the application ends.

Page Breaks

The NewPage method forces the printer to eject the current page and begin subsequent output on the next new page.

The Windows print spooler ensures that each printed page properly breaks at the end of a physical page. Therefore, if the printer's page length is 66 lines and you print 67 lines, the 67th line will appear at the top of the second page of output. There are times, however, when you need to print less than a full page on the printer. You can release that incomplete page for printing using the NewPage method (shown previously in Table 16.2). To use NewPage, simply apply the Newpage method to the Printer object like this:

```
Printer.NewPage
```

Remember that you actually print to the Windows print spooler and that your application's output methods don't directly control a physical printer. Therefore, NewPage tells the print spooler to go to a new page when the print spooler arrives at that location in the output.

Don't forget that you're working with printers that support many fonts and font sizes. You can always determine, in advance, how many lines of output will fit on a single page as long as you first check the value of the following formula:

```
intNumLinesPerPage = Printer.Height / Printer.TextHeight("X")
```

As explained in Table 16.3, the Height property determines the height, in twips, of the page, or in whatever measurement value you want to use. The TextHeight property determines the full height of a printed character (including leading, which is the space directly above and below characters). TextHeight measures the height in twips if you haven't changed the scale using the ScaleMode property.

For printed reports, you'll rarely use the ScaleMode method. If you need to change the scale of measurement, however, you'll have to change the scale back to twips before calculating the number of output lines per page, like this:

```
Printer.ScaleMode = 1
```

ScaleMode accepts values defined in Table 16.3.

TABLE 16.3. THE ScaleMode VALUES.

Value	Named Literal	Description
0	vbUser	A user-defined value
1	vbTwips	Measured in twips (the default)
2	vbPoints	Measured in points
3	vbPixels	Measured in pixels (the smallest unit addressable by your printer)
4	vbCharacters	Measured in characters (120×240 twips)
5	vbInches	Measured in inches
6	vbMillimeters	Measured in millimeters
7	vbCentimeters	Measured in centimeters

Listing 16.4 contains code that prints two messages, one per page of printed output.

LISTING 16.4. MOVING TO THE TOP OF NEW OUTPUT PAGES.

```
1: Printer.Print "The Report begins on the next page..."
2: Printer.NewPage   ' Go to top of new page
3: Printer.Print "The Campaign Platform"
```

You can apply the Print method to your form to print directly on the form without using a control. For example, you can print a title on a form named frmAccts with this statement:

frmAccts.Print Spc(20); "XYZ, Co."

Although you should use controls as much as possible so that the application's code can rearrange and manage the text on the controls, remember to use Print whenever your form needs to hold unchanging text.

Summary

In this hour you learned ways you can route output to your printer. Actually, you have learned here that all Visual Basic output goes to the Windows print spooler and the spooler takes care of speaking to your particular printer.

Creating printed output isn't always simple. With the exception of printing program listings (which you can do by selecting File | Print from the development environment), printing data can take awhile. You must take care of every line and jump to a new page when necessary.

The next hour starts a new part of your tutorial, where you'll create menus and add graphics to your applications.

Q&A

Q I use a network printer sometimes and a local printer at other times, so what do I do to my application to print to either printer?

A Absolutely nothing. Remember that your application sends all output to the Windows print spooler and not to a specific printer. When you see the Print dialog box (the dialog box you can produce with the Common Dialog Box control), you select the printer, and from there you can select either your network or local printer. Windows then determines the best way to get your application's output to that printer.

Q What is the difference between `Spc()` and `Tab()`?

A Both functions send spaces to the `Printer` object, but the functions differ in their starting position. `Spc()` adds spaces from the printer's current position. `Tab()` adds enough spaces to move the printer head to that position on the line, no matter where the printer head currently rests. In addition, if you use a `Tab()` value such as `Tab(20)` but the printer is currently past position 20, Visual Basic adds another line and tabs to column position 20 on the new line.

Workshop

The quiz questions and exercises are provided for your further understanding. See Appendix B for the answers.

Quiz

1. Why does Visual Basic printer output not go immediately to a printer?
2. What happens if the printer isn't online when the user prints something?
3. What is the difference between the `Printer` object and the `Print` method?
4. How can you specify the number of output copies to print?
5. True or false: You can add the `Printer` object to the toolbox.
6. How many spaces does a print zone contain?
7. Why do you sometimes need to use the ASCII-based `Chr()` function when printing?
8. What's the output from the following code?
   ```
   Printer.Print "1";
   Printer.Print "2"
   ```

9. True or false: Using Tab(14) after each variable does the same thing as putting a comma after each variable printed.

10. True or false: You can apply the Print method to a form.

Exercises

1. Write the Print method that prints a Spanish Ñ (with a tilde) on the printer.

2. Write a program that prints ASCII values 32 through 255 on paper when the user clicks a command button.

3. Modify the book publisher application from Hour 15, "Visual Basic Database Basics," to print on paper the current book's title and year when the user clicks a Print command button.

PART V
Sprucing Up Programs

Hour

HOUR 17

Menus and Visual Basic

When you go to a restaurant for the first time, you don't know what to order until the menu arrives. When users use your application, they need a menu so they will know what to order also. Just like a restaurant's customers, your application's new users won't know what they can do. The menu gives them a guide. After they become more familiar with the application, they will also learn various shortcut keys you supply on the menu bar.

Most Windows programs contain common menu commands. Visual Basic is one such program. Many Visual Basic pull-down menus contain the same commands as Microsoft Word and Microsoft Excel. You should follow this pattern as closely as you can. Group your file-related commands on the menu bar's File option so your users will feel right at home with your application. Your application will require some menu options that no other application uses, and your application certainly might not be as complete as VB's, but use as much overlap as you can so your users can adapt as quickly as possible to your application's interface.

Consult the Windows design guide that is available online at
www.microsoft.com for more information about Windows application development conventions.

The highlights of this hour include

- What the Menu Editor does
- How to add a menu bar to applications
- When to code submenus
- How to name menu options
- Where to code menu events

The Menu Editor

Before looking at menu creation, take a moment to familiarize yourself with Figure
17.1's menu components. The rest of this lesson discusses the various components that
make up most Windows menus. In working with Visual Basic, you've already seen these
menu components.

Notice that Visual Basic displays toolbar icons next to menu options that
appear on one of the toolbars. Most of Microsoft's newer products now
show the toolbar icons on matching menu options. You'll learn more quickly
which toolbar goes with which menu item because you'll more quickly associate toolbar button icons to their equivalent menu options. Unfortunately,
you cannot add such icons to your own application menus because Visual
Basic doesn't give you a way to add the icons.

Even Visual Basic programming gurus don't always know that a menu is another control
object just like a command button or a text box. After you add a menu bar to an application, the menu bar and its options are all controls that you can manage from the
Properties window. Even though the menu items are regular controls with properties you
can set, the programming gurus don't often know that because they use a better resource
than the Properties window for creating their menus. Whereas the Properties window is
great for setting normal toolbox control properties, the Menu Editor makes for a better
menu-creation tool.

Menu bar   Menu bar option   Shortcut keystroke

FIGURE 17.1.

The menu components.

View menu options

Toolbar icon

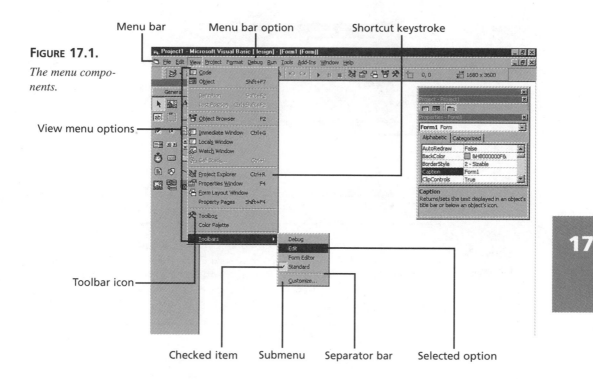

Checked item   Submenu   Separator bar   Selected option

17

The Menu Editor lets you quickly and easily place menu bar items into your application by pushing command buttons and typing a few property values. The Menu Editor contains menu description tools that let you create the application's menu bar, menu commands, and shortcut access keys.

The Menu Editor is a dialog box that you access from the Form window by pressing Ctrl+E or by selecting Tools | Menu Editor from Visual Basic's own menu bar. Figure 17.2 shows the Menu Editor dialog box.

The Menu Editor creates your menu, but you still need to write event procedures that tie menu command selections to actions taken by your application. When the user selects a menu command, Visual Basic generates an event, just as it generates an event when the user clicks a command button. The only event that menu items support is the `Click()` event. Therefore, whether the user selects a menu option with a mouse or with a keyboard, that selection triggers a `Click()` event.

FIGURE 17.2.

Creating a menu with the Menu Editor.

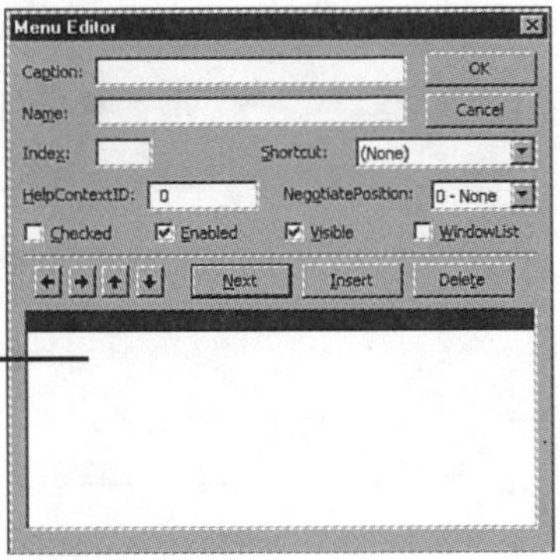

Menu structure appears here as you build the menu

Learning to add menus to your programs involves a mastery of the Menu Editor, and you'll always reopen the Menu Editor if you want to modify an application's menu. After you use the Menu Editor to create the menu, the menu's event procedures work just like the other event procedures that you've been writing throughout this book.

As you'll see throughout the rest of this lesson, the Menu Editor lets you add to applications a menu bar, pull-down menu commands, separator bars (bars that help group menu options), submenus (menus that appear from other menu options), checked items, and shortcut access keystrokes. After you create the menu, you'll write event procedures for each menu option. When the user selects a menu command, that menu command's event procedure will automatically execute.

Sometimes the options on the menu bar's pull-down list are called items or commands. This tutorial uses the more common term, *option*, throughout the text.

Adding an Application's Menu Bar

An application's menu bar is one of the easiest parts of the menu system to add. This section walks you through the steps necessary to add a menu bar. Subsequent sections show you how to add pull-down menu options to each of the menu bar commands.

The Menu Editor makes adding a menu bar to any application simple. Create a new project so that you can practice creating a menu. The menu bar you create will contain the following options:

- File

- Edit

- View

- Help

This tutorial could go into a lot of detail, explaining all the nuances of the Menu Editor. Luckily, you don't need all that preliminary detailed description. The Menu Editor is most easily mastered by jumping in and building a menu from scratch. You don't need a bunch of theory to use the Menu Editor.

Every option on a menu bar, as well as the menu options, submenus, and separator bars that appear when you display a pull-down menu, has properties just as the other controls do. The Menu Editor acts like a dialog box that helps you set menu property values. The Properties window is perfect for the other controls, but as you'll see, menus require a few extra property choices that the other controls don't need. That's why using the customized Menu Editor is simpler than modifying an application's menu through the Properties window.

Perform the following steps to add a menu bar to your new project:

1. Press Ctrl+E to display the Menu Editor. Each menu bar command requires a caption (specified by the Caption property) and a name (specified by the Name property). The other Menu Editor items are optional.

   The additional Menu Editor properties, such as the Enabled property that determines whether the menu item is grayed out and unavailable for certain procedures, as well as a Visible property, which determines when the user can see the menu bar command, are not needed for every option. You'll rarely change these extra property values from their default values for menu bar commands.

2. At the Caption prompt, type &File. The ampersand, as with the other controls' Caption properties, indicates an accelerator keystroke of Alt+F for the File menu item. As you type the Caption value, notice that Visual Basic adds the caption in the Menu Editor's lower section. The Menu Editor's lower half displays the menu bar and the pull-down options as you add them to the menu. The Menu Editor's top half contains a description of individual items in the menu.

17

3. Press Tab to move the focus to the Name text box, and type mnuFile. The application will refer to the File menu bar item by the name mnuFile as needed. In other words, just as a command button might be named cmdPressMe, the menu bar option can be named mnuFile. The three-letter prefix indicates that the mnuFile object is a menu item and not some other kind of control. Your Menu Editor's window should look something like the one in Figure 17.3.

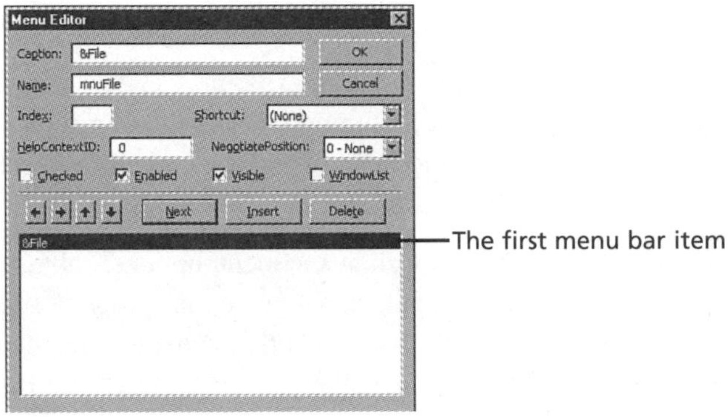

FIGURE 17.3.

The menu bar now has a defined File option.

The first menu bar item

The only accelerator keystroke available for menu bar options is the underlined Alt+keystroke that occurs as the result of the Caption property's underlined letter. Don't attempt to select Ctrl+keystroke from the Shortcut drop-down list box for the menu bar options. Ctrl+keystroke shortcut combinations are available only for pull-down menu options.

Don't press Enter or click the OK button to close the Menu Editor just yet; you need to add the additional menu bar options before closing the Menu Editor's window.

Naming Menu Options

You should follow a standard naming convention when naming menu options.

The event procedures within any Visual Basic application reference menu options by their menu option names. Preface all menu items, both menu bar and pull-down menu items, with the mnu prefix so that you can easily distinguish menu commands from variables and from the other controls as you work within the application's code.

Generally, Visual Basic programmers follow the standard of naming menu bar options with the prefix mnu followed by the name of the item. Therefore, the File option is named mnuFile, Edit is named mnuEdit, and so on.

As you add pull-down options to the menu bar items, preface each option with the mnu prefix as well as the name of the menu bar command, and then append the name of the pull-down menu's item. The File│Exit item would be named mnuFileExit, View│Normal would be named mnuViewNormal, and so on. The names then clearly describe the menu items that they represent. If a submenu appears, append its item name to the parent's name (for example, mnuViewNormalFull).

Follow these steps to complete the creation of a menu bar:

1. Click the Menu Editor's Next command button to inform Visual Basic that you want to add the next item. The lower window's highlight bar drops down to the next line in preparation for the next menu item. The buttons right above the lower window control the addition, insertion, and deletion of menu items from the menu you are building.

2. Type &Edit at the Caption text box and press Tab. Name this second menu bar item mnuEdit. Click the Next command button to prepare the Menu Editor for the next menu bar item.

3. Type &View and press Tab to move the focus to the Name text box. Type mnuView and select Next to prepare for the final menu item.

4. Type &Help and press Tab to move the focus to the Name text box. Type mnuHelp. Your screen should look like the one in Figure 17.4.

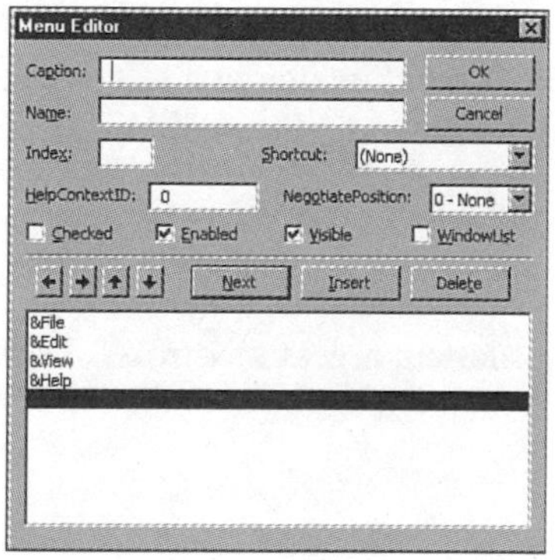

FIGURE 17.4.

The menu bar is now complete with four options.

17

Close the Menu Editor by pressing Enter or clicking the OK command button. Immediately, Visual Basic displays the new menu bar across the top of the application's Form window, as shown in Figure 17.5. The menu bar is the result of your efforts with the Menu Editor.

FIGURE 17.5.

The Form window's new menu bar.

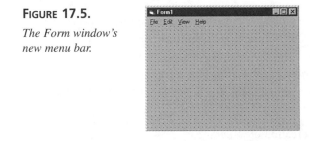

Obviously, the menu is incomplete. The menu bar exists, but no options pull down from the menu bar. You're now ready to add the individual pull-down options to the menu. The next section explains how to complete the File pull-down menu.

Adding Pull-Down Menu Options

Each menu bar command opens a pull-down menu that consists of a series of options, separator bars, access keystrokes, and submenus. The Menu Editor's four arrow command buttons let you indent the pull-down menu commands from their matching menu bar commands to show which items go with which menu bar commands.

Now that you've added the menu bar, you can add the individual options to the pull-down menus. You didn't have to complete the menu bar before completing each pull-down menu. You could have added the File option to the menu bar and then completed the File option's pull-down menu before adding the View option to the menu bar. The order in which you add menu items doesn't matter at all. It is where you place them and how you indent them that determines the order in which the menu items appear.

The File pull-down menu will contain the following items:

- The New command
- The Open command with a shortcut access keystroke of Ctrl+O
- The Close command
- A separator bar
- The Exit command

After you add these submenu items, you can hook up the menu commands to Click() event procedures that you write, as explained in the next section.

Adding pull-down items requires that you follow the same steps you followed when you added the menu bar items in the previous section. The difference is that the Menu Editor options that the previous section ignored, such as the Shortcut option, become more important because you'll apply some of these options to the pull-down menu items. Table 17.1 explains the remaining Menu Editor properties.

TABLE 17.1. THE MENU EDITOR'S REMAINING PROPERTIES.

Property	Description
Checked	Indicates whether a menu item has a check mark next to it. Generally, you'll add check marks to menu options that perform on or off actions, such as a View menu that contains a Highlighted command. The check mark appears when you, at design time or through code, set the menu item's Checked property to True. The check mark goes away (indicating that the item is no longer active or selected) when you set the Checked property to False.
HelpContextID	This is a code that matches a help file description if and when you add help files to your application.
Index	If you create a menu control array rather than name individual menu items separately, this Index property specifies the menu item's subscript within the control array.
Shortcut	This is a drop-down list of Ctrl+keystroke access keys that you can add to any pull-down menu item.
Window List	Specifies whether the menu item applies to an advanced application's MDI (multiple-document interface) document. The menus that you create for this book don't require the use of MDI features.

17

Perhaps the most important command keys on the Menu Editor when you add pull-down menu items are the four arrow command buttons. The left and right arrow command buttons indicate which items go with which menu bar option. In other words, if four items in the lower window are indented to the right and appear directly beneath the File menu bar item, those four indented items will appear on File's pull-down menu. The left arrow removes an indentation level and the right arrow adds an indentation level. The up- and down-arrow keys move menu items up and down the list of menu items, rearranging the order if you need to do so.

The arrow keys make a lot of sense when you see them used. Follow these steps to create the File pull-down menu's submenu:

1. Move the lower window's highlight line to the &Edit menu bar item. Click the Insert command button. You always insert before an item, so to add items to the File menu, you must insert before the Edit menu bar item in the lower window.

2. Click the right-arrow command button. Visual Basic adds four dots (similar to an ellipsis), showing that the newly inserted item will be indented under the File option.

3. Move the focus to the caption prompt and type &New.

4. Press Tab to move the focus to the name prompt and type mnuFileNew.

5. Click Next and then Insert, and click the right-arrow command button to insert another item beneath the New item. Your Menu Editor should look like the one in Figure 17.6. Notice that the File menu bar option now has a pull-down menu; you know this because of the indentation of the New option right below &File.

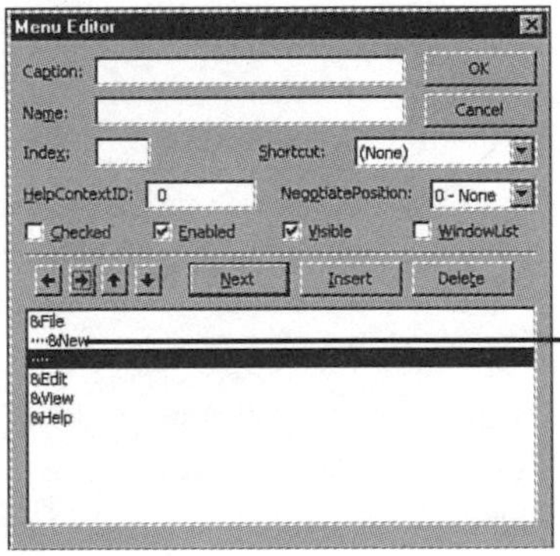

FIGURE 17.6.

The File pull-down menu is gaining additional options.

First File menu option

6. Move the focus to the caption prompt and type &Open. Press Tab and enter the Name property value mnuFileOpen. Rather than add the next item, click the Shortcut drop-down list and select Ctrl+O from the list. When the user now displays the File pull-down menu, Ctrl+O will appear as the shortcut key next to the File | Open menu item.

7. Click Next, Insert, and then the right-arrow command button to make room for the next item. Add the Exit caption with the Name property mnuFileExit. Click Next again and then Insert to insert another item beneath the Close item. You can now add a separator bar.

Separator bars help you break individual pull-down menus into separate sections. Although several options appear on most Windows applications' File pull-down menus, these options don't all perform the same kind of tasks. Some options relate to files, some relate to printing, and the Exit command always appears on the File menu as well. The separator bars help distinguish groups of different items from one another on the pull-down menus.

All separator bars have the same `Caption` property, which is nothing more than a hyphen (-). You must give every separator bar a different name. Usually, the name of the separator bars on the File menu are `mnuFileBar1`, `mnuFileBar2`, and so on. Some programmers prefer to name the first separator bar `Sep1`, the second `Sep2`, and so on, no matter which menu the separator bar appears on.

You must add the separator bars on an indented menu level so that they indent properly beneath their pull-down menus. Follow these steps to add the single separator bar for this lesson's File pull-down menu:

1. Type - (a hyphen) for the `Caption` property and press Tab.
2. Type `mnuFileBar1` for the `Name` property.

There's one more item to add: the Exit item. You know enough to add the Exit option to the File menu. After adding Exit, your Menu Editor should look like the one shown in Figure 17.7.

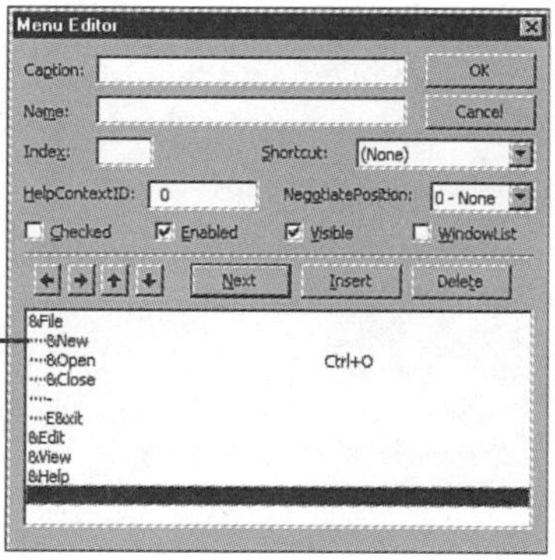

FIGURE 17.7.

The File menu is now complete.

First File menu option

Menu Extras

You don't need to complete all the menu bar options. You already know how to add routine options. If you need to add additional menu elements, however, such as a submenu or a checked item, the mechanics of those additions are about as simple as the items that you added in the previous sections.

To practice adding a checked object, add one checked item to the View pull-down menu bar item. Add an indented option that uses Highlighted for the Caption item and mnuViewHighlighted for the Name. Click the Checked check box. The View|Highlighted option will initially be checked when the user displays the View pull-down menu. Your code can check and uncheck the item by changing the mnuViewHighlighted object's Checked property to True and False.

If you want to add a submenu from a pull-down menu item, add an additional level of indentation. For example, to add a two-option submenu off the File|Open option that gives the user an additional choice of Binary or Text (binary and text are two possible kinds of files), insert a place for the first item right beneath Open and click the right-arrow command button to add a second ellipsis. Type &Binary for the Caption property and mnuFileOpenBinary for the Name property. Insert an additional item beneath that, indented at the same level, and type &Text for the Caption property and mnuFileOpenText for the Name property.

> Your menu has a slight bug now! Go back to the &Open menu option and set the shortcut keystroke back to None. You cannot add a shortcut keystroke to a submenu's parent option.

Now that you've completed the menu (as far as we're taking it here), click OK. When the Menu Editor disappears, you'll see the application's Form window with the menu bar across the top of the screen. Open the File menu and then select Open to see the submenu like the one shown in Figure 17.8. Notice the right arrow next to Open, which indicates that an additional submenu will appear for that option.

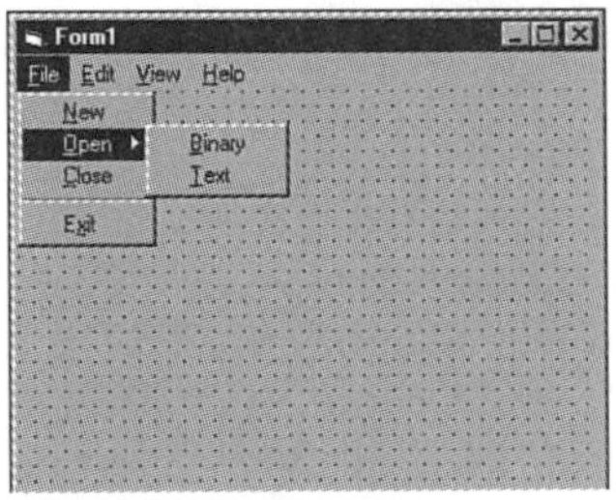

FIGURE 17.8.

The File menu is now complete.

Connecting Menus to Event Procedures

After you've built your menu, you need to tie each menu command to your application. To respond to menu selections, you need to write `Click()` event procedures that you want Visual Basic to execute when the user selects a menu command.

Visual Basic generates a `Click` event when the user selects a menu command. The name of the menu command, combined with `Click()`, provides the name of the event procedure. Therefore, the File|Exit menu item named `mnuFileExit` will generate the execution of the event procedure named `mnuFileExit_Click()`.

Adding the `mnuFileExit_Click()` event procedure requires only that you select that menu command during the program's development. At the Form window, click the File menu bar command. Visual Basic displays the Form window's File pull-down menu. Even though you're not running the program but are working on the program from the Form window, the File menu shows you what happens when the user selects File at runtime.

Click the Exit item on the File pull-down menu. As soon as you click Exit, Visual Basic opens the Code window to a new event procedure named `mnuFileExit_Click()`, as shown in Figure 17.9.

FIGURE 17.9.

The menu option's `Click()` *event procedure.*

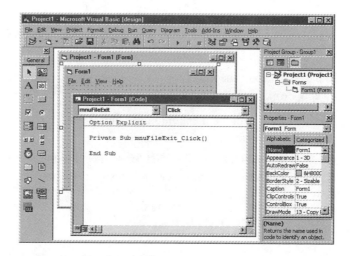

This event procedure is simple to code. When the user selects File|Exit, you want the application to terminate. Therefore, insert an `Unload Me` and an `End` statement to the body of the `mnuFileExit_Click()` procedure and close the procedure by double-clicking its control button. As you can see, adding event procedures requires little more than clicking the menu item and adding the body of the procedure that appears.

17

Although the application is far from complete, you can run the application to see how the menu looks and to test the File | Exit option.

After building your menu, you must tie code to the various menu items by writing `Click()` event procedures that will execute when the user runs the application and selects from the menu. If any menu command duplicates the functionality of other controls, such as command buttons, don't copy the command button's code into the body of the menu event procedure. Instead, simply execute that command button's event procedure from the menu item's event procedure.

> The Menu Editor creates a working menu shell. As you've seen, the Menu Editor won't do more than produce a working menu that responds the way other Windows menus respond. You must write all the code behind all the menu options. If you want a check mark to disappear from a checked menu item (such as this application's View | Highlighted option), your code will have to hide the check mark. The mark won't disappear on its own when the user selects the option.

Copying Menus Between Projects

Here's a tip that you should file away for the day when you want to copy a menu from one form to another project's form file. Although several methods exist, one way that you can accomplish this copy is to perform these steps:

1. Make a backup of the target form where you want to copy the menu.
2. Start the Windows Notepad Editor.
3. Load the form with the menu into the editor. Visual Basic saves form files in a text format that you can load into an editor.
4. Copy all the text that describes that form's menu to the Windows Clipboard. Here is a form's text that describes the previous section's menu:

```
Begin VB.Menu mnuFile
   Caption        =    "&File"
   Begin VB.Menu mnuFileNew
      Caption        =    "&New"
   End
   Begin VB.Menu mnuFileOpen
      Caption        =    "&Open"
      Begin VB.Menu mnuFileOpenBinary
```

```
            Caption          =    "&Binary"
        End
        Begin VB.Menu mnuFileOpenText
            Caption          =    "&Text"
        End
    End
    Begin VB.Menu mnuFileClose
        Caption       =    "&Close"
    End
    Begin VB.Menu mnuFileBar1
        Caption          =    "-"
    End
    Begin VB.Menu mnuFileExit
        Caption          =    "E&xit"
    End
End
Begin VB.Menu mnuEdit
    Caption       =    "&Edit"
End
Begin VB.Menu mnuView
    Caption       =    "&View"
    Begin VB.Menu mnuViewHighlighted
        Caption       =    "Highlighted"
        Checked       =    -1  'True
    End
End
Begin VB.Menu mnuHelp
    Caption       =    "&Help"
End
```

5. Open the target application's form file. Each `Begin...End` block defines an object
   on the form. Locate an `End` statement that completes an object's definition and
   paste the Clipboard's form description there. When you save the file and load the
   form, the menu will be working as it does in the other. You now can write the
   event procedures for the menu options.

Summary

Adding menus to your applications requires only that you master the Menu Editor.
Menus are nothing more than advanced controls with property values that you set using
the Menu Editor. Most menu items require that you specify a `Caption` and `Name` property
as well as indent the item properly under its menu bar command. Optionally, a menu
item might contain a shortcut access keystroke or a check mark next to the item.

The next hour will be really fun—you'll learn how to add colorful graphic images to
your applications.

17

Q&A

Q My application is simple, so do I now need a menu?

A Most applications require a menu, even if the only menu option is File | Exit. The simple applications you've seen throughout this tutorial have rarely had an Exit command button. To close them, you've had to click the application's window close button. You offer users a much more graceful exit if you give them the familiar File | Exit command.

Q How many levels can I use for submenus?

A The Menu Editor supports numerous submenu levels, but menus become much less manageable if you go past two levels of submenus. In other words, a submenu such as File | Open | Text is about as deep as you should go. Your users will find the menu structure too cumbersome to traverse if you add additional submenus. A better option is to create a dialog box if a menu option requires several settings. The dialog box can be a second form with buttons and controls. You can display that form (by assigning `True` to its `Visible` property) when the user clicks the menu option for that dialog box.

Workshop

The quiz questions and exercises are provided for your further understanding. See Appendix B for the answers.

Quiz

1. True or false: Menu items are controls that have properties.

2. True or false: More than one form can have a menu within a single application.

3. What is the most common menu-naming prefix?

4. What would be a good name for an Edit | Select | All menu option?

5. How does the Menu Editor know that a submenu option is part of a menu bar option?

6. True or false: You can add a menu shortcut keystroke to a menu option that produces a submenu.

7. What menu option should all applications use?

8. Why should programmers shy away from using unconventional menu options such as File | Quit?

9. What is the event property used in menu processing?

10. Which property must your application change in order to change the check mark setting on a menu option?

Exercises

1. Create a new project with the following menu bar items: Write, Read, and Listen. Create a Write submenu with these options: Keyboard, Pencil, and Pen. Create a Read submenu with these options: Screen, Book, and Magazine. Create a Listen submenu with these options: Radio and Television.

2. Add menus to the Atm.vbp project that appears in VB's samples folder. On the opening form, add a File | Exit option as well as a Language menu bar option with these pull-down checked choices: English, Italiano, Espanol, Francais, and Deutsch. Don't use special foreign characters unless you can access them easily from your keyboard, and you are used to using them. When the user first starts the application, put the check mark next to the English option but move the check mark (or let the user select a different option) when the user selects an option or clicks the corresponding command button. Add one more menu to the Welcome form that includes a File | Exit option. Unlike the Welcome form's OK button, make sure the menu's File | Exit command on that form completely terminates the application.

17

Hour **18**

The Graphic Image Controls

Take a time-out to have some fun! Almost everybody enjoys working with graphics, and Visual Basic's graphic image controls let you add graphics to your applications. The two primary graphic image tools, the Image control and the Picture Box control, work almost exactly alike to add graphic images to your applications. These tools don't give you the capability to draw lines and circles (other controls do that, as you'll see in the next hour), but you can add graphic images to your applications and manipulate those images with what you learn in this hour's lesson.

The highlights of this hour include

- Which controls display graphic images
- What types of graphic files you can display
- How the Image control differs from the Picture Box control
- When the Toolbar control provides animation techniques

- How to adjust the size of an image contained in a Picture Box or Image control
- How to improve the animation's efficiency so the movement runs more smoothly across your screen

The Image Control

The Image control displays graphics on your Form window. The graphics reside in a file, and the Image control determines how that file's graphic image will appear onscreen.

When you add the Image control to your application's form, you won't see an image of any kind, but rather the outline of a rectangle, as shown in Figure 18.1.

FIGURE 18.1.

The Image control doesn't look like much when you first place it.

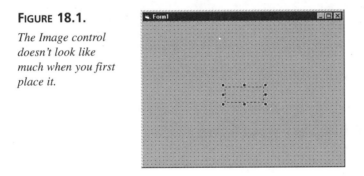

> It's been a while (Hour 1, "Visual Basic at Work") since you saw the location of all the Toolbox window's tools. If you cannot locate the Image control or the Picture Box control for this lesson, remember that all of VB's development environment supports ToolTips, so you can find the correct controls by hovering your mouse pointer over the tools on the Toolbox window. The Picture Box control icon looks like a desert. The Image control icon contains the sun overlooking mountains.

Preparing the Image

A placed Image control doesn't look like a graphic image until you set appropriate properties. The most important property setting is the `Picture` property because the `Picture` property determines which image appears inside the Image control's boundaries on the form. When you click the `Picture` property, Visual Basic displays an ellipsis button you can click to display a Load Picture dialog box (similar to a File Open dialog box).

The Load Picture dialog box displays a list of files with the graphic-related filename extensions shown in Table 18.1.

TABLE 18.1. THE FILE TYPES SUPPORTED BY THE IMAGE CONTROL.

Extension	File Description
.bmp	A Windows bitmap image file
.cur	An animated cursor
.dib	An older bitmap image format
.emf	An enhanced Windows metafile extension
.gif	A Graphic Interchange Format file often used on Web pages
.ico	An icon file
.jpg	The JPEG image format that stores graphics in a highly compressed format
.wmf	A Windows metafile

As long as an image contains one of these filename extensions, you can display that image on your form with the Image control.

 VB comes with several supplied graphic image files that take on Table 18.1's formats. These files are stored in the /Program Files/Microsoft Visual Studio/Common/Graphics folder (provided that you chose to install graphics when installing VB) and further subdivided into categories and file types. When this lesson discusses using one of these graphic files, search the Graphics folder for the image file to load.

18

You can select a graphic file that you want to load into the Image control's Picture property, and Visual Basic displays that image on the form. If you were to select the Coins.wmf file located in the Graphics\Metafile\Business folder, you would see the coin metafile appear like the one shown in Figure 18.2. In the figure, the BorderStyle property is set to 1-FixedSingle so that you'll know where the Image control edges appear in relation to the image.

Sizing the Image

If the metafile had been smaller, the Image control would have decreased its size to capture exactly the image's measurements. The Image control shrinks or enlarges to display the entire image. Therefore, the typical sizing properties such as Width and Height don't always mean much when you place an Image control on the form. The Image control will adjust to hold the entire image that you want to display there.

FIGURE **18.2.**

The Image control enlarges to hold the entire metafile image.

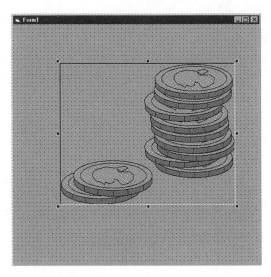

You can try this yourself: Place an Image control on the form and load one of the Bitmap folder images into the Image control's `Picture` property. The Image control shrinks down to the size of a toolbar button to hold the small image.

After you place an image on the form, you can resize the Image control just as you can other controls by dragging its sizing handles out and in. Therefore, after you load an image such as the `Coins.wmf` image, you can adjust the sizing handles to make the Image control smaller.

When you adjust an image's size after you load a graphic image into the Picture control,. the image itself doesn't really shrink or grow, but the Image control shrinks and grows. If you make the Image control's borders smaller, the control will simply truncate or clip the image that doesn't fit in the Image control boundaries. Therefore, the whole image might not appear if the control isn't large enough. If you expand the Image control again, however, the rest of the image reappears so the truncation occurs only visually, but parts of the image itself are not cut off when you shrink the edges. You can enlarge and shrink the image itself; however, you must use a different property, as you're about to see.

The Image control's resizing capability can also make the Image control a nuisance. For example, other images and controls might be in place, and an oversized image would overwrite some of their form area. Therefore, you need a way to control the image's size without clipping the image.

NEW TERM To *clip* or to *truncate* means to hide part of an image with a control's border.

The Stretch property controls the Image control's automatic sizing capabilities. When Stretch is False (the default value), the Image control will expand or shrink to display whatever image you load, but the image inside the Image control doesn't change—it's clipped just as described. If you set the Stretch property to True, the image does enlarge or shrink, depending on the size of the Image control. Therefore, if you want to fit an image into a small space, be sure to turn on Stretch before you adjust the Image control's size.

Figure 18.3 shows a form with two Image controls. One is large and one is small, but they both use the same Coins.wmf image you saw earlier. With both controls' Stretch properties set to True, the images themselves grow and shrink inside their boundaries.

FIGURE 18.3.

The images themselves adjust to the Image control borders.

18

Loading Pictures at Runtime

When your application needs to change the image shown inside an Image control, you cannot simply assign a filename to the Image control's Picture property like this:

```
imgMyFace.Picture = "C:\Handsome.wmf"   ' Not allowed
```

The `Picture` property needs more than a simple assignment. To store a new image in the Image control's `Picture` property, you must use the `LoadPicture()` built-in function. Here is the syntax of `LoadPicture()`:

```
LoadPicture([strFile])
```

`strFile` is a string literal, variable, or control that contains the complete filename and pathname. The graphic image can reside on another computer that your application computer is networked to. When the application gets to the `LoadPicture()` function, the graphic image loads and the picture displays.

To load the `Handsome.wmf` graphic image, you could specify the following line:

```
imgMyFace.Picture = LoadPicture("C:\Handsome.wmf")   ' Allowed
```

If you want to change the image's size before the image appears, you can set the image's `Visible` property to `False` before loading the picture and adjusting the `Height` and `Width` properties. Remember to set the `Stretch` property to `True` if you want the image to resize and not be clipped. After you adjust the size, you then can set `Visible` to `True`, and the image will appear in the size you prefer.

> You can remove an image from an Image control by assigning the `LoadPicture()` function to an Image control's `Picture` property without specifying a filename argument.

The Picture Box Control

If you applied everything you knew about the Image control to the Picture Box control, you could use the Picture Box control. The Picture Box control works almost exactly like the Image control, with these exceptions:

- The Picture Box control supports more properties, events, and methods than the Image control.
- The Picture Box control consumes more resources than the Image control and, therefore, is not as efficient.

The Picture Box control automatically clips the image if it will not fit within the Picture Box control's borders that you set when you placed the Picture Box control.

> You use the Picture Box control to group option buttons into a set just as you can with the Frame control. You then can display a graphic image in the option button background.

Suppose that you placed a rather large Picture Box control on the form but then loaded a graphic file image into the picture box that was much smaller, such as an icon. The Picture Box control would not resize, so the image would appear inside the Picture Box control (see Figure 18.4).

FIGURE 18.4.

The Picture Box control doesn't always shrink to fit.

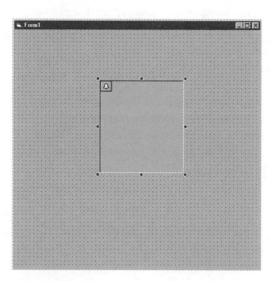

The AutoSize property, normally set to False, determines how the Image control responds to a loaded image's size. If AutoSize is False, the control doesn't resize to fit the image. If, however, you change AutoSize to True, the image control does resize to the image's measurements and doesn't clip. Therefore, the image will always shrink or expand as needed to fit the Image control's size when you set AutoSize to True.

> After you set AutoSize to True, you can manually adjust the Picture Box control's properties in the code. The image will resize along with the picture box's measurements.

18

Use the Align property to determine where on the form the Picture Box control appears. You can dock the control to any side of the Form window control using the Align property values described in Table 18.2.

TABLE 18.2. POSSIBLE Align PROPERTY VALUES.

Property Value	Description
0-None	The Picture Box control appears where you place it in the Form window.
1-Align Top	The Picture Box control appears at the top of the Form window.
2-Align Bottom	The Picture Box control appears at the bottom of the Form window.
3-Align Left	The Picture Box control appears at the left of the Form window.
4-Align Right	The Picture Box control appears at the right of the Form window.

> You can use the Picture Box control to create toolbar buttons, which the Align property docks at the top of the form. By changing the Align property, your code can move the toolbar elsewhere.

Animating Pictures

You can create animated applications using the Picture Box control by duplicating the same techniques used in the stop-animation techniques that movie-makers use for space and monster battles. This section describes the development of a simple animated Form window. After you master these simple techniques, more extensive animation might take more time to develop, but the techniques don't change.

Figure 18.5 shows the running animated application. The application simply floats a changing image across the screen. You'll use an Image control and a Timer control to perform the animation.

The Timer control lets your application time the animation. After every time interval that passes (set in the timer's Interval property), the timer's Timer() event procedure executes. The Timer() event procedure can adjust the image's location (and picture if needed). If you adjust the location every half second or so, the animation will appear to move across the form.

FIGURE 18.5.

The animation appli-
cation sends an
image across the
screen.

Stop-animation techniques are techniques you use to make an image appear onscreen for a fraction of a second before you put a new image in its place or move the image to a different part of the Form window.

To build the application, perform these steps:

1. Create a new project and expand the Form window to a `Height` property of `6840` and a `Width` property of `5910`.

2. Change the form's `Caption` property to `Animated Cartoon`.

3. Place an Image control on the form. Don't worry about the location or size because you'll adjust those values with code. You'll use an Image control for this application instead of a Picture Box control because the Image control is slightly more efficient and you have no need for the extra properties that come with the Picture Box control.

4. Select the `Face02` graphic image located in your `Graphics\Icons\Misc` folder. Remember the full path to this file because you'll have to enter this same path a little later in the application's code.

5. Change the image's `Height` property to `1685` and the `Width` property to `1815`, and change the image's `Name` property to `imgHappy`.

6. Set the image's `Stretch` property to `True` so the happy face resizes like the one in Figure 18.6.

18

FIGURE 18.6.

The happy face is ready for display.

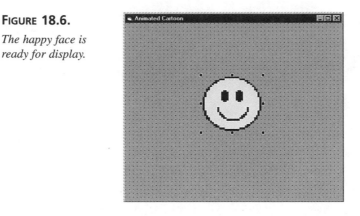

7. Add a Timer control to the form and name the timer tmrAni. Set the timer's Interval property to 500.

8. You must now add the code. Double-click the Form window to open the Form_Load() event procedure. Form_Load() will initialize the image's location. Type the following for the Form_Load() event procedure:

```
Private Sub Form_Load()
  ' Adjust the image's location
  imgHappy.Left = 0    ' Number of twips from
                       ' left of Form window

  imgHappy.Top = 3820 ' Number of twips from
                       ' top of Form window

End Sub
```

9. Add a Timer() event procedure to the Code window. To add the event procedure, you can click the Code window's Object drop-down list to select the Timer control. The Timer() is the only event procedure possible, so Visual Basic opens the Timer() event procedure. You can add code to the event procedure so tmrAni_Timer() looks like this:

```
Private Sub tmrAni_Timer()
  ' Adjust the Left and Top properties
  ' as well as the happy face shown so
  ' that the face appears to float up
  ' and across the Form window.

  ' The first time you declare a Static Boolean
  ' variable, VB initializes it to False
  Static blnFace As Boolean

    ' Add to Left and Top only if room is left
  If (imgHappy.Left < 4800) And _
```

```
        (imgHappy.Top > 500) Then
          imgHappy.Left = imgHappy.Left + 100
          imgHappy.Top = imgHappy.Top - 50
    Else
      imgHappy.Left = 0      ' Restore image's first
      imgHappy.Top = 3820    ' position.
    End If

    ' Change the image displayed

    ' You may need to edit the graphic paths you see below to
    ' match the graphic file locations of your VB installation.
    ' In most cases, simply changing the drive letter from K:\...
    ' to C:\... (or whatever drive VB is installed) will do.

    If blnFace = True Then
        imgHappy.Picture = _
          LoadPicture("K:\Program Files\Microsoft Visual Studio\" & _
            "Common\Graphics\Icons\Misc\Face03.ico")
        blnFace = False
    Else
        imgHappy.Picture = _
          LoadPicture("K:\Program Files\Microsoft Visual Studio\" & _
            "Common\Graphics\Icons\Misc\Face02.ico")
        blnFace = True
    End If

End Sub
```

18

Be sure to put the complete pathname for your computer's Face02.ico and Face03.ico files in the Timer() event procedure's LoadPicture() function calls.

10. Save your project and run your application to see the happy face move across and up the screen. The happy face smiles and grins all along the way.

This animation application is simple, but you now have all the tools you need to produce animation effects. You can smooth the animation by displaying images that don't change as rapidly between time intervals as the two happy faces shown here. In addition, if you compile your application, the animation will run more smoothly than if you run the application from within the development environment. (Compile the program by selecting File | Make. Hour 23, "Distributing Your Applications," explains more about application compilation.)

In addition, you can make the image's movement appear slightly less jumpy if you set the image's Visible property to False at the top of the Timer() event procedure and then set the property back to True before leaving the procedure. Hiding the control before adjusting its location properties seems to improve the control's movement. You might not notice a difference, however, if you run the application on a quick computer, especially if you compile the application.

This application uses the Image control for efficiency, but you would probably see only a little efficiency decrease if you used the Picture Box control instead. Today's computers are fast, and the difference between the controls is not as critical as it once was.

STATIC VARIABLES

This happy face animation application demonstrates a different variable declaration from the ones you've seen so far. The Static statement declares static variables. Although static variables are local to their procedure, they don't lose their values between procedure calls as regular local variables do. Therefore, if blnFace is True when the tmrAni_Timer() event procedure finishes, the next time Visual Basic executes tmrAni_Timer(), the blnFace variable will still be declared and still be True. Visual Basic creates and initializes a static variable only once per program execution, and the static variable retains its value between procedure calls.

The animation application uses the static variable to test which happy face image is showing. If blnFace is True, the event procedure loads the Face03.ico picture into the image and changes blnFace from True to False. On the next event procedure execution, blnFace will still be False, so the event procedure loads the Face02.ico image and changes blnFace to True for the next cycle. The static blnFace variable ensures that a different face shows every time interval.

Summary

You probably had some fun working with the graphic image tools shown in this lesson. You now know how to display graphic file images with the Image control and the Picture Box control. Both controls do basically the same task—display images from graphics files. Their differences lie in the way they display the images when image size becomes an issue; also, the Picture Box control is slightly less efficient but offers more properties, events, and methods.

The next hour further improves your artistic skills. Instead of using prepackaged graphic images, you'll use Visual Basic's drawing tools to draw your own lines, circles, boxes, and other shapes.

Q&A

Q Can I use graphic images other than the ones that Visual Basic supplies?

A Certainly. Both the Image control and the Picture Box control load images from any file that uses one of Table 18.1's graphic file formats. As a matter of fact, Visual Basic's images are fairly limited, and most of them are useful for command button pictures and toolbars but very little else.

Q Did you just say command button pictures? When I click the command button's `Picture` property, no picture appears on the command button, so what's wrong?

A This is as good a time as any to describe how to put pictures on command buttons. After you set the command button's `Picture` property, you must also set the `Style` property to `1-Graphical`. Only a graphical command button can display pictures. The command button works just like before, but now a picture appears. (Erase the `Caption` property if the caption overwrites the picture's image.) You did not learn about command button pictures in earlier lessons because you were not yet familiar with the `LoadPicture()` function. You can use `LoadPicture()` to insert a picture on a command button at runtime if you need to do that. Often, programmers will display a slightly different picture on a command button after the user clicks the button, and you can use `LoadPicture()` to do the same.

Q If speed is no longer an issue, why should I ever use the Image control?

A Although the Image control is slightly more efficient, you are correct in remembering that today's computers are generally fast enough to handle both the Picture Box control and the Image control for any application. If, however, you work in a networked environment or if you set up your Windows desktop to run several applications simultaneously, you will want to utilize all resources as efficiently as possible. Therefore, you might prefer to use the Image control to lessen your computer's load if you don't need the Picture Box control's extra properties, events, and methods.

Workshop

The quiz questions and exercises are provided for your further understanding. See Appendix B for the answers.

Quiz

1. Which two controls display graphic images?
2. Which control is more efficient?
3. What happens if you load a picture into an Image control and the Image control is too small to hold the entire picture (assume default property values)?
4. What happens if you load a picture into a Picture Box control and the Picture Box control is too small to hold the entire picture (assume default property values)?
5. What happens if you load a picture into an Image control and the Image control is larger than the picture (assume default property values)?

6. What happens if you load a picture into a Picture Box control and the Picture Box control is larger than the picture (assume default property values)?

7. What is wrong with this assignment (assume that the filename and pathname are correct)?

    ```
    imgFace.Picture = "C:\DataPics\Flower.Ico"
    ```

8. Which control helps control animation effects?

9. True or false: A static variable is a global variable because its value doesn't change from a procedure's termination to the same procedure's next execution.

10. When does a static variable first get initialized?

Exercises

1. Add a command button to the animation application so that the animation doesn't begin until you click the button. The solution to this exercise might not be obvious at first. (Hint: Consider activating the Timer control in the command button's event procedure.) Put a happy face on the command button and hide the command button so it disappears when the application starts animating the happy face.

2. Change the animation application so that the happy face bounces off all four sides of the Form window.

Hour **19**

Toolbars and More Graphics

In Hour 17, "Menus and Visual Basic," you learned how to add menus to your applications. Many applications use toolbars with buttons that mimic menu options. Toolbars are part of most major Windows applications, and they can be part of yours as well. In addition, you can draw your own graphics on the form. Although VB's graphic-drawing tools are fairly primitive, you can draw lines and circles and other basic shapes to accent and highlight areas of your form.

The highlights of this hour include

- What the Image List control does
- How to add the Toolbar control to the Toolbox window
- Why you must connect the image list to the toolbar
- How to respond to toolbar events
- When to use the Line and Shape controls
- How to accent forms with line-based graphics

Preparing for the Toolbar

The tools that appear on your Toolbox window are called *intrinsic controls*. You can add additional controls to the toolbar. As a matter of fact, you can obtain controls from sources other than Microsoft because many people create controls for Visual Basic.

In Hour 21, "Visual Basic and ActiveX," you'll learn more about how developers create new controls for Visual Basic.

Visual Basic's Professional and Enterprise Edition users can take advantage of an extra control that comes with Visual Basic: the Toolbar control. It comes in a collection of other controls named the Microsoft Windows Common Controls 6.0. To add this set of controls to your toolbar, select Project|Components (Ctrl+T) to display the Components dialog box (see Figure 19.1).

FIGURE 19.1.

Adding more tools to the toolbox with the Components dialog box.

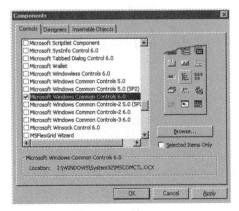

Scroll the box down to the Microsoft Windows Common Controls 6.0 entry and check it. Click OK. When you look at the Toolbox window again, you'll see new controls on the toolbox. Figure 19.2 labels these tools.

You'll probably recognize the purpose of most of these new tools. With these additional tools you can add a status bar to your form and display a progress bar during a long sort or calculation. The Tab Strip control gives you the ability to display a multiple-page dialog box (called a properties sheet or a properties page).

FIGURE 19.2.

The Common Controls package of tools gives you additional power.

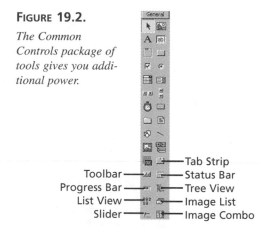

Tab Strip
Toolbar————Status Bar
Progress Bar————Tree View
List View————Image List
Slider————Image Combo

The Image List Control

As you know, a toolbar is a row of buttons with icons on them. The Toolbar control has one slight limitation: It cannot keep track of each image that you place on a toolbar button. Instead, the Toolbar control only works with a special control called an Image List control. Fortunately, the Image List control appears on the toolbox when you add the Microsoft Windows Common Controls 6.0 control set, as you did in the previous section.

Therefore, you might want to practice adding a toolbar to a Form window by opening a new project and then placing an Image List control on the Form window. Expand the Form window slightly so that the Form window is wide enough for a toolbar (approximately 6,645 twips wide).

The Image List control doesn't look like much. Just like the Timer control and the Common Dialog Box control, the Image List control's placed size and location don't matter much because the user will never directly see the Image List control on the form. The user will, instead, see images that the Image List control keeps track of. The Image List control works a lot like a graphic image array. The Image List control holds images from files, and when you're using it for toolbars, the Image List control holds toolbar icons such as the ones in Microsoft Visual Studio's `\Program Files\Microsoft Visual Studio\Common\Graphics\Icons` folder.

NEW TERM   An *image list* is a list of images in an array-like control called the Image List control.

The easiest way to add images to the Image List control is by clicking the Image List control's `Custom` property to display Figure 19.3's custom property pages. This dialog box organizes the Image List control's figures and lets you manage each figure's properties separately.

19

FIGURE 19.3.

Specifying Image List control properties in the Property Pages dialog box.

Although the first page of the Image List control's property pages lets you specify an image's size, you don't need to worry about the size if the graphics files are exactly the size you need to display, just as icon files (with the .ico extension) are. If you use the Image List control to group graphic images of other kinds of files, you'll need to specify each image size if the file size doesn't match the size at which you want to store the image.

Click the Images tab to display the Images page. Here you will build a list of images that will ultimately end up on your application's toolbar. To add some images for this lesson's sample toolbar, click the Insert Picture button and select the icon file named Disk04 located in the \Program Files\Microsoft Visual Studio\Common\Graphics\Icons\ Computer folder. The image will appear in the image list, and its index value will be set to 1, as Figure 19.4 shows.

FIGURE 19.4.

The Image List control now has one image.

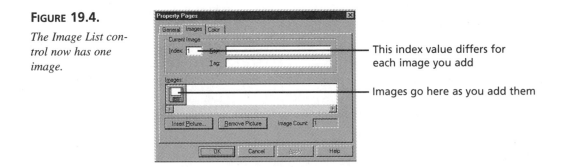

This index value differs for each image you add

Images go here as you add them

Keep inserting images in the following order (from the same folder to keep things simple): Key04, Mouse02, Trash01, and W95mbx01. As you insert the images one at a time, you'll notice that Visual Basic automatically updates the image's Index text box value. After you add the final image, your image list should look like Figure 19.5's list of icons.

FIGURE 19.5.

The Image List control now contains five icon images.

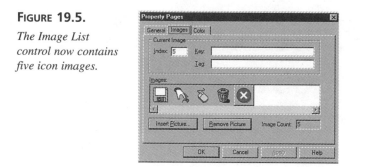

> If you want to change the toolbar's colors from the standard color scheme (typically a gray background just like Visual Basic's toolbars), click the Color tab and select a different color scheme.

Click OK to close the Property Pages dialog box and name the Image List control `imlToolBar` (using the Properties window) so the Toolbar control can reference the images you just stored in the Image List control.

Finalizing the Toolbar

Double-click the Toolbar control to add a toolbar to the top of the form. The toolbar will first appear at the top of the form, which is where most toolbars reside. You can change the `Align` property if you want to place the toolbar against another edge of the form. Change the toolbar's `Name` property to `tlbNew`.

> If you want to give your user a menu choice to place the toolbar elsewhere, the menu selection can change the `Align` property value so the toolbar moves to another location on the Form window.

Click the toolbar's `Custom` property to display the toolbar's Property Pages dialog box, which is shown in Figure 19.6. Although you can set most of the dialog box's properties from the Properties window, you'll find that the Property Pages dialog box makes setting up the toolbox simpler.

19

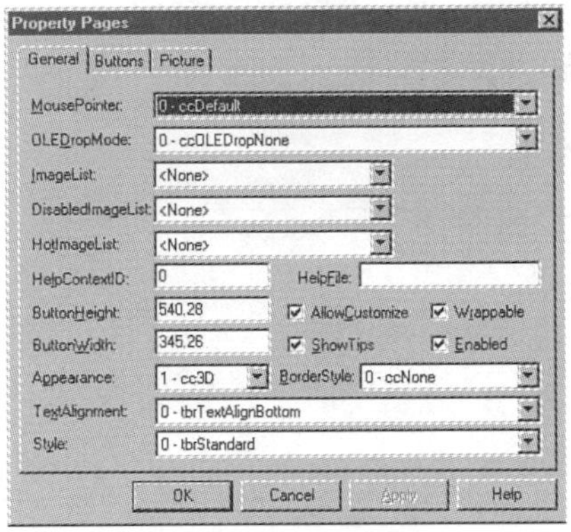

FIGURE 19.6.

*The Toolbar control's
Property Pages dia-
log box.*

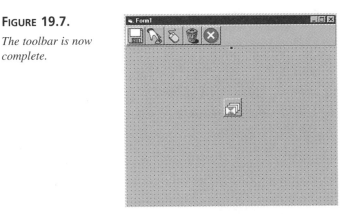

To connect the image list to the toolbar, open the ImageList drop-down list box and
select `imlToolBar` (if other image lists appeared on the form, they would all appear and
you could select the one that goes with the toolbar). Select the `1-ccFixedSingle`
`BorderStyle` property to help distinguish the toolbar from the rest of the form's controls.

To add the toolbar buttons, click the Buttons tab to display the Buttons page. For each
button, click Insert Button and change the Image value to `1` (the first image's `Index`
property value). Also type `Save` for the `Key` value. When you click Apply (to apply the
property values), the first toolbar button will appear with the disk icon that appears first
in the image list.

Continue clicking the Insert Button command button and updating the Image text box.
Use the following values for the last four `Key` values: `Button`, `Mouse`, `Trash`, and `Stop`.
For each `Key` value, increment its Image value by one. When you finish the toolbar buttons, close the dialog box, and the five toolbar buttons with their corresponding icons
from the Image List control will appear (see Figure 19.7).

FIGURE 19.7.

*The toolbar is now
complete.*

You'll use the Key values inside code to determine exactly which toolbar button the user clicks.

Many programmers like to add the same Key values to the ToolTips property as well so that the toolbar supports ToolTip-based help.

Run the application and try the new toolbar. When you click a button, you'll see the button clicking. Now you need to hook up the commands to the buttons. Stop the running application to add the event procedure.

The toolbar acts like a control array. To add code that responds to a toolbar's button click, double-click the Toolbar control to open a new event procedure. The first line appears here:

```
Private Sub tlbNew_ButtonClick(ByVal Button As ComctlLib.Button)
```

The ButtonClick() event is the toolbar's event that occurs when the user clicks a toolbar button. The argument tells your code which button the user clicked so the code can respond accordingly. You must use the argument's Key method to determine the button clicked. The button's Key method returns the string you entered for the toolbar button's Key method. The following code shows an outline of the code you could write that would execute a different procedure depending on the user's toolbar button click:

```
Private Sub tlbNew_ButtonClick(ByVal Button As ComctlLib.Button)
' Respond to button clicks
Dim msgPress As Integer
' Display a message box depending
' on which toolbar button the user clicks
Select Case Button.Key
Case Is = "Save":
msgPress = MsgBox("You pressed Save", , "Save")
Case Is = "Button":
msgPress = MsgBox("You pressed Button", , "Button")
Case Is = "Mouse":
msgPress = MsgBox("You pressed Mouse", , "Mouse")
Case Is = "Trash":
msgPress = MsgBox("You pressed Trash", , "Trash")
Case Is = "Stop":
Unload Me
End
End Select
```

19

Of course, your application would do more than display a message box when the user clicks a toolbar button. More likely you would insert a `Call` statement to call a procedure that handles the toolbar button. If the toolbar's buttons mimic menu selections, as most users design toolbar buttons to do, the `Call` statement can call the corresponding menu item, such as `Call mnuFileExit_Click`.

 If you place the toolbar at the top of the form but the Form window contains a menu (or if you add the menu after you place the Toolbar control), the toolbar will appear beneath the menu and always give room for the menu. The menu's pull-down submenus will always appear on top of the toolbar.

The Line and Shape Controls

The graphics you've worked with in this book have, until now, been graphic images stored in files. The Image and Picture Box controls display graphic images on the form. The toolbar buttons can display icon images. You have yet to see how to draw your own graphics. The rest of this lesson introduces VB's drawing tools.

The Line and Shape controls work together to draw lines, boxes, and all kinds of figures on the form. By placing the controls and setting appropriate properties, you'll be adding flair to applications. The properties of each control that you place on your form determine exactly what kind of image the control becomes.

Here are the primary graphics images that you can draw with the Line and Shape controls:

- Lines
- Rectangles
- Squares
- Ovals
- Circles
- Rounded rectangles
- Rounded squares

Figure 19.8 shows most of these images. By combining these fundamental geometric images and setting appropriate color and size properties, you can draw virtually anything you need to draw on the form.

FIGURE 19.8.

The images that you can draw.

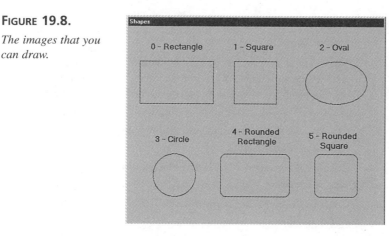

The Line Control

You use the Line control to draw lines of various widths, lengths, and patterns. The Shape control handles the drawing of all other fundamental shapes.

Mastering the Line Control

The Line control contains properties that specify the width and length of lines you draw. In addition, you can change the pattern of each line you draw.

Table 19.1 lists the fundamental property values for the Line control. Table 19.2 contains the values that you can specify for the BorderStyle property. The BorderStyle property determines the pattern that Visual Basic uses to draw the line. By specifying various BorderStyle values, you can vary the line pattern. If you assign a BorderStyle property at runtime, you can either specify a number that represents BorderStyle or use one of Visual Basic's named literals.

19

TABLE 19.1. THE LINE CONTROL'S FUNDAMENTAL PROPERTIES.

Property	Description
BorderColor	Sets the line color.
BorderStyle	Contains one of seven values that specifies the pattern of the drawn line. See Table 19.2 for available BorderStyle values. The default value is 1-Solid. BorderStyle has no effect on lines with BorderWidth greater than 1 twip.
BorderWidth	Specifies the size, in twips, that the line takes.

continues

TABLE 19.1. CONTINUED

Property	Description
DrawMode	An advanced style that determines how the bit patterns of the line interact with the surrounding form's bit appearance. The default value, 13-Copy Pen, works well for virtually all Visual Basic applications.
Visible	Holds True or False, indicating whether the user can see the Line control. You might want to set the Visible property in code so the line appears as a highlighting tool.
X1	Contains the number of twips from the left of the Form window to the start of the line.
X2	Contains the number of twips from the left of the Form window to the end of the line.
Y1	Contains the number of twips from the top of the Form window to the left starting point of the line.
Y2	Contains the number of twips from the top of the Form window to the lower ending point of the line.

TABLE 19.2. THE LINE CONTROL'S BorderStyle VALUES.

Value	Named Literal	Description
0-Transparent	vbTransparent	Background comes through the line.
1-Solid	vbBSSolid	The line is a solid line.
2-Dash	vbBSDash	The line is composed of dashes.
3-Dot	vbBSDot	The line is composed of dots.
4-Dash-Dot	vbBSDashDot	The line is composed of a continuing dash-dot-dash-dot.
5-Dash-Dot-Dot	vbBSDashDotDot	The line is composed of a series of one dash followed by two dots.
6-Inside Solid	vbBSInsideSolid	Same as 1-Solid for lines.

Figure 19.9 shows how various BorderStyle settings affect the lines you draw. BorderStyle determines how a series of dashes and dots compose the line's pattern. (Is this Morse code we're speaking here?)

FIGURE 19.9.

The BorderStyle *property values.*

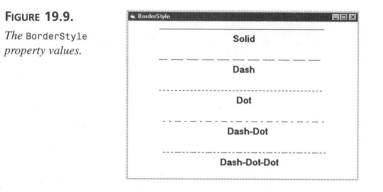

To draw a line, double-click the Line control on the toolbox. A line appears in the center of the form with a handle on each end. To move the line to a different location, drag the center of the line with the mouse. To lengthen or shorten the line, drag either handle on the line. You can raise and lower either end of the line by dragging either end's handle with the mouse.

After you position the line with the mouse in the approximate location at which you need the line to appear, you can fine-tune the line's size and location by setting the various property values. If you're a patient programmer, you can even animate the lines by changing the X1, X2, Y1, and Y2 property settings repeatedly through code.

Figure 19.10 contains the Form window that might be used as a company's front-end form. The various lines help separate controls from the title. As you can see, lines help focus the user's attention.

FIGURE 19.10.

Accenting forms with lines.

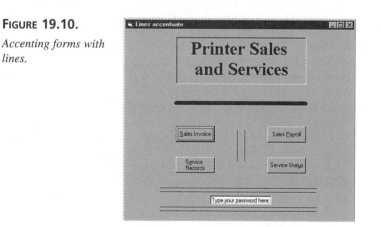

19

Mastering the Shape Control

The Shape control gives you the capability to draw six different kinds of figures on the form. The various shading and color properties help you distinguish one shape from another. Table 19.3 contains the basic properties you'll use for the Shape control. The most important property is the Shape property. The Shape property gives a shape from one of the six fundamental shapes.

TABLE 19.3. THE SHAPE CONTROL'S FUNDAMENTAL PROPERTIES.

Property	Description
BackColor	Specifies a Windows color value that determines the background color of the shape.
BackStyle	Contains either 0-Transparent (the default) or 1-Opaque, which determines whether the background of the form appears through the shape or if the shape hides whatever it covers.
BorderColor	Specifies a Windows color value that determines the color of the shape's bordering edges.
BorderStyle	Contains one of seven values that specifies the pattern of the shape's border. The Line control's BorderStyle values (refer to Table 19.2) provide the shape's BorderStyle possible values as well. The default value is 1-Solid. BorderStyle has no effect on shapes with a BorderWidth greater than 1 twip.
BorderWidth	Specifies the size, in twips, that the shape's outline takes.
DrawMode	An advanced style that determines how the bit patterns of the shape interact with the surrounding form's bit appearance. The default value, 13-Copy Pen, works well for virtually all Visual Basic applications.
FillColor	Specifies a Windows color value that determines the color of the shape's interior lines.
FillStyle	Contains one of eight values that specifies the pattern of lines with which Visual Basic paints the interior of the shape. Table 19.4 contains the possible values for the shape's FillStyle. The default FillStyle value is 0-Solid.
Height	Specifies the number of twips high that the shape is (from the highest point to the lowest point in the shape).
Left	Specifies the number of twips from the form's left edge to the shape's far left edge.
Shape	Contains one of six values that specifies the type of shape that the Shape control takes on. Table 19.5 contains the possible values for the shape's Shape property. The default Shape property is 0-Rectangle.

Property	Description
Top	Specifies the number of twips from the form's top edge to the shape's highest edge.
Width	Specifies the number of twips wide that the shape takes (at the widest axis).

Table 19.4 contains the possible values for the Shape control's FillStyle property. Figure 19.11 shows the various fill patterns that a shape can contain.

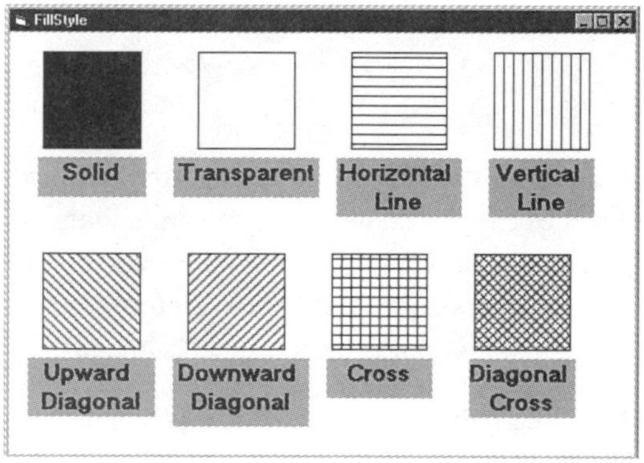

FIGURE 19.11.

The FillStyle property determines the shape's interior design.

TABLE 19.4. THE SHAPE CONTROL'S FillStyle VALUES.

Value	Named Literal	Description
0-Solid	vbFSSolid	Solid color fill with no pattern.
1-Transparent	vbFSTransparent	The shape appears as an outline only.
2-Horizontal Line	vbHorizontalLine	Horizontal lines fill the shape.
3-Vertical Line	vbVerticalLine	Vertical lines fill the shape.
4-Upward Diagonal	vbUpwardDiagonal	Upward diagonal lines fill the shape.
5-Downward Diagonal	vbDownwardDiagonal	Downward diagonal lines fill the shape.
6-Cross	vbCross	Crosshairs fill the shape.
7-Diagonal Cross	vbDiagonalCross	Diagonal crosshairs fill the shape.

19

Table 19.5 contains the possible values for the Shape control's Shape property. Figure 19.8 shows the various shapes that the Shape control can take. Therefore, when you want to place a square on a form, you'll place the Shape control on the form and set the Shape property to 1-Square.

TABLE 19.5. THE SHAPE CONTROL'S Shape VALUES.

Value	Description
0-Rectangle	A rectangle
1-Square	A square
2-Oval	An oval
3-Circle	A circle
4-Rounded Rectangle	A rectangle with rounded corners
5-Rounded Square	A square with rounded corners

Summary

In this lesson you learned how to place toolbars on your application's form and to respond to the toolbar's event procedure. Unfortunately, there isn't enough room to hold every toolbox control, so if you want to use a nonintrinsic control, you must add that control from the Project|Components dialog box. Before you can add a toolbar, you must generate the image list that holds each toolbar's images.

The Line and Shape controls are the primary drawing controls. There are seven fundamental geometric shapes that you can draw. By specifying various properties, you can control how those shapes appear on the form.

Next hour's lesson doesn't discuss a single new control, command, method, property, or event! The next lesson takes you on a tour of Visual Basic's debugging tools that help you test and eliminate bugs from your applications.

Q&A

Q I'm no artist, so why would I want to learn Visual Basic's drawing controls?

A The drawing tools are not for artists. If you want to place a nice art image on your form, use a drawing or paint program designed specifically to help create works of art. You can also download royalty-free images from most online services and the Internet. Place those images on your form with the Picture Box control or the Image control. The drawing tools, although you can use them to draw pictures, are rather primitive, but they do serve to help you accentuate and highlight various parts of a form.

Q **Why can't I use most of the `BorderStyle` properties when the line's width is greater than 1 twip?**

A That's a good question, and there seems to be no great answer. Often, a thick dotted line or dashed line would be welcome for programmers who want to separate parts of a form with such a division. Unfortunately, Visual Basic doesn't support the feature, and hasn't since its very first version.

Workshop

The quiz questions and exercises are provided for your further understanding. See Appendix B for the answers.

Quiz

1. Why must you open the project's Components dialog box before using the Toolbar control?

2. Which control works with the toolbar to produce icon images on the buttons?

3. What does the Image control's `Key` method do?

4. Why does the toolbar's event procedure use an argument?

5. How many shapes can the Shape control produce?

6. Which property determines the pattern of drawn lines?

7. True or false: You should use the `LoadPicture()` function to initialize or change the value displayed with the Shape control.

8. What is the `FillStyle` property used for?

9. True or false: You can change a shape's interior and exterior color.

Exercises

1. Write an application that includes a large Shape control (originally placed as a square) in the middle of the form. Add a command button that reads Change Shape. Every time the user clicks the command button, change the shape to something different.

2. Create a Form window that contains a rectangle with a blue border, red diagonal lines, and a green interior.

19

3. Write an application that draws a yellow happy face in the center of the form. Don't use a graphic image file. Add two toolbar buttons, one with a happy face icon from an icon file and one with a sad face icon. When the user clicks the happy face toolbar button, wink the happy face's eye. When the user clicks the sad face toolbar button, draw a tear coming out of one eye.

HOUR 20

Writing Correct Applications

What is a *correct* application? It is an application that compiles cleanly and runs without errors. Rarely is an application truly correct because some bugs don't appear until late in the life of an application. Other bugs raise their ugly heads as soon as you press Enter after entering a program statement.

This lesson takes you on a tour of Visual Basic's debugging tools. With Visual Basic's integrated debugger as part of the development environment, you can test your applications and locate bugs. Your goal should always be to eliminate as many bugs as possible. Although you cannot always ensure that every bug is gone, you can test your application to eliminate as many bugs as possible.

The highlights of this hour include

- What kinds of errors to watch for
- How to spot mistakes

- When to set a breakpoint
- How to examine variables at runtime
- When to enter single-step mode
- How to use the Immediate window to change program values

Kinds of Errors

You already know that a bug is a program error. Several kinds of bugs exist, however. The kind of error that appears determines how you will fix the bug.

NEW TERM   A *syntax error* is a bug that appears because you misspelled a command or used improper grammar.

Syntax errors are the easiest errors to remove from your program because Visual Basic finds them for you. Take a moment to display the Options dialog box shown in Figure 20.1. (Select Tools | Options to see this dialog box.)

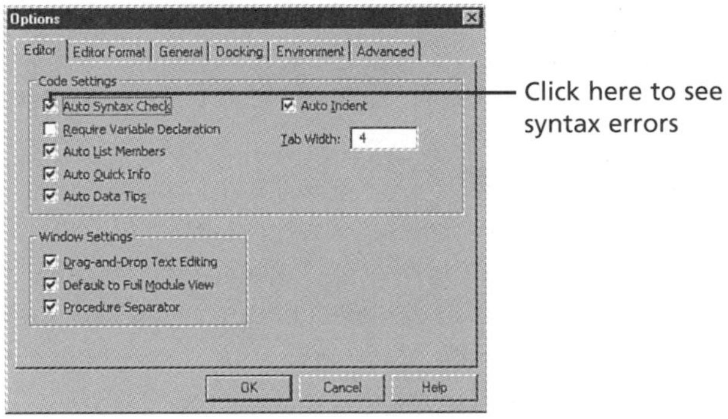

FIGURE 20.1.

Letting Visual Basic find syntax errors for you.

— Click here to see syntax errors

The option labeled Auto Syntax Check turns on and off Visual Basic's automatic detection of syntax errors as you type them. In other words, if the option is set, and you type a statement with a syntax error, the Code window will look over your shoulder and inform you immediately of the error.

Notice what happens in Figure 20.2. The programmer was trying to enter this statement:

```
Private Functiion CalcTotals(x As Integer) As Double
```

FIGURE 20.2.

Visual Basic detected the syntax error.

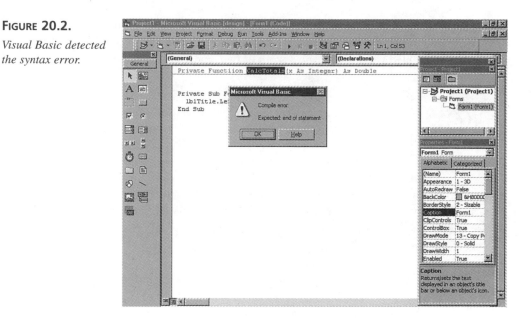

Although it's fairly obvious that the programmer misspelled Function, and it's obvious that the Code window noticed something wrong, here are two things to notice about this automatic syntax check:

- The error message box reads Compile error, not Syntax error.
- Visual Basic highlighted the wrong word! Instead of highlighting the problem word Functiion, Visual Basic highlighted CalcTotals, the name of the function that has no problems.

The error message that appears rarely reads Syntax error because several kinds of syntax errors can occur. The error message Compiler error is less informative than some of the others, but the actual error is secondary to the fact that you typed something incorrectly. Perhaps you misspelled a word (true in this case), left off a quotation mark or a right parenthesis, forgot a built-in function argument list, or failed to end the statement with an underscore when you meant to continue the statement on the next line. When typing code and such an error message box appears, look back at the statement to find the error.

Often, but not always, Visual Basic will highlight the offending part of the statement. In this case, however, Visual Basic failed to locate the exact error. Instead, Visual Basic highlighted the first word found after the error. Visual Basic cannot always detect the

20

exact location of the syntax error because it often has to interpret more of the statement before a problem becomes obvious. Therefore, if you don't see a problem with the current highlighted word, look back a word or two, and you'll find the mistake.

If you don't understand the error message itself, press F1 or click Help at the error message box to read what the online help has to say about the error message.

As you can see, syntax errors are the easiest errors to find. They either show up as you type the program code, or if you've turned off the automatic syntax error check, the syntax errors show up when you try to run or compile the program. Another kind of error, a runtime error, will not show up until you execute the program.

NEW TERM A *runtime error* shows up during the program's execution.

For example, suppose you are calculating an average salary figure, but you make a mistake in the calculation and attempt to divide the total by a variable with zero in it. Division by zero is undefined in mathematics (undefined for the real number system, to be exact), but Visual Basic cannot, when you write the code, know what value the variable will hold. Therefore, only at the time of execution when the division is about to take place can Visual Basic recognize that the division is impossible. Visual Basic will display a runtime error message box such as the one shown in Figure 20.3.

FIGURE 20.3.

A runtime error occurred.

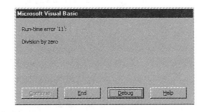

When you're faced with a runtime error, the dialog box gives you these choices:

- Continue
- End
- Debug
- Help

The Continue command button is rarely available because of the severity of most run-time errors. However, with the built-in debugging tools that Visual Basic makes available when you click Debug, you can possibly fix the problem and then continue with the program by clicking Continue. You'll learn all about the debugger in the next section.

If you click End, the program will stop and you'll return to the Code window, where you can locate and fix the problem if you don't need help from the debugging tools. If you want to read more information on the error message itself, click Help to display online help. Figure 20.4 shows the online help that appears when you click Help on the divide-by-zero error.

FIGURE 20.4.

Visual Basic explains the error message.

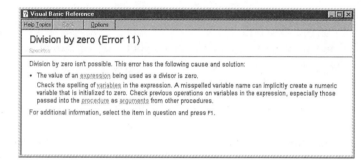

Sometimes you tell the computer to do something that is wrong. The computer under-stands your instructions because no syntax or runtime errors appear, but the computer simply doesn't do what you want it to. In those cases, you've programmed a logic error.

NEW TERM   A *logic error* produces undesired program results, but no error messages appear.

If you've heard people say, "The computer made a mistake," that mistake was most certainly a programmer's or data-entry person's error. In most situations the computer simply does what it was told to do. When the computer zeros out a balance incorrectly, that error is almost always a programmer's logic mistake.

20

Logic errors are the most difficult to locate. Whereas the Code window tells you where a syntax error appeared, and the runtime system tells you when a runtime error appears, you must spot logic errors yourself (hopefully before your application's users spot them) and trace the problem to the source. The development environment's integrated debugger is the most useful tool for finding logic errors.

One of the quickest ways to locate logic errors early is to test your program. When asked for an input value, enter extremely large and extremely small values. Run the application several times, using a series of test data values. If logic errors exist, such testing will almost always make the logic errors surface. After you find all the logic errors, let other people run the program! They can also find problems that you failed to uncover because they will try things you never thought to try. In order to thoroughly test your application, run it with large negative numbers, characters instead of numbers, numbers instead of characters, and control characters.

The Debugger

The debugger gives you a way to search your program's runtime details interactively, looking at variables and trying new values along the way. The *debugger* is the integrated tool that helps you find program bugs.

Visual Basic's Debug menu, shown in Figure 20.5, gives you a good introduction to the debugger's capabilities. Look through the menu and find the Toggle Breakpoint option. Breakpoints provide the time you need to hunt bugs during the application's execution.

FIGURE 20.5.

The Debug menu is ready to help locate bugs.

Debug	
Step Into	F8
Step Over	Shift+F8
Step Out	Ctrl+Shift+F8
Run To Cursor	Ctrl+F8
Add Watch...	
Edit Watch...	Ctrl+W
Quick Watch...	Shift+F9
Toggle Breakpoint	F9
Clear All Breakpoints	Ctrl+Shift+F9
Set Next Statement	Ctrl+F9
Show Next Statement	

Perform all your testing and debugging from within the development environment. Don't compile a program until you remove all the bugs (or until you believe you've removed them all...your users will let you know soon enough if any still exist!). The debugger's facilities are available only from within the development environment.

NEW TERM A *breakpoint* is a halting point in a program; when you run the program, the program executes as normal until a breakpoint is reached, at which time Visual Basic places you in the debugger.

Visual Basic enters the breakpoint mode (sometimes called the break mode) when you halt a program during execution or when execution reaches a breakpoint that you added to the program before you ran it. The Debug menu options are available during the application's breakpoint mode. These are the three modes that a Visual Basic program can be in:

- Design mode
- Runtime mode
- Break mode

Visual Basic tells you which mode is current by displaying the word design, run, or break in the title bar at the top of your Visual Basic screen. When you develop the program, the program is in design mode, as indicated by your title bar; when you or the user runs a program, the program is in the run mode; when you halt a program to use the debugger, the program enters the break mode.

The rest of this lesson is about the break mode. While in break mode, your program retains all variable and control values. Therefore, you can halt the program at any time and look at data values from any line of the code. By comparing the values with what you expect the values to contain, you can find where problems are taking place.

Setting Breakpoints

You'll always enter break mode from the runtime mode. Only after you begin a program's execution will the break mode be available, because only at runtime are the variables and controls initialized with values. Here are the ways that you can move from runtime mode to break mode:

- Press Ctrl+Break during the program's execution at the place where you want to enter break mode. Stopping on one exact line of code is virtually impossible when using Ctrl+Break.
- Select Run|Break from the Visual Basic menu bar during the program's execution.
- Click the Break toolbar button (the toolbar button with two small vertical bars next to the Run button).
- In design mode or during a break mode, set a breakpoint on a particular line at which you want the execution to halt. By setting a breakpoint, you can specify the exact line of code where Visual Basic is to enter break mode.

20

- The menu's Debug | Add Watch dialog box lets you specify a break expression that Visual Basic monitors and uses to halt the program's execution when the expression becomes true.

- If a runtime error occurs, such as the undefined divide-by-zero math operation you saw earlier, Visual Basic enters the break mode at the offending line.

The most accurate and common way to enter break mode is by setting a breakpoint. To set a breakpoint, find the line where you want execution to halt at a breakpoint and set a breakpoint at that particular line of code. The following steps walk you through setting a breakpoint:

1. Load the `Controls.vbp` project that comes with Visual Basic (look in the `Samples` folder).

2. Press F7 to open the Code window.

3. Locate the `opt486_Click()` event procedure.

4. Find the following line of code in `opt486_Click()`:

   `strComputer = "486"`

5. Move the mouse cursor to the line and click the mouse button. The text cursor appears at the mouse click's location.

6. Select Debug | Toggle Breakpoint to set a breakpoint. (You'll see from this menu bar command that F9 is the shortcut key for this command. Also, clicking the toolbar's hand icon would place a breakpoint on this line of code as would clicking to the left of the line.) Figure 20.6 shows how your Code window should appear. Visual Basic changes the color of the line to let you know that a breakpoint will take place on that line during the program's execution.

   You can turn off a breakpoint by selecting Debug | Toggle Breakpoint (or by pressing F9) once again. You can set as many breakpoints as you need throughout a program. Leave this breakpoint in place for now. By setting the breakpoint, you're requesting that Visual Basic halt the program and enter break mode when execution reaches this line of code. Close the Code window and run the program by pressing F5.

The program appears to run as usual. The opening dialog box appears. Click the Option Buttons command button to see what happens when execution reaches the breakpoint. The execution continues, as usual, as long as the breakpoint isn't reached, but when the breakpoint line is reached, execution halts.

FIGURE 20.6.

The breakpoint line is highlighted.

The breakpoint —

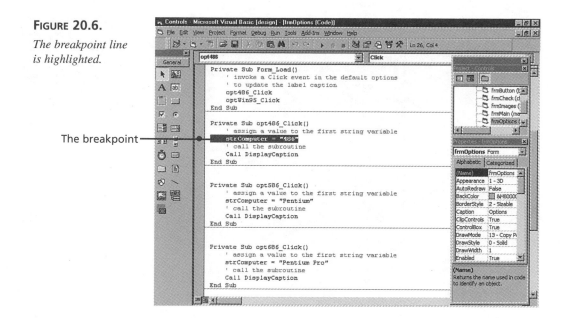

As soon as Visual Basic reaches a breakpoint's line, Visual Basic enters break mode before executing the breakpoint line. The opt486_Click() event procedure assigns a string literal to a string variable and then calls another procedure to load that variable into a label. The breakpoint that you set occurs in the middle of the assignment code.

Follow these steps to see what kinds of things you can do at a breakpoint:

1. Move your mouse to the string variable. After a brief pause, a ToolTip-like message pops up to tell you that the variable contains a null string value (nothing is yet assigned to the string). Drag the mouse to highlight the strComputer variable on the breakpoint's line.

2. Select Debug | Quick Watch. The menu option produces the Quick Watch dialog box. Visual Basic displays the breakpoint line, the variable name, and the current value that's a null string, as shown in Figure 20.7.

3. Click Add to add the value to the Watch dialog box. Whereas the Quick Watch dialog box is useful for looking at a variable at its current location, the Watch dialog box keeps track of multiple variables that update as the program executes.

20

FIGURE 20.7.

Looking at the variable's null value.

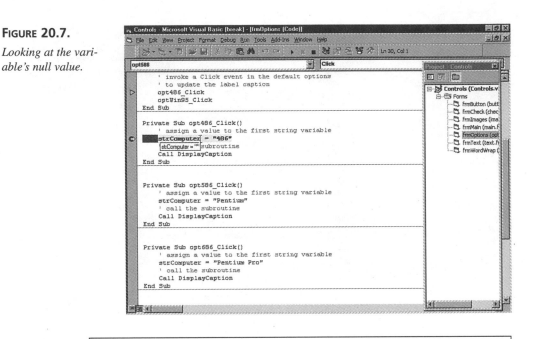

> Notice that the title bar now reads Break before the form name. The title bar shows you that the break mode is in effect.

4. Select View | Toolbars | Debug to display the special floating Debug toolbar. Most tools you need for interactive debugging appear on this toolbar. As Figure 20.8 shows, the Debug toolbar includes its own Quick Watch button. In addition, Figure 20.8 shows you the Watches window, where the variables and controls you want to watch reside.

The difference between the Quick Watch window and the Watches window is that you can, at any breakpoint, highlight a variable and display its value and surrounding code and datatype by clicking the Debug toolbar's Quick Watch button. If you want to keep a running list of watch variables, however, you must add the variables and controls to the Watches window. If you start the program again and hit another breakpoint later (you can set multiple breakpoints), the Watches window still shows the variables and controls you placed there, but the Quick Watch window will no longer appear until you request it again with another highlighted value.

When you single-step through code, you execute subsequent program instructions, one statement at a time, looking at values and testing the logic as you go.

FIGURE 20.8.

Looking at the variable in the Watches window.

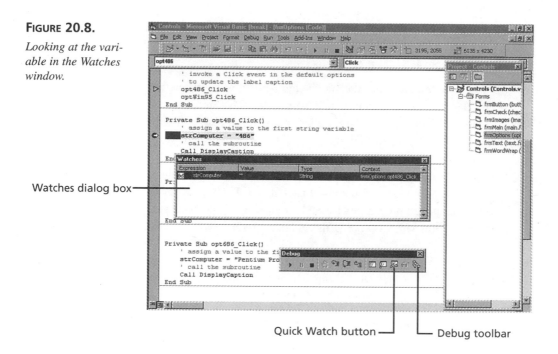

Watches dialog box

Quick Watch button ——— └— Debug toolbar

5. Usually, the programmer will single-step through a few lines of code after reaching a breakpoint. To step through the code one line at a time, you can choose the Debug | Step Into option (or press F8). As you single-step though the code, Visual Basic highlights the next line of execution. At any point during the single-step process, you can examine variables and controls with the Quick Watch dialog box and add them to the Watches window.

Stepping Through Code

One of the most powerful debugging features is the single-step feature mentioned at the end of the previous section. At the breakpoint you set, only one additional statement (other than remarks, which don't execute) resides in the procedure, and that statement is a procedure call to another procedure named `DisplayCaption()`.

The Debug menu's Step Into option (also available on the Debug toolbar) executes each statement in the program, including all the statements in procedures called. Therefore, if you single-step through the code from the breakpoint, the `DisplayCaption()` procedure executes (you can follow the yellow highlight to see the execution). After you step

20

through the `DisplayCaption()` procedure, control returns to the `opt486_Click()` procedure that called `DisplayCaption()`, and then you can single-step back to the procedure that called `opt486_Click()`.

If you want the effects of the single-step without going through every line of code, you can select the Debug menu's Step Over option. The Step Over option won't single-step through subsequent procedures called, but will run each call individually without single-stepping through the lines in the procedures. In other words, you can single-step through the next subroutine procedure's `Call` statement (or function call), but when you then single-step, control doesn't go into that procedure; the procedure executes as normal and then you get the single-step control back again. The Step Over option is useful when you've debugged procedures called by the current procedure and you don't want to waste additional time single-stepping through a procedure you've already debugged.

> The Step Over option is very useful when a procedure calls, in a loop, another procedure several times. The first time through the loop, you might want to single-step through the called code. In subsequent loop iterations, you might want to select Step Over; the code inside the procedures executes, but you won't wade through it line by line.

The Debug menu's Step Out option executes the rest of the current procedure without executing the procedure in single-step mode. When the current procedure finishes and control returns to the procedure that called the current procedure, execution begins once again in single-step mode.

> During the line-by-line execution, you can place additional breakpoints. Every time you click a line and press F8 (to toggle the breakpoint), Visual Basic adds a new breakpoint to the line. Therefore, a program can contain multiple breakpoints. In subsequent executions, you can run the program until it gets to a breakpoint, analyze values, click Start to run the program to the next breakpoint, analyze values, and so on. The breakpoints, therefore, help you get to the problem areas quickly without stepping through the rest of the code.

The Call Stack Shows Where You've Been

At any point during the debugging session, you can click the Debug toolbar button's Call Stack button to display the Call Stack window (see Figure 20.9).

FIGURE 20.9.

The Call Stack window lists all called procedures.

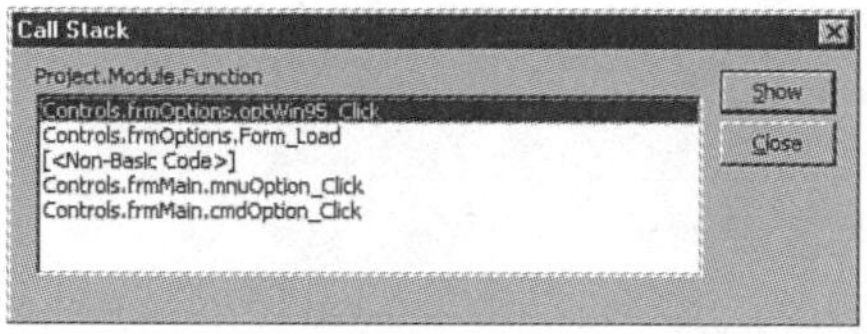

Call Stack

Project.Module.Function

Controls.frmOptions.optWin95_Click
Controls.frmOptions.Form_Load
[<Non-Basic Code>]
Controls.frmMain.mnuOption_Click
Controls.frmMain.cmdOption_Click

Show
Close

The Call Stack window shows where your program execution has traveled. In addition, any non–Visual Basic routines, such as Windows routines that sometimes take over, appear in the Call Stack window. The call stack keeps a running list of all procedures executed, even if the same procedure executes multiple times.

Inside the debugger's break mode, you'll only see the Code window and its related Debug windows that you display. If you want to see the program's actual output, press Alt+Tab to switch to the application's running window.

Suppose that a variable contains an incorrect value but you're not exactly sure where the error is occurring. You could set a breakpoint at every line of code that changes the variable. When you run the program, you'll look at the contents of that variable before and after each breakpoint's line of execution. If the first breakpoint seems to initialize the variable properly, you don't have to single-step through the code until the next breakpoint is reached. Instead of single-stepping, you can select Run | Continue or press F5 to return the execution to its normal runtime (and real-time) mode. When Visual Basic reaches the next breakpoint, the code halts, and you can continue to examine the variable.

At a breakpoint, you can add not only variables but Watches window expressions as well. Suppose that a variable is to maintain a count of customers, but somewhere in your code a negative value appears in the variable. You can debug this problem by adding a watch expression such as `intCustCnt < 0` to the Watches window. To do this, right-click the window and select Add Watch to display the Add Watch dialog box (see Figure 20.10). Click the window's Break When Value Is True option button. You can then run the programs, and Visual Basic enters break mode at any line that causes the variable to become negative.

20

The breakpoints and watch dialog boxes that you can request while debugging your code give you tremendous power in analyzing variables and watching for specific results. You can look at the contents of variables and controls to make sure that data is being initialized the way you expect. Also, the Add Watch dialog box lets you set up expressions that Visual Basic watches for during the program's execution. If the values of those expressions ever become true or change, Visual Basic halts the code at that line and lets you analyze values using the Watches window.

The Immediate Window

At any breakpoint you can select View | Immediate Window (Ctrl+G) to request the Immediate window (sometimes called the *Debug window*). The Immediate window is a special window in which you can directly type Visual Basic commands and view and change variables and control values during a program's execution.

For displaying variables and controls, apply the `Print` method (see Hour 16, "Printing with Visual Basic") to view variables and controls. When you use Print in the Immediate window, Visual Basic sends the output to the Immediate window and not to the `Printer` object, as you saw in Hour 16. For example, suppose that you set a breakpoint during a variable's assignment, as described in the previous sections, and you pressed Ctrl+G to open the Immediate window. The Immediate window recognizes simple Visual Basic commands and methods such as `Print` and assignment statements.

Figure 20.11 shows what happens if you print the value of `strComputer` after the variable is assigned the string value. Unlike the Quick Watch dialog box, the Immediate window has room to display multiple lines if you display a multiline control such as a text box. You can resize and move the Immediate window. Although they must use the `Print` command instead of simply clicking a variable or control, many programmers prefer to display values from the Immediate window instead of the Quick Watch dialog box. The Immediate window displays the entire value and contains a vertical scrollbar so that you can scroll through the values printed in the window.

FIGURE 20.11.

The Immediate window displays the values of variables.

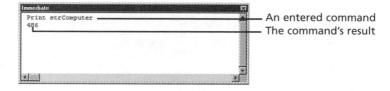

An entered command
The command's result

The Immediate window's scrolling and resizing features are so handy that some Visual Basic programmers prefer to send messages to the Immediate window at runtime rather than use the Quick Watch dialog box. For example, if you want to see the value of certain arguments when called procedures execute, you can add the `Print` methods at the top of those procedures that send the argument values to the Immediate window automatically as the program executes. When you get the bugs out of the program, you can remove the Print commands so that the Immediate window stays closed.

To print to the Immediate window, preface the `Print` method with the special `Debug` object. The following command, executed anywhere from an application's code, prints the values of two variables with appropriate titles in the Immediate window:

```
Debug.Print "Age:"; intAgeVal, "Weight:"; intWeightVal
```

All the `Print` method's options, including semicolons, commas, and `Tab()` and `Spc()` functions, work inside the Immediate window just as they do for the `Printer` object described in Hour 16. Be careful to specify the `Debug` object before the `Print` method, however. If you omit `Debug`, Visual Basic prints the output directly on the form itself!

The Immediate window recognizes assignments that you make to variables and controls. For example, suppose you know that a certain variable wasn't initialized properly earlier in the execution, but you still want to finish the program's execution as if the variable had its proper value. If you need to, you can assign that variable a new value directly within the Immediate window using the assignment statement. When you resume the program's execution, either in single-step or in runtime mode, the variable, from that point in the program, will contain the value that you assigned to it.

20

Summary

In this hour you learned ways you can test and debug your applications. Several kinds of bugs exist and Visual Basic can find some bugs for you. Other bugs appear at runtime and they can be frustrating. Fortunately, the interactive debugger lets you step through your program one line at a time if needed, examining variables and controls to make sure that the expressions and input are as expected. After you eliminate as many bugs as possible, you can then compile and distribute the code.

The next hour begins a new part of the book that teaches more advanced subjects. You will learn how your Visual Basic program can interact with other kinds of applications.

Q&A

Q How much testing should I perform?

A As much as needed and then some. Consider the alternative: If you don't debug your program, your users will find the bugs. A user is rarely happy about such things (users can be so picky!). The more thoroughly you test a program, using extreme values as described in this lesson and trying all the program branches (entering data that makes each leg of each If execute at least once), the less likely a bug will slip through testing.

Workshop

The quiz questions and exercises are provided for your further understanding. See Appendix B for the answers.

Quiz

1. Which errors are the easiest to find?

2. Which errors are the hardest to find?

3. If you write a program and, during execution, the program halts and displays an error message telling you that a disk drive doesn't exist, what kind of error just occurred?

4. How can you tell the current program mode?

5. What is a breakpoint?

6. What are three things you can do at a breakpoint?

7. How do you single-step through a program?

8. True or false: While using the debugger, you have no access to your program's Output window.

9. What's the quickest way to see a variable's value at a breakpoint?

10. What method displays values in the Immediate window?

Exercises

1. Larry the Visual Basic programmer wants to send values to the Immediate window right before he reads a disk file. Here are some statements Larry uses to print to the Immediate window:

```
Print lblFileName.Caption
Print intNumRecs, intNumFields
Print strCompName
```

Larry isn't having success. Instead of the Immediate window, these values all seem to appear on the form itself! Help determine what Larry is doing wrong so he can view the values in the Immediate window.

2. Load the `Controls.vbp` sample project. Single-step through the project beginning at a breakpoint that you set in `Form_Load()`'s last statement. The program uses data in a different way than normal because the program uses a resource file to hold its strings. By moving all its data out to a resource file, the strings can be easily translated to other languages, and the program only needs to be recompiled. Without a resource file, a programmer would have to search the Code window for all strings and possibly miss some. Use the single-step mode to learn how the resource file and its related built-in functions operate.

20

PART VI

Advancing Visual Basic Applications

Hour

Hour **21**

Visual Basic and ActiveX

Look in a bookstore and you'll find many thick books that discuss ActiveX. ActiveX is Microsoft's new open technology that is supposed to merge the desktop with the Internet seamlessly. Although that lofty goal is probably thrown around too lightly today, it's true that ActiveX takes component technology a step forward. Although Visual Basic programmers have been used to drop-in controls since Visual Basic's version 1.0, ActiveX controls give programmers on all PC development systems similar abilities and the controls can communicate with each other and with applications without regard for the development language being used.

Because this lesson is only an hour long, it can only expose the tip of the ActiveX iceberg. Nevertheless, by the time you finish this lesson, you'll have a better idea of what ActiveX is, how Visual Basic supports ActiveX, and how ActiveX takes its predecessors, OLE and custom controls, to their next step.

The highlights of this hour include

- Why ActiveX controls are important today
- Where ActiveX controls come from
- How to install ActiveX controls in your Toolbox window
- How to bring OLE objects into your application
- How to convert a form to an ActiveX document

ActiveX: The Tools You Use

In Hour 12, "Dialog Box Basics," you learned how to add the Common Dialog Box control to Visual Basic's Toolbox window. In Hour 19, "Toolbars and More Graphics," you added additional tools to produce a toolbar and an image list. The tools that you added are examples of ActiveX controls.

An ActiveX control is a control you can add to Visual Basic's Toolbox window. If the Toolbox window doesn't contain the control you need, you might find an ActiveX control that suits your purpose, and you can add that control to the Toolbox window for use in your application.

ActiveX controls are not unique to VB. You can add an ActiveX control to a Web page, to a Delphi project, or to a Visual C++ project.

All the controls you find in Visual Basic's Components dialog box (shown in Figure 21.1) are ActiveX controls. Search through the dialog box now to locate controls that interest you. You might never use all the controls, but some you'll use many times (such as the Toolbar control).

FIGURE 21.1.

Visual Basic comes with many ActiveX controls.

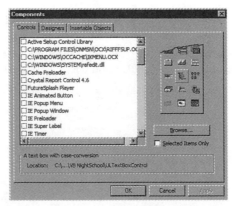

LOCATING ACTIVEX CONTROLS

As you look through the controls, you'll find a Marquee control that displays moving text across a form, a Calendar control, a Charting control, a Modem Communications control, and several others, including some Internet controls you'll read about in this book's final lesson. By the way, all the Internet controls also work for intranets, the intracompany networked connections that are so prevalent today.

When you add many of the controls, such as the Marquee control, to your Toolbox window, you can probably figure out which properties to set from the Properties window, but the majority of the controls support too many esoteric properties, events, and methods for you to figure all of them out without help. Visual Basic's Books Online reference describes these additional ActiveX controls so you can get help with a control when you need help.

The Components dialog box isn't the only place you'll find ActiveX controls. If you click the Component dialog box's Browse command button, you can search your hard disk for other controls. If, for example, you subscribe to the Microsoft Network online service, your Microsoft Network folder will contain some ActiveX controls you can use.

Many vendors sell ActiveX controls, and you can search Microsoft's Web site for additional information. Many online services and Internet pages offer free or shareware ActiveX controls that you might want to try as well. Search the Internet using some of the search engines available for a list of ActiveX sites.

Previous versions of Visual Basic supported these extra controls, but Visual Basic used to work only within a 16-bit environment. Therefore, the tools the Visual Basic programmers used were 16-bit tools called VB custom controls. A custom control was a control you added to your Visual Basic Toolbox window to gain additional power.

As the need for tools grew and as other programming platforms such as Visual C++ began requiring such extra tools, these other platforms began supporting the use of VB custom controls. If a Visual C++ programmer wanted a Text Box control, he had to locate a Visual Basic Text Box control file and add the text box to Visual C++'s development environment. (Those C++ programmers are always playing catch-up to Visual Basic programmers!)

The 16-bit VB custom controls use .vbx for their filename extensions. Visual Basic version 6 can't use these 16-bit controls because version 6 supports only 32-bit controls.

21

NEW TERM *Encapsulation* refers to a package of data and code that works like a small program. A control is encapsulated.

Soon, shortcomings of the VB custom controls began surfacing and their capability for
taking advantage of new technology, such as 32-bit operating environments, became
obvious. Microsoft developed a new control standard called OCX controls. One of the
nice things about VB custom controls was their capability to work between and inside
several programs even if the programs that used them weren't Visual Basic programs.
The controls were encapsulated so that the programming language only needed to know
the properties, methods, and events supported by the controls to use the controls. The
OCX controls, so called because of their .ocx filename extensions, kept all the advantages of 16-bit controls but also worked inside the 32-bit environment.

NEW TERM *OLE* (short for Object Linking and Embedding) refers to the process of inserting
linked and embedded objects in one application that another application created.

Along the way, the distinction between OLE and OCX controls became blurred. An OLE
process used a custom control to do its job, and the OCX controls further refined the
OLE process so that a programmer could embed a complete application written in Visual
Basic inside a Visual C++ program. In addition, the user could even drag an Excel worksheet into a Word document, and that worksheet not only became another data item
inside the document, but also the worksheet was active; when the user clicked the worksheet, Excel's menus appeared in place of Word's. That Excel worksheet was nothing
more than an advanced OCX control.

ActiveX controls are OCX controls that take these drag-and-drop and drop-into-code
concepts even further. An ActiveX control can appear on a Web page for anyone to use
(if the page is ActiveX-enabled and the user's browser is also; most Web browsers are
ActiveX-enabled today). In other words, if a Web page contains an ActiveX control,
even if that control is a complete Visual Basic application turned into an ActiveX control
(no size limitation for controls exists), the users who view the Web page see the application and interact with it as if they were running it from their own hard disk. ActiveX controls took the concept of OCX controls to the Internet. Now, if you want a special tool
such as a command button on your Web page, you can just place an ActiveX command
button control on the Web page during the page's development, and your page's users
will be able to click the command button.

> Microsoft seems to be making a push for all code to be these kinds of
> ActiveX controls. Future operating systems are supposed to be ActiveX-
> based. All programs will, in effect, be ActiveX controls. Therefore, you can
> embed any application within any other and borrow technology instead of
> reinvent it. Future programming, in theory, will involve building and com-
> bining prewritten ActiveX controls. ActiveX controls of an application can be
> distributed among multiple computers using DCOM.

Don't throw out your Visual Basic programming language skills just yet, however. The
ActiveX control as a total solution is still theory and is only partially available and working today in reality. Your Visual Basic skills are not only going to be needed in the future
as ActiveX controls gather steam, but your Visual Basic programming skills are going to
be needed even more as companies retool their applications and turn applications into
such controls.

Building ActiveX Controls With VB

You can use Visual Basic to easily build your own ActiveX controls. If you like command buttons but you wish they would support a special event or property that your
application needs, you can write your own command button control as an ActiveX control, and then use that control as if Visual Basic came with it. You can add the control to
your own application's toolbox (through the Project|Components dialog box) and set its
properties from the Properties window.

To build an ActiveX control, start Visual Basic and select to create an ActiveX control. If
you already have Visual Basic running, remove the current project and select File|New
from the menu bar to select to create an ActiveX control. Your Visual Basic environment
will now look like Figure 21.2.

The initial name that VB gives to the control you build is UserControl1; hence the Name
property value and the name in the Project window. Most of the tools, windows, and
menu objects are exactly the same for the ActiveX control.

21

FIGURE 21.2.

Building an ActiveX control with Visual Basic.

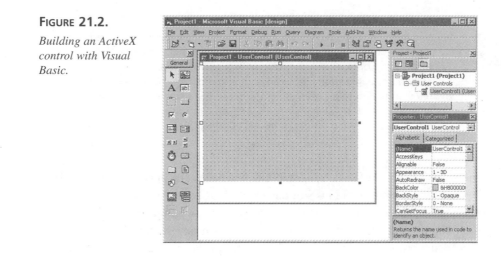

Custom controls are tedious to create. Not only must you know Visual Basic and all its language and inner workings (as you do now), but you also need to understand the way ActiveX controls are built, and you must understand the wizards available with VB 6 that help you build the controls. Although you'll need to get some fairly heavy training before you learn to build ActiveX controls, consider the following points:

- Many ActiveX controls are based on existing controls. If you were going to create a new kind of command button, you'd start with the regular command button and build on it. You would place a command button in the center of the Form window and add functionality to the command button to turn it into your own control.

- If you are building a complex control that contains several additional controls, you can place all the foundation controls on the Form window and work with them to build the complex control.

NEW TERM *Inheritance* refers to the capability of object-oriented languages (such as C++) to base new capabilities on existing language capabilities or controls.

- Although Visual Basic doesn't support true inheritance, a wizard is available in VB 6 to let you select functionality from existing controls and put that functionality into your new ActiveX control.

- After you design the control, you must design its interface. VB 6 comes with wizard technology that helps you add properties, events, and methods to the control.

- Your new ActiveX control will be capable of mimicking existing controls in all
  ways. Therefore, if you later add your new control to an application's Toolbox
  window, the Properties window will display that ActiveX control's properties,
  including support for drop-down list boxes from which fixed property values are
  available for selection. In addition, you'll see your ActiveX control's pop-up statement syntax appear inside the Code window editor when you add methods to the
  control.

> This lesson cannot possibly describe how to build an ActiveX control in an
> hour. Actually, it would take an entire book to do so. But you'll get a
> glimpse of what's involved from this section.

OLE Processing

You can place objects into your application that aren't normally considered to be
ActiveX controls. Although you should stick with true ActiveX controls when possible,
you can use the Toolbox window's OLE control to drop items from several different
applications onto the form window.

For example, suppose that you want your user to be able to see a Microsoft Excel work-
sheet on your form and interact with the worksheet as if the worksheet were a regular
Visual Basic control. Add the OLE control to your Form window. As soon as you do, the
Insert Object dialog box appears, as shown in Figure 21.3.

FIGURE 21.3.

*Adding objects from
other applications.*

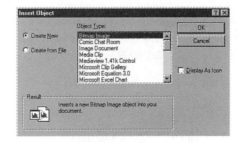

> As you install Windows applications on your computer, Windows keeps a list
> in its Registry of OLE candidates. The Registry contains an entry that tells the
> system your Paint program's data is available as an OLE object. The list of
> applications you see in the Insert Object dialog box comes from the Registry.

21

The Insert Object dialog box gives you the choice of inserting an existing Excel work-sheet object (by clicking Create From File) or creating a new object from scratch (by clicking Create From New). You will only be able to create objects if you have those applications on your system, but as stated earlier, your Registry knows what is installed, so only those applications appear in the Insert Object dialog box.

Creating Inserted Objects

If you elect to create the new object from scratch, you can choose that option and double-click the object type (which, in this example, will be an Excel worksheet). Visual Basic loads a blank object into your OLE control as shown in Figure 21.4. You'll also notice that Visual Basic menus change to Excel menus.

FIGURE 21.4.

You can create an Excel worksheet in the middle of the form window.

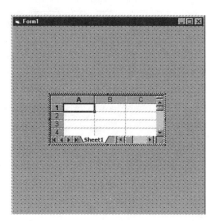

After you create the worksheet, click the Form window outside the worksheet area and you can continue placing the other controls and completing your application. When you finish, run the application to see the worksheet embedded in the form.

Although your users won't be able to edit the worksheet automatically, if they double-click the worksheet embedded in the form, an Excel menu will appear across the top of the form and the users can change and enter new values in the worksheet.

Inserting Existing Objects

Instead of inserting new objects that you must create at design time, you can insert exist-ing objects, such as Excel worksheets. When you select the Insert Object's Create From

File option (see Figure 21.5), Visual Basic changes the Insert Object dialog box to the file browsing dialog box.

FIGURE 21.5.

Selecting a work-sheet to insert.

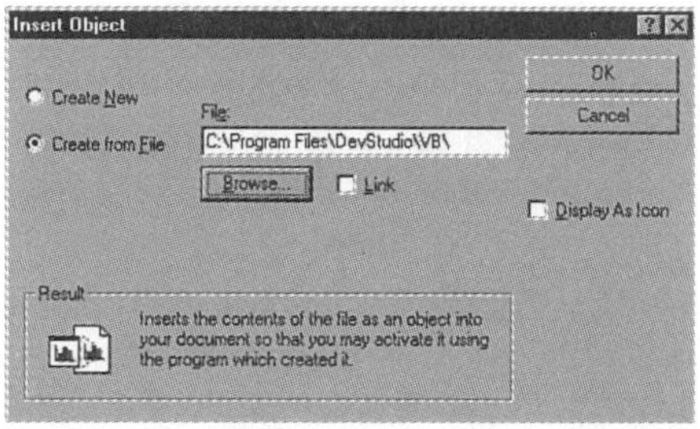

 To *link* an object means that your application will contain a pointer to the object. If the object ever changes, your application's form will reflect those changes. The object isn't stored with your application, but the link to the object is.

 To *embed* an object means that your application gets a copy of the object. Therefore, if the original object changes, that change won't be reflected in your application until you or your user make the same change to the application's object. The object is stored with your application so if something happens to the original, no link exists to be broken.

The Link option informs Visual Basic that you want to link the new object and not embed it. You can choose to link or not depending on how current the object must be with the original object's file.

> Click the Display As Icon option if you want the object to appear as an icon on your form when the user runs the application. If you don't click this option, the object (in this case, an Excel worksheet) appears on your Form window as a small worksheet.

When the user runs your application, she can double-click the worksheet (or the icon) to add Excel menus to the Form window and to change the worksheet.

ActiveX Documents

21

NEW TERM An *ActiveX container* is an application, such as Internet Explorer, that can display and activate ActiveX documents.

ActiveX documents are difficult objects to create from scratch. An ActiveX document must be contained within an ActiveX container application such as Internet Explorer. If you have Internet Explorer, try this: Start Internet Explorer but don't log on to the Internet as you might normally do. Open a Word document. If you've never tried this, you might be surprised at the results. Internet Explorer can display the Word document, formatted completely, and you can edit the document as if it were shown inside Word. Figure 21.6 shows such a document embedded inside Internet Explorer.

FIGURE 21.6.

Internet Explorer is an ActiveX container program.

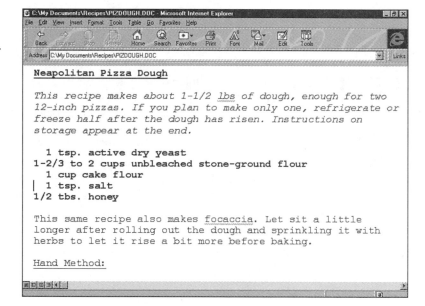

You have access to Word's menus inside the ActiveX container. You can also right-click over the text to see Word's pop-up menu. Misspelled, foreign, and abbreviated words are underlined as possible misspellings, and you can highlight and format text by pressing Word's typical formatting keystrokes (such as Ctrl+B to boldface text).

NEW TERM When an ActiveX container *activates* an ActiveX document, all the document's usual controls and features become available.

A Word document is an ActiveX document. An ActiveX container such as Internet Explorer can display and let you work within the ActiveX document. ActiveX documents are going to become more important as the Internet becomes more important. The more you work within a Web browser, the more likely it will be that you'll want to view data from another source, such as a Word document. When you're working with an ActiveX document, you don't have to start Word to read the document.

Visual Basic's Professional and Enterprise Editions include a wizard that converts your forms to ActiveX documents. Although the wizard cannot convert complete applications to ActiveX documents, you can convert forms with all their features.

> Surprisingly, if your form contains OLE controls, even ActiveX-based OLE controls, those controls don't convert to the ActiveX document.

To run the wizard, called the VB ActiveX Document Migration Wizard, you must add the wizard to your Add-Ins menu by following these steps:

1. Select Add-Ins | Add-In Manager to open the Add-In Manager dialog box (see Figure 21.7).

FIGURE 21.7.

Adding the wizard to the Add-In Manager.

Add-In Manager		
Available Add-Ins	Load Behavior	OK
DTC Framework Registrar		Cancel
Package and Deployment Wizard		
ResEdit.Connect		
Source Code Control	Startup / Loaded	
VB 6 ActiveX Ctrl Interface Wizard		
VB 6 ActiveX Doc Migration Wizard	Loaded	
VB 6 Add-In Toolbar		
VB 6 API Viewer		
VB 6 Application Wizard		
VB 6 Class Builder Utility		
VB 6 Data Form Wizard		
VB 6 Data Object Wizard		
		Help

Description: VB 6 ActiveX Document Migration Wizard

Load Behavior:
☑ Loaded/Unloaded
☐ Load on Startup
☐ Command Line

2. Select the entry labeled VB 6 ActiveX Doc Migration Wizard, check the Loaded/Unloaded check box, and close the dialog box. The wizard now appears on your Add-Ins menu when you display the menu.

3. Open the application that contains the form you want to convert to an ActiveX document.

4. Select Add-Ins | ActiveX Document Migration Wizard to start the wizard.

5. After you click Next at the introductory dialog box, select the form you want to convert to an ActiveX document.

6. Generally, you'll select all the defaults, so click Finish to complete the migration.

7. Close the ending dialog boxes. Run the application to create the ActiveX document file.

21

Do you remember the animated form with the happy face moving up the form from Hour 18, "The Graphic Image Controls"? If so, you'll enjoy seeing it again, only this time as the ActiveX document in Figure 21.8.

FIGURE 21.8.

You can convert any form to an ActiveX document!

Summary

You've now been taken on a whirlwind tour of ActiveX. This hour summarizes ActiveX and how ActiveX fits in with Visual Basic programming. ActiveX controls are becoming more important as Internet-based use grows because of the strong interaction ActiveX controls have with ActiveX-enabled Web browsers.

The next hour covers another fairly advanced issue: Visual Basic objects. By learning how to work with objects through code, you'll be able to increase the capabilities of your applications.

Q&A

Q I don't write programs for the Internet, so why should I worry about ActiveX controls?

A As you have learned in this lesson, not all ActiveX controls are designed for the Internet. Every control you add to your Visual Basic 6 Toolbox window is an ActiveX control. You really don't have to worry much that the control is an

ActiveX control, and you don't have to worry about the system technology behind ActiveX controls to use these controls. The nice thing about ActiveX controls is that they act just like other controls and have properties, events, and methods you're used to programming.

Q Again, I don't write for the Internet, so why should I worry about ActiveX documents?

A ActiveX documents are becoming more and more important. Some extremely reliable sources predict that future operating systems will be little more than an Internet and ActiveX document browser. If so, forms that you create will need to be readable for that super browser, and the browser will primarily consist of an ActiveX container application. Therefore, if you want to write applications for future operating environments, you'll want to be able to convert the forms in those applications to ActiveX documents.

Workshop

The quiz questions and exercises are provided for your further understanding. See Appendix B for the answers.

Quiz

1. Which came first: OCX controls, ActiveX controls, or VB custom controls?

2. How do you add ActiveX controls to your Toolbox window?

3. Where can you get additional ActiveX controls?

4. True or false: Programmers in other languages, such as Visual C++, can use ActiveX controls created by VB 6.

5. If you design an ActiveX control that works and looks somewhat like an existing control, what can you do to speed the development of the new control?

6. What is the difference between an inserted object and an embedded object?

7. How does the user of an application with an embedded OLE object activate that object for editing?

8. What is the difference between an ActiveX document and an ActiveX container?

9. What is an example of an ActiveX container that many Visual Basic programmers use already?

10. What must you do to convert a form to an ActiveX document?

21

Exercises

1. Create a new project and add two OLE controls to the form. Place a linked Word document in one and place an embedded Word document in another. Run the application, double-click each object, and manage the objects from within the application to see the effects. Start Word and modify the object, and then rerun your application to see the change reflected in one of the objects. (If you don't use Word, you can use WordPad or another word processor as long as that word processor appears inside the Insert Object dialog box.)

2. In this lesson's final section you saw Hour 18's animation form converted to an ActiveX document. Run the VB ActiveX Document Migration Wizard to do the same for another single form application created in a previous chapter and display the created ActiveX document in Internet Explorer.

HOUR 22

Object Basics

Considering that Visual Basic isn't a true object-oriented language (because of its lack of inheritance features), Visual Basic sure uses a lot of objects! Everything seems to be an object in Visual Basic, including forms, windows, toolbox tools, and ActiveX controls.

This lesson discusses several of the more advanced programming topics that surround objects. By the time you finish this lesson, you will better understand how objects fit into the Visual Basic environment.

The highlights of this hour include

- How to access the system objects
- What distinguishes a class from an object
- When to shortcut code with With...End blocks
- How to create your own collections
- Why OLE automation gives your application tremendous power
- How to make Word work from inside Visual Basic

The System Objects

You've worked with several Visual Basic objects already. The `Printer` object is an object you use with a `Print` method to send output to the printer, as in the following statement:

```
Printer.Print Tab(15); "Company Balance Sheet"
```

In addition, you've seen the `Debug` object when printing to the Immediate window like this:

```
Debug.Print "intVar is "; intVar
```

In both cases, the object represents an item outside your application's scope. The printer and the Immediate window are not your application's; therefore, Visual Basic uses objects to represent them. The `Printer` object doesn't reference any particular printer; rather, the `Printer` object references the current Windows printer. The `Debug` object represents the Immediate window.

| NEW TERM | A *system object* is an object defined by Visual Basic that lies outside your program's immediate scope.

The `Printer` and the `Debug` objects are system objects predefined by the Visual Basic system. Although a command button on your form is an object, the command button isn't a system object because the object didn't really exist before you placed the command button on the form—only its pattern existed on the Toolbox window.

Table 22.1 lists all the predefined system objects your applications can work with.

TABLE 22.1. THE SYSTEM OBJECTS AND THEIR METHODS.

Object	Description	Methods
App	Your current application	The `EXEName` method returns the application's filename. `Path` returns the application's path. `Title` returns the primary startup form's title bar text. `Previnstance` returns `True` or `False` to indicate whether another instance (copy) of the application is currently running.
ClipBoard	The Windows Clipboard	The method `Clear` erases the Clipboard. `GetData` returns the graphic image stored on the Clipboard. `GetFormat` returns the format of the Clipboard object. `GetText` returns the text on the Clipboard. `SetData` copies a graphic image to the Clipboard. `SetText` copies text to the Clipboard.

Object	Description	Methods
Debug	The Immediate window	The method `Print` copies information, at run-time, to the Immediate window (only possible in Visual Basic programs you run from Visual Basic's development environment).
Printer	The system printer	Provides printer support.
Screen	The user's screen	`FontCount` returns the number of fonts the current screen supports. `Fonts` contains a list of all the screen's possible font names. `Height` returns the twip height of the screen area. `MousePointer` holds (or determines if you specify a new one) the shape of the mouse cursor. `TwipsPerPixelX` returns the number of possible horizontal twips. `TwipsPerPixelY` returns the number of possible vertical twips. `Width` returns the width, in twips, of the screen.

Use these objects and methods to return information about the objects. For example, you could append the current application pathname to a string variable like this:

```
strFullName = App.Path & "\" & "Afile.dat"
```

Although you won't use the system objects in every application, they do come in handy when you're performing interaction with the Windows Clipboard or the screen.

> The `Screen` object's measurements differ depending on the video card, resolution, and monitor your user uses. Therefore, the `Screen` object, available at runtime, represents the entire Windows Desktop. If you want to center a form in the middle of the user's screen, you could place these statements at the beginning of the `Form_Load()` event procedure:
>
> ```
> frmName.Left = (Screen.Width - frmName.Width) / 2
> frmName.Top = (Screen.Height - frmName.Height) / 2
> ```
>
> You can also use the Form Layout window to position a form.

Program Objects

NEW TERM   A *class* is a packaged object, with behaviors and properties that describe members of the class.

Objects that you create with your application are objects that are members of a particular class. For example, an option button class defines properties, events, and methods that all members of the option button class support. In other words, even though your application may contain five option buttons, and even though all five of those option buttons differ in one or more of their properties (such as Caption), they are all members of the same class. A command button can never be a member of the option button class because a command button's properties, events, and methods differ from an option button's.

You can test for membership within any given class. The class forms a hierarchy and all members of the class take on the class properties, events, and methods. One of the reasons for a class test is that you can pass to procedures not only variables, but also controls. The following procedure receives a command button as its only argument:

```
Public Sub GetIt(cmdClick As CommandButton)
```

Some procedures can be multipurpose. In other words, a procedure might change the BackColor property of whatever object you pass to that procedure. Use the As Object argument declaration as follows to make the procedure multipurpose:

```
Public Sub ChangeColor(objOnForm As Object)
```

You haven't seen the Object keyword until now, but you can declare not only arguments as Object datatypes, but variables as well, like this:

```
Dim objAnything As Object
```

The objAnything variable can now represent an object.

Your application's code can create any object needed at runtime. In other words, you could declare an array of five option buttons like this:

```
Dim ctlOpButtons(1 To 5) As New OptionButton
```

The New keyword tells Visual Basic to create five new option buttons. If you want to base a new object on an existing object, you only need to change the properties that differ in the new object from the old one. The following statement declares a new form based on an existing form named frmAcctsPay:

```
Dim frmNewForm As New frmAcctsPay
```

Notice that if you place an existing control name after the New statement, Visual Basic declares a new object based on an existing one. If you use a control's class name (such as CommandButton, Form, OptionButton, or Label), Visual Basic declares a new control with all default property values (except for the Name property, which you set with the Dim statement as you declare the control). You then can specify the property values that you want for your new object.

Use the `If TypeOf...Is` programming block to test for an object's datatype. The following `If` generates `True` if the object stored in `objAnything` is a text box:

```
If TypeOf objAnything Is TextBox Then
```

In addition to being a keyword command, Visual Basic supports the `TypeOf()` function that returns the object type of its argument.

Knowing about an object's class lets Visual Basic accept the following code that contains a `With` keyword block:

```
With lblTitle
    .Caption = "Accounts Payable"
    .Alignment = vbRightJustify
    .Font.Size = 15
    .Font.Bold = True
    .Left = 25
    .Right = 0
    .Width = 1000
End With
```

If you must set more than two or three properties in code, use `With`, which tells Visual Basic that all objects without an object qualifier are label objects. Without the `With` keyword, you would have to type the object's name all through the assignments, like this:

```
lblTitle.Caption = "Accounts Payable"
lblTitle.Alignment = vbRightJustify
lblTitle.Font.Size = 15
lblTitle.Font.Bold = True
lblTitle.Left = 25
lblTitle.Right = 0
lblTitle.Width = 1000
```

Using Collections and Object Arrays

In earlier lessons you learned about control arrays that you can declare. By declaring an array of five Option Button controls that all have the same name, you can set property values for one, and all the others gain the same properties. Your application will distinguish between the controls by the control array subscript.

NEW TERM A *collection* is a set of all objects of the same datatype. In addition to the control arrays, you can work with collections. A collection differs from an array because your application may contain three command button arrays but only one `Controls` collection. The `Controls` collection refers to every control used in your application.

Table 22.2 describes common Visual Basic collections.

TABLE 22.2. SOME OF THE COLLECTIONS YOU CAN MANAGE.

Collection	Description
Controls	All controls within your application
Forms	All forms within your application
Printers	All printers connected to your system

The collections support several methods that you can use to manage the collection. Table 22.3 lists some of those methods.

TABLE 22.3. SOME METHODS YOU CAN APPLY TO COLLECTIONS.

Method	Description
Add	Adds items to collections
Count	Returns the number of items in a collection
Remove	Deletes items from a collection
Item	References a collection element

> You can create your own collections, and some of Table 22.3's methods are more useful to you when you work with your own collections than when you work with the supplied collections. For example, you'd never add an item to the Printers collection because Windows defines that collection from your system's installed printer list.

Suppose that you want to display all controls on the form, even some that might be hidden from other procedures that executed previously. Although you could set each control's Visible property to True, the following loop makes for an easier display of the controls:

```
For intCtr = 0 to Controls.Count-1
   Controls(intCtr).Visible = True
Next intCtr
```

The For Each statement makes the loop even simpler. The zero-based collection subscript requires that you loop through the Count-1 subscript, which is a little confusing.

22

Substitute `For Each` to clarify things and to let Visual Basic take care of the subscripting like this:

```
Dim ctlControl As Control
For Each ctlControl In Controls
    ctlControl.Visible = True
Next ctlControl
```

Notice that you must declare a control variable so that the `For Each` statement has a place to load each control in the collection.

Suppose that you add forms to that same application and you want to make all controls visible on all the forms. The `Forms` collection makes such a task simple if you use the following nested loop:

```
Dim ctlControl As Control
Dim frmMyForms As Form
For Each frmMyForms In Forms
    For Each ctlControl In Controls
        ctlControls.Visible = True
    Next ctlControl
Next frmMyForms
```

If you want to create your own collections, you'll be able to work with them just as you work with the supplied collections. You'll have to declare and manage the collection yourself, but after you build a collection, you can operate on all the collection items more easily than if they were separate or part of a control array.

Given that the `Collection` keyword is itself a defined object, you can declare a collection like this:

```
Public colNewCollect As New Collection
```

If you don't use `Dim`, but use either `Private` or `Public` to declare collections, declare the collections in the `general` section of a module so that the `Public` or `Private` keyword determines the scope (either project- or module-level availability).

> The previous `Public` statement declares a new collection class but doesn't declare any specific members of that collection. To use a `Collection` object, you must define the specific items to go in the collection.

If you use `Dim` and declare a new collection inside a procedure, only that procedure has access to the collection. Often such a local collection is wanted, but be aware that other procedures cannot use the collection.

After you define the collection in the general section, you can create the collection's specific instances. Listing 22.1 declares collection members and shows you how to use the methods to add and manage the collection.

LISTING 22.1. CREATING AND MANAGING A COLLECTION.

```
 1: Dim colPeople As New Collection
 2: Dim intCtr As Integer
 3: Dim m As Integer     ' MsgBox() return (not used)
 4:
 5: colPeople.Add "George"
 6: colPeople.Add "Sandra"
 7: colPeople.Add "William"
 8: colPeople.Add "Sue"
 9: colPeople.Add "Terry"
10:
11:  ' Print the collection
12: For intCtr = 1 To colPeople.Count
13: m = MsgBox("The next name is " & colPeople(intCtr))
14: Next intCtr
15:
16:  ' Add another person if you wish
17:  ' As you can see, you don't need to
18:  ' concern yourself with running past a
19:  ' maximum subscript value as you
20:  ' would with arrays.
21: colPeople.Add "Kay"
22:
23:  ' The following should display 6 people
24: m = MsgBox("There are " & Str(colPeople.Count) & _
25: " in the collection.")
```

Here is the output from this code:

```
The next name is George
The next name is Sandra
The next name is William
The next name is Sue
The next name is Terry
The next name is Kay
There are 6 in the collection.
```

As you can see, a collection's index value begins at 1, not zero, as is the case for arrays and control arrays. The mixture of starting subscripts provides yet another reason for using For Each to step through such items.

22

The previous discussion shows how you can use the Add method to add new items to the collection. You don't have to worry about a maximum subscript. The problem, however, is that with Add's default method format, you cannot add new collection items except to the end of the collection. In addition, you cannot remove specific items, except for the final collection item, from the collection with Remove.

NEW TERM   A *named argument* is an argument known by its name and not by its specific position within an argument list.

Add supports a named argument, Before, that lets you insert new items into a collection before an existing item. In effect, Visual Basic shifts all the subsequent items down in the list. If you want to add a new name to the beginning of the People collection, code the following:

```
People.Add "Robert", Before:=1
```

Don't use a regular assignment statement when assigning named argument values; instead, use the special := named argument assignment operator.

The collection now looks like this:

```
Robert
George
Sandra
William
Sue
Terry
Kay
```

If you want to remove the third name, you can do so like this:

```
People.Remove 3   ' Deletes the 3rd item
```

Introduction to OLE Automation

NEW TERM   *OLE automation* refers to the capability of one application to declare and use ActiveX objects that are actually created by other applications.

As you learned in Hour 21, "Visual Basic and ActiveX," the overall distinction between OLE and ActiveX is becoming blurred. Nevertheless, OLE and ActiveX do work well together to support OLE automation. Although this section only scratches the OLE automation surface, you'll probably be surprised at what OLE automation can accomplish.

More and more programmers are calling OLE automation Active
Automation due to ActiveX's impact on OLE automation.

Suppose that your application needs to create data files for Excel or Word. Using the normal file access routines you learned in Hour 15, "Visual Basic Database Basics," makes
such file creation extremely tedious and bug-prone. How can you find the data format
required by Word?

With OLE automation, your Visual Basic application can actually borrow Excel or Word
and, behind the user's back without ever showing the other application, make Excel or
Word (or any other OLE automation-compatible application) create the data file for you.
When finished, the data file will reside on the disk and no traces of the other application
will be left. Your user will believe your application created the data file.

Your development computer must have a copy of the OLE automation's
application before you can test your application. Also, your user must have a
copy of the OLE automation application. Without Word, for example, you
cannot use OLE automation to create a Word document.

To create a Word data file using OLE automation, you must first create an object variable
that can reference the Word OLE automation application. Declare such an object variable
like this:

```
Public objWordApp As Object
```

Always use a global variable for OLE automation objects. The variable references a completely different application outside your application's workspace.
Therefore, the variable is truly global to your application's other variables.

objWordApp is an object variable that represents the entire Word OLE automation application. The rest of the code will use this application's reference object variable to perform the data-generation task. Nothing about objWordApp lets Visual Basic know that the
object is the Word application, so the following statement will link the object variable to
Word:

```
Set objWordApp = CreateObject("Word.Application.8")
```

The 8 is a property that uses Office 97's Word instead of earlier versions. Before Office 97, which technically contains Word version 8, Word used a language called WordBasic for its automation language. Word 8 uses Visual Basic, which is sometimes called Visual Basic for Applications.

Notice that this isn't a normal assignment statement. The Set keyword tells Visual Basic not to store a value in objWordApp because the Word application isn't a value that you could put into a variable. Set tells Visual Basic to *reference* the Word application. objWordApp works like a link to Word. Visual Basic will, through OLE automation, transfer functions you apply to objWordApp to the Word application. The CreateObject() function actually starts Word (in the background) and prepares the OLE automation link.

> If Word is already running, CreateObject() starts another copy of Word. If you want to use the currently running Word, use GetObject() instead of CreateObject() to borrow the running copy of Word. You can test to see if Word is already running like this:
>
> ```
> Set objWordApp = GetObject("", "Word.Application.8")
> If objWordApp Is Nothing Then    ' True if not running
> Set objWordApp = CreateObject("Word.Application.8")
> End If
> ```

The null string at the beginning of GetObject()is necessary. If you want to open an existing Word document and work on that document inside Visual Basic, you'll insert the path and filename to that document as the first argument. If you want to use Word to create a new document, leave the null string for the first argument.

Keep in mind that OLE automation is fairly extensive and that you can, through your Visual Basic application, make Word do anything you could do at the keyboard with Word. Therefore, the OLE automation can trigger Word's menus, format text, and save files. You'll apply methods, most of which match Word's menus, to perform these tasks.

Listing 22.2 shows you a complete code set you could use to create a Word document named MyWord.Doc.

LISTING 22.2. OLE AUTOMATION CODE THAT USES WORD TO CREATE A WORD DOCUMENT.

```
1: Dim objWordApp As Object
2:
3: ' Create a Word document and add text to it
4: Set objWordApp = GetObject("", "Word.Application.8")
```

continues

LISTING 22.2. CONTINUED

```
 5: If objWordApp Is Nothing Then    ' True if not running
 6: Set objWordApp = CreateObject("Word.Application.8")
 7: End If
 8: objWordApp.Documents.Add ' Add a document to the collection
 9:
10:  ' The title will have a blank line after it
11:  ' Move the cursor to the next line (simulate the
12:  ' user pressing Enter) by sending the vbCrLf named
13:  ' literal to the document
14: objWordApp.Documents(1).Content.Font.Size = 28
15: objWordApp.Documents(1).Content.Font.Bold = True
16: objWordApp.Documents(1).Content.InsertAfter _
17: Text:="Why go to Italy?" & vbCrLf & vbCrLf
18:
19:  ' The body of the document is next
20: objWordApp.Documents(1).Range.InsertAfter Text:= _
21: "Italy sells the best ice cream in the world." & vbCrLf
22: objWordApp.Documents(1).Range.InsertAfter Text:= _
23: "Italy has the best architecture in the world." & vbCrLf
24: objWordApp.Documents(1).Range.InsertAfter Text:= _
25: "(Oh, and did I mention the ice cream?)"
26:
27:  'Save the document
28: objWordApp.Documents(1).SaveAs "c:\MyWord.Doc"
29:  ' Close the Word document
30: objWordApp.Documents(1).Close
31:  ' Quit the Word application
32: objWordApp.Quit
```

One of the new features of Visual Basic 6.0 is the capability for CreateObject() to specify an object on another machine. Please refer to online help for all the details.

Listing 22.2 contains a lot of strange-looking properties, events, and methods such as InsertAfter and Range. These are Word-based Visual Basic objects, properties, events, and methods. Although you haven't seen most of these before, you can probably guess what each statement does. (No range is set up by the code, so Range refers to the cursor's current position in the document.)

After running Listing 22.2 (perhaps from an event procedure you tie to a command button), you can open Word and load the MyWord.Doc document created from Listing 22.2. You'll see that the document is fully Word compatible; it should be because Word created it from your application's OLE automation commands. Figure 22.1 shows a Word screen with the document open.

FIGURE 22.1.

The Word document that Visual Basic created with OLE automation.

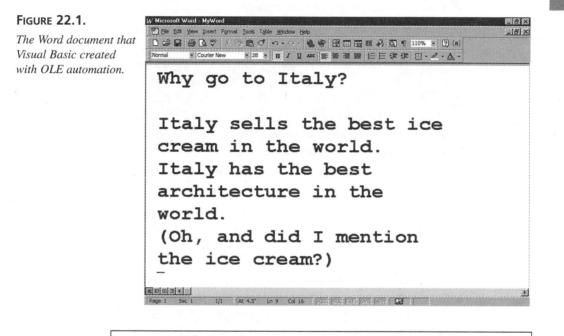

Why go to Italy?

Italy sells the best ice cream in the world.
Italy has the best architecture in the world.
(Oh, and did I mention the ice cream?)

You must be intimately familiar with the OLE automation application before you can work with it through Visual Basic objects. Often the other application offers online OLE automation support information so you can use that application in an OLE automation setting. You can get help with Word's OLE automation language by starting Visual Basic for Applications from Word's Tools menu and viewing the help files there.

Summary

You now understand more about objects and how to access them from within Visual Basic. In programming terms, an object is a packaged set of properties and code, and that's exactly what Visual Basic objects such as controls are. You set a control's properties and run methods to manipulate those objects. The object model gives you the ability to pass controls and other objects, test an object's type, and create your own collections that often make object programming easier than programming arrays.

The next hour explains how to prepare your application for distribution now that you've learned how to write powerful applications.

Q&A

Q Why are collections better than arrays?

A Collections are not better than arrays in all cases. If you need to keep track of 100 integer temperature values, keep those values in an integer array. The array is efficient and you can work with the array using loops as you are used to doing. A collection is nice when you don't know how many items will appear in the group, especially when those items are objects such as controls and not simply regular datatypes. The collection can grow to any size and the methods you use on the collection make for easy programming because you don't have to keep track of the highest item in the collection yourself.

Q What is the real difference between OLE and OLE automation?

A OLE lets users edit objects from other applications inside a Form window. The cross-application platforms that OLE provides let you embed a `Paint` object in your application without having to code drawing methods that perform as `Paint` objects perform. Before OLE automation, however, regular OLE did not give your Visual Basic application the capability to control the serving application. Applications that support OLE automation can now expose all their internal properties, events, and methods (if they're not OLE automation compatible, they will have no properties, events, or methods) to applications such as Visual Basic. Visual Basic, therefore, can make Access manipulate database tables or make Excel manipulate a named range in a worksheet. Although you must do some extra work on the front end to code the OLE automation, your applications become much more powerful because they borrow technology from these other applications.

Workshop

The quiz questions and exercises are provided for your further understanding. See Appendix B for the answers.

Quiz

1. What are three system objects?
2. What is the difference between a class and an object?
3. What happens when you use the `New` keyword inside an object declaration?

22

4. True or false: `TypeOf` is both a statement and a function.

5. True or false: You can pass objects such as controls and forms as arguments to procedures.

6. What is the index value for a collection's first item?

7. How can you insert a new item at the beginning of a collection?

8. Which OLE automation function should you use to initiate OLE automation when the OLE automation application is already running on the machine?

9. What is the new term being used more frequently for OLE automation?

10. True or false: As long as you know the OLE automation language, you don't need the OLE automation application installed on your machine to use OLE automation with that application.

Exercises

1. Write a procedure that decreases the font size of all controls on all forms by 50%. Use a system object to accomplish the change.

2. If you use Word, Excel, or any other OLE automation–compatible application (as all the Office 97 products are), start that application and search the online help for information on that application's properties, events, and methods used in OLE automation. The more you know about that application's internals, the more easily you can integrate that application and borrow its power for your own applications. If the application is an Office 97 application, search the online help for the Visual Basic help to see how to start Visual Basic. (Visual Basic is often called Visual Basic for Applications in application help files. Visual Basic for Applications [or VBA] is the same language as Visual Basic.) Start the application's Visual Basic editor to see a development environment that looks like Visual Basic's own development environment. Open the application's Object Browser to receive an Explorer-like view of that application's properties, events, and methods. Search the Object Browser's online help for extensive OLE automation help.

Hour **23**

Distributing Your Applications

Now that you've become a top-notch Visual Basic programmer in less than 24 hours, you're ready to learn how to distribute your applications to other users. If you've installed professional software, you've seen first-rate installation front ends that let the user install software as painlessly as possible. It's your turn to create such a front end with Visual Basic's help.

The highlights of this hour include

- Why you should compile your final application
- How to start the install creation routine
- When to create dependency files
- Where Setup installs the application
- How to uninstall the application

Compiling Your Application

NEW TERM To *compile* an application means that Visual Basic translates the application and all its projects into an executable file.

Before you distribute your applications, test them thoroughly using the testing and debugging tools you learned about in Hour 20, "Writing Correct Applications." When you are satisfied that you've removed as many bugs as possible, you are ready to compile the application.

You'll want to compile your application for these reasons:

- Your application will load and run faster.
- Your user won't need the Visual Basic development environment to run the application.
- The application is more secure because compiled programs are more difficult to change than uncompiled source code such as that which you run inside the development environment.

Compiling an application is often called *making a project.*

When you compile your project, Visual Basic gathers all the project files together and converts those files into a single executable file. (Sometimes, depending on the project, an extra file or two are needed in addition to the executable file.) The executable file has the .exe filename extension, and your users can run the application from the Start menu's Run option or from an entry they add to the Start menu.

To compile your application, select File | Make and select a location from the Make Project dialog box that appears. When you click OK, Visual Basic compiles the program. You can now exit Visual Basic and run the program from the Start menu's Run command.

Setting Project Properties

Before you compile a program, you can take a moment to set some project properties that determine how the program compiles. When you click the Options button in the Make Project dialog box (instead of clicking OK to start the compile), Visual Basic displays Figure 23.1's Project Properties dialog box.

FIGURE 23.1.

*Setting project
properties before
compiling.*

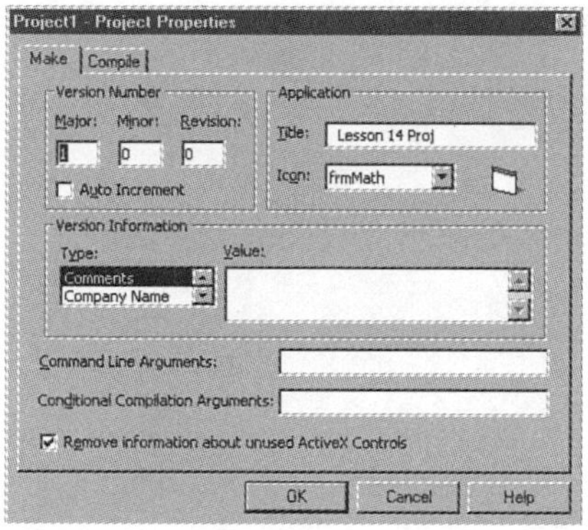

23

> The Project Properties dialog box you see when making an executable is a
> scaled-down dialog box from the Project Properties dialog box you see
> when you choose Project | Properties.

NEW TERM   *Version control* refers to the capability of Visual Basic to assign version numbers,
such as 1.01, 1.02, 2.00, and so on, to compiled code.

If you plan to update your application in the future and distribute subsequent versions,
set the Major, Minor, and Revision version number text boxes. The versioning values let
you distinguish between compiled versions. You might want to place the version number
in your application's Help | About dialog box.

> If you plan to issue several versions, consider checking the Auto Increment
> check box and Visual Basic will update the versions for you at each compila-
> tion.

In addition to the versioning information, consider locating an icon that you want displayed on the Start menu and on the taskbar that represents your program. The only
catch is that you cannot set the application's icon from the Icon list box. The Icon list
box lets you select a form name from your project. If your project contains only a single
form, that's the only form that appears in the list box. The form's Icon property holds the
icon filename, and when you select that form in the Project Properties dialog box, its
icon becomes the compiled application's icon.

When you click the Project Properties dialog box's Compile tab, you'll be able to set
additional properties, as shown in Figure 23.2.

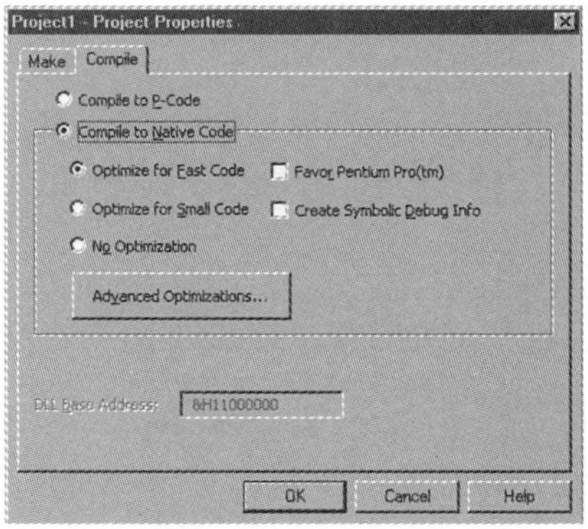

FIGURE 23.2.

Additional project properties you can set.

Generally, if you go to the trouble of compiling the application, you'll want to make sure the option labeled Compile to Native Code is selected. If you compile as p-code using the top option, your application will run more slowly and require a runtime .dll file that you must distribute along with your application.

P-code is an interpreted language that works beneath some compiled Visual Basic applications. P-code, which stands for pseudocode, tells the system what your application wants to do next. *Native code*, on the other hand, is a machine language that your computer understands directly without the need for a time-consuming interpreted language such as p-code. Versions of Visual Basic before 5.0 could not compile applications into native code, so programmers had to use p-code. P-code still exists for compatibility, but you'll always want to compile into native code for the fastest execution speed your application can achieve.

By clicking the Advanced Optimizations command button, you display another set of options, as shown in Figure 23.3. There is one problem with this set of options: Although they produce a more efficient running application, the application checks less for runtime errors. You will want to set one or more of these advanced options only if you have thoroughly tested your application.

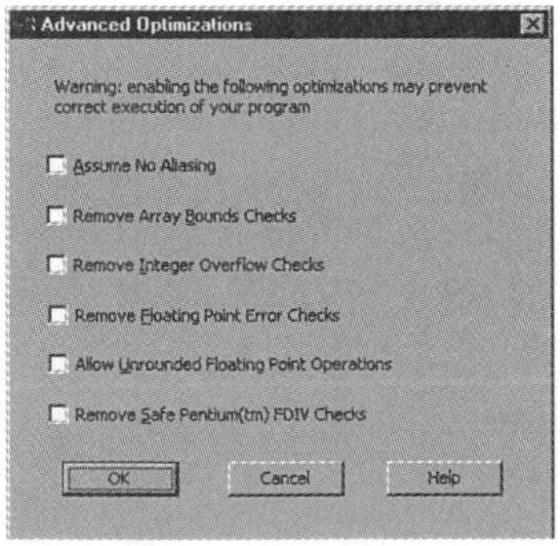

FIGURE 23.3.

These options request less runtime error checking.

> You are safer using one or more of the advanced optimization options if your application uses no floating-point arithmetic or if it heavily uses arrays.

Setting Up Your Application

NEW TERM The *Package And Deployment Wizard* is a wizard that turns your compiled application into a complete installation disk set.

After you test and compile your application, you are ready to create the distribution set of files that your user uses to install the application. Visual Basic supplies the Package And Deployment Wizard to help you turn your application into distributable disks.

Not every application should be installed from disks, and the Package And Deployment Wizard creates a distribution set for just about any kind of installation, such as for CD-ROM installations and for networked computer users who want to install the application from a server. Actually, the Package And Deployment Wizard performs several tasks, including the following:

- Compresses files so your installation's disk files consume less space than the installed application
- Generates an uninstall configuration so that the users who install your application can remove your application and all its related files at a later date
- Creates a disk set of installation files, even spreading extra-large files over multiple disk volumes if needed
- Generates a setup program for users who install the application
- Generates a hard disk installation set so that you can copy the setup application onto a CD-ROM (if you have the appropriate hardware) or install the application over a network to other users
- Creates a special setup distribution so that you or other users can install the application across the Internet

Starting the Package And Deployment Wizard

After you compile your application, you can distribute it by starting the Application Setup Wizard from the Windows Start menu. Locate the Start menu from which you normally start Visual Basic, but instead of starting Visual Basic, start the program named

23

Package And Deployment Wizard to display the wizard's opening dialog box, shown in Figure 23.4. The Package And Deployment Wizard is likely going to be found in the Tools folder of the Visual Studio Start menu folder. Click the Browse button to select the Visual Basic project you want to distribute. The Package And Deployment Wizard offers you the following options:

- By selecting the Package button, you can generate a setup program and, optionally, set up a dependency file to ensure that needed files are included with your application. These needed files might be ActiveX control files or help files. Although all your forms and code compile into an executable, several external files aren't included with your compiled application, including the help files and resource files.

- If you will be deploying your distribution file to a distribution site such as an Internet server, click the Deploy button.

- Use the Manage Scripts button to make modifications to Package And Deployment Wizard scripts that you have already created.

For most applications, you will be distributing for the immediate future, so you will select the Package button. After selecting a project, press the Package button to proceed with this tutorial.

FIGURE 23.4.

The Package And Deployment Wizard's opening dialog box.

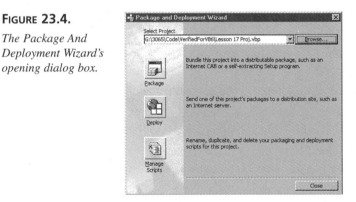

The Package And Deployment Wizard must know exactly which files to include with the installed set of disks. Even though the Setup Wizard installs your application's executable program, the Package And Deployment Wizard must search your application's project file (the application's project filename extension is .vbp, as you might recall) to get a list of all related files.

NEW TERM A *dependency file* is a reference file that determines which files are needed by other files. For example, an application might require an ActiveX control to execute, and that ActiveX control would be a dependency file for the application.

If the Visual Basic project you selected has not yet been compiled, the Package And Deployment Wizard will give you the chance to compile it before proceeding any further. You will then be asked to select a Package type for the distribution package. Choose to create a Standard Setup Package.

When prompted, select the folder in which the distribution package will be assembled. The VB Package And Deployment Wizard will then analyze your application and determine which other files should be distributed with your application so that it executes properly. Until you are more familiar with what various files selected by the Package And Deployment Wizard for distribution do, leave all the selected files the same and proceed to the next dialog box.

The Package And Deployment Wizard will prompt you for the distribution type with the dialog box shown in Figure 23.5. The Distribution Type dialog box tells the Package And Deployment Wizard how to build the setup program. The Single File option installs the setup routine to a single hard disk file, which you then could copy to a CD-ROM (if you have the appropriate hardware). The Multiple Files option is ideal for installing the setup files onto one or more floppy disks.

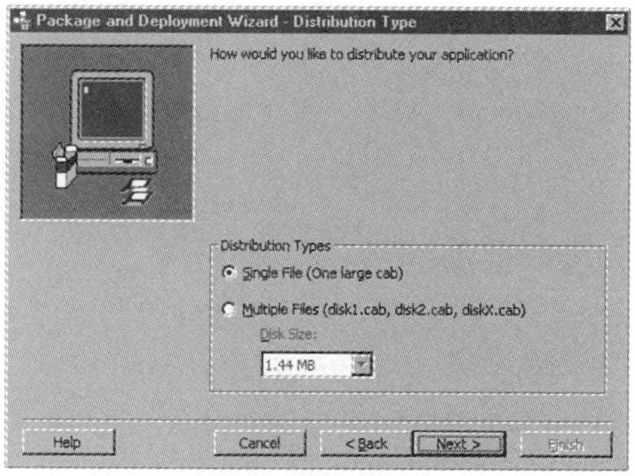

FIGURE 23.5.

Telling the Package And Deployment Wizard how you want the installation distributed.

When the dialog box shown in Figure 23.6 appears, use it to give the installation program a title. It is a good idea to include your application's version number here along with the title.

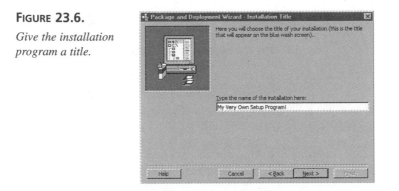

The dialog box in Figure 23.7 is used to select a start menu group and an icon for your application. If you want, you can make modifications to the default values.

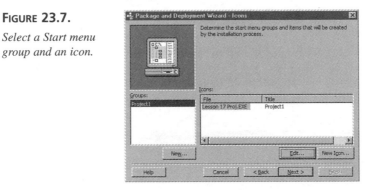

In the next dialog box, the Package And Deployment Wizard will give you the opportunity to modify the individual location of various individual files in the distribution package. After examining the default locations, proceed to the next dialog box. It is recommended that you do not change the default location (System32 folder) of shared DLL files. For most applications that you will be building in the immediate future, you can leave the same default options of subsequent dialog boxes.

Depending on various other capabilities of your applications (database access, for example), you might see additional Package And Deployment Wizard dialog boxes. Finally, the Package And Deployment Wizard will give you the option of saving the settings you specified for this project in a script file. This will make things easier for you the next time you want to use the Package And Deployment Wizard to create a distribution file for a newer version of the same project. After specifying a script name, click the Finish button and sit back and watch the Package And Deployment Wizard perform its magic.

Running Setup

Make sure that you test your setup installation to ensure that the installed application performs the way you expect. If you forgot a dependency or didn't even know your application required one (this is common, so expect it), your installed application won't run correctly. You then can begin to trace the problem, such as adding an ActiveX control file to the dependency list if the control is missing.

To run the installation, select the Start menu's Run command, click Browse to locate the Setup.exe file, and click OK.

The installation routine won't overwrite existing files on the target computer if the target computer already has newer files that have the same filename. If the installation routine finds such a file, the routine will ask the user for permission to overwrite the current file or leave the newer file intact. Most of the time the user should leave the existing files to preserve newer versions of their software, especially ActiveX controls.

Uninstalling the Application

NEW TERM An *uninstall* routine removes the application, including all related files, from the computer.

One of the best features of the setup routine is its ability to create an uninstall routine for the application. To uninstall the application, select Settings | Control Panel from the Windows Start menu and double-click the Add/Remove Programs icon. Your installed application will appear in the list of applications available for removal. Click the Add/Remove command button, and the uninstall process begins.

Summary

This hour explains how to create an installation routine for the applications you distribute. Your users will get a bulletproof installation routine that ensures all necessary files are installed to the user's system so that your application runs properly. Of course, first you'll have to test the application to ensure that the bugs are out before you distribute the installable application to users. Not only does the setup routine install the files, but the setup routine also creates an uninstall routine with which your users can remove all files related to the application.

The next hour describes how to write Internet-aware applications that integrate the application with the Web.

Q&A

Q Why should I go to the trouble of creating a distribution file for my application when it runs just fine when I execute its executable file?

A Although your executable file might run just fine on your computer, the computer that was used to actually develop the project, it might not run by itself on another computer due to the lack of files required by your application. For example, if you use a certain ActiveX control, that ActiveX control may have dependency files. When you use the Package and Deployment Wizard to distribute your applications, you can ensure that you distribute your applications with all the required files.

Workshop

The quiz questions and exercises are provided for your further understanding. See Appendix B for the answers.

Quiz

1. What are three advantages to compiling an application?

2. True or false: You must run the File | Compile option to compile the program.

3. Why might you use version control?

4. How do you designate an icon for an application?

5. True or false: You can create the installation routine from Visual Basic's development environment.

6. What is a dependency file?

7. True or false: The Package And Deployment Wizard can create an installation routine for the Internet.

8. Why does the Package And Deployment Wizard offer two ways to store the setup routine on your hard disk (in a single folder or multiple folders)?

9. What happens if the installation routine finds a newer version of a file it's about to install?

10. How does the user uninstall the installed application?

Exercise

Change the form icon from Hour 18, "The Graphic Image Controls," to one of the happy face icons used in the project. Compile the project and make sure that the compiled application uses the icon for the project icon. Create an installation routine for Hour 18's animation application. Install the application using the setup routine. Run the application (look in the Program Files folder for the application) to make sure everything works well. If you need to change something, re-run the Package And Deployment Wizard. After you create a successful installation, open the Control Panel and uninstall the application.

23

HOUR 24

Online Visual Basic

At the end of this hour, you will be able to add powerful Internet features to your VB applications. Internet programming is not simple. If you look through a bookstore, you will see shelf after shelf containing thick programming guides that teach how to build Internet applications.

Visual Basic programmers have been writing Internet-based programs for a while, but before version 5, Visual Basic programmers had to do a lot more work than they now have to do with Visual Basic 6.0. You'll see that adding Internet Web access requires only that you follow the steps in a simple wizard.

The highlights of this hour include

- Why both intranet and Internet programming support are vital
- Where to find Internet programming tools in Visual Basic
- How to request Internet support from the VB Application Wizard
- What to expect from the wizard's Web browser
- Which ISP requirements a user needs before he can access the Internet with your application

Follow the Wizard to the Web!

As mentioned in the introduction, Visual Basic 6 makes Internet access extremely simple. Way back in Hour 2, "Analyzing Visual Basic Programs," you learned how to start the VB Application Wizard that created an application shell for you. You now know enough of the Visual Basic language to create a shell and modify the application with specific code so that the application does the work that you need.

 An *intranet* is a localized version of the Internet and is sometimes used as a local area network's protocol system.

> You can use Visual Basic's Internet connections to build routines and applications that access both the Internet and your own company's intranet. The intranet is becoming the interface of choice by many companies whose employees access the Internet. After all, shouldn't the computer down the hall from you be as simple to access as a computer around the world? Instead of using a separate networking software solution, many companies prefer to leverage their existing Internet tools. You'll be able to build simple intranet applications with Visual Basic by the time you finish this lesson.

> You must have Microsoft's Internet Explorer 3.0 or later installed on your system before you can create Visual Basic applications with Internet access. (Internet Explorer 4.0 or later is highly recommended.)

One of the wizard's dialog boxes gives you access to the Internet. Try it yourself by following these steps:

1. Start a new project.
2. From the New Project dialog box (shown in Figure 24.1), double-click VB Application Wizard to start the wizard.
3. Read the dialog boxes and click Next as you follow the wizard's application design. Accept all the default values on each dialog box and pause when you come to the dialog box labeled Internet Connectivity (see Figure 24.2).

NEW TERM A Web *browser* is a program that lets you display and interact with colorful Web pages on the Internet.

FIGURE 24.1.

Click here to start the wizard and add Internet support.

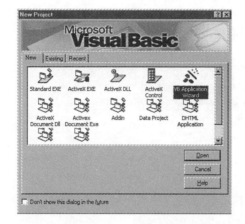

FIGURE 24.2.

This wizard dialog box requests Internet support.

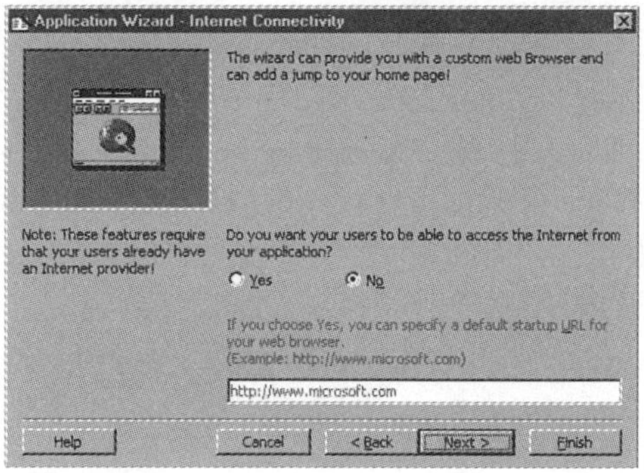

NEW TERM   *URL* (*uniform resource locator*) is an Internet Web site address where you can point a Web browser. URLs generally begin with *http://* (which stands for *Hypertext Transfer Protocol*). URL addresses can also specify an FTP (File Transfer Protocol) document or even another document that resides on your computer or on another networked disk.

4. Click Yes to request Internet support. In addition, enter a default URL in the text box. If you don't change the default URL, the Web browser will go to Microsoft's home page when the application's user displays the Web browser the first time.

   If your company has a home page, you might want to enter that home page's URL in the text box. If you want to make your users really smart, point them to Macmillan Publishing's home page at `http://www.mcp.com`.

5. When you complete the Internet dialog box, continue clicking Next until you get to the final wizard dialog box. Click Finish to complete the wizard and watch the wizard generate your application. So far, nothing looks different from the wizard you used to create an application in Hour 2.

Close the wizard's summary dialog boxes and run the application. Figure 24.3 shows the resulting Internet-enabled application.

FIGURE 24.3.

Where's the Internet?

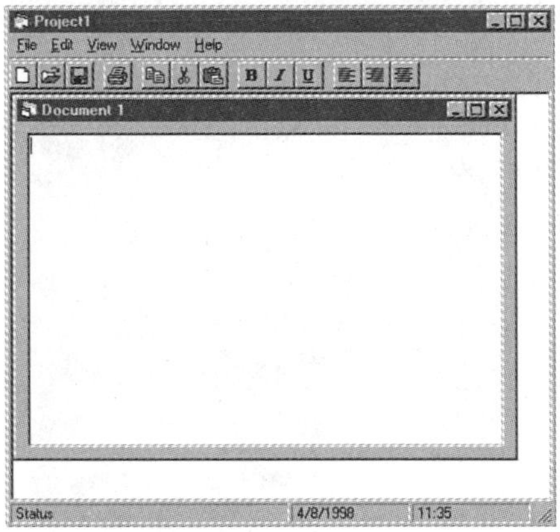

Obviously, something is wrong because the application doesn't look anything like an Internet application. When you ran the wizard, you accepted a lot of dialog box default values. The wizard didn't generate an Internet application only, but rather an application that happens to contain Internet access.

Select View | Web Browser. The application will load the Web browser form and send the application to the Internet through your Internet Service Provider (ISP).

Your Users Need an ISP

An *ISP* is an Internet service that you and your users use to connect to the Internet. You might even work for a company that contains the hardware needed to be its own ISP. If your PC has Internet access, you'll have no trouble using the application you create.

Therefore, when you distribute your application, if the application has Internet access, you'll need to warn the users that they, too, must have an ISP to use the application with the Internet. Again, if your users are workers within your own company that already provides Internet access to PCs, you'll have no problems distributing your applications.

Using the Browser

When you select View | Web Browser with your generated application, your application will attempt to make an Internet connection through your ISP. Generally, this means that you'll have to log on to the Internet by issuing your username and password. For example, if you subscribe to the Internet using The Microsoft Network online service, you'll see Figure 24.4's Sign In dialog box right after you select View | Web Browser.

FIGURE 24.4.

You must connect to your ISP.

Obviously, anyone who runs your application must also log in to her ISP, and her ISP login dialog box will appear in place of this Sign In dialog box if she uses a different ISP.

After you (or your application's user) log in to the ISP, the application displays the Web browser and the Web page you set as the default (see Figure 24.5).

FIGURE 24.5.

Your application now contains a Web browser.

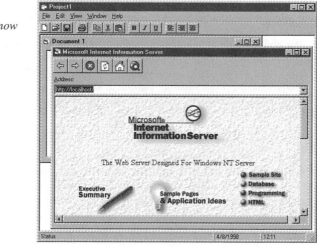

24

The Web browser includes the standard browsing tools that you are used to if you've ever used a browser. You can perform all the following tasks from your application's browser:

- You (or your application's user) can click the Web page's hotspots to jump to related Web pages.
- You can enter a new URL in the Address text box to see a different site.
- You can browse backward through the pages you've seen by clicking the toolbar's Back button.
- Once you back up, you can return to a Web page by clicking the toolbar's Forward button.
- If a Web page takes a long time to load its graphics, you can click the toolbar's Stop button to freeze the page at its current loaded state. (Usually the text will load long before all the graphics load and you might not need to view the rest of the page's graphics.)
- You can refresh a Web page that you've stopped from loading or refresh to see new information by clicking the toolbar's Refresh button.
- The toolbar's Home button takes you to the home page set up for your ISP (not the URL you entered in the wizard's text box). You can select View | Options | Navigation to set a different home page.
- Click the toolbar's Search button to locate other sites on the Internet.

All this is possible and you never coded one programming statement to gain the Internet functionality!

NEW TERM *Java* is a Web-based programming language similar to C++. Java adds interactivity to a Web page.

> The browser that the wizard generated is Java-enabled because it is based on Internet Explorer, which is Java-enabled. Your application won't get all the functionality of the full-functioned Internet Explorer, but you will get most of the vital features such as Java and Web browsing.
>
> If you use additional components in your VB application, those components have to be distributed/deployed along with the executable application.

Click the browser's drop-down Address text box, shown in Figure 24.6, to go back to any specific Web page you've visited during your browsing session.

FIGURE 24.6.

You can review the sites you've visited.

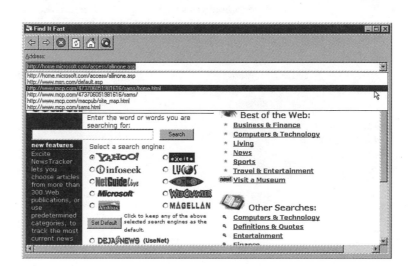

NEW TERM   *VBScript* is a Web page scripting language that you can use to activate Web pages by adding intelligence to Web pages to interact with the user.

By the way, now that you've mastered Visual Basic, you know almost everything there is to know about VBScript. Therefore, you'll be able to work as a Web page programmer with just a little extra training in VBScript and HTML coding. For a great text that explains how to use VBScript, pick up a copy of either *Sams Teach Yourself VBScript in 21 Days* or *Laura Lemay's Web Workshop: ActiveX and VBScript* (both by Sams Publishing).

When you finish browsing the Web, you can close the Browser window and continue with your application. Obviously, the wizard's application is still just a shell. Nevertheless, the most functional part of the application is the Web browser, and you can see how simple Visual Basic makes it to drop a browser into an application.

Did you notice how many new tools the wizard added to your Toolbox window to support the Web browser? Close the application and look at the toolbox. You'll see additional tools, labeled in Figure 24.7, that help the application do its tasks. Although the Web browser is simple, the wizard did put its parts together. Although Visual Basic supplies a Web Browser tool (see Figure 24.7), the tool requires other support tools to have an object such as the drop-down Address list box.

FIGURE 24.7.

The Web Browser tool requires several other controls to do its job.

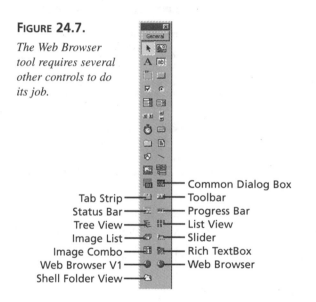

To help your application's users, you'll need to add more features to the Web browsing portion of your application. For example, the application doesn't have a logoff feature. Perhaps you could add a menu to the browser and include common options found in most browsing menus.

Looking Through the Other Tools

When you select Project | Components and look through the list of tools you can add to the Toolbox window, you'll find several Internet-related tools. For example, all the controls that begin with the words *Internet Explorer* are Internet Explorer–like controls you can add to an application. Table 24.1 briefly describes these tools.

TABLE 24.1. INTERNET AND MICROSOFT INTERNET EXPLORER–RELATED COMPONENTS.

Component	Description
IE Animated Button	An animated display showing Internet Explorer's connection.
IE Popup Menu	A menu control that appears on the Web page.
IE Popup Window	A tabbed window control that opens a new connection window.
IE Preloader	A control that preloads a site before the visible Internet access begins.
IE Super Label	A Web page label.
IE Timer	A clock control that provides timing operations for Internet services.
Microsoft Internet Controls	The Web browser control you used in the previous wizard's application.
Microsoft Internet Transfer Control 6.0	The transfer protocol control to transfer files between Internet computers.
Microsoft Winsock Control 6.0	The Windows connection to common Internet protocols.

NEW TERM *FTP* stands for *File Transfer Protocol* and refers to one computer's capability to log on to the Internet and exchange files with another user's computer.

NEW TERM *Winsock* is the Windows interface to inter-computer data communication.

You'll also find several FTP and Winsock controls that help you encapsulate advanced Internet applications into packages you can use as a standalone Web browser or, more commonly, as a Web browser you can make available in the middle of your application for your application's users to use when needed. These extra controls are fairly advanced, so read the extensive online documentation that Visual Basic provides for Web applications in the Books Online reference sets.

Summary

In this hour you quickly learned how to achieve Internet and intranet connectivity from within the Visual Basic applications you write. If your application needs a Web browser, the VB Application Wizard will take care of the details. If you need more, you can add additional functionality to your application.

This hour's lesson completes this 24-hour tutorial. You should take a few days' rest before returning to the keyboard to write the next killer application that outsells Microsoft Office. Good luck with Visual Basic and with your programming future!

Q&A

Q Why does Visual Basic come with all the Internet Explorer controls?

A The VB Application Wizard doesn't add a comprehensive Web browser to an application. Instead, the VB Application Wizard adds a usable Web browser that works well as a drop-in tool but performs with mediocrity as a standalone Web browser or as a full-featured browser. Therefore, you might be able to incorporate the other controls into the final application you build.

Workshop

The quiz questions and exercises are provided for your further understanding. See Appendix B for the answers.

Quiz

1. Which has the broader scope: an intranet or the Internet?

2. Which online connection—an Internet, an intranet, or both—can the VB Application Wizard support?

3. True or false: The computer on which you develop your Visual Basic application with Internet support must have Internet Explorer 3.0 or later.

4. True or false: The computer on which your application executes must have Internet Explorer 3.0 or later.

5. What is an ISP used for?

6. True or false: The computer on which you develop your Visual Basic application with Internet support must have an ISP.

7. What makes a Java-enabled Web page different from one that has no Java code?

8. Why are extra support tools needed when an application already uses the Web Browser tool from the Toolbox window?

9. True or false: The VB Application Wizard generates a Web browser that you can use to log on to the Internet's Web pages. When you finish viewing the Web pages, you can click a button to log off the browser but remain inside the generated application's code.

10. What are three ways to display a Web page that you previously displayed from the Web browser in the same session?

Exercise

Use File | Print to print all the Web browser form's code. You'll see that the wizard generated a lot of code and that some of the code is fairly tricky. By studying the code, you'll see that these Internet controls can be difficult to program and that the wizard takes much of that difficult task off your shoulders.

24

PART VII

Appendixes

Appendix

APPENDIX A

Operator Precedence

Table A.1 lists the operator preference order. The table includes the operators grouped by their type of operation.

TABLE A.1. VISUAL BASIC'S ORDER OF OPERATORS.

Arithmetic	Comparison	Logical
Exponentiation (^)	Equality (=)	Not
Negation (-)	Inequality (<>)	And
Multiplication and division (*,/)	Less than (<)	Or
Integer division (\)	Greater than (>)	Xor
Modulus arithmetic (Mod)	Less than or equal to (<=)	Eqv
Addition and subtraction (+, -)	Greater than or equal to (>=)	Imp
String concatenation (&)	Like, Is	

APPENDIX B

Answers

Hour 1 Quiz

1. To develop Windows applications
2. Programming languages are now visual to handle Windows environments.
3. BASIC (stands for Beginner's All-Purpose Symbolic Instruction Code)
4. Form window
5. The Form window holds the application's form background and all its user controls, such as command buttons. The Form Layout window lets you adjust the Form window's location on the user's screen when the user first executes the application.
6. True

Hour 1 Exercise

No answer is necessary.

Hour 2 Quiz

1. Windows programs are visual and include graphic elements the user interacts with to control the program. In addition, Windows programs respond to events, whereas text-based programs guide the user more rigidly and the programs control the user's next move.

2. Events occur during your application's execution and usually, but not always, occur in response to the user's action, such as a mouse button click or a keystroke.

3. The Project window's component filenames use common filename extensions such as .vbp and .bas, but Visual Basic doesn't use filename extensions when referring to those components.

4. Compilation

5. The control's event procedures determine the code that executes when an event occurs.

6. False

7. Control property changes show themselves at design time and at runtime, whereas event procedures execute only at runtime.

Hour 2 Exercise

No answer is necessary.

Hour 3 Quiz

1. Double-click the control on the Toolbox window to place the control on the form quickly.

2. The sizing handles let you move the control and change its size.

3. Hold down the Ctrl key when you click each control, or lasso multiple controls by dragging a square around them with the mouse.

4. True (such as the Top and Left properties)

5. The Caption property sets the form title.

6. A control is a type of object; objects also can include the form, menus, and other application components.

7. Add ToolTips to controls when you place the controls on the form.

8. A dialog box appears when you click a control property's ellipsis to let you fill in multiple values related to the control property.

Hour 3 Exercises

1. You can retrieve the code from the CD-ROM that accompanies this book. After you retrieve the source code, please look for a project named Lesson 3 Exer 1.

2. You can retrieve the code from the CD-ROM that accompanies this book. After you retrieve the source code, please look for a project named Lesson 3 Exer 2.

Hour 4 Quiz

1. False; the focus appears at runtime, not at design time.

2. True

3. Labels

4. Set the control's Cancel property to True.

5. The Enabled property

6. Labels don't directly interact with users.

7. The label expands horizontally before you have a chance to set the WordWrap property. WordWrap does you no good when the label is so long no wrap is necessary.

8. The form might not be large enough to hold multiple autosizing labels that hold a large amount of text.

Hour 4 Exercises

1. The code can be retrieved from the CD accompanying this book. After you retrieve the source code, look for a project named Lesson 4 Exer 1.

2. The code can be retrieved from the CD-ROM that accompanies this book. After you retrieve the source code, look for a project named Lesson 4 Exer 2.

B

Hour 5 Quiz

1. A datatype describes the kind of data a variable can hold.

2. A string holds zero or more characters, whereas a Boolean datatype holds only one of two values, True or False.

3. Option buttons and check boxes

4. A literal's value never changes.

5. 12Months, 85

6. The plus sign performs addition and concatenation. In addition, the equal sign assigns values as well as tests for equality.

7. Fixed-length strings set a limit on the number of characters they can hold.

8.   a. 8

       b. 8

       c. 32

       d. 24

Hour 5 Exercises

1. ```
Dim strFirst As String
Dim strLast As String
Dim intAge As Integer
Dim sngTaxRate as Single
Dim blnMarried As Boolean
```

2. You can retrieve the code from the CD-ROM that accompanies this book. After you retrieve the source code, please look for a project named `Lesson 5 Exer 2`.

# Hour 6 Quiz

1. A message box is not a control, but a dialog box that appears when needed to get information from the user. A text box is a control that resides on the form.

2. A text box stays on the screen longer, in most cases, than an input box.

3. When you use a named literal instead of placing literal values throughout an application, it's easier to make modifications to the code. Named literals are more intuitive to people who maintain your code than values of named literals.

4. The apostrophe and the `Rem` statement are both remarks.

5. Remarks are for people who look at your program code.

6. Modality determines how the dialog box reacts to the user's input.

7. You can display one of four icons in a message box.

8. False; you can return a maximum of one value from a function.

9. The input box returns the default value if the user does not change the default value.

10. True
```

Hour 6 Exercises

1. ```
' Programmer name: Julie Russell
' Date: November 27, 1999
' This program calculates sales taxes
' based on the customer sales values
```

2. ```
varAge = InputBox("How old are you?", "Age Request", "25")
```

Hour 7 Quiz

1. Comparison operators return Boolean results and perform no math.

2. The ASCII table determines the order of character comparisons.

3.   a. True

       b. True

       c. False

       d. False

4. Code the `Else` portion if you want to specify execution for the `If`'s false comparison result.

5. True

6. `Select Case`

7. `Case expr1 To expr2`

8. The statement following the `End Select` executes.

9. Every statement in the code block executes if that leg of the `Select Case` executes.

10. The `End Else` should be `End If`.

B

Hour 7 Exercises

1. ```
If (A > 3) And (B > 10) Then
      lblAns.Caption = "Yes"
End If
```

2. ```
If (X >= 10) And (Y < 20) Then
```

Hour 8 Quiz

1. Your program might need to repeat one or more statements.

2. Four

3. False; they check for the condition at different locations in the loop.

4. The `Do...Loop While` loop continues as long as the condition is `True` and the `Do...Loop Until` loop continues as long as the condition is `False`.

5. The `Do Until` checks its condition at the top of the loop.

6. `Val()` converts string values to numbers.

7. True, if you use a negative `Step` value.

8. 10 times

9. 1

10. False; `Exit` supports several forms, including an `Exit` that exits the current subroutine, an `Exit` that exits the current function, and an `Exit` that exits the current loop.

Hour 8 Exercises

1. You can retrieve the code from the CD-ROM that accompanies this book. After you retrieve the source code, please look for a project named `Lesson 8 Exer 1`.

2.
```
Dim strAge As String
Dim intAge As Integer
Dim intPress As Integer

Do
    strAge = InputBox("How old are you?", "Age Ask")
    ' Check for the Cancel command button
    If (strAge = "") Then
        End    ' Terminate program
    End If
    intAge = Val(strAge)

    If (intAge < 10) Then
        ' The user's age is too low
        intPress = MsgBox("Your age is too low!" _
                   vbExclamation, "Error!")
    ElseIf (intAge > 99) Then
        ' The user's age is too high
        intPress = MsgBox("Your age is too high!", _
                   vbExclamation, "Error!")
    End If
Loop While ((intAge < 10) Or (intAge > 99))
```

Hour 9 Quiz

1. The `StartUpPosition` determines the form's initial location on the screen.

2. So the user can quickly move to the text box next to the label

3. Enter `ToolTipText` properties when you add controls because you are more familiar with the controls' purpose at that time.

4. A control array is a collection of controls that have the same name and many similar properties.

5. Visual Basic assumes that you want to add a similar control, and control arrays often hold similar controls.

6. Lock the text in a text box when you don't want the user to be able to change the text.

7. Unload the form and then issue the `End` statement.

8. A runtime error occurs because you cannot divide by zero.

9. True; `Caption` is a label's default property. Of course the wording differs, but the statements perform the same action.

10. A function procedure returns a value to the calling procedure, whereas a subroutine procedure never returns a value.

Hour 9 Exercises

1. You can retrieve the code from the CD-ROM that accompanies this book. After you retrieve the source code, please look for a project named `Lesson 9 Exer 1`.

2. You can retrieve the code from the CD-ROM that accompanies this book. After you retrieve the source code, please look for a project named `Lesson 9 Exer 2`.

Hour 10 Quiz

1. At runtime

2. The `AddItem` method

3. The `ListCount` method

4. True

5. 3

6. Specify the `Style` property to change a combo box style.

7. False; users cannot enter items into a drop-down list box.

B

8. A collection of variables with the same name

9. 9

10. True

Hour 10 Exercises

1. You can retrieve the code from the CD-ROM that accompanies this book. After you retrieve the source code, please look for a project named `Lesson 10 Exer 1`.

2. You can retrieve the code from the CD-ROM that accompanies this book. After you retrieve the source code, please look for a project named `Lesson 10 Exer 2`.

Hour 11 Quiz

1. False

2. The clicked option becomes the selected option button, and the one that was selected no longer is selected.

3. The item might be temporarily unavailable.

4. The check box becomes selected, and any others that were already selected are still selected.

5. True

6. Any control can go on a frame.

7. The `SmallChange` property determines the amount of scrolling that takes place when the user clicks the scroll bar arrows; the `LargeChange` property determines the amount of scrolling that takes place when the user clicks the scroll bar on either side of the scroll thumb.

8. The `Value` property changes when the user clicks the scrollbar.

9. False; the Timer control triggers events every time a fixed number of milliseconds pass.

10. False; through programming you can make a single Timer control any timed interval.

Hour 11 Exercises

1. The `Index` value that you use in the `Select Case` will be the argument passed to the procedure.

2. The form requires no frame because the user can select multiple check boxes at once, unlike option buttons.

3. Set the Timer control's Interval property to 1000. Use an If at the start of the timer's event procedure so that the label's size grows no larger than 70 points.

Hour 12 Quiz

1. 6

2. Programming is easier and your applications are more consistent with each other and with other Windows applications your users already know.

3. True

4. False; these actions are available all from one control, the Common Dialog Box control.

5. The Filter property controls the filename extensions that appear.

6. ShowColor, ShowFont, ShowHelp, ShowOpen, ShowPrinter, and ShowSave

7. The Flags property is not set.

8. Check the FileName property.

9. False

10. The Printer dialog box does no printing but only sets up printing.

Hour 12 Exercises

1. No answer is necessary.

2. You can retrieve the code from the CD-ROM that accompanies this book. After you retrieve the source code, please look for a project named Lesson 12 Exer 2.

3. No answer is necessary.

4. You can retrieve the code from the CD-ROM that accompanies this book. After you retrieve the source code, please look for a project named Lesson 12 Exer 4.

B

Hour 13 Quiz

1. Your programs are easier to write and easier to maintain when you write structured code.

2. False; structured programming puts off details.

3. True

4. The keyword should be `Sub`.

5. If the procedure uses no arguments, `Call` is optional.

6. `X` is module global and `Y` is project global. The variables would be the same if they appeared in an external module.

7. Don't include the array subscript.

8. The arguments are local to the calling procedure, so the called procedure needs to know the datatypes being passed.

9. By the passed argument list

10. `ByRef` is the default argument passing process, so if you want to pass by reference, you don't need to specify the `ByRef` keyword. If, however, you want to pass by value, you must specify `ByVal`.

Hour 13 Exercises

```
1. Public Function By10 (ByRef intVal As Integer) As Integer
       By10 = intVal * 10
   End Function

2. Public Sub LblSng (ByVal a1 As Single, _
                      ByVal a2 As Single, ByVal a3 As single)
      lblSng1.Caption = a1
      lblSng2.Caption = a2
      lblSng3.Caption = a3
   End Sub
```

Hour 14 Quiz

1. None; the built-in functions are part of the Visual Basic language.

2.   a. abc

    b. efg

    c. bcd

    d. bcdefg

3. A statement

4. A function

5.   a. 20

    b. 20

    c. -2

    d. -3

6. 10

7. 12:56

8. A thousands separator is used at each thousand's place in a number. For example, a comma appears as this number's thousand's separator: 45,419.12.

9. False; use Format() to display your dates in the format you want them to appear.

10. True

Hour 14 Exercises

1.
```
Dim strASCII As String(256)
For intCtr = 0 To 255
    StrASCII(intCtr) = Chr(intCtr)
Next intCtr
```

2.
```
Public Sub getTime()
    Dim dteTimeIn As Date
    Dim dteTimeOut As Date
    Dim lngSec As Long
    Dim intMin As Integer
    Dim intHours As Integer

    dteTimeIn = InputBox("What time did you check in?", "Check In")
    dteTimeOut = InputBox("What time did you check out?", "Check Out")
    lngSec = DateDiff("s", dteTimeIn, dteTimeOut)
    intMin = DateDiff("n", dteTimeIn, dteTimeOut)
    intHours = DateDiff("h", dteTimeIn, dteTimeOut)

    lblSecWorked.Caption = lngSec
    lblMinWorked.Caption = intMin
    lblHoursWorked.Caption = intMin/60
End Sub
```

3.
```
' You may want to add input validation to ensure
' that the user enters a reasonable age.
Public Sub getTime()
    Dim dteBirth As Date
    Dim intYrsRetire As Integer
    Dim intAge As Integer
    Dim Msg As Single

    Do
        dteBirth = InputBox("When were you born?", "Birthday")
    Loop Until IsDate(dteBirth)

    intAge = DateDiff("yyyy", dteBirth, Now)
    If intAge >= 65 Then
```

B

```
            Msg = MsgBox("Congratulations on a long life!" _
                   , vbExclamation, "It's great!")
         Else
            intYrsRetire = 65 - intAge
            Msg = MsgBox("You have only " & intYrsRetire & _
                   " years to retire!", vbExclamation, "Soon...!")
         End If

      End Sub
```

Hour 15 Quiz

1. A database is an organized collection of one or more tables of records.

2. A record is a row, and a field is a column from a file.

3. A table is a file in a relational database.

4. The file is overwritten.

5. The file is added to.

6. All open files

7. False; only for the tables you want to work with

8. If the user changes the bound control, the underlying database value changes also.

9. An option button or a check box

10. Use the VB Data Form Wizard

Hour 15 Exercises

```
1. Public Sub WriteValues()
      Open "c:\friends.dat" For Output As #1
      Write #1, "George", 35, "912-3344"
      Write #1, "Elaine", 31, "649-1999"
      Write #1, "Jerry", 34, "912-5712"
      Write #1, "Kramer", 38, "747-1123"
      Write #1, "Newman", 32, "648-2900"
      Close #1
   End Sub

   Public Sub ReadValues()
      Dim strName(6) As String
      Dim intAge(6) As Integer
      Dim strPhone(6) As String
      Open "c:\friends.dat" For Input As #1
      For intCtr = 1 to 5
         Input #1, strName(intCtr), intAge(intCtr), _
                   StrPhone(intCtr)
```

```
      Next intCtr
      Close #1
      ' Code goes here that processes data
End Sub
```

2. You can retrieve the code from the CD-ROM that accompanies this book. After you retrieve the source code, look for a project named Lesson 15 Exer 2.

3. No answer is available.

Hour 16 Quiz

1. The output goes to the Windows print manager.

2. An error message box appears.

3. The Printer object receives data sent by the Print method.

4. Specify the Copies property.

5. False

6. 14

7. Use Chr() to print special characters on the printer.

8. 12

9. False

10. True

Hour 16 Exercises

1. `Printer.Print Chr(165)`

2. ```
   For intCtr = 32 to 255
      Printer.Print Chr(intCtr)
   Next intCtr
   ```

3. See the project named Lesson 16 Exer 3 on the CD-ROM.

Hour 17 Quiz

1. True

2. True

3. mnu

4. mnuEditSelectAll

5. The indentation determines the menu level.

B
   ```

6. False

7. File | Exit

8. The user will not adapt as quickly to your application.

9. Click

10. The `Checked` property

Hour 17 Exercises

1. You can retrieve the code from the CD-ROM that accompanies this book. After you retrieve the source code, look for a project named `Lesson 17 Exer 1`.

2. The answer is not available, so that copyright information can be maintained in Visual Basic's prepackaged `Atm` example.

Hour 18 Quiz

1. The Picture Box and Image controls display graphic images.

2. The Image control is more efficient than the Picture Box control.

3. The Image control will shrink to measure the same size as the loaded picture.

4. The Picture Box control doesn't resize to measure the same size as the loaded graphic image.

5. The Image control enlarges to display the entire image.

6. The Picture Box control doesn't enlarge to display the full image, but rather, clips the image.

7. The assignment is missing the `LoadPicture()` function.

8. The Timer control helps you control animation effects.

9. False; only local variables can be static.

10. Visual Basic initializes static variables at compile time, so the first time through the procedure, the variable has an initial value.

Hour 18 Exercises

1. Set the Timer control's `Enabled` property to `False` in the Properties window. In the `Click` event procedure, set the `Enabled` property to `True` to begin the animation. Be sure to set the command button's `Style` property to `Graphical` before putting the happy face on the button.

2. No answer is available.

Hour 19 Quiz

1. The Toolbar control doesn't appear as an intrinsic control on the Toolbox window.
2. The Image List control
3. The `Key` property determines which string returns when a toolbar button is clicked.
4. The argument value determines which toolbar button is clicked.
5. 7
6. `BorderStyle`
7. False; `LoadPicture()` is for the Picture Box and Image controls.
8. The `FillStyle` property determines the interior pattern of shapes.
9. True. You can set the shape's border and interior colors.

Hour 19 Exercises

1. You can retrieve the code from the CD-ROM that accompanies this book. After you retrieve the source code, look for a project named `Lesson 19 Exer 1`.
2. You can retrieve the code from the CD-ROM that accompanies this book. After you retrieve the source code, look for a project named `Lesson 19 Exer 2`.
3. You can retrieve the code from the CD-ROM that accompanies this book. After you retrieve the source code, look for a project named `Lesson 19 Exer 3`.

Hour 20 Quiz

1. Syntax errors are the easiest to find.
2. Logic errors are the hardest to find.
3. A runtime error occurred.
4. Visual Basic's title bar tells the current mode.
5. A stopping point during a program's execution where all variables are kept active.
6. Look at the variables, add variables to the Watches window, single-step through the rest of the program, add other breakpoints, remove breakpoints, or terminate the execution.
7. Click the Debug toolbar's Step Through button at any breakpoint. You can also press F8 to step into the next line or press Shift+F8 to step over the line.
8. False

B

9. Click the Quick Watch button or rest the mouse pointer over the variable to see its value.

10. The `Print` method displays values in the Immediate window.

Hour 20 Exercises

1. Larry is not printing to the `Debug` object.

2. No answer is necessary.

Hour 21 Quiz

1. VB custom controls

2. Use the Components dialog box.

3. From the Internet and online services such as CompuServe, and you can also write your own

4. True

5. Use the existing similar control as a basis for the new ActiveX control.

6. Nothing

7. The user can double-click the embedded object or its icon.

8. An ActiveX document is an application that an ActiveX container is capable of displaying during execution as a child process.

9. Internet Explorer is an ActiveX container.

10. Run the VB 6 ActiveX Document Migration Wizard to convert a form to an ActiveX document.

Hour 21 Exercises

1. No answer is available, so that copyright information can be maintained for Word and WordPad.

2. No answer is needed. Run the wizard to convert the application to an ActiveX document.

Hour 22 Quiz

1. `Form`, `Printer`, and `Screen`

2. A class defines objects, and an object is a single instance of a class.

3. Visual Basic creates a new object.

4. True

5. True

6. One

7. Use the Before named argument to insert items at the beginning of a collection.

8. GetObject()

9. Active Automation

10. False

Hour 22 Exercises

```
1. Public Sub FontDecrease()
       For intCtr = 0 to Controls.Count - 1
           Controls(intCtr).Font.Size = Controls(intCtr).Font.Size _
                                         / 2
       Next intCtr
   End Sub
```

2. No answer is necessary.

Hour 23 Quiz

1. The program loads and runs faster, is more secure, and doesn't require Visual Basic's Development Environment to run.

2. False; use the Make option.

3. To maintain records of multiple versions of an application

4. Use the form's icon located in the form's Icon property.

5. False; you must run the installation routine from the Start menu.

6. A dependency file is a file needed by an application's installation to install and execute properly. The dependency file specifies the names of all the files the application requires, such as certain fonts, controls, and ActiveX files.

7. True

8. In case you want to copy the installation to floppy disks

9. The installation routine gives the user a chance to save the newer version.

10. The user can run the uninstall routine from the Control Panel.

B

Hour 23 Exercise

No answer is necessary; no source code changes from the original application.

Hour 24 Quiz

1. The Internet
2. The VB Application Wizard supports both.
3. True (Internet Explorer 4.0 or better is highly recommended)
4. True (Internet Explorer 4.0 or better is highly recommended)
5. An ISP is used to gain Internet access.
6. Only if you want to test the Internet-based application do you need an ISP. In most cases, you should have an ISP.
7. Java-enabled Web pages are more active than non–Java pages. For example, a Java-enabled Web page can contain a multimedia video clip that runs on the user's own computer. The Java application's runtime speed isn't dependent on download speed because a Java application executes on the end user's machine.
8. The Web Browser tool requires a toolbar and an Image List.
9. False; you must add a logoff routine.
10. Click the Back button, display the pull-down URL list box, type the URL address in the text box, or select the Open dialog box and type the URL of the page you just browsed.

Hour 24 Exercise

No answer is necessary as this exercise simply directs a process.

APPENDIX C

Using the CD-ROM

The CD-ROM that accompanies this book contains all the authors' source code and examples from the book, as well as many third-party software products.

Windows 95/NT 4 Installation Instructions

1. Insert the CD-ROM into your CD-ROM drive.
2. From the Windows 95/NT desktop, double-click the My Computer icon.
3. Double-click the icon representing your CD-ROM drive.
4. Double-click the SETUP.EXE icon to run the installation program.
5. The installation program creates a program group with the book's name as the group name. This group contains icons to browse the CD-ROM.

If Windows 95 is installed on your computer and you have the AutoPlay feature enabled, the SETUP.EXE program starts automatically when you insert the CD into your CD-ROM drive.

System Requirements

This CD-ROM contains the Microsoft Visual Basic Control Creation Edition. Some of the features of Visual Basic 5 discussed in this book may not be usable with the Control Creation Edition. The Control Creation Edition is provided to enable you to become familiar with the Visual Basic environment and to create your own ActiveX controls.

The following are the minimum system requirements for the Visual Basic Control Creation Edition:

- A personal computer with a 486 or higher processor
- Microsoft Windows 95 or Windows NT Workstation 4.0 or later
- 8MB of memory (12MB is recommended) if running Windows NT Workstation
- The following hard disk space:

  Typical installation: 20MB

  Minimum installation: 14MB

  CD-ROM installation (tools run from the CD): 14MB

  Total tools and information on the CD: 50MB

- A CD-ROM drive
- A VGA or higher-resolution monitor (SVGA is recommended)

INDEX

H

I

J-K

M

Make Project dialog box, 386
making projects, *see* **compiling applications**
math hierarchy, 93
math operators, 91-94
operator precedence, 93
Max property (scrollbars), 191
MDI (multiple-document interface) Form windows, 16
Me object, 157
memory, unloading forms from, 157
menu bar, 14
Menu Editor, 288-290
arrow command buttons, 295
menu bars
adding to applications, 290-292
checked objects, adding, 297
naming menu options, 292-294
pull-down menu options, adding, 294-297
properties, 295
menus
components, 288
connecting to event procedures, 299-300
copying between projects, 300-301
menu bars
adding to applications, 290-292
checked objects, adding, 297
naming menu options, 292-294
pull-down menu options, adding, 294-297

message boxes, 99-100
intType value, 101-102
modality, 102
MsgBox( ) function
format, 101
named literals, 101-102
return values, 103-104
methods, 163
Add (collections), 374
AddItem (list boxes), 171
Circle (Printer object), 274
Clear (list boxes), 171-172
common dialog boxes, 206-207
Count (collections), 374
EndDoc (Printer object), 274, 280-281
Item (collections), 374
KillDoc (Printer object), 274
Line (Printer object), 274
List (list boxes), 171
ListCount (list boxes), 171-172
NewPage (Printer object), 274, 281
PaintPicture (Printer object), 274
Print
controls, 276
expressions, 276-277
literals, 275-276
multiple values, 277-278
Printer object, 274-280
spacing control, 279-280
variables, 276
PSet (Printer object), 275
Remove (collections), 374
RemoveItem (list boxes), 171

Scale (Printer object), 275
ScaleMode (Printer object), 281-282
ScaleX (Printer object), 275
ScaleY (Printer object), 275
TextHeight (Printer object), 275
TextWidth (Printer object), 275
Microsoft Internet Controls, 405
Microsoft Internet Transfer Control, 405
Microsoft Web site, 288
Microsoft Winsock Control, 405
Mid statement, Mid( ) function comparison, 233
Mid( ) function, 232
Mid statement comparison, 233
milliseconds, 193
Min property (scrollbars), 191
mnu prefix, 292-293
modality (message boxes), 102
Mode values (Open statement), 248
modules
adding, 161
external, 216-217
form, 78-79
standard, 31, 78-80
mouse, focus, 60
MousePointer property, assigning a named literal, 49
moving controls, 42-43
MsgBox statement, 100
MsgBox( ) function, 99-101
format, 101
intType value, 101-102
named literals, 101-102
return values, 103-104

radio buttons, 184
reading file data
  Input # statement,
  253-254
  Line Input # command,
  254
records, 254
relationship results
  (comparison operators),
  115
Rem statements, 107-108
remarks, 106
  apostrophe remarks,
  109
  Rem statement,
  107-108
Remove method (collec-
  tions), 374
RemoveItem method (list
  boxes), 171
return values, MsgBox( )
  function, 103-104
Right( ) function, 232
rounding up fractions,
  239
RTrim( ) function, 232
running applications,
  28-30
runtime errors, 338-339

S

Scale method (Printer
  object), 275
ScaleHeight property
  (Printer object), 273
ScaleLeft property
  (Printer object), 273
ScaleMode method
  (Printer object),
  281-282
ScaleMode property
  (Printer object), 273
ScaleTop property
  (Printer object), 273
ScaleWidth property
  (Printer object), 273

ScaleX method (Printer
  object), 275
ScaleY method (Printer
  object), 275
scientific notation, 83
Screen object, 371
scrollbars, 190
  properties, 190-191
  thumb, 191
SDI (single-document
  interface), 16
Select Case statement,
  122-125
  additional formats,
  125-127
Set keyword, 379
setting breakpoints,
  341-345
Shape control, 330-332
shapes, drawing, 330-332
  fill options, 331
  options, 330-331
shortcut forms, If
  statement, 118
Shortcut property, 295
simple combo boxes, 174
Simple dialog box, 16
Sin( ) function, 231
sines, returning, 231
Single datatype, 82
  converting to, 239
single-document
  interface (SDI), 16
single-stepping, 345-346
  Step Out option, 346
  Step Over option, 346
sizing
  controls, 42-43
  images, 307-309
skeleton programs, 34
SmallChange property
  (scrollbars), 191
Sorted property
  combo boxes, 175
  list boxes, 170
spaces, removing
  leading, 232
  trailing, 232
Spc( ) function, 279-280
Standard Edition (Visual
  Basic), 10

standard functions,
  216-218
  see also functions
standard modules, 31,
  78-80
  see also modules
standard procedures, 216
  see also procedures
standard subroutines,
  216-218
  see also subroutines
starting Visual Basic,
  11-13
StartUpPosition
  property, 149
statements
  apostrophe remarks,
  109
  assignment, 139
  Beep, 140
  ByVal, 225
  Call, 215
  Close, 250-251
  Dim, 86-87
  Else, 119-120
  End If, 117-119
  Exit, 142-143
  If, 117-119
    shortcut form, 118
    testing multiple
    conditions, 122
  If...Else, 119-120
  Input# statement,
  253-254
  Mid, Mid( ) function
    comparison, 233
  MsgBox, 100
  New, 372
  Object, 372
  Open, 247-250
    format, 248
    Mode values, 248
  Option Explicit, 86
  Public, 86
  Rem, 107-108
  remark statements, 106
    apostrophe remarks,
    109
    Rem statement,
    107-108

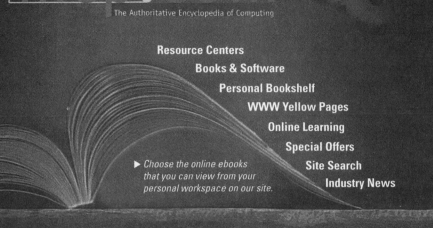

Sams Teach Yourself VBScript in 21 Days

—Keith Brophy and Tim Koets

With this book, you learn how to use VBScript to create living, interactive Web pages. This unique scripting language from Microsoft is taught with clarity and precision, providing the reader with the best and latest information on this popular language. This book teaches advanced OLE object techniques and explores VBScript's animation, interaction, and mathematical capabilities. The accompanying CD-ROM contains all the source code from the book, as well as examples of third-party software.

Price: $39.99 USA/$56.95 CAN   *New–Casual*
ISBN: 1-57521-120-3   *720 pages*

Laura Lemay's Web Workshop: ActiveX and VBScript

—Paul Lomax and Rogers Cadenhead

ActiveX is an umbrella term for a series of Microsoft products and technologies that you can use to add activity to Web pages. Visual Basic Script is an essential element of the ActiveX family. With it, you can add animation, multimedia, sound, graphics, and interactivity to your Web site. This book is a compilation of workshops that show you how to use VBScript and other ActiveX technologies in your sites. The CD-ROM contains the entire book in HTML format, along with a selection of the best ActiveX development tools, scripts, templates, backgrounds, borders, and graphics.

Price: $39.99 USA/$56.95 CAN   *Casual–Accomplished*
ISBN: 1-57521-207-2   *450 pages*

Sams Teach Yourself Database Programming with Visual Basic 6 in 21 days

—Curtis Smith

The book presents a step-by-step approach to learning what can be a critical topic for developing applications. Each week focuses on a different aspect of database programming with Visual Basic. In addition, you study advanced topics such as SQL data definition and manipulation language, and issues for multiuser applications such as locking schemes, database integrity, and application-level security.

Price: $45.00 USA/$64.95 CAN   *New–Casual–Advanced*
ISBN: 0-672-31308-1   *900 pages*

Sams Teach Yourself More Visual Basic 6 in 21 Days

—Lowell Mauer

This book provides comprehensive, self-taught coverage of the most sought after topics in Visual Basic programming. It goes beyond the basics of Visual Basic 6.0 and delves into each topic to a level that you can apply to your own programs. The book includes complete coverage of database applications and uses real-world applications to demonstrate specialized programming.

Price: $35.00 USA/$50.95 CAN   *Beginner–Intermediate*
ISBN: 0-672-31307-3   *700 pages*

Add to Your Sams Library Today with the Best Programming Books

The easiest way to order is to pick up the phone and call

1-800-428-5331

between 9:00 a.m. and 5:00 p.m. EST.

For faster service, please have your credit card available.

ISBN	Quantity	Description of Item	Unit Cost	Total Cost
1-57521-120-3		Sams Teach Yourself VBScript in 21 Days	$39.99	
1-57521-207-2		Laura Lemay's Web Workshop: ActiveX and VBScript	$39.99	
0-672-31308-1		Sams Teach Yourself Database Programming with Visual Basic 6 in 21 Days	$45.00	
0-672-31307-3		Sams Teach Yourself More Visual Basic 6 in 21 Days	$35.00	
		Shipping and Handling: See information below.		
		TOTAL		

Shipping and Handling

Standard	$5.00
2nd Day	$10.00
Next Day	$17.50
International	$40.00

201 W. 103rd Street, Indianapolis, Indiana 46290   1-800-835-3202 — FAX

Book ISBN 0-672-31306-5

MISCELLANEOUS

If you acquired this product in the United States, this EULA is governed by the laws of the State of Washington.

If you acquired this product in Canada, this EULA is governed by the laws of the Province of Ontario, Canada. Each of the parties hereto irrevocably attorns to the jurisdiction of the courts of the Province of Ontario and further agrees to commence any litigation which may arise hereunder in the courts located in the Judicial District of York, Province of Ontario.

If this product was acquired outside the United States, then local law may apply.

Should you have any questions concerning this EULA, or if you desire to contact Microsoft for any reason, please contact the Microsoft subsidiary serving your country, or write: Microsoft Sales Information Center/One Microsoft Way/Redmond, WA 98052-6399.

LIMITED WARRANTY

NO WARRANTIES. Microsoft expressly disclaims any warranty for the SOFTWARE PRODUCT. The SOFTWARE PRODUCT and any related documentation is provided "as is" without warranty of any kind, either express or implied, including, without limitation, the implied warranties or merchantability, fitness for a particular purpose, or noninfringement. The entire risk arising out of use or performance of the SOFTWARE PRODUCT remains with you.

NO LIABILITY FOR DAMAGES. In no event shall Microsoft or its suppliers be liable for any damages whatsoever (including, without limitation, damages for loss of business profits, business interruption, loss of business information, or any other pecuniary loss) arising out of the use of or inability to use this Microsoft product, even if Microsoft has been advised of the possibility of such damages. Because some states/jurisdictions do not allow the exclusion or limitation of liability for consequential or incidental damages, the above limitation may not apply to you.

3. **UPGRADES.** If the SOFTWARE PRODUCT is labeled as an upgrade, you must be properly licensed to use a product identified by Microsoft as being eligible for the upgrade in order to use the SOFTWARE PRODUCT. A SOFTWARE PRODUCT labeled as an upgrade replaces and/or supplements the product that formed the basis for your eligibility for the upgrade. You may use the resulting upgraded product only in accordance with the terms of this EULA. If the SOFTWARE PRODUCT is an upgrade of a component of a package of software programs that you licensed as a single product, the SOFTWARE PRODUCT may be used and transferred only as part of that single product package and may not be separated for use on more than one computer.

4. **COPYRIGHT.** All title and copyrights in and to the SOFTWARE PRODUCT (including but not limited to any images, photographs, animations, video, audio, music, text, and "applets" incorporated into the SOFTWARE PRODUCT), the accompanying printed materials, and any copies of the SOFTWARE PRODUCT are owned by Microsoft or its suppliers. The SOFTWARE PRODUCT is protected by copyright laws and international treaty provisions. Therefore, you must treat the SOFTWARE PRODUCT like any other copyrighted material except that you may install the SOFTWARE PRODUCT on a single computer provided you keep the original solely for backup or archival purposes. You may not copy the printed materials accompanying the SOFTWARE PRODUCT.

5. **DUAL-MEDIA SOFTWARE.** You may receive the SOFTWARE PRODUCT in more than one medium. Regardless of the type or size of medium you receive, you may use only one medium that is appropriate for your single computer. You may not use or install the other medium on another computer. You may not loan, rent, lease, or otherwise transfer the other medium to another user, except as part of the permanent transfer (as provided above) of the SOFTWARE PRODUCT.

6. **U.S. GOVERNMENT RESTRICTED RIGHTS.** The SOFTWARE PRODUCT and documentation are provided with RESTRICTED RIGHTS. Use, duplication, or disclosure by the Government is subject to restrictions as set forth in subparagraph (c)(1)(ii) of the Rights in Technical Data and Computer Software clause at DFARS 252.227-7013 or subparagraphs (c)(1) and (2) of the Commercial Computer Software—Restricted Rights at 48 CFR 52.227-19, as applicable. Manufacturer is Microsoft Corporation/One Microsoft Way/ Redmond, WA 98052-6399.

7. **EXPORT RESTRICTIONS.** You agree that neither you nor your customers intend to or will, directly or indirectly, export or transmit (i) the SOFTWARE or related documentation and technical data or (ii) your software product as described in Section 1(b) of this License (or any part thereof), or process, or service that is the direct product of the SOFTWARE, to any country to which such export or transmission is restricted by any applicable U.S. regulation or statute, without the prior written consent, if required, of the Bureau of Export Administration of the U.S. Department of Commerce, or such other governmental entity as may have jurisdiction over such export or transmission.

←

terms of this EULA; and (2) you may permit your end users to reproduce and distribute the object code version of the files designated by ".ocx" file extensions ("Controls") only in conjunction with and as a part of an Application and/or Web page that adds significant and primary functionality to the Controls, and such end user complies with all other terms of this EULA.

2. DESCRIPTION OF OTHER RIGHTS AND LIMITATIONS.

a. **Not for Resale Software.** If the SOFTWARE PRODUCT is labeled "Not for Resale" or "NFR," then, notwithstanding other sections of this EULA, you may not resell, or otherwise transfer for value, the SOFTWARE PRODUCT.

b. **Limitations on Reverse Engineering, Decompilation, and Disassembly.** You may not reverse engineer, decompile, or disassemble the SOFTWARE PRODUCT, except and only to the extent that such activity is expressly permitted by applicable law notwithstanding this limitation.

c. **Separation of Components.** The SOFTWARE PRODUCT is licensed as a single product. Its component parts may not be separated for use by more than one user.

d. **Rental.** You may not rent, lease, or lend the SOFTWARE PRODUCT.

e. **Support Services.** Microsoft may provide you with support services related to the SOFTWARE PRODUCT ("Support Services"). Use of Support Services is governed by the Microsoft policies and programs described in the user manual, in "online" documentation, and/or in other Microsoft-provided materials. Any supplemental software code provided to you as part of the Support Services shall be considered part of the SOFTWARE PRODUCT and subject to the terms and conditions of this EULA. With respect to technical information you provide to Microsoft as part of the Support Services, Microsoft may use such information for its business purposes, including for product support and development. Microsoft will not utilize such technical information in a form that personally identifies you.

f. **Software Transfer.** You may permanently transfer all of your rights under this EULA, provided you retain no copies, you transfer all of the SOFTWARE PRODUCT (including all component parts, the media and printed materials, any upgrades, this EULA, and, if applicable, the Certificate of Authenticity), and the recipient agrees to the terms of this EULA. If the SOFTWARE PRODUCT is an upgrade, any transfer must include all prior versions of the SOFTWARE PRODUCT.

g. **Termination.** Without prejudice to any other rights, Microsoft may terminate this EULA if you fail to comply with the terms and conditions of this EULA. In such event, you must destroy all copies of the SOFTWARE PRODUCT and all of its component parts.

←

1.   **GRANT OF LICENSE.** This EULA grants you the following rights:

   a.   Software Product. Microsoft grants to you as an individual, a personal, non-exclusive license to make and use copies of the SOFTWARE for the sole purposes of designing, developing, and testing your software product(s) that are designed to operate in conjunction with any Microsoft operating system product. You may install copies of the SOFTWARE on an unlimited number of computers provided that you are the only individual using the SOFTWARE. If you are an entity, Microsoft grants you the right to designate one individual within your organization to have the right to use the SOFTWARE in the manner provided above.

   b.   Electronic Documents. Solely with respect to electronic documents included with the SOFTWARE, you may make an unlimited number of copies (either in hardcopy or electronic form), provided that such copies shall be used only for internal purposes and are not republished or distributed to any third party.

   c.   Redistributable Components.

   (i)   Sample Code. In addition to the rights granted in Section 1, Microsoft grants you the right to use and modify the source code version of those portions of the SOFTWARE designated as "Sample Code" ("SAMPLE CODE") for the sole purposes of designing, developing, and testing your software product(s), and to reproduce and distribute the SAMPLE CODE, along with any modifications thereof, only in object code form provided that you comply with Section d(iii), below.

   (ii)   Redistributable Components. In addition to the rights granted in Section 1, Microsoft grants you a nonexclusive royalty-free right to reproduce and distribute the object code version of any portion of the SOFTWARE listed in the SOFTWARE file REDIST.TXT ("REDISTRIBUTABLE SOFTWARE"), provided you comply with Section d (iii), below.

   (iii)   Redistribution Requirements. If you redistribute the SAMPLE CODE or REDISTRIBUTABLE SOFTWARE (collectively, "REDISTRIBUTABLES"), you agree to: (A) distribute the REDISTRIBUTABLES in object code only in conjunction with and as a part of a software application product developed by you that adds significant and primary functionality to the SOFTWARE and that is developed to operate on the Windows or Windows NT environment ("Application"); (B) not use Microsoft's name, logo, or trademarks to market your software application product; (C) include a valid copyright notice on your software product; (D) indemnify, hold harmless, and defend Microsoft from and against any claims or lawsuits, including attorney's fees, that arise or result from the use or distribution of your software application product; (E) not permit further distribution of the REDISTRIBUTABLES by your end user. The following **exceptions** apply to subsection (iii) (E), above: (1) you may permit further redistribution of the REDISTRIBUTABLES by your distributors to your end-user customers if your distributors only distribute the REDISTRIBUTABLES in conjunction with, and as part of, your Application and you and your distributors comply with all other

END-USER LICENSE AGREEMENT FOR MICROSOFT SOFTWARE

Microsoft Visual Basic, Control Creation Edition

IMPORTANT—READ CAREFULLY: This Microsoft End-User License Agreement ("EULA") is a legal agreement between you (either an individual or a single entity) and Microsoft Corporation for the Microsoft software product identified above, which includescomputer software and may include associated media, printed materials, and "online" or electronic documentation ("SOFTWARE PRODUCT"). By installing, copying, or otherwise using the SOFTWARE PRODUCT, you agree to be bound by the terms of this EULA. If you do not agree to the terms of this EULA, do not install or use the SOFTWARE PRODUCT; you may, however, return it to your place of purchase for a full refund.

SOFTWARE PRODUCT LICENSE

The SOFTWARE PRODUCT is protected by copyright laws and international copyright treaties, as well as other intellectual property laws and treaties. The SOFTWARE PRODUCT is licensed, not sold.